SUB HUNTERS

AUSTRALIAN SUNDERLAND SQUADRONS IN THE DEFEAT OF HITLER'S U-BOAT MENACE 1942-43

ANTHONY COOPER

FONTHILL

This book is dedicated to all those swallowed up by the sea.

Front cover image: C/10 photographed in Plymouth harbour in 1944–45, exemplifying the armament upgrades introduced to all aircraft over the turn of 1943–44: evident are the twin-gun nose turret, two of the four gunports in the nose for the pilot-aimed forward-firing armament, and the open galley hatch further aft for a 'galley gun' each side—all .303. (*Ross McMurtrie via Neil McMurtrie*)

Fonthill Media Language Policy

Fonthill Media publishes in the international English language market. One language edition is published worldwide. As there are minor differences in spelling and presentation, especially with regard to American English and British English, a policy is necessary to define which form of English to use. The Fonthill Policy is to use the form of English native to the author. Anthony Cooper was born and educated in Brisbane; therefore British English has been adopted in this publication.

Fonthill Media Limited
Fonthill Media LLC
www.fonthillmedia.com
office@fonthillmedia.com

First published in the United Kingdom and the United States of America 2020

British Library Cataloguing in Publication Data:
A catalogue record for this book is available from the British Library

Copyright © Anthony Cooper 2020

ISBN 978-1-78155-832-4

The right of Anthony Cooper to be identified as the author of this work has been asserted by him in accordance with the Copyright, Designs and Patents Act 1988.

Typeset in 10.5pt on 13pt Sabon
Printed and bound in England

Contents

Introduction

Two Australian flying boat squadrons, Nos 10 and 461, during the pivotal period of 1942–43, played leading parts in the defeat of the German U-boats. These two units fought their war from British bases, with No. 10 based at Mount Batten in Plymouth Harbour, and with No. 461 based first alongside No. 10 at Mount Batten, then in Poole Harbour, Dorset, and finally at Pembroke Dock, Wales. Their crews flew four-engined Sunderland flying boats on twelve-hour patrols over the Atlantic to 'seek, find, and kill' U-boats. It was their job to stop enemy submarines making their passages across the Bay of Biscay between their bases on the west coast of France and their patrol areas across the Allied convoy routes in the Atlantic.

No. 10 was the senior squadron, and by 1942, it had grown into one of the pre-eminent anti-submarine squadrons in British service. By contrast, No. 461 Squadron was the offspring of No. 10, formed in April 1942 from a small cadre of personnel donated by the senior unit. These two Australian squadrons fought a common campaign within RAF Coastal Command: crews from both units hunted the same U-boats over the same contested waters of the Bay of Biscay, and similarly fought for their survival against attacks by the same German aircraft. The details of these two squadrons' U-boat kills and aircraft losses are given in Appendix I and II.

This book rests first and foremost upon the official records and crew reports generated by the squadrons themselves, but also upon the work of researchers, historians, and memoirists, whom I acknowledge here with admiration and appreciation. Both squadrons received good unit histories, K. C. Baff's *Maritime is Number Ten* for No. 10, and for No. 461, Ivan Southall's *They Shall Not Pass Unseen*, as well as *The Anzac Squadron* by Norman Ashworth. In addition, squadron members' memoirs provide personal perspectives: Les Baveystock's *Waves at My Wingtips*, Phil Davenport's *Hurrah for the Next Man*, and Ed Gallagher's *PS: Love Me?* In addition, contemporary researchers have cross-referenced Axis and Allied primary sources to corroborate, contest, or correct the claimed outcomes of the various air-sea and air-to-air combats: Chris Goss has provided data on the losses and claims of the German aerial opposition, in *Bloody Biscay*, while a community of U-boat researchers has provided extensive hard information, published for example in Axel Niestle's *German U-boat Losses*, Kenneth Wynn's *U-boat Operations*, and Clay Blair's *Hitler's U-boat War*. I am in debt to all these for their adjudications of results.

In the time period covered by this book, besides the anti-submarine operations mentioned above, both Nos 10 and 461 Squadrons were engaged in anti-shipping operations as well as transport operations between England and Gibraltar. Some combats occurred in the course of the Australian Sunderlands' anti-shipping operations, but no ships were sunk by either squadron and no aircraft lost in the course of these few attacks upon ships. I have chosen not to focus upon these operations, as they were subsidiary to the main anti-submarine campaign, which is the focus of this narrative.

In this book, I refer to individual aircraft by their callsign, composed of the individual letter followed by the squadron number, for example, W/10 or M/461. This convenient protocol follows wartime convention, by which each squadron assigned an individual identity letter to each of its aircraft, which would be painted prominently on the flanks of its hull. Thus, W/10 was the callsign for that particular Sunderland on the strength of No. 10 Squadron identified by the individual aircraft code 'W'. See Appendix III for aircraft particulars. In this book, many pilots are referred to as 'captains'; this is not an air force rank, but rather a job description, namely the pilot designated as being in command of that aircraft and crew.

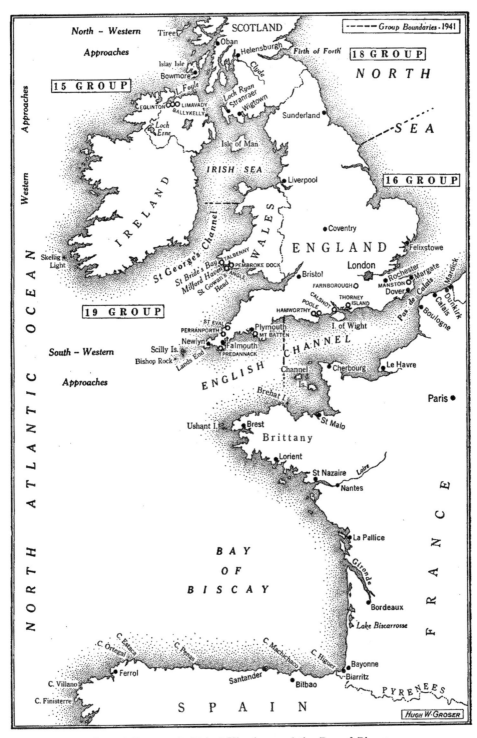

Coastal Command: United Kingdom and the Bay of Biscay.

1

Battle in the Bay

By the summer of 1943, Hitler's U-boat offensive against Allied convoys in the North Atlantic was facing a rout at the hands of the Allied navies and air forces. Since 1940, Grand Admiral Karl Dönitz had been waging an extended campaign to win the 'tonnage war', by sinking more ships than the Allies could build. This had gone well in 1942, with a happy hunting time for his U-boats along the US Eastern Seaboard, which saw 609 ships sunk, totalling 3.1 million tons. However, since those glory days, the fortunes of the German U-boat arm had turned sharply downwards, plumbing a new nadir over April and May 1943, when Allied forces sank fifty-three U-boats in the Atlantic. Under the shock of these losses, on 24 May, Dönitz ordered his boats out of the North Atlantic, temporarily ceding to the Allies uncontested control of the convoy routes between Britain, North America, and the Mediterranean. This defeat did not mean that the campaign had ended, however: Dönitz sailed another forty-eight U-boats into the Atlantic in June, although he sent them to patrol less fiercely-contested waters, such as the South Atlantic and Caribbean. Even then, nine of these boats in the June sailings were sunk.[1]

Four of these June losses were sunk in the Bay of Biscay, as were seven of the May losses, showing that this waterway was a focus point for Allied anti-submarine operations.[2] Indeed, the Bay was the 'black pit' of the U-boats' war, the hard-fought-over transit zone for U-boats on passage between their Flotilla bases and the wide oceans that played host to the convoys.[3] After the fall of France in June 1940, most of Germany's operational U-boat Flotillas had shifted port from the harbours on Germany's Baltic and North Sea coasts to the French Atlantic coast harbours of Brest, Lorient, St Nazaire, La Pallice, and Bordeaux. From those ports, the broad waters of the Bay provided direct access to the heavily-trafficked North Atlantic. Drawn to all this ship traffic, the U-boats repeatedly sallied from their French ports, returning thence afterwards for refuelling, re-ammunitioning, re-victualling, and crew rest and recreation. This metronomic submarine traffic made the waters of the Bay a target-rich environment for Allied anti-submarine aircraft and naval hunter-killer task forces.

In an attempt to interdict this U-boat traffic, RAF Coastal Command had been mounting air patrols over the Bay since 1941, but it was only after the major strengthening of its units, equipment, weapons, doctrine, and training over the winter of 1942–43 that the air effort finally gained enough heft to start achieving the results long hoped-for. It helped that the 'Trident' Conference, held in Washington during May 1943, further increased the resources allocated to Allied anti-submarine forces in the decisive year of the war. Led by President Roosevelt and Prime Minister Churchill, the British and American war leaders affirmed that to ensure the safe build-up of Allied forces in Britain for what became known as D-Day the next year, the war against the U-boats had to be pursued 'with every possible means'. RAF Coastal Command was to mount 'an all-out series of intense hunter-killer operations' to defeat the threat to eastbound troop convoys.[4] This directive specifically emphasised the Bay of Biscay, where the Allied air effort was directed by the RAF's No. 19 Group, a specialised anti-submarine air force that was headquartered at Plymouth, with its air units operating from bases throughout the south-west corner of the British Isles.

Hitler saw the Atlantic Front as Germany's western defensive perimeter against the Western Allies, where the U-boat service took pride of place as 'the only offensive branch of Axis warfare against the Anglo-Saxon enemies'.[5] Therefore, Dönitz knew that despite his rising losses, his U-boats would have to continue their campaign to interdict the transatlantic trade-routes that were bringing the plentiful resources of the USA to the European Theatre of Operations. In July 1943, Dönitz resumed the campaign by sailing forty-eight boats on war patrols, seventeen of which were tasked with intercepting convoys across the North Atlantic. Meanwhile, he prepared to return his boats to the North Atlantic in force, starting with a surprise offensive in September. His U-boat Command also beef-up its boats' anti-aircraft (AA) gun armament: all boats sailing in July had augmented AA armament, and furthermore all were despatched in group sailings, in order to fight off any Allied air attacks with intensive and co-ordinated gunnery.[6]

It was during this resumption of the campaign that, over 27–28 July, a group of six U-boats set out from their Biscay ports to make their passage across the Bay into the Atlantic. In accordance with the new strategy, they sailed in two groups of three for mutual protection. These boats were sailing into a violent collision with the submarine hunters of Coastal Command: of the six boats, only two would make it through the Bay of Biscay and out into the Atlantic, and only one would make port again.[7]

By the morning of 30 July 1943, one of these U-boat trios, comprised of *U-461*, *U-462*, and *U-504*, had almost sailed beyond range of Allied air patrols—but not quite. The three boats, all with the new, beefed-up AA armament, were to stick together for mutual protection until such time as they passed beyond range of Coastal Command aircraft from England; at that point, they could split up and set course individually to carry out their assigned war patrols. That morning, they were cruising westward on the power of their twin diesel engines, recharging their batteries so that they could avoid Allied air patrols by continuing the voyage underwater by running on their electric motors. The German U-boats were typical of all other diesel-electric submarines of the Second World War in having a bank of batteries to drive the boats' electric motors for submerged running, with diesel engines for running on the surface and simultaneously recharging the batteries. This repetitive cycle of surfaced battery recharging and submerged battery discharging was the basic operating rhythm for submarines of the era, before the introduction of nuclear power plants in the Cold War era. The previous month, Dönitz had set new tactics for his boats in transit through the Bay: they were to make the passage submerged, surface only to recharge batteries, sail in groups, and if caught by Allied aircraft while on the surface, to fight it out with their AA batteries.[8] Time would prove these tactics wrong, but *U-461*, *U-462*, and *U-504* were sailing in accordance with these instructions.

After sailing from Bordeaux on the 28th, *U-461* and *U-462* had rendezvoused at sea with *U-504*, along with an escorting force of three destroyers. The surface warships had shepherded the three submarines across the exposed inshore waters of the Bay of Biscay, but by the morning of the 30th, the three U-boats had to continue their passage unescorted, the destroyers having turned back the night before. Unbeknown to the Germans, the presence of this destroyer escort had inadvertently focussed malevolent Allied attention upon this particular U-boat sailing. *U-459* had been sunk by a Wellington on 22 July, and some of the forty-one survivors picked up by the Polish destroyer *Orkan* had loose lips, naively mentioning to their captors about the destroyer escort that had accompanied their boat over the first part of the passage.[9]

The Admiralty's Submarine Tracking Room was already decrypting the German Navy radio signals pertaining to the destroyers' comings and goings from the Biscay ports, and now had the final piece of the jigsaw to understand the significance of these sailings. By the time the destroyers *Moewe*, *Kondor*, and *T19* sailed from La Pallice on 27 July to rendezvous with the three submarines, the Admiralty was able to deduce what was happening by reading the pre-sailing inter-harbour wireless traffic. Indeed, the Royal Navy's Western Approaches HQ had pre-empted the U-boat sailing by ordering a Royal Navy U-boat hunter-killer task force, the 2nd Support Group, to sail from Plymouth on the 23rd. This support group was comprised of five sloops under the command of the famous U-boat hunter, Capt. F. J. 'Johnny' Walker, RN. The presence in the western Bay of Biscay of a task force of anti-submarine surface warships was a recent innovation in the campaign, Walker's Support Group having been formed only six weeks before. This force had already collected its first scalps, having on 24 June sunk two U-boats and seriously damaging the third after being homed to an earlier group sailing by Coastal Command aircraft.[10]

Before sailing, the escorting destroyer *Moewe* embarked a 'B-Dienst' wireless intercept team, and before midnight on the first night, this team monitored enough RAF wireless traffic to tally a cumulative total of thirty-two British aircraft on patrol through the preceding afternoon and during that night. Despite this intensive air search effort, the small flotilla of German submarines remained undetected until the morning of 30 July, by which time the three destroyers were racing back to La Pallice at 24 knots. Having so far eluded British detection by maintaining radio silence and communicating only by signal lamp, at 9.22 a.m. that day, the *Moewe* transmitted a wireless message to base, reporting the destroyers' drop-off of the three U-boats seven hours earlier. Intercepted at once by the British Y-Service, this signal was decrypted by the British codebreakers at Bletchley Park within hours, quickly enough for Walker's 2nd Support Group to receive new orders at 1 p.m., directing the warships to head north to intercept the three submarines in their deduced position.[11]

After their destroyer escort departed, the three U-boats had sailed submerged until dawn, on a set heading and at set engine revolutions, and running at different depths to avoid collision. Although safe from patrolling Allied aircraft, this submerged passage seriously slowed down the boats' progress to westward, as *U-461* and *U-462* cruised at only 2 knots underwater, compared to their 12 knots on the surface. However, the slow transit was deemed justifiable, as radar-equipped Allied aircraft had frequently demonstrated the capability to track surfaced U-boats at night, and then to appear suddenly out of the dark to attack them with depth-charges. This was because, by now, No. 19 Group had five of its squadrons equipped with centimetric ASV III radar, the transmissions of which were undetectable by U-boat radar warning receivers. In accordance with instructions from U-boat Command, the three boats surfaced after dawn in order to recharge their batteries while cruising together on the surface under diesel power, protected by their combined gun batteries.[12]

U-461 and *U-504* surfaced on cue that morning and rendezvoused successfully, but *U-462* did not at first appear. While the two boats sailed together and recharged, their bridge parties anxiously scanned the horizon for the other boat. Having recharged their batteries, *U-461* and *U-504* were about to submerge when a lookout spotted *U-462* in the distance, flashing a signal by searchlight; the missing boat had belatedly found the rendezvous. By the time she joined up, much time had been lost, and worse than that, *U-462* signalled that she had not yet recharged her batteries: this boat's batteries were already weakened after months of strenuous operations, and so had been especially depleted by the previous night's submerged sailing under battery power; the worn-out batteries were also slow to recharge, and therefore the third boat needed extra time on the surface to charge them sufficiently to support yet another bout of submerged running.[13]

Korvettenkapitän Wolf Stiebler, *U-461*'s captain and the senior officer in the group, was tempted to submerge and leave *U-462* to her fate, but exactly in accordance with Dönitz's latest tactical instructions, he knew that the other two boats would just have to wait for his tardy consort to recharge, in the meantime sailing in company to protect each other with their anti-aircraft guns.[14] The three U-boats' combined armament of about fifteen 20-mm automatic AA guns was certainly formidable enough to deter and defeat aircraft attack. Under the umbrella of their own gun batteries, the three boats thus sailed west, in a position about 150 miles north-west of Cape Ortegal in Spain, with *U-461* leading the other two boats in a V-formation, *U-462* to starboard and *U-504* to port.

Sunrise had brought fine weather and good visibility, and therefore heightened the aircraft danger. Although it was their third morning at sea, the three boats were still within 500 miles of Plymouth, and Sunderland aircraft from that base had the range to fly more than 600 miles out to sea to patrol across the U-boats' path, each bearing a load of eight deadly 270-pound depth-charges. Another day's sailing was needed for the boats to sail beyond the range of Allied anti-submarine aircraft patrols from south-west Britain, and so the daylight hours of 30 July would be critical for the mission's success. All three U-boats were fitted with Metox radar warning apparatus, which gave indications of radar transmissions up to 30 miles away, but by the summer of 1943, the Bay was so swamped by Allied aircraft patrols that a surfaced U-boat was always in range of radar transmissions. As a result, the set gave incessant alarms, which therefore often came to be ignored by the boats' command teams.[15] Moreover, U-boat commanders had fallen prey to the erroneous belief that the British aircraft were able to home upon the electronic emissions of the Metox set, such that by May 1943, many had lost confidence in it sufficiently to discontinue its use altogether.[16] Whatever the explanation aboard these three U-boats, while running on the surface across the Bay on the morning of 30 July, their command teams were reliant upon visual search for aircraft warnings.

The three boats were still running on the surface, their officers impatiently waiting for *U-462* to complete her battery recharging, when at 9.50 a.m., one of the lookouts on *U-461*'s conning tower called out a sighting of an approaching Sunderland flying boat. By then, *U-462* had only been charging for about half an hour, so her batteries were still too depleted to submerge.[17] Within minutes, *U-461* transmitted an aircraft contact report to U-boat Command. This transmission was picked up by the approaching British warships of the 2nd Support Group, which used their high-frequency direction finding (HF/DF) equipment to obtain a bearing upon the transmission, and to change course towards it, steering 225 degrees.[18]

The unwelcome, yet not unanticipated, appearance of an enemy aircraft presented *Korvettenkapitän* Stiebler with an acute tactical conundrum: his three boats needed to be submerged for safety against aircraft, but now that they had been spotted by an enemy aircraft, it was too late to dive. His boats would now have to stay together on the surface and oppose any air attack with their combined AA armaments and the boats' inherent manoeuvrability. This decision fulfilled *Grossadmiral* Dönitz's order of 1 May to his U-boat flotillas to sail together while within range of Allied land-based aircraft, and to fight it out on the surface, and was also in accordance with Stiebler's own tactical preferences as an experienced operational U-boat commander: after luckily surviving two previous air attacks while commanding *U-461*, he now considered that the only effective answer to aircraft attack was plentiful AA gunfire, as 'a diving U-boat is the airman's delight, like a sitting bird'.[19, 20] This was a realistic appreciation, for it took two minutes to submerge a Type XIV U-boat like *U-461*: one minute for the men on the upper decks to get below and another minute to submerge the boat to a safe depth of 30 metres.[21] During this awkward interval, the boat had no means of fighting back and was indeed a sitting target to any aircraft able to reach her position within that timespan: thus any aircraft within 5 miles would be able to bomb her unopposed.

The captains of both *U-461* and *U-462* had recently had some sobering personal experiences of air attack. *U-462*'s commanding officer, forty-one-year-old *Oberleutnant* Bruno Vowe, was not as experienced as Stiebler, and as an ex-merchant mariner and pre-war ranker in the German Navy, he had only been commissioned in 1939, and so *U-462* was his first command. It could not have been a reassuring thought to recall that his boat had been attacked by Allied aircraft on both her previous patrols: during her sixth patrol, on 21 June, she had been strafed by RAF Mosquitoes, and her gun-crew on the 'bandstand' had been badly hit, with one man killed and four wounded. And during her most recent patrol, on 2 July, she had been attacked by an RAF Liberator: in that instance, Vowe had crash-dived his boat to escape, but the Liberator had arrived in time to straddle the boat with its salvo of 270-pound depth-charges. One bomb hit the forward hull in a direct hit and then bounced into the water to explode alongside, causing considerable damage to her tanks; but once again, the tough pressure hull had withstood it. The damage was such that *U-462* had had to abort that mission and return to Bordeaux for repairs. That Liberator attack had occurred 80 miles off Cape Ortegal, and so within 70 miles of his position on 30 July. After these experiences, it is unlikely that Vowe viewed the impending air attacks on the morning of the 30th with equanimity.

Stiebler was a more experienced submarine commander, but he too had had some close shaves in *U-461*. On her second patrol, in August of the previous year, she had suffered a heavy attack by an RAF Sunderland, the depth-charges of which had exploded so close that the boat had her 'deckboards torn to shreds, its instrument glasses broken, lights extinguished and depth gauges smashed'. More recently, on her fifth patrol, she had been heading home, running on the surface at night, when she was suddenly ambushed out of the darkness by an RAF Wellington.[22] The depth-charges fell wide, but after these experiences the officers and men could hardly have formed a reassuring assessment of the U-boats' ability to elude aircraft attack.

Aboard *U-461*, as soon as the Sunderland was sighted on the morning of 30 July, the aircraft alarm was broadcast on the boat's loudspeaker. The gun crews raced up the ladder from the control room below, to man their action stations, moving aft from the conning tower to ready the 20-mm AA guns on the submarine's 'bandstand' gun platforms. *U-461* and *U-462* each mounted one twin 20-mm to port and starboard, on the upper bandstand just abaft the bridge, and one quad 20-mm mounting a few metres further back, on the lower bandstand. Once all three of *U-461*'s gun crews had taken their positions, the boat had a total of fourteen men posted on her conning tower and bandstands. The other forty-six souls aboard remained down below: in the control room directly underneath the conning tower, to operate the hydroplanes, rudders, pumps, tanks, compasses, and periscopes; in the engine room, tending the two supercharged diesels; in the motor room, tending the boat's electric system; in the sick bay, to prepare for possible casualties; in the wireless room, to operate the wireless set connecting the boat to U-boat Control in Paris; and in the listening room to operate the passive sonar equipment. All these men relied upon those on the upper deck to fight off the air attacks.

U-461 and *U-462* were not attack submarines, but submarine tankers, on passage to a position off the Cape Verde Islands to refuel torpedo-armed attack boats destined for operations in the Indian Ocean. The U-tankers' only armament was their AA guns, as their corpulent hulls were packed with tankage for 618 tons of fuel, enough to keep twelve Type VII U-boats at sea for four extra weeks.[23] During *U-461*'s five previous patrols, her crew had tallied a total of sixty-one submarine refuellings; for example, during her previous patrol (in April), *U-461* had refuelled thirteen U-boats while operating in a refuelling area in the South Atlantic, south of the Azores.[24]

Unlike *U-461* and *U-462*, *U-504* was an attack boat and therefore faster and handier, but she was for now inconveniently tied to the slower speed of the Type XIV boats for the duration of their joint passage through the Bay. For obvious reasons, the capacious U-tankers were referred to within the submarine service as *Milchkühe* (milk cows), and like dairy cattle, they were not fast movers: at maximum power from their twin 1,600-hp diesel engines, they did only 14 knots on the surface, compared with the 18 knots of the attack boats. Although a slender Type VII attack boat like *U-504* took only twenty seconds to crash-dive, and so had a good chance of getting away, here she was obliged to play the role of AA escort to two clumsy milk cows, so could not exploit her superior handiness. Aboard *U-504*, *Korvettenkapitän* Wilhelm Luis and his crew of fifty-two men had good reason to be apprehensive when they heard the aircraft warning, as well as resentful towards their heavier, more vulnerable consorts for tying them down.

When the Sunderland appeared, these three U-boats were proceeding in formation on a course of 250 degrees, running at the Type XIVs' economical speed of 10 knots. The flying boat orbited around the submarines, staying about 5,000 yards away, safely out of range of their 20-mm guns. On *U-461's* bridge, Stiebler used a 70-cm rangefinder to assess the range of the orbiting Sunderland, while his watch officers, *Oberleutnant* Herbert Ludewig, *Leutnant* Frank, and *Oberstfähnrich* Carston Schröck, swept the horizon with their binoculars to look for further aircraft and identify targets for the guns. In *U-461's* wireless room, the wireless operators monitored the Sunderland's coded sighting report radioed back to base, followed by its continuous homing signal on the frequency of 385 Kilohertz. *U-461's* crewmen were experienced enough to know what this meant: other aircraft would now be heading for them, drawn to the spot by the Sunderland's homing signal. The U-boats had no voice radio for inter-communication, so the officers on *U-462* and *U-504* kept an eye out for colour-coded semaphored signals from *U-461's* bridge— red or green for turns to port or starboard respectively.

By 11 a.m., the three boats' bridge teams were tracking two four-engined aircraft around the horizon, and by 11.30 a.m., the number of aircraft in sight had grown to three. Although *U-462* had by now recharged her batteries, it was too late. Stiebler's initial tactical conundrum had now become more acute: with three aircraft within easy attacking distance, it was now triply unsafe to submerge; the U-boats were irrevocably committed to fighting on the surface. At 10.15 a.m., *U-461* transmitted another aircraft report to base, which too was picked up by the 2nd Support Group, which obtained a bearing on HF/DF and altered course again, approaching at the sloops' maximum speed of 18 knots.[25]

The Sunderland that the U-boat officers had initially been watching as it flew around them in a broad circle was Fg Off. Stan White's 'R-for-Robert' from No. 228 Squadron, based at Pembroke Dock in South Wales. White had been drawn to the area by an earlier sighting report from Liberator 'O-for-Orange' of No. 53 Squadron, captained by a Canadian, Fg Off. W. J. Irving, which had passed by among the broken clouds, unsighted by the U-boats. Also unseen by anyone aboard the U-boats, at 10.45 a.m., a German Ju 88 twin-engined fighter appeared among the haze and cumulus clouds to make a firing pass at White's Sunderland. This forced White to climb away and hide in cloud; he also jettisoned his depth-charges in his alacrity to escape the fighter and was thus no longer able to directly harm the U-boats. The fighter had evidently diverted to the scene from its regular patrol beat in response to Stiebler's wireless message requesting air cover, but the U-boats were now too far out to sea for further air support to arrive, as they were two and a half hours' flying time from the fighter base at Bordeaux. By then, it would all be over, one way or the other. White's now bomb-less Sunderland R/228 made itself useful by homing other aircraft to the scene by radio.[26]

Drawn by the homing transmissions, the next aircraft to arrive was a Liberator from the 19th Anti-Submarine Squadron, one of two USAAF bomber units temporarily attached to RAF Coastal Command to beef up the Allied anti-submarine air offensive, and flying out of RAF St Eval in Cornwall.[27, 28] A Catalina from No. 210 Squadron had also arrived; it noted the U-boats' position, and then headed away to make visual contact with the ships of the 2nd Support Group, to guide this force of warships to the U-boats. The U-boat captains and the listening U-boat Command ashore remained unaware of the presence of the British warships, which maintained radio silence, still hidden below the horizon. At 11.33 a.m., *U-461* transmitted another aircraft report to base, this time specifying four enemy aircraft. The listening signalmen on the ships of the 2nd Support Group obtained a bearing on their HF/DF, and Walker altered course to 243 degrees, steaming right up the U-boats' wake.[29]

Although four aircraft were now orbiting the U-boats, not one of them had made an attack, their pilots acutely aware of the peril posed by the three boats' combined flak barrage. Meanwhile, the aircraft sought to establish communication with each other, in an effort to arrange a concerted attack.[30] None of the aircraft captains wanted to make a solo bombing run; relative safety could only lie in distracting and dividing the U-boat gunners by mounting simultaneous attacks. The aircraft thus exchanged signals over the heads of the U-boats, whether by HF voice radio or by tapping out Morse code with their visual signalling lamps, but satisfactory communications had yet to be established by the time a second Sunderland arrived. This was 'U-for-Uncle' from the Australian-manned No. 461 Squadron. It was thus a numerical coincidence that the German submarine, *U-461*, was now heading for a violent collision with the Australian Sunderland, 'U/461'.

This Sunderland's captain, Flt Lt Dudley Marrows, had never even seen a U-boat before, let alone attacked one, despite being a veteran airman on his thirty-seventh operation in command.[31] At 10 a.m., Marrows had been more than seven hours into his patrol, almost 700 miles from his base at Pembroke Dock in South Wales. By that time, his Sunderland was heading home, making for the navigational waypoint of Cape Finisterre, on the north-western extremity of Spain. Marrows was flying his Sunderland north along the Spanish coast, staying 3 miles offshore to avoid infringing the sovereignty of this neutral country, when his wireless operator, Fg Off. Pete Jensen, received O/53's first sighting report about the three U-boats. Jensen recalled that it had been a 'beautiful day' so far; the crewmen were so close to Spain that they were vicariously enjoying the perfect beach weather, using their binoculars to observe the bathers on the beaches.[32] As 'U-Uncle' headed north, she was low on fuel, and almost 200 miles from the reported position of the U-boats. Because of this, Marrows did not see how the radioed U-boat sighting reports could be applicable to him, for he did not believe the submarines would remain surfaced long enough for him to reach them. Prudently ignoring the wireless messages, he set course for the Scilly Isles, *en route* to home, adhering to his original flight plan. Then Jensen delivered a message from base, explicitly directing U/461 to proceed to the U-boats' position. Marrows would now have to comply, but his aircraft had only five hours' patrol time left (just enough to get home with safe fuel reserves), so the Sunderland's safe airborne endurance of twelve and a half hours would be stretched to its limit in making this detour.

There followed a discussion on the flight-deck between Marrows, his first pilot, Plt Off. 'Jimmy' Leigh, his navigator, Fg Off. 'Jock' Rolland, and his Irish flight engineer, Sgt 'Paddy' Watson, RAF, about the aircraft's fuel state and the fuel implications of this diversion off-course to the west. Marrows's conclusion was that 'we were really at the end of our outward endurance.'[33] The navigator used his slide rule to check and recheck his calculations about fuel consumption, fuel remaining, headwind component, ground speed, and elapsed time, and then told Marrows to 'Cruise as economically as you can ... if you have to make an attack you'll need every gallon to get home.'[34] Setting the engines to zero boost gave a minimum fuel consumption of 30 gallons per hour per engine, at which rate they needed 500 gallons just to make the English coast. Marrows recalled that it had been a 'frightening responsibility' for Rolland to get these calculations right, to ensure that they really could make it home afterwards.[35]

After almost two hours' cruising, meanwhile monitoring the other crews' amplifying sighting reports, Marrows arrived in the target area just before 11.48 a.m., flying at 2,000 feet for 'maximum U-boat sighting range'. Beside him, in the co-pilot's seat, Jimmy Leigh was scanning the band of sea below the horizon through the binoculars. From 15 miles away, he spotted the U-boats, still sailing west in V-formation, initially misidentifying them as destroyers. Seeing two four-engined aircraft circling around the U-boats, Marrow turned to join them in their orbit. The flight engineer, Paddy Watson, recalled a 'nerve-racking anti-clockwise circling of the U-boat pack, with more and more Sunderlands and Liberators joining the circus'.[36] Sunderland R/228 and the Catalina departed because of fuel considerations, leaving two Liberators (the British O/53 and the American A/19), two Halifaxes from 502 Squadron, and Sunderland U/461. With the threat escalating, the three U-boats now broke off their attempt to sail away to the west and began to circle warily to ward off the impending bomb runs. Stiebler's strategy seems to have been to see off the expected wave of air attacks with AA fire, and then to submerge one by one once the aircraft used up their depth-charges, leaving the rapidly-diving *U-504* to last. This strategy was sound in principal, but with so many aircraft about, there would be a lot of depth-charges to use up.

Although Sunderland U/461 arrived more than two hours after the first Allied aircraft made contact with the three U-boats, even so the Australians had still arrived early enough to witness the first attack. Immediately after joining the circuit, Marrows's crew saw a Halifax make an attack run at 1,000 feet over one of the outer U-boats. This was aircraft 'B' of 502 Squadron, which attacked at 11.48 a.m., dropping three of the RAF's new 600-pound anti-submarine bombs; it flew through a blizzard of tracers from the submarines' AA guns, took some flak hits in its tail, and departed the scene damaged. At the flight engineer's panel on U/461, Paddy Watson let curiosity get the better of him: he turned away momentarily from his gauges and switches and looked over his shoulder to get a view of the action up ahead through the windscreen, seeing 'many white puffs of smoke, little grey balloons, ahead of us'.[37] Having peered ahead past his wireless sets at the same scene, Jensen knew that the Halifax and Liberator were both faster, more modern machines than the Sunderland, so after watching the Halifax's attack, he thought, 'well that precludes us.'[38] Marrows seemed to agree, remarking over the intercom after watching the AA, 'Hell, look at that flak. We cannot make it through that.'[39]

However, the crew also knew that they had no time to wait around for something better to happen. Not only did the Sunderland's fuel state demand minimum delay in the target area before resuming its passage to the navigational waypoint of the Scilly Isles, but the RAF aircraft in the area had been transmitting continuously for two hours, drawing the attention of the German radio monitoring service to the concentration of RAF aircraft over the threatened U-boats. In fact, at 11.19 a.m., U-boat

Command had signalled the three boats that nine Ju 88 fighters were inbound to their position, but only due to arrive at 2 p.m.[40] At the flight engineer's panel aboard U-Uncle, Watson was unable to stop his mind straying from his engine and fuel gauges to anxious thoughts about Ju 88 fighters hurrying from the coast of France towards his slow, conspicuous, and vulnerable flying boat.

Jensen had just started comforting himself with the thought that U/461's role would be limited to homing the warships onto the U-boats, when he was dismayed to hear the klaxon sounding, the signal for the depth-charge racks to be run out. They were going in to attack after all! In a state of incredulity, he then overheard Marrows talking calmly to Leigh, starting with, 'We'll take the port one Jimmy,' and finishing with, 'Get ready to take over if I'm hit.' Metaphorically chained to his wireless set, Jensen sat there in silence, thinking that the two pilots sounded like 'maniacs' as they discussed this near-suicidal attack.[41] Of course, Marrows knew it was dangerous, having watched the U-boats firing their full AA broadsides, but he also knew that if he was going to attack, it had to be now: 'Eating up fuel, time running out'. From the command seat up front, Marrows was unaware of the doubts and horrors of back-seater crewmen like Jensen who were obliged to remain silent at their posts. Indeed, as the captain weighed up his options, he had felt buoyed by the men in the back: 'Could feel the support of the crew'.[42] Marrows had made contact over the HF voice radio with the captain of the American Liberator, and the two had agreed upon a co-ordinated attack, so he was now committed to going in.[43] Both aircraft banked, turned in, and dived.

Marrows turned U-Uncle to go in from astern against the same U-boat the Halifax had just attacked—it was *U-462*. At once, all three submarines wheeled in unison to present their broadsides to him. Jensen craned his head to look out over the pilots' heads, seeing the swathe of shell explosions bursting in front of the Liberator: '… what a barrage! It looked like a brick wall'. He estimated, quite accurately, that the three boats were firing with a total of twelve 20-mm guns. Given the fury of this fiery fusillade, Jensen was unsurprised to see the Liberator abort its bomb run, bank sharply away, and then head away from the U-boats' flak tracers. The barrage of flak bursts in front of his own aircraft was similarly so intimidating that Marrows turned away early before entering the killing zone of close-range automatic gunfire. Nonetheless, the Sunderland came close enough before turning away for Jensen to hear 'shrapnel rattling on the hull like hail with incessant loud bangs as pieces of shrapnel were picked up by the props and flung against the hull'.[44] Marrows realised that the U-boats, travelling at 12 knots, could turn much tighter than could his Sunderland at 150 knots; therefore, there seemed no way of avoiding their massed batteries of flak guns.[45] He turned his aircraft out of gun range and briefly reconsidered his limited options.

As Marrows mulled over his tactical conundrum, other decisions in other cockpits were being made: the die was being cast by others. It was almost twelve o'clock, and one after the other, the two Liberators and one Halifax banked inwards towards the U-boats and committed themselves to attack runs. At almost the same moment, the masthead lookouts on the ships of the 2nd Support Group sighted the U-boat conning towers on the horizon. Aboard the *Starling*, Capt. Walker hoisted the Nelsonian flag signal, 'Hoist General Chase.'[46] Meanwhile, the three aircraft in turn went in against *U-462*: first in was Bill Irving's Liberator O/53, the aircraft which had located the U-boats in the first place and initially helped home the other aircraft to the spot. Marrows was hanging back, but as the three U-boats manoeuvred to meet the attack, he saw that their formation was becoming more ragged, and that the gunners on all three boats were concentrating their fire upon the RAF Liberator. With the German gunners distracted, it was now or never. He rolled in about a mile behind the Liberator, calling on Jimmy Leigh to apply full power: 'Right, give me the lot, Jimmy. We're going after him'.[47] With the throttle levers fully forward, Marrows dived and jinked, trying to get some speed from the aircraft before they got in close. He got down to sea level as rapidly as possible, levelled out just above the waves at a point about 1,000 yards out from the nearest submarine, and turned to line up on the boat on the left flank of the formation. To show how disordering the U-boats' evasive turns had by now become, this outer boat was Wolf Stiebler's *U-461*, which had somehow lost its central position. Moreover, Stiebler's consort, *U-462*, was now so close off his starboard bow that *U-461* was unable to make an evasive turn away from the Sunderland to present her maximum AA armament towards the incoming aircraft. Because Marrows came in from *U-461*'s port quarter, the hull of this boat would mask the fire from the other two boats. Thus U-Uncle was facing the firepower of only one submarine, not three.

Marrows had played his best hand, but still needed to survive the bomb run, and then to bomb accurately. As his Sunderland bored in over the waves at 50 feet, trailing streams of black, rich-mixture smoke from all four exhaust stacks, he had two gunners in the nose of the aircraft to take care of the U-boat's flak guns: Sgt Fred 'Pierre' Bamber in the nose turret, with a single .303-inch Vickers K-gun, and Sgt Allan 'Bubbles' Pearce, armed with an American .30-inch Browning rigged to fire out of the nose bomb-aiming hatch. Pearce was 'a noted competitive rifle shooter pre-war', but both men had only about five seconds' worth of firing from their 100-round magazines.[48] To make up for the firepower deficiency, both guns were loaded with a heavy mix of tracer rounds to give the Germans the impression that the Sunderland had more guns than it actually possessed. One or both of Marrows's nose gunners opened fire at what the German bridge crew estimated was 1,000 yards—an extreme range for a rifle-calibre gun—and remarkably got hits at once.

The Germans' 20-mm automatic cannon outranged the Sunderland's rifle-calibre machine guns, but the U-boat gunners were unable to exploit this range advantage: they fired over open sights, standing on a platform that rolled and pitched as they made their aiming adjustments by hand. Somehow the gunners on the Sunderland and on the U-boat opened fire at one another simultaneously, and either Pearce or Bamber got hits with his first burst. A spray of .303 rounds struck *U-461*'s bandstand with remarkable precision, killing both loaders on the quad 20-mm and jamming the mounting so that it could not traverse. The most formidable flak weapon on the boat had thus been knocked out before it had fired more than a few rounds. Further bursts of .303 lashed the conning tower, severely wounding two of Stiebler's officers. Signalman Korbjuhn, the gunner on the U-boat's port single 20-mm, remained unscathed, firing until he ran out of ammunition with the Sunderland only 100 yards away: he had difficulty adjusting his fire for range, with bursts going over and under the Sunderland before getting a couple of hits in both wings.[49, 50] One of the 20-mm rounds struck the aircraft's bomb carriage on the underside of the port wing and then exploded against the rear wing spar, while another shell explosion caused an electrical fire. Luckily, neither hit degraded the combat capability of the aircraft or crew. By contrast, through their accurate shooting with their 'puny' rifle-calibre machine guns, Bamber and Pearce had very effectively suppressed *U-461*'s return fire and got Marrows and the rest of the crew safely through the Sunderland's highly perilous approach run.

In the cockpit, Marrows was not too busy lining up on the U-boat and judging his height, lay-off angles, and closure rate to notice what his gunners were doing, exclaiming over the intercom, 'Bloody good shooting Bubbles'. There was no bombsight in the Sunderland for such mast-height attacks as this, so the pilot had to judge it all instinctively by eye. He held the Sunderland low over the waves, then pulled up to clear the submarine's conning tower, releasing a stick of seven depth-charges as the submarine disappeared underneath the nose. As he went over the top, he obtained a fleeting impression of 'upturned faces, figures ... German gunners falling and throwing themselves about'.[51] His bombing was perfect, a textbook 'straddle', with two depth-charges splashing into the water close on either side of the U-boat, which at that second was turning to the right in an evasive turn. This turn brought the forward hull right over the top of the two depth-charges that had fallen to starboard, and these sank to their pre-set, 25-foot depth and then exploded close underneath the forward hull.

On the conning tower, Stiebler felt his boat sink under his feet in seconds: he later reported that '*U.461* went down like a stone'. Inside the boat, the crewmen had been anxiously listening over the loudspeaker to reports from the conning tower about one aircraft attack after the other. Soon after hearing the fifth report of an incoming aircraft, 'Suddenly there was a tremendous explosion and a wall of water rushed into the control room from forward.' One of the men in the control room thought that the bows had been blown clean off; he at once leapt for the ladder to the conning tower hatch. Although he was 'a strong athletic type', it was 'only with the greatest exertion' that he 'managed to haul himself up through the conning tower hatch, for water was already pouring down it'. This was the only man to escape alive from inside the hull of the submarine; as soon as he emerged from the hatch, he heard Stiebler order 'abandon ship'.[52]

Aboard Sunderland 'U-Uncle', Marrows's mind switched from killing to staying alive. Having pulled up to bomb, he knew that he was now no longer masked from the fire of the other two U-boats, so pulled the Sunderland into such a violent, steeply-banked turn that none of his gunners could lift their heads up and look outside the turn to see what had happened to their U-boat victim. Navigator Jock Rolland was the only crewman who saw anything in the seconds after bombing; at his action station beneath the midships astrodome, as the Sunderland heeled through its steep turn, he saw 'the U-boat slide forward under the water, with quantities of orange coloured froth and scum issuing, apparently from the fore part'. As Marrows eased the turn, the rear gunner fired some bursts from long range at the sinking wreck, shouting over the intercom, 'We have split him in half, skipper.'[53] By the time the Sunderland had rolled out of its turn and was heading away out of danger, the boat was gone; the crew counted about twenty-five men in the water, in the middle of a dirty pool of scum.

As *U-461* was sinking, *U-462* too was heading for the bottom. She had soaked up attack after attack from the Halifaxes and Liberators, in the cover of which Marrows had made his one, deadly attack upon *U-461*. Almost simultaneously with Marrows's attack, Halifax 'S' of 502 Squadron, captained by Fg Off. August van Rossum, a Dutchman, made his second bomb run upon *U-462*. At 11.58 a.m., he bombed remarkably accurately from 3,000 feet, dropping a single 600-pound anti-submarine bomb so close to the submarine's starboard quarter that the boat was left running out of control, going in circles with a jammed rudder, unable to dive because of a distorted rear torpedo hatch, and with water flooding into her stern compartment and engine room.

With further attacks coming in from Van Rossum's Halifax and from the persistent US Liberator, Vowe decided to scuttle his boat to save his crew, encouraged to do so by the 4-inch shells that started splashing into the water—the ships of the 2nd Support Group had opened fire from 5 miles away. *U-462*'s earlier flak gunnery had been good enough to hit Liberator O/53 so badly that Fg Off. Irving had headed away after his attack, steering straight for the nearest land in neutral Portugal. But before she left, O/53 had made a big contribution, for it had been Irving's attack in particular which Marrows had exploited to make his sudden attack on *U-461*.

At 12.14 p.m., Vowe ordered *U-462*'s sea vents to be opened and for the crew to abandon ship. Two minutes later, the submarine was dead in the water, sinking slowly on an even keel, with the men jumping overboard to take to their dinghies. With smoke streaming from the open hatch, *U-462*'s conning tower slipped beneath the water fifteen seconds later, before the Royal Navy ships' gunners had found the range.[54]

After his attack on *U-461*, Marrows orbited the scene to ascertain results, and then went back for a low pass, in an act of chivalry dropping one of the Sunderland's three pneumatic dinghies into the water beside his victim's survivors. The Sunderland circled around again, and the crew saw that the dinghy had inflated successfully and that German survivors were dragging themselves out of the oily water to board it. With Rolland reminding the pilots that the aircraft's fuel was dangerously low, Marrows set course for the Scilly Isles. Jensen transmitted a signal to the 2nd Support Group that there were German survivors in the water to be picked up.[55]

The violent breaching of *U-461*'s hull had consigned most of her crew to a sudden death. Only fifteen out of her sixty men survived. When Marrows's crew counted heads in the water on their final pass, they over-estimated the number of live swimmers, perhaps misled by the bodies of dead men and the flotsam that floated among them. All the U-boat's survivors but one had been on the conning tower or the bandstands; for them, the upper deck had simply dropped away beneath their feet, leaving them treading water with their heads above the oil slick. Four men had been killed on the submarine's upper decks before it sank away: besides the two gunners on the quad 20-mm killed in the Sunderland's first burst, the second lieutenant, *Leutnant* Falk, had also been hit by machine-gun fire while standing in the conning tower, and died from his wounds, as did the helmsman, *Oberststeuermann* Klimaszewski.[56] The first lieutenant, *Oberleutnant* Herbert Ludewig, had been wounded so severely by .303-rounds that he was left too severely injured to talk.[57]

Stiebler's party of swimmers had been greatly relieved when the returning Sunderland passed by overhead without strafing them, and even more so when it dropped a dinghy instead. The fitter men succeeded in swimming over to it, inflating it, and paddling it back. Stiebler had the four wounded men, including his critically injured first lieutenant, put aboard the dinghy. The other eleven stayed in the water, holding on to the lifeline that ran around the circumference of the dinghy. All U-boat crews wore lifejackets full-time while transiting through the Bay, but the survivors nonetheless would have had no chance of surviving in the water overnight if they did not get hold of the dinghy. When the British warships appeared above the horizon, the men might have hoped that they were to be rescued, but Captain Walker and his captains had U-boat killing on their minds instead. Rescuing enemy survivors could wait.

U-504 had dived to save herself when she saw her two consorts sinking. After her submergence, only the heads of U-boat survivors remained on the surface of the water as visible evidence of the so-recent presence of the three submarines. Unfortunately for *Korvettenkapitän* Luis and the crew of *U-504*, he had in fact left his dive too late. Capt. Walker, on the bridge of HMS *Kite*, had obtained a good visual bearing upon the point of the U-boat's disappearance, and from there he commenced a coordinated underwater sonar search with his five ships. His sonar operators obtained a good contact at 50 fathoms depth, and then the attack commenced. Aboard the sloops, it took almost five hours of assiduous listening, plotting, manoeuvring, and depth-charging, but the hunt ended with a pool of oil rising to the surface, within which floated wreckage and remains, including a 'uniform jacket, a human lung, and some well-cured bacon'.[58] All fifty-three men aboard *U-504* died.[59]

During this extended assault, the survivors of *U-461* were in the water only a few hundred yards away, floating in their lifejackets, subject to the fearful shock waves of nearby depth-charge explosions. All five of the sloops took turns to depth-charge *U-504*, probably dropping well over 100 charges in total.[60] The swimmers 'suffered excruciating pain from the force of nearby underwater explosions'.[61] Once Walker had made sure of the third U-boat, he permitted his ships to pick up the traumatised survivors from the other two German U-boats. Happily, the *Woodpecker*, *Kite*, and *Wren* were successful in picking up all sixty-four men of the *U-462*'s crew, as well as the fifteen survivors from *U-461*.

Marrows's decent action in dropping one of his aircraft's dinghies for the *U-461* survivors had probably saved lives, but it would give rise to cool deliberations up and down Coastal Command's command chain. Three days later, No. 19 Group HQ issued an instruction to all squadrons, laying down that aircraft were not to drop their dinghies to enemy survivors, in view of the acute threat they themselves faced from enemy fighters. As we shall see, the Bay of Biscay was not only a place where RAF aircraft preyed upon U-boats, but also a place where they themselves, in their turn, were preyed upon by Luftwaffe fighters. In this dangerous environment, the air commanders set the reasonable and rational prioritisation that aircraft dinghies must be kept for their own crews.

Job done, Marrows's Sunderland headed home at its most economical speed. Despite their submarine kill, there was minimal triumphalism or elation among the crewmen aboard, but rather great anxiety about their aircraft's fuel state. Paddy Watson, the flight engineer, as anxious as navigator Jock Rolland about it, had already drained all the remaining fuel from the outer wing tanks into the inner, main tanks in each wing. Checking the contents of these, he delivered to Marrows his assessment that, 'we would never make Pembroke Dock!' The Scillies provided the closest friendly land, but there was even some doubt whether they would reach there before the aircraft ran out of fuel. It was thus a very troubled crew that headed home, 'firmly saddled with the realisation' that they might not make it after all.

It did not help that they ran into yet another U-boat on the way home. Marrows 'jumped almost with fright' when Watson, now standing watch in the nose turret, suddenly shouted into the intercom, 'U-boat on the starboard bow!' Marrows could not see it initially, and replied with, 'It can't be, Paddy,' incredulous that there could be so many U-boats to see in one day, after seeing none for eight months. Then a stunned silence ensued when he spotted the submarine, 1½ miles away. After that brief hiatus came his abrupt announcement to the crew, 'I'm going straight in! Get the bomb out!' To avoid any extra fuel consumption, Marrows dived straight at the U-boat to drop his sole remaining depth-charge.

The resultant attack dive turned into a desperate physical struggle to pull up to avoid crashing into the sea in front of the U-boat: both pilots had to heave together on their control wheels to raise the nose; the aircraft 'cleared the U-boat by inches' as 'the horrified German gunners flung themselves on the decks'. Even after winding the tail trim right back to help hold the nose up, the pilots had to continue sweating and straining to hold their control yokes back just to maintain normal flight. In this way, they 'bullied' the aircraft back up to 1,000 feet, and it was only then, with some air between his keel and the sea, that Marrows got his eyes free enough from his immediate predicament to check the positions of all levers and switches in the cockpit; discovering to his chagrin that, in his shock and hurry, upon commencing the dive he had accidentally knocked the lever forward to engage the autopilot!

Watson had sprayed the conning tower with bursts of .303 on the run-in but did not shoot as accurately as Pearce had done an hour earlier, for the U-boat's flak gunners put a burst right under the wing-root, spraying the area with shell splinters, and setting alight the electric traversing motor of the bomb-carriage. After hearing over the intercom, 'Galley to control. We're on fire in the bomb-room,' Pearce was relieved by the assistant engineer at the flight engineer's panel, so that he could hurry down the ladder into the galley to attend to the fire in the adjoining compartment. He used the extinguisher to douse the burning motor, plugged himself into the intercom to report 'Fire out', then went back up the ladder to resume his station.[62]

After the alarm of this unanticipated action, and the undesired extra fuel consumption occasioned even by this short attack, the crew were now even more discomforted about U-Uncle's fuel state and their chances of making the Scillies. Maximum range was obtained by so reducing the engine power settings as to fly at minimum airspeed: accordingly, Watson asked Marrows to cruise at only 115 knots. By this means, they extended their airborne endurance sufficiently to alight at St Mary's in the Scillies at 3.15 p.m., with what Watson calculated to be perhaps fifteen minutes' worth of fuel left in the tanks (about 30 gallons).[63] Once 'U-Uncle' was secured to a buoy, the crew undertook a laborious refuelling using 4-gallon cans brought out to their mooring in a launch: even if they only took 300 gallons (enough for a two-hour trip), such a refuelling would take seventy-five fuel cans, with each can passed by hand in through the door, up the ladder to the upper deck, out on to the wing through the astrodome hatch, and then poured into each wing's main tank.[64] After refuelling, U/461 took off for the one-hour trip back to Pembroke Dock, arriving there at almost 6.30 p.m., after which the weary crew withstood a debriefing in the ops room, followed by celebrations in the squadron messes. Jubilation came with safety.

With an explosive shell hole in its port wing spar, Marrows's submarine-killing Sunderland, 'U-Uncle', was condemned as unairworthy, but was patched up well enough at Pembroke Dock to be made flyable again, and on 24 August was flown away to Belfast for repairs by her manufacturer, Short Brothers. She had flown seventeen operations with No. 461, being one of the oldest aircraft in the squadron, one of the four early-model Mk II aircraft used by the squadron during 1943. She never returned to the unit but survived to serve out the rest of her time with the RAF until 1945.[65] Marrows's crew was allocated a new replacement Mk III Sunderland, coded 'E'. Two months later, No. 461 received a visit from the great Capt. 'Johnnie' Walker, RN, who was so pleased with the numerical coincidence of U/461 sinking *U-461* that he went out of his way to visit Pembroke Dock, making a presentation of a piece of wreckage from *U-461* picked up by HMS *Woodpecker*.

Although it is invidious to single out contributors to the combined triumph of sinking three U-boats, it was Irving's Liberator O/53 that had first alerted other aircraft to the passage of the three U-boats on the surface, and that two hours later had drawn the flak to enable Marrows's successful attack. It was White's Sunderland R/228 that had corrected an initial positional error and homed the other aircraft in. After that, it was Marrows's U/461 that had made a highly meritorious bomb run and killed *U-461* single-handedly in one pass; while van Rossum too had bombed with commendable accuracy to cripple *U-462* and ensure her demise by rendering her incapable of diving. Walker's task force of hunter-killer warships had demonstrated great expertise by tracking *U-504*'s underwater movements and killing her while she tried to hide in the deep, but even Walker had been reliant upon the aircraft for the submarine contact in the first place. Beyond that, the entire action had been dependent upon Bletchley Park's decryption of the German destroyer flotilla's wireless traffic, and upon the acumen of the Admiralty's Submarine Tracking Room in correctly deducing the context of those signals. Marrows and his crew can be seen as the spearhead of a huge inter-service collaboration, upheld and enabled by an organisational effort involving thousands of people in multiple locations.

Suspended in the centre of all this propitious context, it had certainly been Marrows's lucky day nonetheless, for three other Australian Sunderland crews had been out that day patrolling the area, but all missed out on the action through the usual operational contingencies of timing, route, and location. Of these, Fg Off. Dick Gray from 10 Squadron took off in Sunderland H/10 during the early afternoon, in time to witness the rescue of the U-boat survivors: at 6.05 p.m., he arrived over the scene of the battle earlier that day to find two Royal Navy warships stopped in the water, picking up the German survivors. No. 10 Squadron's former commanding officer (CO), Grp Capt. Jim Alexander, had come aboard 'H' for the ride. Now serving as the CO of RAF Mount Batten, he had never seen a U-boat during his short time with the squadron, and was too late to see one now, forced to content himself with viewing the aftermath of the handiwork of the junior Australian squadron.

The destruction of an entire group of three U-boats was rightfully hailed as a breakthrough moment for Coastal Command as a whole. Air Marshal John Slessor sent a signal through his whole command, praising all participants for their 'brilliant combined action', but singling out Marrows for choosing 'the exact moment' when the U-boat gunners were distracted by firing at the Liberator, and for bombing from only 50 feet to 'make sure of a "kill"'. Slessor geed up his men with the declaration that they had 'beaten all previous records and have shewn that the enemy cannot hope to get away with it by passing through the bay in packs and fighting back on the surface.... It is difficult to exaggerate the importance of these operations to the whole issue of the war. Keep it up.'[66] It was not for nothing that Slessor declared July 1943 to be the 'black month for the Axis in their U-boat campaign', for out of the seventeen boats which the German U-boat Command had despatched in July for North Atlantic patrols, eleven were sunk that month by the squadrons of No. 19 Group.[67, 68] The passage of the Bay had become a death-ride for the U-boats.

2

Sunderlands

The Short S.25 Sunderland flying boat was the largest British aircraft to be operated in numbers within the wartime RAF and was a fine machine broadly representative of the technological state-of-the-art in the immediate pre-war era. Flying boats were a well-established aircraft category at a time when good airfields remained rare or non-existent in many parts of the world; thus, it was logical to configure an aeroplane to land and take-off from water, rather than from *terra firma*.

By the outbreak of the Second World War, flying boats had grown immensely in size, power, and performance to become large, modern, capable monoplane machines like the Sunderland. In broad terms, this aircraft was of 30 tons maximum take-off weight, was propelled by 4,000 horsepower, and, with 2,000 imperial gallons of fuel, it could heft a 1-ton bombload on missions of more than twelve hours' duration. Its capacious hull not only provided buoyancy, but housed three hydraulically powered gun turrets; crew positions for up to twelve crewmen; a bomb-room with an electrically-operated winch and retractable bomb racks; banks of smoke floats, sea markers, and flares; reconnaissance cameras; pneumatic dinghies; a galley with a gas stovetop; a wardroom for taking meals; bunks for off-duty crewmen; an anchor, anchor chain, bollard, and drogue sea anchors; and even a bathroom with a flushing white porcelain toilet, and a sink with running water and a shaving mirror.

The internal appointments of the Sunderland were sufficiently homely to permit crewmen to live aboard the aircraft overnight, in bad weather keeping an eye out for water in the bilges or for dragging on the anchor. The Sunderland's interior appointments were Spartan by civil airliner standards, but off-duty crewmen in the galley could use the primus stove to fry up staples like chops, sausages, and eggs to go with fresh bread or toast; such meals could even go three courses, including a soup and a sweet; and the wardroom was always the place to go for hot tea, coffee, or cocoa, as well as the only place in the aircraft where a man was officially permitted to sit and smoke. Thus the Sunderland allowed its crewmen to dine in civilised fashion, sitting together around the wardroom table, using good cutlery and china—which all too often the crewmen had purloined from a range of pubs, guesthouses, and tea rooms in Devonshire, Pembrokeshire, and Dorset! The on-board watch crew could also use the aircraft's powerful wireless to tune into a wide range of foreign radio stations—for example, during one such duty, No. 10 Squadron wireless operator Percy Smith tuned into not only American radio stations from Pittsburgh, Pennsylvania, and Rutherfordton, North Carolina, but also enjoyed the transgressive thrill of listening in to stations from the Axis side, such as Turin radio and the Berlin stations, DXD and DJB.[1]

The domestic facilities of the Sunderland's spacious interior stemmed from its design ancestry as a close relative of its stablemate, the Short S.23 'Empire Flying Boat'. This pre-war airliner type was designed and built for the Empire Air Mail routes stretching between England and Australia. These 'Empire' boats were even larger than the Sunderland, with wider hulls to encompass the passenger cabins, freight compartments, bar, galley, toilets, and smoking rooms necessary to meet the high-maintenance needs of the pre-war era's well-heeled air-travellers. In broad terms, the Sunderland can be seen as a slimmed-down but heavier, more densely-packaged, military version of its airliner cousin.

Design commonality meant that the Sunderland also shared the Empire boats' weaknesses. It had too much structural weight, which cut down the proportion of its gross weight that could be given to fuel, hence limiting its airborne range and endurance.[2] Also its hull bottom was prone to rupture in heavy water landings, and its wingtip-float struts and attachments were too delicate, judged to be the aircraft's weakest point, as they were apt to fail in heavy seas, dropping the wing into the water and causing the loss of the aircraft.[3] Other contemporary flying boats used different configurations to improve on these aspects: for example, the Sikorsky designs featured a slim hull suspended by struts beneath a parasol wing; these machines reaped the reward of lower structural weight, hence a higher fuel fraction, and so longer range.[4] The Sunderland's American contemporary, the Catalina, represented this competing design philosophy.

When the Sunderland was designed in the mid-1930s, it was to be a 'jack of all trades' combat aircraft, suitable for a range of air-to-ground, air-to-sea, and air-to-air combat roles. Moreover, the Sunderland was also designed to be suitable for service not only in British home waters but throughout the Empire. For example, the first RAF squadron to receive the new aircraft was No. 230, stationed at Singapore. The Sunderland was thus designed from the outset not primarily for anti-submarine patrols, but for finding, photographing, and attacking enemy shipping on the high seas, and for defending itself in air combat with enemy aircraft. As a result of this broad specification, the aircraft entered the war in 1939 as perhaps the most operationally versatile and well-armed flying boat of its time. Sunderlands in the first half of the war reconnoitred seaways, attacked submarines, bombed enemy ships, defended friendly ships against enemy bombers, fought off fighter attack, transported VIPs over long distances through contested skies, and rescued shot-down aircrew from the sea. The pressure of real operations also showed the aircraft's vulnerabilities. Sunderlands entered the war in 1939 with a defensive armament of seven .303-inch machine guns, but by 1942, the need for up-gunning was obvious, and thus by 1943, extra guns were appearing on operational Sunderlands.

The Sunderland in its mature, mid-war Mk III form was a capable warplane, able to carry a ton of depth-charges to a point in the ocean 600 miles from base, there to conduct a three-hour search, and then return to base after a twelve-hour flight, still with a couple of hours' fuel reserves aboard as a safety margin. In 1942–43, the bombload was usually eight 270-pound depth-charges, set to explode at a depth of 25 feet—a killing depth for a U-boat running on the surface. Like all other maritime patrol aircraft in Coastal Command from 1941 onwards, Sunderlands used search radar to detect and track submarines on the surface, giving their crews the ability to find and attack their prey even in bad weather and heavy seas, when visual searching was impracticable.

Sunderland Crew Roles

Visual searching with the 'Mk 1 Eyeball' remained a vital practice, however, not least because even if the U-boat was initially detected by radar, it was still necessary to make a confirmatory visual sighting before making an attack. For visual lookout, the co-pilot in the right-hand pilot's seat used a pair of binoculars to sweep the sea arc below the horizon, sharing the visual searching across the forward hemisphere with the bow gunner, who traversed his turret left and right across his allocated arc. The search arcs across the rear hemisphere were covered by the other two turret gunners: in the midships turret, positioned high up on the aircraft's back, and in the tail turret, both of whom similarly traversed their turrets from left to right across their allocated arcs. There were thus four men engaged on full-time lookout duties at any one moment on a patrol: the three turret gunners and the co-pilot. A fifth set of eyes came into play while the aircraft was within range of enemy fighters, when the 'off-duty' pilot would stand beneath the astrodome, at the rear of the flight-deck, scanning the clouds and sky for airborne danger.

Men could only maintain the sharp focus necessary for effective lookout if they were relieved regularly, and thus every hour the men changed position, according to a set crew roster. The three pilots took turns serving as the pilot in control (in the left-hand seat), then swapping by turn to the right-hand co-pilot's seat, to the fighter lookout position in the astrodome, to the radar set, or to some other duty, such as fetching sandwiches and hot cocoa from the galley. Despite the outward egalitarianism of this rotation, it was skewed in favour of the captain and first pilot: the captain only rarely left the flight-deck, while the lowly second pilot usually obtained only brief turns at the controls during safe passages of the flight; he was typically regarded by the captain as his 'dogsbody', employed on an as-needed basis to fulfil odd-jobs, such as encoding or decoding wireless messages, moving through the hull checking on the other crewmen in their posts, or going aft to prepare a flare, sea marker, or smoke float for dropping.[5] The navigator was the only crewman who did not rotate roles at all: he officially served full-time as navigator from start to finish of each flight, metaphorically chained to his chart table on the flight-deck, moving only as far as the adjacent astrodome to measure the azimuth of a heavenly body for his next calculation of latitude.[6]

Besides the three pilots and the navigator, the other seven or eight men in the crew stood one-hour 'tricks' in a constant rotation, with one man off-duty every hour and the other six standing watch at one of six positions: wireless, radar, flight engineer's panel, nose turret, midships turret, and tail turret. Within the Australian Sunderland squadrons, this group was typically composed of a broad range of trade musterings, such as engine fitters, airframe riggers, air gunners, wireless operator/air gunners, wireless mechanic/air gunners, flight engineers, and armourers. In the typical Australian crew, these were enlisted men, ranging in rank from leading aircraftman to flight sergeant, while the pilots and navigators were typically of officer rank, ranging from pilot officer to flight lieutenant. As a result, once ashore, the pilots and navigator lived and socialised apart in the officers' mess, while the 'back-seaters' lived and socialised in the airmen's and sergeants' messes. A crew was thus integrated in the air but segregated on the ground.

The air gunners stood at the bottom of the crew totem pole, not included in the one-on-one pre-flight briefings accorded to the specialist members, during which the captain and first pilot were briefed on all the particulars of the mission, the navigator worked out his flight-plan, the wireless operators received their sets of frequencies, stations, and schedules, and the flight engineers rechecked the fuel and saw to the completion of any last-minute work by Maintenance Flight. While all this brain work was going on, it was the air gunners who were obliged to go out to the boat early, installing and loading all the guns, and generally getting the boat shipshape for flight. They also took the flight rations out to the aircraft, stowed these in the galley, and during the flight boiled the water for the production of hot drinks, cooked the meals, and washed up in the sink. Before and after take-off and landing, it was the gunners who stood in the bow hatch with a boathook for the seamanlike duties of mooring and unmooring, and likewise prepared and deployed the canvas sea anchors out of the galley hatches while taxiing. At the completion of each flight, they stayed aboard the aircraft with the flight engineers to remove, clean, and stow the guns, as well as anything else that needed to be done to make the boat shipshape again before they could go ashore after the officers.[7] When a couple of men were needed to stay on-board as boat-guard, to keep an eye on leaks, operate the petrol-driven pump, or watch the mooring in windy conditions, this task too was allocated to the gunners.[8]

Of course, in a 'pilot's air force' like the RAF and RAAF, an organisation run by pilots for pilots, there could never be any doubt that the captain and first pilot stood at the top end of the totem pole.[9] This was especially so in the Coastal Command flying boat fraternity, where these qualified pilots enjoyed the prestige of membership in the metaphorical 'Flying Boat Union'.[10] Militarily, the captain was, after all, the aircraft commander, and the first pilot his deputy, and both were moreover officers, in a crew typically dominated numerically by enlisted airmen.

However, the navigator was arguably as highly positioned as the pilots on the status hierarchy. Not only was he too an officer, but because there was only a single navigator in each crew, he was personally indispensable for the safe conduct of any flight beyond sight of land. Moreover, he was typically regarded as the brains of the crew, even by the pilots. This attitude was associated with the navigator's mastery of the esoteric mysteries of navigation, maintaining an accurate 'dead reckoned' plot using the myriad inputs of astronomical observations, radar beacons, light houses, medium-frequency direction-finding, direction-finding loop-aerial fixes, drift measurement, and radar detection of islands and headlands.[11] Although most navigators had joined the air force for pilot training, only to endure the disappointment of being 'scrubbed' from pilots' course, after that setback their training was similarly lengthy and thorough to that of their pilot colleagues, and like them, navigators typically shared the pilots' officer status (this was certainly so in the Australian Sunderland squadrons), which underlined their joint status as the executive cadre within a crew.[12]

The reputation navigators enjoyed for knowledge and intelligence was also reflected in their higher levels of educational attainment and higher social status: whereas only 16 per cent of RAAF wartime-trained wireless operator/air gunners had completed senior high school or higher, the proportion for pilots was 40 per cent, while that for navigators was 58 per cent. Similarly, whereas only 51 per cent of wireless operator/air gunners came from white collar or professional backgrounds, the proportion for pilots streamed on to multi-engined aircraft was 74 per cent, while that of navigators was 79 per cent.[13]

The exclusivity of the navigator fraternity conferred privileges as well as responsibility: the navigator did not need to get his hands dirty on menial tasks aboard the boat like mooring, but could enter the aircraft like a high priest of aeronautical exactitude, carrying his holy 'gen bag', which was 'weighted with authority' from its load of esoteric objects: charts, books, sextants, slide rule, protractors, dividers, pencils, rubbers, and sharpeners. When newly posted-in 461 Squadron navigator Plt Off. 'Ossie' Pederick started helping the enlisted airmen in mooring-up the boat, he was 'very smartly told by the "navigators' union" that navigators didn't do such things'.[14] After that rebuke, upon boarding the aircraft, he withdrew like his other navigator colleagues to the splendid isolation of the chart-table, leaving the gunners to get on with it.

While on an operational flight, a typical rotation of roles for the wireless operator/air gunners was to start at the wireless set, followed by a trick at the radar set, followed by lookout duty in one of the gun turrets, and then back to the wireless to start over again. Both the wireless and radar sets were mounted on the flight-deck, immediately behind the pilots' seats, with the wireless in a purpose-designed station to port, and the radar to starboard, crammed into an improvised workspace curtained-off between the back of the co-pilot's seat and the front of the navigator's chart table. The ASV (air-to-surface vessel) radar equipment was a late-arriving innovation, adapted to aircraft use after the design of the Sunderland. For the crewmen, taking a turn on the radar set came after doing a turn on the wireless because the operator's eyes needed to be attuned to dim lighting conditions in order to better discern and interpret the ghostly green glows, traces, and smudges on the tiny cathode ray tube. After an hour in the wireless operator's hole, his eyes were sensitised to the dimly-lit displays of the electrical equipment, and hence right for the radar. It was only after being relieved at the radar set that the crewman's 'night vision' could be freely ruined by exposure to the blinding sunlight of the gun turret. For the fitters and flight engineers, a typical role rotation would take in a spell at the deeply-recessed flight engineer's panel, then at the radar, then a spell in one of the gun turrets. Within each eleven- or twelve-man crew, one or two men were also rostered off each hour so they could eat a meal in the wardroom, make a brew in the galley, or take a 'kip' on one of the bunks.

At this stage of the war, there was no separate aircrew 'trade' of radar operator; indeed, the radar equipment of the day was so secret that it was not even mentioned by its name (ASV) but by the cover term, 'special equipment'. A crew's roster of radar operators was therefore not limited to men with a wireless qualification but was composed of a selection of approved men from any random combination of trades, such as second pilots, flight engineers or air gunners. Members of various aircrew specialisations were simply trained to operate the radar set, and became *de facto*, undesignated, off-the-record radar operators—and sworn to secrecy about this aspect of their duties. Within each crew, only selected crewmen were put on the radar because the RAF had realised that some men had the gift for this and some did not, and that within the limits of the set's technical characteristics, the detection of targets was a measure of operator proficiency.

An Example Sunderland Crew

The men who manned the Sunderlands of Coastal Command in the middle of the war can be exemplified by Dudley Marrows's crew from the previous chapter. There we found Marrows himself sitting in the left-hand command pilot's seat; like most captains, he bore the responsibility for his aircraft and crew by flying most of the flight in the command seat. Like the captain's chair on a warship's bridge, this was the aircraft's nerve centre, at the apex of the tactical information inputs provided by the co-pilot, navigator, wireless operator, radar operator, and flight engineer, all of whom were clustered closely beside or behind the captain's seat. Beyond that, he was the central point within the intercom system, through which he received and responded to information via the disembodied voices of his three turret gunners and the fire controller in the astrodome. Given the luxury of time, the captain metaphorically stood at the head of a triune war council, whereby tactical choices were deliberated between himself, the co-pilot and navigator—as well as the flight engineer, for in long flights far out to sea, most decisions had to factor in an up-to-the-minute fuel calculation. The first three members of this 'brain trust' were almost always officers; the latter was almost always a sergeant, but despite that, he needed to be included in the discussions for his intimate knowledge of the contents of the aircraft's fuel tanks. Despite a certain amount of informal in-cockpit conferencing, it was the captain who made the decision and took the responsibility for what followed. He was usually the most experienced airman in the crew, so could credibly lead his men into danger, literally leading them from the front.

By the end of July 1943, Flt Lt Dudley Marrows had been flying operations with No. 461 for more than a year, captaining his own crew since November 1942. He had enlisted in the RAAF in October 1940, obtained his pilot's wings in 1941, completed a Sunderland conversion course early in 1942 at No. 4 OTU in Scotland, and arrived on the new squadron in June 1942. He joined the unit as a low-hours twenty-four-year-old pilot, but he grew rapidly in operational stature: by 30 July 1943, he was captaining his thirty-seventh operation, only a couple of missions away from finishing his tour of operations.

In the right-hand co-pilot's seat was Marrows's first pilot, Plt Off. Clifford 'Jimmy' Leigh, a twenty-three-year-old Melbournian who had enlisted in April 1941, joining No. 461 as a green sergeant pilot in January 1943. He had flown five operations as a second pilot before being commissioned in the following June, for the RAAF preferred its Sunderland pilots to be of officer rank rather than of sergeant rank, as was otherwise normal in the wartime air force. Having thus been rapidly elevated to officer status, Leigh had been trained up to fly the Sunderland solo, and on 30 July was flying his debut operation as first pilot.

Plt Off. Pearce Taplin flew as Marrows's second pilot on 30 July, flying his ninth operation since joining the unit in February 1943; he had only flown with Marrows once before, back in March. This was because the second pilot was not a regular member of a crew, as he flew with a different crew almost every flight as part of his on-the-job-training; only upon qualification to first pilot would he become a regular member of a crew. Taplin, from the town of Moora, north of Perth, was at thirty-one years old—unusually old for a newly-graduated pilot—the second-oldest man in the crew. The essential difference between the two co-pilots in a Sunderland crew was that the first pilot had qualified to fly the aircraft solo, whereas the second pilot had not. The captain would give the second pilot spells at the controls to help him gain this qualification, but while flying in the operational area, the captain and first pilot would occupy the pilots' seats for most of the time, leaving the second pilot to carry out ancillary duties further aft in the fuselage. Despite his relatively lowly position within the flight-deck hierarchy, the second pilot was nonetheless an officer, and thus part of a crew's officer cadre concentrated at the front of the aircraft. In the action of 30 July, Taplin was operating the radar, and thus close to the nerve centre of the aircraft.

The other member of the flight-deck officers' club was the navigator, Fg Off. John 'Jock' Rolland. Despite being one of the youngest members of the crew, this twenty-two-year-old from Sale in Victoria was a more experienced operational airman even than the captain. Rolland had joined up in March 1941 and had initially been posted to the senior Australian Sunderland unit, No. 10, flying half a tour of operations with that unit through early 1942 before being posted to the newly-created No. 461 in July of that year. He thus joined the unit at its inception as one of its most experienced airmen, at first serving as navigator in Bert Smith's crew, within which Dudley Marrows had served as first pilot. Marrows and Rolland thus went back some way as an operational team. By 30 July 1943, Rolland was, like Marrows, coming to the end of his tour.

Behind the officers' club on the flight deck, the rest of a Sunderland crew were typically NCOs, but Marrows's crew harboured an outstanding exception in Fg Off. Pete Jensen the wireless operator. The flying officer rank of both Rolland and Jensen, outranking Leigh and Taplin, pointed to their relative seniority, in a crew where both co-pilots held the lowest commissioned rank of pilot officer. Jensen had joined the RAAF in February 1941; after arriving in England, he had completed a course on Sunderlands at 4 OTU, then begun his operational career with No. 10, flying with that unit throughout 1942, before getting posted in No. 461 in early 1943. By July 1943, he was thus a veteran of Coastal Command's war, and probably the most operationally-experienced man in the crew. Trained as a wireless operator/air gunner, he had been a typical product of the Empire Air Training Scheme by graduating as a sergeant, but had then been commissioned in 1942, groomed by the squadron's executive officers to be appointed squadron gunnery officer at the conclusion of his operational tour. To qualify for this role, in December 1942, he was sent off to attend a course on gun turrets with the Parnell Armament School at Yate, and in March 1943 completed a course with the Central Gunnery School at Sutton Bridge. Like Rolland, Jensen was by the end of July 1943 on the verge of completing his tour and would stay on the unit afterwards to lead its gunnery department and would be duly promoted to flight lieutenant at the end of the year, in accordance with these executive responsibilities.

Behind the five officers stood a team of five sergeants, but the modest rank of these men belied some formidable experience and proficiency. Sunderland crews included two flight engineers, who took turns at the flight engineer's panel at the rear of the flight-deck. There the duty engineer monitored the gauges for the aircraft's critical systems (engines, fuel tanks, hydraulics, electrics), warned the pilots of any instrument indications 'in the red' and gave the skipper instructions to shut down or throttle-back ailing engines; he also switched between fuel tanks and calculated and recalculated actual fuel consumption and projected endurance, passing these data to the navigator and captain for deliberation and decision. The flight engineers' duties and responsibilities did not end when the crew went ashore at the end of a flight: one of the two engineers would spend most days aboard the moored flying boat, inspecting, checking and adjusting her systems, and supervising the work of the fitters, riggers, and mechanics from Maintenance Flight who came aboard to complete maintenance tasks.

Marrows's senior flight engineer was the only non-Australian in the crew, Sgt 'Paddy' Watson of the RAF. This Irishman had considerable mechanical ability, having been a motor mechanic in Dublin before joining the RAF in January 1941, and having served as an engine fitter in the ground crew before becoming a flight engineer in mid-1942. He was so well thought-of that he was commissioned after finishing his tour, staying on the unit and becoming its flight engineer leader with the rank of flight lieutenant. Marrows's crew was thus built around a formidably-proficient core of four departmental specialists, each of whom was so experienced as to be on the cusp of finishing his tour: Marrows, the captain; Rolland, the navigator; Jensen, the wireless operator/air gunner; and Watson, the flight engineer.

The second flight engineer was also no newly-qualified greenhorn: Sgt Allan 'Bubbles' Pearce was one of two RAAF tradesmen in Marrows's crew who had volunteered for aircrew, the other being Sgt Fred 'Pierre' Bamber, a flight rigger who like Pearce now served as a jack-of-all-trades air crewman. These men served as air gunners, with Bamber manning the nose turret, and Pearce the improvised gun in the nose hatch. Both had solid ground-crew technical backgrounds, and a common mature age of twenty-nine years old. These two men were the only members of Marrows's crew who had enlisted in the regular RAAF. Except for the sole RAF member, Paddy Watson, everyone else was a 'hostilities-only' airman who had enlisted and been trained within the wartime Empire Air Training Scheme (EATS). With three regular airmen on-board, all with solid ground trade backgrounds, Marrows's crew was as well served in its strong cadre of expert NCO technicians as it was in its cadre of experienced and qualified aircrew officers.

The other two sergeants in Marrows's crew were typical of the wireless operator/air gunners trained within the EATS: Sgt Charles 'Bunny' Sidney and FS Horace Morgan. Sidney, the tail gunner, was the oldest man in the crew, a thirty-two-year-old from Sydney. Morgan was the opposite, a twenty-one-year-old from Yangan in Queensland who served as the second wireless operator and took turns in the midships turret.

In the 30 July 1943 action against *U-461*, Pearce and Bamber were manning their guns in the nose; Marrows and Leigh were at the controls in the cockpit; Jensen and Taplin were just behind the pilots on the wireless and radar sets respectively; Rolland and Watson were behind Taplin, at the navigator's desk and flight engineer's panel; while Morgan and Sidney were in the midships and tail turrets.

Overall, Marrows's crew was experienced and highly proficient, and would have been the envy of virtually any squadron of the period. The excellent result they achieved on 30 July 1943 was thus not coincidental. However, it was also a lucky crew: not only did these men win fame by sinking *U-461*, but they avoided getting shot down in the process, and then they got home safely; finally, luck smiled upon all of them by seeing them through to the end of the war alive. Statistically, this was a luckt result for members of the Sunderland aircrew cohort who went through the dangerous times of 1942–43, as we will see.

Marrows and Rolland continued their long-lasting flying partnership by getting posted back to Australia to fly Sunderlands on transport flights between Australia and New Guinea until the end of the war. Both Leigh and Taplin graduated to captaincy in late 1943, and piloted operations with No. 461 through 1944; indeed, Leigh flew forty-eight ops, the second highest total for any squadron captain, and was still on the staff of No. 461 at the end of the war, as was Pearce, who by that time had been commissioned. Another three of the men finished the war instructing in specialist schools: Sidney at the Sunderland operational training unit in Britain, and Jensen and Morgan on the staff at a wireless air gunnery school in Australia.

Australian Flying Boats in Britain

It was only accidental that Australian crews ended up flying war operations from England in Sunderlands, for the RAAF had originally destined them for service in Australia. When the Australian Minister of Defence Mr G. A. Street announced in May 1939 that the RAAF would purchase nine of the new flying boats from Short Brothers at Rochester in Kent, these aircraft were intended to spearhead the expansion of the service's home defence capability as war with Japan loomed.[1] The RAAF had wanted a squadron of flying boats as far back as 1921.[2] It had identified the requirement for a flying boat squadron in a 1935 force review, and in the same year had defined the operational doctrine for this flying boat force.[3] It was to operate from forward bases on New Guinea, New Britain, and New Ireland, maintaining long-range patrols against Japanese incursions into the northern approaches to Australia.[4] The RAAF's Sunderland-equipped squadron was thus slated to fulfil exactly the same function as its Catalina-equipped sisters, Nos 11 and 20 Squadrons, actually performed over the early months of the Pacific War in 1941–42.[5]

In 1938, the RAAF began the process of selecting and acquiring a modern seaplane type, as part of the same pre-war expansion and modernisation process that saw the service re-equipped with Lockheed Hudson patrol bombers. By that time, Japan had already launched its protracted war upon China, so the writing was on the wall for war in the Pacific. The then-commander of the RAAF, Air Vice-Marshal Richard Williams, specified the selection of a large, modern, multi-engined seaplane for the air force's envisaged wartime role of patrolling Australia's northern approaches. The role included both reconnaissance tasks like locating and shadowing Japanese ships, as well as strike roles such as bombing their ships and forward island bases. Large seaplanes were seen as the answer to Australia's needs because of the lack of airfields across this remote and extensive theatre of operations; seaplanes could putatively 'land anywhere'. Although Williams thought that the American type, the Consolidated Catalina, was the best aircraft for the job because of its greater range and excellent Pratt & Whitney engines, his successor, Air Marshal Stanley Goble, instead chose the British equivalent, the Short Sunderland.[6] Whatever the relative merits of these aircraft types, the RAAF would arguably get the best of both worlds, for by 1942, it had two squadrons operating the Sunderland in European skies, simultaneously with two squadrons operating the Catalina in the Pacific theatre.

On 1 July 1939, No. 10 Squadron formed at Point Cook, outside Melbourne, created out of the 'Seaplane Squadron' of the resident unit, No. 1 Flying Training School. Throughout the interwar years, the RAAF's seaplane element at Point Cook had subsisted there in vestigial fashion, employing a small collection of obsolete British biplane types of modest flight performance and very limited operational capability. None of these short-ranged machines were capable of making any significant contribution to real war operations around the northern coast of Australia, but they did serve to maintain a tradition of seaplane flying proficiency within the pre-war RAAF. Thus, there were trained seaplane pilots available to be posted to No. 10 and despatched to England to take possession of the Sunderlands and fly them back to Australia.

Upon arriving in England, these pilots would find the Sunderland an impressive and imposing aircraft: back at Point Cook, they had trained on single-engined Seagull V amphibians with a take-off weight of only 3 tonnes, giving an operating radius of less than 200 miles, but here was a 'seemingly gigantic' aircraft with four engines, a 112-foot wingspan, a take-off weight of 22 tons, and an operating radius of 600 miles. By the end of July 1939, the first group of seven pilots had commenced their conversion to modern flying boats at RAF Calshot, on Southampton Water; from mid-August they were receiving on-the-job training on Sunderlands, accompanying British crews on operational patrols. In September, the Australians took delivery of their first Sunderland from the Short Brothers factory at Rochester in Kent, and thereafter set about taking possession of their machines one by one, making them ready to be ferried back to Australia.[7] Each aircraft cost the Australian government £49,225.[8]

The RAAF's plans for Sunderlands over New Guinea were interrupted by Hitler's invasion of Poland on 1 September and Britain's consequent declaration of war upon Germany on the 3rd, followed by Australian Prime Minister Robert Menzies's similar declaration on the 4th. In response to the altered situation, on 20 October, the Australian War Cabinet cancelled the planned return of No. 10 Squadron to Australia; the unit was now committed to the defence of Britain.[9] Back in Australia,

Wg Cdr Joe Hewitt, commander of the RAAF's newly established flying boat base at Rathmines on Lake Macquarie, had been driving his men hard in getting the base ready to receive the Sunderlands from Britain. Frustratingly, the sudden change of policy now left him with only a single Seagull amphibian to use at the new base.[10] Meanwhile in England, No. 10 had hitherto existed as a skeleton unit only, with just enough men in England to fly the nine aircraft home. Now that the squadron was committed to war service in England, the RAAF would have to find the men to bring it up to full wartime strength. This would take time: by the end of December 1939, the unit was possessed of its full complement of nine Sunderlands, but its total personnel strength of 213 was less than half of wartime squadron establishment.[11]

The deployment of No. 10 to Britain's war against Germany was a down-payment towards an intended 'Australian Air Expeditionary Force'. According to this scheme, the RAAF would raise six new squadrons and deploy them as a vertically-integrated force alongside the RAF, commanded by RAAF officers. However, the outcome of negotiations between Britain and the Dominions at Ottawa in November 1939 completely overturned this concept too: instead of sending expeditionary air forces to fight alongside British forces, the Dominions would now provide airmen to fight within the British air force. The expeditionary force was thereby cancelled, leaving No. 10's ongoing deployment to England as a faint echo of the original idea, namely as a fully-RAAF unit fighting alongside the RAF in Britain, rather than inside it.[12]

Wartime Organisational Politics for the RAAF

Once Australia signed on to the terms of the EATS in December 1939, the RAAF was committed to transforming itself into an immense training organisation to supply trained and semi-trained aircrew for service with the RAF. Britain's air force was thus reconceived as, in effect, an imperial air force, commanded by British officers but manned by men from throughout the empire. Australia had agreed to provide 36 per cent of the Dominion sub-total.[13] Thus the RAAF's main wartime task became the creation, staffing, and running of flying schools in Australia: Grp Capt. George Jones was given the job of creating thirty-three new training schools throughout the country, from Bundaberg to Benalla, from Camden to Cunderdin.[14] Once the system was up and running, Australia was committed to graduating 306 pilots, 186 navigators, and 314 wireless operator/air gunners every four weeks for service within the RAF's global war-fighting organisation.[15] Enabled by aircraft and equipment shipped from Britain, the RAAF certainly proved to be an effective training organisation, for by December 1941, it had despatched 6,472 aircrew and 2,294 ground crew for service with the RAF.[16]

Article XV of the EATS agreement obliged Britain's Air Ministry to give consideration to the Dominions' national aspirations, authorising each Dominion to form some national squadrons within the RAF. Each of these national units would be manned by the particular Dominion's own EATS graduates, while the bulk of their trained men went to RAF units. Canada, New Zealand, and Australia would duly form the first of their Article XV squadrons in early 1941, and by 1944, Australia would have ten such squadrons deployed in Britain. Article XV thus became the default framework for any Canadian, Australian, and New Zealand squadrons that were formed in Britain. In the wake of this arrangement, No. 10 was left as the sole regular RAAF squadron in Britain, organisationally divorced from the coming wave of Australian Article XV units formed within the RAF.

As a relic of an earlier dispensation, the initial cohorts of 10 Squadron's personnel were 'the best the RAAF had to offer'.[17] The initial pilot cadre sent out from Australia as aircraft captains and executive officers indicates the squadron's status as the flagship unit of the RAAF: of the eight pilots, all but two were senior men of flight lieutenant rank or above, with many of these going on to have noted careers as wartime commanders. On its part, the RAF would generously provide the plum location of Mount Batten as the base for the new Australian squadron—perhaps an in-kind reciprocation for Australia's generosity in committing such a fine unit to Britain's defence. RAF Mount Batten was a comfortable, fit-for-purpose, pre-war flying boat base conveniently located at Plymouth, with three flying boat slipways, three hangars, and co-located headquarters, workshops, and messes.[18]

Well connected by railway to London, the men were close enough to the big city to spend short leaves there. The busy entertainment program pursued by LAC Percy Smith, a wireless operator who joined the squadron in 1940, can be taken as representative of such visits: during a single short leave, he visited Australia House, Duncannon Restaurant, St James's Palace, The Ritz, Aldgate Pump, the Tower of London, the Empire Rendezvous Overseas Club, Whitbread Brewery, the Beaver Club, *The Sydney Morning Herald* office, Capt. Scott's Antarctic exploration ship, the *Discovery*, moored at the Thames Embankment, St Paul's Cathedral, and Westminster Abbey; he also dined at Mansion House with the Lady Mayoress of London. For even shorter leaves, there were day trips out of Plymouth to local sightseeing spots like Dartmoor, cultural sites like Buckfast Abbey in Devon, picturesque towns like Totnes and Dartmouth, and beachside coastal towns like Penzance and St Ives in Cornwall, and Paignton in Devon.[19]

With other Coastal Command squadrons dispersed to dreary wartime bases in remote Scotland, Northern Ireland, and Wales, Plymouth's comparatively good weather and convenient amenities made No. 10 the envy of the RAF flying boat community. The symbolical, political, and diplomatic dimensions of No. 10's deployment in Britain were reflected in the early visit to the squadron of Britain's Foreign Secretary Anthony Eden accompanied by Australian High Commissioner and former Australian Prime Minister Stanley Bruce.[20] Despite the overarching tone of imperial *bonhomie*, Australia would pay its way, meeting the annual cost of £430,000 for the RAF's logistical upkeep of its squadron, in accordance with the terms set by the EATS.[21]

No. 10's status as the sole squadron of the regular RAAF in Britain would prove useful to the Air Board in Melbourne in furthering the careers of its permanent officers: this one unit provided an avenue for hand-picked officers to acquire valuable operational experience, much-coveted decorations, promotions, and seniority in higher rank—all advantageous in progressing up the career ladder back home. In addition, it provided a useful flow of operationally-experienced officers of senior rank who, on return to Australia, could be usefully posted to command roles in the Pacific Theatre. Examples of tour-expired 10 Squadron officers who took up key posts in what became the South West Pacific Area were Grp Capt. W. H. Garing, DFC, who in 1941–42 served as senior air staff officer in North East Area HQ in Townsville; Wg Cdr W. N. Gibson, DFC, base commander of RAAF Port Moresby in 1942; Wg Cdr C. W. Pearce, DFC, operations director at Moresby in 1942; and Sqn Ldr J. A. Cohen, DFC, who commanded No. 11 Squadron in its early war operations over New Guinea. Without these operationally-experienced and capable officers, the home-based RAAF would have had to rely upon commanders with no operational experience at all during Australia's war emergency of 1942.

However, this supply of officers from No. 10 was much fewer than the RAAF wanted, for there was a conflict of interpretation within the RAAF command structure over the application of the EATS agreement. Career officers like Grp Capt. Joe Hewitt (who had been slated for the initial command of No. 10 but unluckily lost his spot after suffering an injury) ached to go overseas to get operational experience within the wartime RAF, but with only a single Australian flying boat squadron overseas the vacancies were strictly limited. Ambitious RAAF senior officers wanted Australian officers to be appointed to command roles within the wider RAF, but the British head of the RAAF, Air Marshal Sir Charles Burnett, quashed such aspirations by limiting such arrangements to only a few exchange postings per year. Burnett considered that the two units of the regular RAAF overseas, No. 10 Squadron in Britain and No. 3 (Fighter) Squadron in Egypt, provided an adequate outlet through which permanent RAAF officers could obtain operational experience. The result was that almost all of the RAAF's most eligible officers saw out the war without exercising command in war operations.[22] By the end of 1941, only two senior officers—both having served with No. 10 and obtained wing commander rank—had accrued considerable operational experience. All those who were senior to them had none.[23]

No. 10 Squadron's Early Growth to Operational Maturity

In February 1940, No. 10 attained initial operational status, and in April moved to its wartime operational base at RAF Mount Batten in Plymouth Sound. The men appreciated the purpose-built facilities of their 'fine' new base: as a pre-war RAF station, it had 'excellent living quarters' and 'splendid maintenance facilities'; while its location on the outskirts of Plymouth provided 'good recreational facilities' for men off-duty.[24] Flt Lt 'Dick' Cohen was impressed by Mount Batten's 'big and beautiful' hangars and comfortable messes. However, he did not like the confined space of the Cattewater mooring area, which was 'quite dangerous to get in and out of' in a taxiing Sunderland; experience was needed in taxiing to avoid 'bumping into other aircraft of the squadron'. Indeed, Mount Batten was in fact far from perfect: Plymouth harbour was 'very crowded with some very big ships', which posed significant hazards to flying boats taxiing to and from the runways.[25] The open waters of Plymouth Sound also became 'distinctly rough' when the wind was from the south; also, the ring of barrage balloons around the much-bombed port hemmed-in the flying boats' circuit area, obliging the pilots to make unusually tight approaches.[26]

For the first two years of its existence in Britain, 10 Squadron flew a varied program of operations, from convoy patrols to long-range transport flights between Britain and her Mediterranean bases. This diffuse effort reflected the fact that 1940–41 was a time of shortage and scarcity for RAF Coastal Command: with three of its Sunderland squadrons deployed overseas, by mid-1941, only Nos 10 and 201 Squadrons remained in the UK over this period, and these were hard-stretched to cover their widely-spread operational taskings.[27] In this context, No. 10 had to operate detachments away from its home base, despite having as few as seven Sunderlands on squadron strength: during 1941, the Australian unit operated not only from Mount Batten but also from Oban on the Firth of

Lorn in Scotland, from Pembroke Dock on Milford Haven in Wales, and from Loch Erne in Northern Ireland; this was in addition to peripatetic operations between England and Gibraltar, Malta, or Alexandria. By the end of April 1941, squadron strength had reached a total of 348 personnel, and its aircraft had accumulated a total of 6,752 flying hours. A year later, No. 10 had risen to a strength of 502 personnel, having by now flown a total of 11,199 operational hours, and having lost four aircraft in crashes, with the equivalent of two full crews killed or captured.[28] By then, they considered themselves 'a pretty good unit'.[29]

So far, the tangible operational return for these losses and all this effort was a part contribution to the loss of one U-boat, and the outright sinking of another. The first incident occurred on 1 July 1940, when *U-26* was so seriously damaged by a sustained depth-charge attack from the corvette HMS *Gladiolus* that she used up all her battery power and so was unable to submerge; caught in this situation when HMS *Rochester* steamed in to make a new series of depth-charge attacks, the German captain surfaced his boat and ordered his crew to scuttle her and abandon ship. She was in this parlous state when a 10 Squadron Sunderland attacked her: Flt Lt 'Bill' Gibson's second salvo of depth-charges landed a hull-length away from the submarine, after her crew had opened her sea socks to scuttle her. *U-26*'s crew was rescued by the *Rochester*.[30] Gibson's attack was very unlikely to have damaged the U-boat, although it had probably confirmed the German captain's decision to scuttle his boat before it could be captured by the Royal Navy.[31]

More than a year later, on 10 September 1941, Flt Lt Athol 'Artie' Wearne from the same squadron was seven hours into a patrol in the Bay of Biscay, more than 400 miles out to sea from Bordeaux, when a submarine was spotted on the surface, only 1,000 yards away. Wearne turned to descend and attack, and as he did so, the submarine submerged. However, the blue green shape of the submerged hull was still visible beneath the water ahead of its surface wake, allowing Wearne to drop a salvo of depth-charges, two of which landed so accurately that he reported them as direct hits. A large reddish-brown patch appeared in the water 100 yards from the point of the explosions, followed by a film of oil three minutes later. The Sunderland crew returned home to report that they had attacked *U-77*, believing that they had read '77' painted on the side of the conning tower.[32] Because Admiralty intelligence tracked *U-77* on operations until its final loss in 1943, the 'kill' was not awarded.[33] In fact, however, U-Boat researchers Axel Niestlé and Eric Zimmerman concluded in 2004 that the submarine attacked was not *U-77* but the Italian *Alessandro Malaspina*. She was lost with all hands.[34] Thus 10 Squadron went through the war with one U-boat kill credited to Gibson, and none to Wearne, whereas in fact it was the reverse.

By the new year of 1942, an inter-generational change was occurring among No. 10's aircraft captains: the unit's founding pilots had become 'tour-expired' after a two-year tour of duty, displaced by a cohort of less senior captains. This succeeding generation of captains had attained command status under the tutelage of their seniors during more than a year's operational flying, having joined the squadron as raw new-graduate pilot officers in 1940, and then progressively gained experience and capability while crewing in co-pilot roles. By now, this second generation of 10 Squadron captains had grown into the status of proficient and experienced operational airmen: men like Sqn Ldr Reg Burrage (the squadron's acting flight commander) and Flt Lts Geoff Havyatt, M. L. 'Buck' Judell, Reg Marks, Tom Stokes, Dave Vernon, Sam Wood, and Eddie Yeoman. Each of these senior pilots in turn would complete their operational tours through the course of 1942, after accruing in the region of 1,200–1,600 Sunderland flying hours. By that time, they themselves had been understudied in turn by a 'third generation' of captains, the men who would take 10 Squadron's war into the decisive battles of 1943.[35]

The turn of the year from 1941 to 1942 had brought the outbreak of war against Japan in the Pacific Theatre, with its depressing, humiliating, and alarming litany of defeat and disaster for the Allies: the loss of Malaya, Singapore, Burma, the Philippines, the Netherlands East Indies, and the mandated territory of New Guinea. Australia was the Commonwealth country most immediately affected by the suddenly-real Japanese threat, finding itself in dire need of a larger, more modern, and more effective frontline air force for its own defence, as distinct from a training organisation to supply the manpower needs of a war on the other side of the globe. Back in 1939, the Australian government had made No. 10 available to Britain on the proviso that it could be withdrawn to Australia if the need arose. The crisis in the Pacific at the beginning of 1942 constituted just such a contingency, leading to government discussion of 10 Squadron's return to Australia to fulfil its original purpose of reconnaissance across Australia's vulnerable northern maritime approaches. However, the Air Ministry in London was loath to lose what had become one of its most experienced Sunderland squadrons, one which moreover was the only such squadron remaining in No. 19 Group for critical long-range patrols across the Bay of Biscay. Accordingly, the British made an immediate counter offer: they would provide the home-based RAAF with the *quid pro quo* of nine extra Catalinas. Further reassurance came with the RAAF's success in purchasing a fresh batch of 105 Hudson reconnaissance bombers in America. Thus mollified, Australian authorities conceded to the maintenance of the *status quo ante*, so No. 10 would remain in England.[36]

A Second Australian Sunderland Squadron

With No. 10's ongoing presence in Britain settled, on 7 April 1942, RAAF Overseas HQ in London received advice from RAF Coastal Command HQ to the effect that a second Australian Sunderland squadron, No. 461, was to be formed around a nucleus provided by No. 10. Moreover, this had to be done in a hurry: 'The necessity of forming this Squadron as quickly as possible cannot be over-emphasised'. The stated urgency stemmed from the fact that in the preceding months, Coastal Command's strength had been badly depleted as a result of the diversion of squadrons overseas to meet the escalating demands of the war in the Mediterranean, and to stem the flow of Allied reverses in the new, inconveniently-timed war against Japan. As a result of these redeployments and reallocations, by March 1942, No. 19 Group in the southwest of Britain had been reduced to a mere three squadrons for its vital anti-submarine patrols across the Bay of Biscay, leaving No. 10 Squadron as its sole squadron of long-range aircraft, sharing Biscay skies with one squadron each of medium-range Whitleys and short-range Hudsons.[37] This force was too weak to fulfil 19 Group's assigned task of interdicting the transit routes between the U-boat bases in the Bay of Biscay and their patrol areas in mid-Atlantic. Coastal Command squadrons in Britain had been left with a total of only fifty-one Catalina and Sunderland flying boats in operation, so No. 10 Squadron alone constituted almost 20 per cent of the RAF's diminished front-line force of flying boats in the British Isles.[38]

The formation of a second Australian flying boat squadron would therefore be a welcome addition to 19 Group's force of anti-submarine aircraft, as part of a conscious build-up of Coastal Command towards the point where its strength would at last be equal to its assigned tasks. Coastal Command's commander, Air Chief Marshal Sir Philip Joubert de la Ferté, had been urging this force expansion upon his superiors, having on 19 February 1942 warned about the parlous state of his weakened command and the critical state of the battle against the U-boat menace. Joubert's argument was that 'though the war against Germany might not be won in the Atlantic, it would certainly be lost unless the U-boat was mastered'.[39] Admiral Sir Dudley Pound, the First Sea Lord (the professional head of the Royal Navy), agreed with this logic, declaring in March 1942 that 'if we lose the war at sea we lose the war.'[40] Such argumentation was well timed, for the first half of 1942 was the U-boats' second 'Happy Time' in the course of their long, drawn-out campaign in the Atlantic, sinking 609 ships in nine months off the American Eastern Seaboard.[41] Moreover, by then Germany had stepped up U-boat production to 20 per month, so that 292 U-boats were in commission by the beginning of May.[42] Numbers like these spelt trouble for the ongoing viability of Britain's transatlantic supply convoys, thereby endangering the viability of future Allied offensives against Germany. However, Air Chief Marshal Joubert argued that given adequate aircraft and resources, his command could defeat the U-boat threat to Britain's logistical lifeline across the Atlantic.[43] By now he was winning the argument, for by April 1942, the chiefs of staff agreed to the transfer of four squadrons of medium bombers from Bomber Command to Coastal Command.[44] Moreover, for the crucial operations against the U-boat transit lanes through the Bay of Biscay, the Air Ministry agreed to triple the strength of 19 Group to nine squadrons, of which the new Australian squadron was to be one.[45]

No. 10 Squadron was not officially advised of the new squadron's imminent formation until 13 April, but rumours had already made their way to Mount Batten from RAAF HQ in London as early as March, predating by some weeks the official advice from 19 Group HQ.[46] To organise the formation of the new squadron, Sqn Ldr Reg Burrage from No. 10 was appointed as its temporary CO. He was an excellently-credentialed, twenty-four-year-old, pre-war RAAF regular officer from Melbourne, who had commenced duty with 10 Squadron in November 1940, accrued more than a year's operational experience, and by April 1942 was acting in the role of 10 Squadron's flight commander. On 15 April, 10 Squadron's CO, Wg Cdr A. X. 'Axle' Richards, despatched Burrage to Coastal Command HQ at Northwood on the outskirts of London to find out all he could about the formation of the new Australian squadron.

At Northwood, Burrage attempted to press upon his British superiors 10 Squadron's wish for both Australian squadrons to be co-located at Mount Batten but was politely rebuffed, evidently because of British suspicions of Australian empire-building. He succeeded in obtaining an audience with no less a personage that Air Chief Marshal Joubert himself, but returned to Mount Batten almost empty-handed on 19 April, having acquired the impression that HQ in fact had no detailed plan for the formation of the new unit. Burrage next day descended upon 19 Group HQ, which was conveniently located at Mount Wise, almost directly across Plymouth Sound from Mount Batten. Again, Burrage succeeded in gaining access to the top of the hierarchy, finding an audience with the group commander, Air Vice-Marshal Geoffrey Bromet. Here Burrage discovered some hard information at last, namely the tantalising fact that there were already three Sunderlands moored at RAF Pembroke Dock awaiting collection by No. 461. However, there was little to go on beyond that: Bromet's senior air staff officer, Grp Capt. Deipth, was unable even to advise where the new unit would be based. As Burrage recalled: 'The SASO didn't seem to be able to give us much advice as to how things were to proceed, the role the squadron was to perform and its ultimate location'.[47]

Burrage had visited both of the responsible headquarters and gone right to the top at each place in his quest for specific information and instructions, but had come away unenlightened; on the contrary, he had gained the impression that there was in fact little hurry at headquarters level in relation to the formation of the second Australian flying boat unit, despite the rhetorical 'urgency' in the original instruction to proceed. Consistent with this deflating impression, RAAF HQ in London was warned that 461 would be getting only one crew per month as each batch of airmen graduated from No. 4 OTU, the RAF's flying boat crew training unit at Invergordon in Scotland. Moreover, it seemed that the predicted slow build-up of aircrew strength within the new squadron would be matched by a similarly slow build-up of the squadron's aircraft strength: after its initial allocation of three aircraft, further arrivals were expected to arrive only at intervals, as the production of Sunderlands was lagging severely behind demand.[48] Overall, the impression was one of evident contradiction between rhetoric and action in 461's creation. This was consistent with the experience of the first Australian bomber squadron to be formed in England a year previously, when No. 455 Squadron had found that there was a similarly wide gap between the stated intention of creating a new Australian squadron in a hurry, and the halting arrival of aircraft and crews.[49]

Despite 10 Squadron's request to have 461 based alongside it at RAF Mount Batten, and despite Coastal Command's initial statement of such intent, on 20 April a signal arrived at Mount Batten advising that the new unit would instead be based at Poole.[50] This was formerly a civilian flying boat base situated on the shore of Poole Bay, on the outskirts of Bournemouth, in Dorset. Despite previous civilian use of Poole as a take-off and landing area for BOAC's Empire flying boats, the essentials for an operational RAF squadron base were simply not yet evident: the slipway was not yet constructed, so the boats could not be brought out of the water for servicing, and indeed there was no room ashore for hangars.[51] After completion of the essential slipway and hard-standing (no hangar was built), the new base would be duly opened in August 1942 as RAF Hamworthy, but even then, Poole Harbour's five seaplane runways lacked the sea room and clear approaches to allow take-offs and landings in poor visibility or at night, as the narrow alighting areas were tightly encroached by islands, jutting headlands, and shallows.[52] Mount Batten, by contrast, had four hangars, extensive hard-standings, three slipways, three runways inside the breakwater, and an unencumbered take-off run heading straight out to sea.

Because of these obvious shortcomings, the officers of 10 Squadron considered the decision to base the new squadron at Poole 'illogical'. No. 461's caretaker CO, Reg Burrage, 'didn't want that to happen at all', and tried to change the commanders' minds. When he flew into Poole on 30 April with an inspection party led by Air Vice-Marshal Bromet, he found that the harbour channels had an 'exceptionally strong tidal current'; all he could see were 'mud banks, narrow channels ... and little scope for long take-off runs'. When Bromet asked him his opinion, Burrage told him bluntly that it was 'unsuitable as an operational flying-boat base', an unwelcome comment that was reportedly greeted by 'some scowls' among Bromet's retinue of staff officers from Group HQ.[53] To compound the disagreement, the officers of No. 10 interpreted the choice of the airline flying boat base at Poole as a sign that No. 461 would be relegated to the role of a transport squadron, leaving the more glamorous combat flying to No. 10. Provoked by the rumour, Burrage wrote a letter of protest to RAAF Overseas HQ in London, the commander of which, Air Vice-Marshal Frank McNamara, made some discreet inquiries at Coastal Command HQ, and asked Air Chief Marshal Joubert to put things right by sending a signal to 461 Squadron denying that it would be a transport squadron.

Whatever the technical merits of the new squadron's assigned base, in April 1942, Poole was not yet ready to host an RAF flying boat squadron, so No. 461 would not move there until the RAF facilities were made ready; meanwhile, it would remain temporarily co-located with No. 10 at Mount Batten. In the meantime, Coastal Command HQ requested the senior unit to make available to the junior outfit as many of its 'EATS' aircrew as it could spare, while retaining for itself its permanent RAAF aircrew. No. 10 Squadron regarded with 'sorrow and anger' the requirement to split itself in two to create the new unit, because it viewed the new EATS unit through a filter of strong organisational snobbery. Thanks to No. 10's unique status as a regular RAAF squadron and Australia's flagship outfit in Britain, its members regarded themselves as 'an exclusive club', 'a gathering of the chosen few'. They knew that they were obliged to help stand No. 461 up on its feet, but it would be a 'reluctant birth'.[54]

Attitudes within No. 10 towards the new Article XV unit reflected an oddity of Australia's military organisation in the Second World War, namely the national predilection for splitting its armed forces into bifurcated manpower pipelines. This phenomenon was most plainly seen in the Australian Army, which in the Second World War fielded a conscripted home-defence 'militia' army, as well as the separately-organised and separately-recruited Australian Imperial Force (AIF), an overseas expeditionary army manned by volunteers. Similarly, through 1940–

42, the RAAF trained and manned two air forces in parallel: the EATS organisation as well as the regular 'home defence' RAAF organisation. Given the huge scale of the RAF's needs, the EATS men constituted the majority of the personnel in the RAAF's manpower pipeline, placed on a separate training pathway towards service within RAF squadrons, and given special eight-digit service numbers to mark their status as hostilities-only servicemen. Meanwhile, a much smaller stream of men, identified by different service number conventions, were recruited and trained to man the 'RAAF' proper. In Britain, this bifurcated streaming of personnel was reflected in the fact that No. 10 was an RAAF unit administered from RAAF HQ in Melbourne, whereas No. 461 was to be a standardised RAF unit administered by the British Air Ministry, just like any other such Article XV unit—such as the Australian-manned 460 bomber squadron, in England at the same time. Thus, the new unit was to be staffed with Australian EATS aircrew graduates, rather than by members of the regular RAAF. By contrast, No. 10 was to be preserved as a prized flagship unit of the RAAF, by preference manned by RAAF personnel sent out separately from Australia, although it was permissible for any manning shortfalls to be made up by cherry-picking EATS men from the RAAF's personnel pool at Bournemouth.

Given these fine jurisdictional niceties, RAF Coastal Command anticipated that the RAAF would object to its request for 10 Squadron to donate men to 461 Squadron. To soften the blow and pre-empt the objections, Coastal Command HQ pointed out that No. 10 already had a surplus of aircrew; indeed, that it already had a very generous allocation of thirty-six pilots on strength, of whom fourteen were fully qualified captains able to operate both by day and night. Given that the squadron had only nine Sunderland aircraft on strength, each of which required only three pilots, this point seems not unreasonable. However, the RAF authorities could not actually direct the RAAF unit to transfer airmen over to the new unit, because No. 10 was a unit of the RAAF, rather than an Article XV squadron within the RAF as No. 461 was. In its signal of 16 April, Coastal Command HQ only 'suggested' that the EATS aircrew component of the senior squadron be so transferred. Nonetheless, the RAF anticipated ultimate RAAF compliance, for while arguing its case with No. 10, it was meanwhile separately advising No. 461 that its aircrew cadre would be formed around the 'surplus' EATS pilots donated by No. 10.

The senior Australian unit did indeed co-operate in these plans, but because it took its administrative instructions from RAAF HQ, not from the RAF, its cooperation in the suggested arrangement was constrained in both scope and timing. No. 10's CO, Wg Cdr 'Axle' Richards, declared that he 'made the training organisation and experience of No 10 freely available to the new unit', but this did not mean he could be open-handed in the provision of trained and experienced personnel.[55] Indeed, on 21 April, No. 10 advised Coastal Command HQ that it had in fact no 'surplus' EATS aircrew, and that its release of a 'nucleus' of aircrew to No. 461 was conditional upon the arrival of a draft of RAAF aircrew from Australia to replace the men thus posted away; once these newcomers were present and trained, the aircrew made surplus would be released. No. 10 would not compromise its privileged position as a regular RAAF unit by giving away its permanent RAAF members to a mere Article XV unit, even an Australian one!

Despite the pedantry of RAAF personnel policy, the formation of No. 461 went ahead nonetheless, for symbolic purposes on Anzac Day, 25 April.[56] As remembered by the 461 Squadron originals, the new outfit started when 'A handful of 10 Squadron types moved into a small wooden hut on the shores of Plymouth Harbour and began to fit the bits together'.[57] The 25th was Australia's *de facto* national day, and hence No. 461 was sometimes referred to by the press as the 'Anzac squadron'. The new outfit was formed around a tiny nucleus of staff detached from 10 Squadron: besides acting CO Reg Burrage, Fg Off. Ron Gillies was appointed as 461's flight commander and Plt Off. Stan Nichol as the navigation officer. The junior rank of all these officers provides further evidence of the ambivalent level of support provided by 10 Squadron, which had certainly not donated its best-qualified officers to take up these vital posts at the core of the needy new squadron. For example, twenty-two-year-old Gillies had been flying operations for more than a year, but had only recently risen to captaincy status, and was thus by no means among the most senior pilots available: in No. 10, such executive roles as his would have been filled by much more-experienced officers of flight lieutenant or squadron leader rank. Despite Gillies's modest seniority, he proved to be a good choice: regarded as 'one of the best chaps in 10 Sqdn', he was a hard worker and proved to be an effective flight instructor.[58]

Similarly, No. 461's ground staff was built around the few men of only junior rank who were donated as an act of charity by No. 10: the orderly room was to be set up by FS A. V. Shepherd, while the Operational Flight was to be built around veteran air-crewmen Sgt Sol Abadee. The latter was well-chosen, being a famous man on 10 Squadron through his purported feat of shooting down two Ju 88s in one action with only 120 rounds of .303 from his tail turret guns. One of 10 Squadron's wireless operators, Sgt Ed Gallagher, also went across to the new squadron, induced by the intimation from his superiors that 'promotion should be rapid'. Once on No. 461, however, he found it 'pretty hard work', with 'umpteen fellows to train in the arts and guile of operational flying'. During the early training flights with 'sprog' crews, Gallagher had to be a jack-of-all-trades: 'fitter, rigger, Operator and what-not'. It was a testimony to the versatility of seasoned flying boat crewmen like him that they were able to impart skills far outside their own narrow trade specialisation: for example, as a wireless operator/air gunner, Gallagher not only had to teach the new men the seamanship skill of mooring up, but he also had to teach fitters and riggers how to do their specialist jobs aboard the aircraft; as well as showing the new flight engineers how to prime and start a Pegasus engine![59] The neediness of the trainees was hardly surprising, given that, according to Ron Gillies, they had 'never seen a flying-boat in their lives before arriving at Mount Batten'. Gillies himself had to rush trainee back-seaters through one morning's program of ground training, then that very afternoon take them out onto the water for circuits and bumps with the new pilots, using that morning's batch of 'trained' air-crewmen as flight crew! During these initial training flights, sometimes Gillies found that he had to be in three places at once: in the cockpit to supervise the trainee pilots taxiing the aircraft to the runway (itself a non-intuitive skill); back at the flight engineer's panel to help the flight engineer orientate himself to his dials, gauges, levers, buttons, and switches; and down in the bow compartment to check that the sprog crewmen had secured the nose turret and dogged the front hatch in place.[60]

By now, two of 461 Squadron's Sunderlands were moored in the Cattewater off Mount Batten: Ron Gillies had delivered 'B' on 22 April and 10 Squadron's Flt Lt Dave Vernon delivered 'D' on the 25th. With no maintenance crew yet at No. 461, it was 10 Squadron staff who helped to make B/461 ready for 461's first flight on the 24th: Reg Burrage test-flew her that day for No. 461's first local flight. These first two squadron aircraft were both built by Blackburn at Dumbarton in Scotland, and both drew approval for their nicely finished appearance: when D/461 arrived, she drew a crowd of admiring onlookers, one of whom was No. 10's CO, Wg Cdr Richards, who declared, 'Behold, the birth of a squadron!' This portentous impression was given added emphasis when the broad sides of the new squadron's Sunderlands were painted up with 461's own newly-allotted squadron code letters (UT), distinguishing them from the RB-coded aircraft of 10 Squadron moored nearby.[61] Striving to build up his new squadron, on 1 May, Reg Burrage was pleased to see his third Sunderland, 'A', flown in from Pembroke Dock, and duly took her for her first test flight on the 6th.

Training could soon commence, and on 11 May, Ron Gillies was replaced in the squadron flight commander role by a pilot of greater seniority and experience, Sqn Ldr Colin Lovelock, RAF. This British officer was a thirty-year-old, flying boat professional and an experienced Sunderland captain, having flown an operational tour with No. 204 Squadron, served for nine months as a Sunderland instructor at No. 4 OTU at Invergordon, and also served as a staff officer with No. 15 Group Coastal Command, which at the time operated three squadrons of Sunderlands at Lough Erne.[62] Even the self-satisfied ex-10 Squadron types quickly recognised that Lovelock knew 'more about flying boats than anyone in sight'.[63] He had an ideal CV for the role and would prove to be a pivotal officer in working up the new Australian flying boat squadron as an autonomous unit. He was described by foundation wireless operator/air gunner, Sgt Ed Gallagher, as the 'Stationmaster of the new squadron', suggesting that he knew everything that was going on there as well as the precise time it was happening. He also had the pleasing ability of securing the willing cooperation of subordinates without patronising them (not necessarily a common characteristic for pre-war regular officers): when Sgt Les Baveystock joined the squadron in October as a new pilot, he found Lovelock (by then CO, as we shall see) 'courteous and friendly' towards him.[64] Even back-seater NCO airmen further down the pecking order seemed to have received the same courtesy, for Ed Gallagher categorised Lovelock as 'a very nice chap'.[65]

Four days later, another British officer, Wg Cdr Neville Halliday, RAF, arrived to assume command from Reg Burrage, whose tour would expire the following month, after which he would return to Australia. Halliday was described sympathetically as 'a nice young man with a moustache and a fluffy head of hair'.[66] He was a thirty-year-old, pre-war regular who had graduated from the RAF College at Cranwell in 1929; he had a good flying boat background, having flown Saro London flying boats with No. 209 Squadron in the early 1930s, but he had not operated seaplane types since, until he was suddenly required to undertake the Sunderland conversion course at No. 4 OTU in preparation for his posting to No. 461. An officer of such deep air force experience, impressive seniority and relevant professional background was no doubt an appropriate choice to build a new squadron from scratch, but he was not current on operational flying and was significantly inexperienced in the operation of modern, multi-engine monoplane types like the Sunderland.[67] He also arrived on the unit unsure of himself after a succession of staff postings; and also 'unsure of Australians', sensitive to the fact that he was the token 'Pom', dropped into the role of leading a unit dominated by opinionated ex-10 Squadron people. Like many COs, he tried to get on with his Australians by being friendly but could not 'rise over his aloneness' as he tried to bring people together to surmount the infant unit's teething problems.[68]

The Politics of RAAF Personnel Policy in Britain

The appointment of this non-Australian officer to command the new Australian squadron, on top of the earlier appointment of Lovelock as the CO's deputy, was the result of an unresolved dispute within the RAAF over the application of the EATS agreement. Soon after the inception of the scheme, in March 1940, Australia's Minister for Air Jim Fairbairn had emphasised his understanding that the scheme allowed for regular RAAF officers to obtain commands with Article XV squadrons.[69] In other words, this meant that the RAAF could use Australian-manned squadrons within the RAF, such as No. 461, as an avenue for the career development of its professional officers. The problem was that the recently-appointed commander of the RAAF, Air Marshal Sir Charles Burnett, RAF, was a British officer and 'an Empire man' who put RAF interests ahead of those of the service he now commanded.[70] He ruled out any such interchange of officers between regular RAAF units like No. 10 and Article XV squadrons like No. 461.[71] Burnett seems to have been supported in this pedantic ruling by the responsible Australian leaders in London, namely High Commissioner Stanley Bruce and the acting commander of the RAAF Overseas HQ, Air Vice-Marshal McNamara. Australia's Attorney General and Minister for External Affairs Dr H. V. 'Bert' Evatt, on the basis of the impressions he gained during his visit to London in May 1942, accused both these pre-eminent Australians of 'going over to the English'. The undiplomatic foreign minister evidently considered that both men had 'gone native' by being in London too long.[72] The RAAF's most senior officer, Air Marshal Richard Williams, would have agreed: in January 1943 during a visit to London prior to taking up his new post as RAAF representative in Washington, he 'came away with little confidence of anything being done' to further RAAF interests in Britain, and considered that Bruce was not interested in pursuing the issue of advancing RAAF administrative autonomy *vis à vis* the RAF.[73]

For now, it was thus Burnett who got his way, rather than Evatt; the careers of 10 Squadron's permanent officers would continue their ordained courses from Australia to England and then back to Australia again, and the RAF would just have to come up with officers of its own to fill the command vacancies in the new Australian-manned squadron. Demarcation boundaries like this between the RAAF's own pure-bred offspring, No. 10, and its bastard, RAF-sired progeny, No. 461, would result in vastly differing levels of staffing, experience, and operational efficiency between the two otherwise closely-affiliated Australian squadrons throughout the first year of 461's existence, as we shall see.

With this demarcation dispute at command level, it followed that neither the RAF nor RAAF put forward a suitably qualified Australian for the command of No. 461, despite the steady stream of permanent RAAF officers who had completed their tours with No. 10 by the end of 1941. Such recently tour-expired ex-10 Squadron officers with the requisite rank, seniority, professional background, and recent operational experience for command roles within No. 461 included Sqn Ldr Ivan Podger, DFC, and Flt Lt Vic Hodgkinson, who were both returned to Australia in early 1942, and Wg Cdr Ern Knox-Knight (who had already served as 10 Squadron C.O.) and Sqn Ldr Hugh Birch, DFC, both of whom were posted to desk jobs at RAAF Overseas HQ in London in December 1941. All four qualified officers were slated for posts within strictly-RAAF units, so would not be loaned to an RAF organisation like No. 461.

The result was two British officers were left at the head of the new Australian unit. Fortunately, although RAAF HQ had not seen fit to release a tour-expired RAAF officer for either command role, the RAF had been generous in its selections, for both Halliday and Lovelock would prove to be hard-working officers who would lead from the front in getting their aircraft online, their crews trained, and the squadron operational. As always, it was the task of the squadron officers to make it work despite the planning deficiencies of the higher-level headquarters. And despite No. 10's RAAF-imposed obligation to withhold its best-qualified personnel, the senior Australian unit nonetheless acted both as a donor and a training unit to help get No. 461 on its feet. For example, at the end of April, when three new pilots arrived at Mount Batten posted to No. 461 fresh from Australia (Plt Offs Henry Osborne, David Laurenti, and Raleigh Gipps), they were attached at first to No. 10 so that the senior unit could convert them to the Sunderland and provide on-the-job operational training until the new unit was ready to receive them. The same applied to the new squadron's founding navigators: Stan Nichol, No. 461's squadron navigation officer, was joined on 6 May by Plt Off. John Watson, fresh from Coastal Command's No. 3 School of General Reconnaissance. Watson would understudy the more experienced Nichol, commencing his on-the-job training that same day alongside the latter during a flight with a 10 Squadron crew.

Summer 1942 Operations

No. 461's fourth Sunderland was flown in from Pembroke Dock on 13 May by Plt Off. Bruce Buls, a partly-trained first pilot now transferred to the unit from No. 10. As an EATS graduate who had not yet qualified for captaincy, he was surplus to requirements at No. 10, ripe for transfer to No. 461. The new unit still had barely enough aircrew for a single eleven-man Sunderland crew, but flight training commenced in earnest on that same day, when Reg Burrage took a training crew on a five-hour out-and-back navigation exercise to Fastnet Rock off the south-west coast of Ireland. With two aircraft generally available for flight on any given day, training flights ensued on a daily basis, captained either by Reg Burrage, Colin Lovelock, or Ron Gillies—the latter being the designated training captain. On 25 May, a month after the squadron's official formation, nine new pilots arrived, like Buls donated by No. 10: Russell Baird, Bill Dods, Harry Cooke, Robert Hosband, Fred Manger, 'Bert' Smith, Colin Steley, Colin Walker, and John Weatherlake. No. 10 Squadron had released these men as surplus to its requirements, eligible for transfer to the new Australian Article XV squadron in belated fulfilment of RAF Coastal Command's original request: all were pilot officers, the most junior officer rank in the air force; all except Walker were freshman pilots who had been fulfilling the lowly second pilot role within 10 Squadron crews; all but one were EATS personnel rather than permanent air force, in accordance with the RAAF personnel policy of keeping the two personnel streams separated.

Despite their very limited level of training and flying experience, in the straitened situation of artificially-induced personnel shortage within 461 Squadron, half of these new pilots would now be rushed straight through to captaincy. Only three of this cohort of pilots had even qualified for solo flight in the Sunderland, thereby most lacked even the modest level of experience that would qualify them even for first pilot status within 10 Squadron, let alone captaincy. This founding generation of No. 461's captains would nonetheless live up to 10 Squadron's legacy, as we shall see. However, three of the ten new pilots posted-in from No. 10 would not survive their tour of duty at the sharp end of No. 461's operations.

The six least-qualified of these newly posted-in pilots had evidently barely touched the flight controls of a Sunderland during their second pilot roles with 10 Squadron crews before joining No. 461, leaving Gillies and Lovelock with the task of getting them qualified for solo day flying (in visual flight conditions). Another new pilot, Plt Off. Phil Davenport, arrived via a separate route: upon arrival from Australia, he had been detached away from Bournemouth's Personnel Reception Centre to RAF Dyce in Scotland to do a beam approach training course. After that he joined the squadron with 190 hours in his logbook. This figure shows how low-hours these newly graduated pilots were. However, compared to the other new pilots posted in from No. 10, Davenport was unusually well-qualified because of his completion of the blind approach course: on the strength of this extra training he would fly only eight operations as second pilot before graduating to first pilot, having by then clocked-up 150 hours on Sunderlands.[1]

On 29 May, the new unit received external validation when No. 461's newly-joined aircrew officers received a visit from Britain's Secretary of State for Air Sir Archibald Sinclair, an influential government minister and an architect of Britain's air strategy. No. 461 was given the arbitrary target date of 1 July for the attainment of operational status, and the only way for the squadron to meet this deadline was to expedite and truncate training pathways. But even that was dependent upon aircraft availability, and with only a skeleton maintenance staff, inexperienced junior leaders, and many bugs to be ironed out aboard the unfamiliar new aircraft, there were many days when not a single aircraft was serviceable to fly. Wg Cdr Halliday had to put himself on the roster as a training captain alongside Lovelock and Gillies, just as his predecessor, Burrage, had done before him. Halliday led from the front by taking a trainee crew on a navigation exercise to the Scilly Isles, off the south-western tip of Cornwall, which was a standard training trip for 'sprog' crews flying out of Mount Batten or Pembroke Dock.

Crew training was pursued in three stages: firstly, the lowest-hours pilots were taken through a program of daytime 'circuits and bumps' at Mount Batten, to get them up to daytime solo status on the Sunderland. Then, starting on 30 May, Ron Gillies commenced a short, sharp, and intense program of night flying at Pembroke Dock for the more advanced pilots. 'PD' was preferable to Mount Batten for night take-offs and landings because there was less shipping to contend with at the Welsh port than at busy Plymouth. This was an important factor under wartime conditions as the flying boats taxied with navigation lights off, and with the flare-path lights similarly doused between take-offs and landings to avoid attracting unwanted attention from the Luftwaffe. Under the expedited training syllabus dictated by the squadron's rushed timeline towards operational qualification, two nights of 'circuits and bumps' at Pembroke Dock was sufficient for a new trainee to attain night qualification, and five of the pilots were thus successfully checked-out, a precondition for captaincy. This night training might have been compressed, but it was intensive: each of these nights was a sustained and intense work-out for the trainee pilots, a monotonous and fatiguing succession of take-offs, circuits, landings, and take-offs again, from dusk to dawn. It was also a wearing schedule for the back-seater flight engineers and wireless operators who had to go along for the ride: Ed Gallagher was soon sick of 'those damned night landings' that went on until 2 or 3 a.m. and rejoiced whenever the weather was too bad to fly. On those occasions, he took solace by 'downing a jug or three with the boys' in the sergeants' mess.[2]

The last stage of crew training was when the newly-graduated captains took their crews to Pembroke Dock to undertake bombing and gunnery courses under the tutelage of instructors from No. 4 Armament Instruction Group at nearby RAF Carew Cheriton. The instruction involved ground tuition in aircraft recognition, and fifteen hours of flying as a crew, during which they dropped dozens of practice bombs from minimum height and fired thousands of .303 rounds at target drogues towed tamely behind Lysander aircraft. For the air-to-air gunnery exercises, individual gunners were allocated a specific gun, which was loaded with rounds dipped in paint of a unique colour; the resultant colour-stained bullet holes on the drogue enabled each gunner's hits to be scored separately. The gunners fired competitively, with 30 per cent hits considered good shooting against the 'sitting target' of the non-manoeuvring drogue. The crews' armourers were also kept busy during these flights, for the pilots dropped sixty practice bombs per training sortie, which required the crewmen in the bomb-room to load and reload these 11-pound bombs on to the bomb-racks, eight at a time, while straining to remain upright in the 'bucking kite'. The airmen learnt their skills by performing the required evolutions under supervision until minimum standards were demonstrated (for example, rounds on target, or accuracy of aircraft recognition). Pilots also practised simulated depth-charge attacks upon submarines: the Royal Navy provided a 'tame' submarine for this purpose, and while one crew performed its practice attacks, another crew would spend the day gaining an impression of the exercise from the navy's perspective, watching the other crew's attacks from an armed trawler. This duty was popular not only because it was 'interesting' to spend a day at sea for a change, but also because the trawler's coxswain plied the appreciative airmen 'with rum at intervals'.[3]

Through this training regime, captains-under-training like Buls, Walker, Smith, and Manger were paired off with second pilots under training like Cooke, Dods, Hosband, Steley, and Weatherlake. The resultant pilot teams would become the kernel around which full crews would be built, each of which when ready would be assigned their 'own' aircraft. For example, when Bruce Buls's crew line-up was announced on 20 June, they were assigned to aircraft A/461. Wireless Operator Ed Gallagher had flown with Buls during the training flights, and he was pleased to be allocated to his crew, impressed by Buls's ability: 'He can handle these Sunderlands better than anyone I've flown with', 'He'll do me for a captain ...' In this manner, four complete crews were built up. Strong unit camaraderie was already forming: when Buls graduated as a night captain on 14 June, both officers and men gathered together at the Bristol Castle pub in Devonport for a 'good party' in celebration.[4]

No. 461 seems to have acquired this culture of informal comradeship across the barrier of rank from No. 10: Sgt Gallagher recalled that while serving with the senior unit before his posting to No. 461, his NCO mates had 'a party in town' on the night of 17 April, and that aircrew officers 'Cooke, Egerton, Brown, and Jensen came along' to drink with the enlisted men. Naively, Gallagher considered this inter-rank fraternisation to be peculiarly Australian: 'I don't think the Pongos [British] understand how we Aussies mix together. The idea of an officer drinking with anyone who has no commission is beyond them'. Aside from such parochial hyperbole, it seems that the new squadron evolved a frank, businesslike culture with little exaggerated deference shown by the other ranks towards the officers: for example, after 'a few beers' in the sergeants' mess on the night of 24 October, Gallagher 'in a fit of cholera' rang the then-squadron flight commander, Sqn Ldr Raban, to 'tell him' to take him off duty NCO duties, as he had done it too often already. Raban 'apologised' and asked Gallagher to suggest another candidate for duty NCO; Gallagher gave him the name of his 'particular *bête-noir*, the laziest bastard in the squadron', and the problem was thus solved by negotiation.[5] Contrary to Gallagher's earlier sweeping generalisation, it is worthy of note that the evidently very approachable Raban was a British officer!

No. 461's training provided a wearying flying commitment for its trio of training captains, Gillies, Lovelock, and Halliday, who had to work up to eighteen hours a day. The artificially-forced pace of the pilot training is attested by Ron Gillies, the squadron's night flying instructor, who reflected that one of the first 461 Squadron pilots whom he trained-up as an aircraft captain, Colin Walker, had flown with him on 10 Squadron only a couple of months earlier, but only as a lowly second pilot. He had certainly not expected to be training Walker up for captaincy so soon! Like the others, Walker was pushed through to captaincy at a tempo that was very rushed compared to the more measured norms of 10 Squadron. With this background, Gillies 'felt sorry for the trainees who didn't have sufficient experience on the Sunderland, even in daylight, to be doing what was asked of them'. Nonetheless, he found they coped better than expected, and he even made the unlikely claim afterwards that not one of them had frightened him at any time during his numerous training 'hops!'[6]

The squadron underwent a rite of passage on 2 June, when Colin Lovelock was returning with a trainee crew from a navigation exercise to the Scillies: at 9.50 p.m., 2 miles north of the Eddystone lighthouse and only fifteen minutes from home, his Sunderland was attacked by an Me 109 fighter. Fortunately, the German pilot was keener on getting back on the ground before nightfall than on shooting down the Sunderland, for he made only one ineffectual pass before heading home to France at speed. No one on the Sunderland's flight-deck even saw the Messerschmitt go past. One of the trainee pilots, Plt Off. Phil Davenport, was at the time idly looking out a side window at the ocean below, and suddenly saw a turmoil of churned-up water on the surface of the sea. He assumed it was a shoal of baitfish, but it was in fact a spray of cannon shells fired from above by the 109. Upon being told by the rear gunner that an enemy fighter had dived at them from 'out of the sun', Davenport realised that he and his fellow trainee crewmen were 'truly babes in the war'.[7]

Three new pilots joined No. 461 on 9 June, all freshmen straight from Australia, without having come through 10 Squadron or any other form of post-graduate training, and so earmarked for second pilot roles. These men had been sourced from the personnel reception centre at Bournemouth, which was the holding unit for semi-trained aircrew arriving in Britain from the EATS training schools overseas. This unit became one of the main sources of 461's aircrew, which only heightened the training commitment within the squadron, as new arrivals from here had neither attained previous operational experience nor undertaken operational training. A source of better-trained aircrew was the Sunderland conversion unit, No. 4 OTU, at Invergordon in Scotland; early arrivals from here included two pilots, Plt Offs Dudley Marrows and Roger Barker.

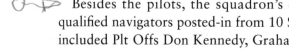 Besides the pilots, the squadron's crew rosters were filled out by qualified navigators posted-in from 10 Squadron during June–July: these included Plt Offs Don Kennedy, Graham White, Harry Winstanley, and Don Stewart. As with the pilots, the more experienced navigators would

tutor these freshmen navigators on their duties and procedures in the course of actual operational flights, in order to qualify them to serve unsupervised as full-time navigators within their own crews. Similarly, the newly-arrived second pilots were apprenticed to the newly-qualified captains. By now, these budding captains had begun taking their crews out on unsupervised non-operational flights: for example, Bruce Buls took his crew out on a navigation exercise over the sea on 8 June, and Fred Manger followed on 9 June. Less-advanced trainee captains were only trusted to take their crews on short daytime navigation exercises around the south-west coast of the British Isles: for example, Colin Walker's crew flew to Pembroke Dock and back over 13–14 June, and Bert Smith was allowed to ferry Sunderlands between Pembroke Dock and Mount Batten on the 21st and 24th.

No. 461 Commences Operations

Right on schedule, on the first day of July, 461 Squadron was duly declared operational. Nominally, this met the challenging deadline set by Coastal Command HQ, but in truth, the unit's operational status remained heavily qualified by its aircrews' incomplete training. With only three operational crews, those of Manger, Smith, and Walker, the understrength unit made a respectable start, nonetheless, flying nine sorties in the first fortnight. Wg Cdr Halliday led from the front by captaining the very first operation on 1 July, flying his patrol in very challenging weather conditions, with 10/10th cloud extending right down to the surface of the sea. The squadron's second sortie came early on the 3rd, when Fred Manger departed in a night take-off for an anti-shipping patrol. The CO was again airborne on this sortie, demonstrating a nice balance of delegation and moral example by accompanying the crew as supernumerary, but no doubt casting a watchful eye over proceedings on the flight-deck in his part-time role as a training captain.

The debut of the new squadron did not go unnoticed in Australia: Sgt Ed Gallagher was sent clippings from the *Brisbane Telegraph*, which had reported factually that No. 461's aircrew complement at the time of writing comprised, besides the CO, one flight lieutenant, five flying officers, twenty-three pilot officers, and one flight sergeant (Gallagher). Brisbane's *Courier Mail* also publicised the new unit, by naming the men from Brisbane who had transferred across from No. 10.[8] Well cued by RAAF Public Relations, the press in Australia showed sustained interest in the Australian squadrons in England, reporting such developments in detail.

No. 461's first missions were directed towards the Bay of Biscay, and this set the geographical focus for the squadron's operations over the next year and a half. The mouth of the Bay stretched 300 miles from the tip of Brittany Peninsula in France to Cape Ortegal in Spain, and so Bay patrols by Mount Batten-based Sunderlands involved long flights out to an operating radius of more than 600 miles—for example, to the Spanish port of San Sebastian, at the end of the Sunderlands' patrol line, via the standard dogleg course out to sea to avoid the Luftwaffe fighters at Brest. In executing their debut sorties, No. 461's freshman crews successfully completed flights of up to twelve and a half hours' endurance, thereby showing how effectively the unit's hard-working training captains had drilled them in the engine and fuel management procedures of their complex aircraft.

More than that, No. 461's first sorties were noteworthy for the sharp hazards encountered by the squadron's newly-minted crews, leaving the men in no doubt about the risks they ran as operational Sunderland crewmen. On 6 July, Fg Off. Bert Smith departed in A/461 at 4.13 a.m. on an anti-submarine patrol in the Bay of Biscay, and by 7.10 a.m. had reached far enough into the Bay to start performing low-altitude visual surveillance of Spanish fishing boats. By then, he was also getting close enough to the Luftwaffe's fighter base at Bordeaux-Merignac to attract Luftwaffe attention: at 8 a.m., a Junkers Ju 88 was spotted 5 miles off the Sunderland's port beam. Smith dived away, but the Ju 88 was much faster and caught up, making repeated firing passes. Although the German pilot pressed home his attacks as close as 200 yards before breaking away at the end of each pass, he nonetheless failed to get a single hit on the manoeuvring Sunderland, and at length gave up and headed for home. Smith was thereby able to resume his patrol, and regained the coast of England without further incident, but the encounter served as a vivid reminder of the threat posed by German aircraft off the enemy coasts.

A Celebrated mid-Ocean Rescue

Two days later, on 8 July, Wg Cdr Halliday faced a very different, but no less real hazard: that of landing a Sunderland on the open sea. A two-engined Whitley patrol bomber had force-landed in the sea, and an RAF aircraft had on the previous evening located the crew dinghy and reported its position within the Bay of Biscay. On the night of the 7th, Halliday received an operational order from HQ to launch an Air-Sea Rescue (ASR) mission next morning, with instructions to 'Land and recover survivors'. Not one of Halliday's captains was experienced enough to perform this mission, so he volunteered to lead the mission himself. The trouble was that he was no better qualified himself, being a low-hours Sunderland pilot who had so far failed to convince his Australians of his mastery over the Sunderland.[9] The next problem was aircraft availability: only the newly-arrived E/461 was available, but this was the aircraft allocated to Bruce Buls's crew, and it was then so new it had not even been tested properly, so was not yet graded as operational. Halliday took the aircraft anyway, and also took Buls's crew with him, who had volunteered to a man.[10] He left 'Bullsie' himself behind, to the latter's consternation: in the close-knit fraternity of a settled crew line-up, no pilot liked letting an outsider take 'his' crew, and no crew liked being captained by an outsider. After a four-and-a-half-hour transit flight, the Sunderland arrived overhead the reported position, about '300 miles out in the Atlantic', and at 1.50 p.m. commenced a square search. After more than an hour of searching, the second pilot, Plt Off. Russ Baird, spotted a smoke puff ahead, which on closer investigation proved to be a signal cartridge fired from a yellow dinghy 3 miles away.

At that moment, the off-watch crew members were just sitting down in the galley to a 'lovely feed of steak and sausages', but everyone was called to their stations, so the meal had to go back on the stovetop. Halliday made a low pass over the dinghy, saw that it contained six live occupants, then orbited around it to assess the conditions: he considered the weather good, with a surface wind of only 3–4 knots over a slight swell. However, perspectives on this varied: Sgt Ed Gallagher, a veteran wireless operator/air gunner with 400 Sunderland hours, looked down at the same sea and thought the idea of alighting upon it 'terrifying'.

Nonetheless, the resolute Halliday decided to alight to pick up the survivors. He made a careful approach, and luckily put the Sunderland down on the water 'beautifully'.[11] It touched down at 75 knots along the crest of a wave, with Halliday heaving deftly upon the wheel to keep the port float out of the surging wavetop—if they lost the float, then they too would go into the water. Once the Sunderland's hull was 'down, safe and sound', 'gliding into the trough', Plt Off. John Weatherlake, the first pilot, turned his face to Halliday's with a look of appreciative admiration for having pulled off so smooth a landing on the open sea. Halliday returned the glance, his relief at having got down safely balanced with the silent gratification of having proven to his men that he 'did know how to fly' after all.[12] The navigator, Fg Off. Fred Gascoigne, got up on top of the hull, sitting in the open astrodome hatch, to guide Halliday towards the dinghy; he told him to taxi on a course of 200 degrees, as 'I believe it lies in that direction'. Straight after that, the dinghy appeared, half a mile on the port bow. After that, it proved harder than expected to get the dinghy alongside the hatch on the starboard side of the after hull. Knowing it would be disaster if the yawing aircraft with its viciously spinning propellers veered across the dinghy, Halliday aborted a series of approaches, each time turning away about 50 yards off upon recognising that it was becoming unsafe.

Weatherlake broke the impasse by getting out of the co-pilot's seat and then stripping his clothes off at the rear of the flight-deck. He told 'the boss' he was volunteering to take a rope and swim to the dinghy. Halliday, said stiffly, 'I can't say I like the sound of that, Weatherlake'. The co-pilot replied, 'I can't say I like the sound of it myself, sir'.[13] Meanwhile, Russ Baird, the first pilot, crawled out along the top of the wing in bare feet, stripped to his underpants in case he slipped off into the sea, secured by a rope tied-off around his waist.[14] Standing poised on the very end of the wing tip, he coiled the rest of the rope and threw it as far as he could. It fell into the water short of the dinghy, but the dinghy crewmen had enough energy left to paddle furiously towards it. One of them grabbed the knotted end and held it above his head cheering. Weatherlake, by now standing naked in the open rear hatch, had been reprieved and could go back upstairs to put his clothes back on. Baird retreated from the slippery wingtip, braced himself and started pulling on the rope, hauling the dinghy in under the wing so that Gallagher and the others could get it alongside and 'drag 'em in through the rear hatch'.[15] Once the dinghy occupants were inside and the hatches shut, Halliday turned into wind and took off successfully, evening out the bumps by running down-swell.

The survivors were Sgt Robert Stewart and his crew, who had ditched at 4.30 p.m. the previous day after their Whitley suffered an engine failure.[16] Although a twin-engine aircraft, the Whitley could not maintain height on one engine, so engine failure meant a forced-landing in the sea. They told the Sunderland crew that they had spent a miserable night vomiting with sea sickness as their dinghy bobbed over the waves, that they had run out of food, and that it was their very last signal pistol cartridge they had fired to attract the attention of the passing Sunderland. Once aboard, the tired Whitley crewmen were soon put on the road to recovery, however, attacking the problem in order of priority: 'Food can wait, a smoke first'. After a cigarette in the wardroom, they tucked into the Sunderland crew's warmed-up meal of steak and sausages, watched perhaps somewhat enviously by their off-watch hosts: as Gallagher related, 'We went without dinner but no one grumbled'. Then the survivors collapsed into the deep sleep of utter exhaustion, jumbled against each other in the wardroom like a stack of kit bags in a train station. Gallagher tapped out a coded message to base, 'Returning with six passengers, one slightly injured'.[17]

More than that, they had proved themselves: Halliday, the self-conscious new CO, had proved himself by pulling off a skilful open-water landing and take-off; the tyro crew had proven themselves by navigating accurately, and using crew teamwork to rescue the Whitley crew; and the green new squadron had proven itself by pulling off a famous feat and making a name for itself within Coastal Command.[18] Upon returning and mooring up at Mount Batten, the Sunderland crewmen saw 'doctors and ambulances' waiting on the pier, and went ashore with 'swelled heads' to find themselves suddenly 'heroes'. Next day, the crew was paraded before Air Vice-Marshal Bromet, who dropped in from nearby 19 Group HQ to shake hands with each man and tell them what 'a fine show' it was. After that came a procession of Australian 'press reps' to the station to interview the crew and get the story. A few weeks later, the men read about it all in the *Illustrated* and the *Daily Sketch*, the latter regaling its readers with 'another instance of the value of the little rubber dinghy and the giant flying boat in saving airmen's lives'.[19] The men themselves were delighted to have been involved in the rescue: Sgt Gallagher considered it, 'the best deed I'll ever do in this war'.[20]

Although this successful rescue was a splendid result, it set a bad precedent for the future: alighting a Sunderland upon the sea in mid-ocean was a risky undertaking, the successful accomplishment of which remained substantially dependent upon an often-indeterminate conjunction of good conditions, good judgment, and good fortune. No. 461's airmen would unfortunately discover the indiscriminate truth of this to their own cost. For now, however, the official approbation and public recognition of their feat had glorified the act of landing upon the sea to pull off a rescue, and this imposed implicit moral pressure for its repetition.

No. 461 in the Shadow of No. 10

No. 461's growth in operational capability was shown by the expansion of its aircraft inventory in July to eight Sunderlands. The new unit's expanding capabilities were also shown by its ability to produce two sorties per day on 11 July and three each on the 15th and 16th, which were comparable to No. 10's sortie output. On the 17th, both Australian Sunderland squadrons received visits from four Australian journalists representing Australian Consolidated Press and the *Truth* newspaper. The accompanying RAAF public relations officers from RAAF HQ at Kodak House in London, Sqn Ldr Tart and Flt Lt Guthrie, set up interviews for the journalists with squadron personnel, to provide the journalists with material for the stories that RAAF Public Relations and the media agencies 'required'. Meanwhile the squadron's preparations for assuming its full operational role continued: Sqn Ldr Lovelock took John Weatherlake's crew to Pembroke Dock for the Armament Training Camp at Carew Cheriton in mid-July, as a waypoint in their progress towards operational status; while the CO flew repeated day-trips into Poole to check on preparations for his unit's arrival at its assigned base.

Despite this good progress in getting No. 461 operational, the RAAF's bifurcated personnel policy left a yawning gap in experience and proficiency levels between its two Sunderland squadrons. This can be shown by a comparison of the operational experience of both squadrons' captains at this point in the story. Excluding the CO and flight commander, No. 461 Squadron would enter September 1942 with eight captains on its operations roster, of whom five had moderate experience: Plt Offs Bruce Buls, Fred Manger, and Col Steley and Fg Offs Bert Smith and Col Walker. These were the squadron's founding generation of captains, each of whom had by now captained between nine and thirteen operations since the squadron started operational flying in July. Besides these five moderately-experienced captains, there were three newly qualified captains just starting out: Fg Offs Bill Dods and Harry Cooke and Plt Off. Robert Hosband.

In comparison with No. 461, 10 Squadron had ten captains on its flight roster, of whom six had captained in the region of thirty operational patrols, a level of operational experience far beyond their 461 Squadron colleagues. These 10 Squadron veterans were Flt Lts Eddie Yeoman, Sam Wood, Dave Vernon, Graham Pockley, and Reg Marks and Plt Off. Tom Egerton, each of whom had between twenty-seven and thirty-six operations to their credit. The flight lieutenant rank of most of these 10 Squadron captains marks them out as senior airmen within the Coastal Command pecking order: by contrast, No. 461 had no captain sufficiently senior to carry this rank. There were two more 10 Squadron captains with substantial operational experience, namely Flt Lt Ron Gillies and Plt Off. Terry Brown, each of whom had captained nearly twenty operations. Besides these, No. 10 also had two newly-qualified captains, Fg Off. George Miedecke and Plt Off. Kerv Beeton. However, even this latter suggestion of inexperience is misleading within the 10 Squadron context, as both these officers had been flying in co-pilot roles from 1941 onwards, and therefore were experienced operational airmen.

In the pre-war RAF, flying boat pilots had typically served five-year apprenticeships in co-pilot roles, obliged by the unwritten rules of the so-called 'Flying-Boat Union' to wait for 'year after year for their own boat'. The cadre of incumbent captains who thus so zealously policed the entry qualifications for membership of their 'union' were as a result of this exclusivity a select and highly experienced band of senior airmen, seasoned veterans of operating seaplanes in a marine environment.

Although wartime conditions necessarily accelerated the process, No. 10's captains had so far similarly served lengthy apprenticeships (and under wartime conditions too), thus proving themselves worthy holders of their metaphorical 'union cards'. By contrast, not one of 461 Squadron's captains would have 'made the grade' to be accepted into membership.[21] In summary, while No. 10 had great personnel depth and a wealth of operational proficiency, No. 461's much greener pilots just had to catch up, required to ascend a much steeper learning curve much more quickly. No. 461 had been disadvantaged by the RAAF's obstinate differentiation throughout 1942 between the career pathways of permanent air force officers on the one hand and hostilities-only EATS airmen on the other. In the meantime, each of 461's newly-minted captains knew just how green he was, but each also pulled off the confidence trick expected of them: Ivan Southall recalled his inner voice telling him to 'Wear the cheery smile, boy, cultivate the cheery word to deceive the crew—and the Commanding Officer...'[22] Behind the forced show of breezy confidence, captains shouldered their duties very seriously: Russell Baird from No. 461 had four members of his crew under nineteen years old, and 'felt terribly responsible for them'.[23]

10 Squadron's Summer of U-boat Attacks

While No. 461 was gaining experience and working up to operational proficiency, 10 Squadron had maintained its normal operational tempo, with its ten operational crews flying more than 100 patrols over May–June 1942. This provided much opportunity for obtaining contact with U-boats. Indeed, June brought unusually good opportunities to deliver attacks upon enemy submarines, including three of the most effective submarine attacks delivered by No. 10 so far. On the 5th, No. 10 launched two anti-submarine sorties, with Flt Lt Sam Wood taking off in U/10 at 11.25 a.m. After a two-hour transit flight to the patrol area, he commenced his 'beat' at 3.45 p.m., starting from a position about 200 miles out to sea from the U-boat base at La Pallice. Almost at once, Wood's radar operator announced a radar contact 8 miles off the starboard bow. Wood turned towards the contact, flying in a cloudless sky at 5,000 feet, and almost immediately spotted a fully-surfaced submarine dead ahead. At once he pushed the nose of the Sunderland down and dived without any further ado upon the submarine's beam. However, the U-boat crew spotted the incoming aircraft and commenced to dive, so that the submarine had been submerged twenty-five seconds by the time Wood went over the top at 50 feet. This was just within attack parameters, so he dropped a full salvo of eight depth-charges into the water 130 yards ahead of the swirl left on the surface of the sea at the point of the boat's disappearance.

The visibility was so clear and the sea so calm that Wood could judge the point of bomb release perfectly, and a minute after the depth-charge detonations, the disturbed water surface was broken by the U-boat's bow, which rose out of the sea at a 40-degree angle and then lurched forward to reveal the whole submarine lying stationary on the surface. The upper deck forward of the conning tower was awash, the stern was sitting proud of the water, and the boat was listing 15 degrees to port, leaving a slick of escaping diesel oil. A large air bubble 25 feet in diameter appeared alongside the conning tower, and the boat lay there dead in the water for ten minutes while the Sunderland roared backwards and forwards overhead. With all depth-charges expended in the first pass, Wood was reduced to having his gunners spray the hull and conning tower with a total of 2,000 rounds of .303-inch machine-gun fire. The U-boat's gun crews started emerging from the conning tower in the intervals between the Sunderland's overhead passes, and then opened fire with the 20-mm AA gun when Wood came back in; they got hits on the Sunderland before Wood turned away to avoid the gunfire. After that, Wood contented himself with wide orbits beyond gun range. The damaged U-boat got underway again and did a series of 'figure eights' on the surface at low speed, with smoke and steam issuing from the engine compartment in the rear hull. Then it gradually increased speed to 8 knots, and finally submerged. Wood's wireless operator had tapped out an attack report, indicating that the U-boat was severely damaged, but without fresh depth-charges or the arrival of a fresh aircraft there was no way of delivering the *coup de grâce*.

Wood had attacked *U-71*, which had departed La Pallice on 4 June for its seventh war patrol. The captain, *Kapitänleutnant* Walter Flachsenberg, recalled that his inexperienced lookouts had failed to look into the glare of the sun and so failed to spot the diving Sunderland until it was almost too late, and that the depth-charges had exploded around his just-submerged boat in a tight, well-aimed concentration. With ruptured tanks in the after hull, the boat lost buoyancy and started descending stern first. Flachsenberg blew water ballast tanks and only just 'caught the boat' before it plunged beyond its maximum pressure depth, hence its dramatic bow-first reappearance on the surface. Having resurfaced, it took two hours of frenetic work to make the boat capable of diving again. After that, he headed straight back to La Pallice for repairs.[24]

The Sunderland's search for the resubmerged *U-71* ended when the gunners spotted a Focke Wulf 200 patrol bomber a mile away off the Sunderland's port quarter at 7.35 p.m. This aircraft belonged to

Bordeaux-based III./KG40, 10 Squadron's equivalent unit within the Luftwaffe's Atlantic Air Command, with up to twenty Fw 200 Condors on strength.[25] This unit was responsible for long-range patrols in support of the U-boats, and so its aircraft were frequently encountered as they ranged across the Bay. These four-engined German patrol bombers had a formidable forward-firing armament, with 20-mm guns in the dorsal turret and in the ventral sponson, and this particular Condor was flown aggressively enough to take advantage of its firepower, making repeated attacks from beyond the effective range of the flying boat's .303-inch guns. The German gunners were unusually accurate, hitting the Sunderland repeatedly, including severing the hydraulic line to the tail turret. Without power actuation, the turret was 'pretty hopeless' under manual control, and so the rear gunner, LAC Colin Mills, had the greatest difficulty getting his sights upon his target.[26] However, Wood's gunners got hits too, for by the time the enemy bomber finally broke off and headed away towards the French coast, it had suffered one crewman killed and one wounded.[27] In return, there were five large cannon holes and eighty small ones in the Sunderland, but the German gunfire had luckily missed the Sunderland's fuel tanks, engines, flight controls, and crew, and so Wood was able to fly home safely, making a night landing four hours later at Mount Batten.

Two days later, on 7 June, two of No. 10's crew took off into the darkness of 1.30 a.m., despatched on concurrent anti-submarine patrols to the southern reach of Bay of Biscay, each loaded with the Sunderland's maximum anti-submarine bombload of eight depth-charges. By 7.12 a.m., Plt Off. Tom Egerton was patrolling off the northern coast of Spain, flying X/10 at 1,500 feet, when a submarine came into sight 5 miles away off the starboard beam. Egerton ordered the wireless operator to transmit a submarine sighting report and dived his Sunderland upon it from out of the sun. However, this submarine's lookouts were observant, for at a range of 3,000 yards the incoming Sunderland was greeted by a bright red flash from the 100-mm gun on the submarine's foredeck, followed by the black smoke of its shell burst, much closer. As he dived the Sunderland at the submarine, Egerton had to press on through machine-gun tracers; the enemy gunners got hits upon the Sunderland, but Egerton held his line and laid his stick of eight depth-charges across the still-surfaced boat. His closest depth-charge exploded close by the submarine's starboard side, with the others so close that the columns of white water from the detonations almost obscured the boat from sight. After the bursts subsided, the U-boat started zigzagging, but still it did not submerge. As the Sunderland circled at a safe distance, Egerton discovered that two of his crew had been hit in the exchange of fire: Sgt 'Cec' Keane had suffered a superficial wound in his right shoulder, while LAC Keith Miller suffered multiple shrapnel wounds in his chest; fortunately, his wounds too were superficial.[28] Egerton had the wireless operator transmit an attack report, and after orbiting for half an hour, at 7.40 a.m. he saw a second Sunderland approach.

This was Flt Lt Eddie Yeoman's A/10, which, after receiving Egerton's radioed sighting reports, had headed for the scene of the action. At 7.40 a.m., he was flying west along the northern coast of Spain, passing Santander, when the crew spotted what they were looking for: first they saw the other Sunderland a mile away, closer to the coast; then, three minutes later, they saw what they identified as an Italian submarine, 6 miles away. Yeoman circled around it, but as he did so, his Sunderland was unexpectedly taken under accurate AA fire from the submarine's expertly-manned 100-mm gun, suffering hits in its tail. Yeoman responded to the flak not by turning away but by going straight into the attack. The submarine's gunners continued to shoot accurately as the Sunderland came in, with one explosive shell piercing the bottom plating of the hull; it exploded under the galley with such force that the bomb doors in the hull sides could not be closed afterwards. The armourer, Sam Pile, was lucky to escape only with wounds in both legs from this shell explosion.[29] The whole crew were lucky to be still alive and their aircraft still airborne, with four engines still turning. In reply, Yeoman's nose gunner sprayed the up-rushing submarine's conning tower, silencing its return fire as the Sunderland swept in to bomb. Yeoman brought his aircraft in from the submarine's beam, roared overhead at 80 feet and accurately straddled it with a stick of seven depth-charges (the eighth hung up). Two of these charges exploded close alongside the hull amidships.

Egerton's watching crew saw a large flash as A/10 bombed and a cloud of black smoke so thick that they feared Yeoman's crew had been blown up by the explosion. However, the Sunderland reappeared from the smoke and headed away to the north, leaving the submarine behind, dead in the water. Yeoman's aircraft had already been at minimum fuel when it arrived, so after the attack, he set course at once on the 650-mile return trip to Plymouth. As he turned away, his crewmen saw the submarine turning left through the wide patch of disturbed water left by their depth-charge bursts, and saw a torpedo launched from the rear torpedo tubes and run erratically, porpoising out of the water—the submarine crew had probably jettisoned the boat's four stern torpedoes to reduce weight in the flooded after compartments. As Yeoman headed north, he was pursued by an Arado Ar 196 floatplane, which swung from one rear quarter to the other to make repeated attacks. Each time it was greeted by tracers from the four .303s wielded by the tail gunner, Sgt John Harrison, and at length it gave up and went home, without having scored a hit.

Yeoman had a signal transmitted to base advising that his aircraft had a large hole below the waterline and requesting a team of ground crew to stand by to beach the aircraft immediately. Six hours later, he alighted at Mount Batten, the crew having in accordance with standard alighting procedure closed and secured the watertight doors to confine the flooding to the galley compartment. Once safely waterborne, A/10 taxied in towards the slipway, allowing ground-crewmen to wade out into waist-deep water to fit the beaching wheels. The aircraft was immediately hauled up out of the water on to the hard-standing for repairs to the bottom plating. Sunderland A/10 flew again nine days later, on 16 June.

The submarine was the Italian *Luigi Torelli*, and she had gotten much the worst of the exchange, suffering such severe flooding aft that by 7.54 a.m., her bow was sticking out of the water at a 45-degree angle. The boat had sailed from La Pallice on 2 June, bound for a patrol off the Bahamas. By the time of the Australian Sunderlands' attacks on 7 June, she had already been damaged three days earlier, having been ambushed at night by a Wellington from No. 172 Squadron while sailing on the surface 70 miles off the Spanish coast. At that time, the boat's commander, Lt Augusto Migliorini, had headed his damaged vessel back towards France, sailing along the neutral Spanish coast only 6 miles offshore to gain some protection from Spain's neutrality. However, with the gyro compass wrecked and the steering mechanism damaged, the boat ran too close to the Spanish shore at Cape Peñas and went aground on rocks. She was subsequently towed by Spanish tugs into the port of Aviles, where she was beached on a sand bank to effect repairs. The Spanish authorities declared that in accordance with international law, the Italian boat had twenty-four hours to leave the harbour or she would be interned. Accordingly, at midnight on 6 June, Migliorini managed to get his boat underway at 4 knots to head for repairs at Bordeaux, this time hugging the Spanish coast only 3 miles offshore.[30] This would force the RAF to violate Spanish neutrality in order to make an attack on her.

It was in this crippled condition that the *Luigi Torelli* was caught by Egerton and Yeoman the next morning, having departed from Aviles, yet still unable to submerge. Thus, the Italians had fought it out on the surface with guns by necessity. They found the Sunderlands' 'strafing' of their conning tower 'vicious', with the captain and another officer wounded, and one man killed. After Egerton's aircraft finally departed the scene, Migliorini saw that his boat would surely sink if he did not beach her, and by desperate measures, the crew kept her upright and afloat long enough to beach her on a sand bar in Santander harbour.[31] There, the RAF photographed the stranded submarine at low tide, as she lay on her side in the middle of a wide slick of spilling diesel fuel.

To finish the job, Egerton was briefed for an attack upon her the next day with eight 250-pound bombs, but while taxiing for take-off, he received a cancellation message from the ops room: the British Foreign Office had vetoed the attack, rightly considering that such a flagrant violation of neutrality would imperil relations with Spain. The RAF could console itself with the consideration that an interned submarine was almost as good as a sunken submarine; indeed, on 13 June, No. 10 Squadron received a message from the Admiralty congratulating both crews for attacks that had resulted in the 'internment' of the Italian submarine.[32] However, having made their boat seaworthy again, the enterprising Italians managed to elude the 'loose' Spanish surveillance: while being towed across the harbour for the boat to be handed over to the Spanish navy, Migliorini had his crew start one of the submarine's diesels, then slipped the tug's towline and headed straight out to sea. On 15 July, the *Luigi Torelli* finally reached Bordeaux for proper repairs.[33]

Only four days after Egerton's and Yeoman's attacks upon the Italian submarine, early on the morning of 11 June, two crews departed Mount Batten on anti-submarine patrols. This time it was Flt Lt Eric Martin who had the luck to encounter a U-boat. He was flying W/10 at 2,000 feet off the Spanish coast when the crew spotted a fully-surfaced U-boat, 5 miles off the port bow, running on a south-easterly course at 8 knots. Martin circled around behind it and dived in from astern, attaining such complete surprise over the boat's lookouts that he laid his stick of six depth-charges across the target without any AA fire in return. After the splashes of the explosions subsided, the boat lay almost dead in the water, wallowing in a pool of scum and listing so far to starboard that the Australians could see almost the whole port side of her hull. As the Sunderland orbited around its crippled prey, the crew's armourer, LAC Guthrie Hore, was working as rapidly as he could to run the empty bomb racks back inside the hull, to winch the two remaining bombs on to the bomb racks, and to run the racks out again. The aircraft had been armed for a multi-purpose mission, with six depth-charges (for submarines) and two 250-pound bombs (for ships). The bombs were unlikely to be effective as anti-submarine weapons, as they would explode too deep and thus too far from the submarine hull to do significant damage, but Hore nonetheless rearmed the Sunderland. Meanwhile, the damaged U-boat got underway again, then slowly submerged. The crew's disappointment lasted only a minute, when the submarine unexpectedly broke the surface again, as *U-71* had done a week earlier. This was their second opportunity.

By now, Hore had reloaded the Sunderland's bomb racks, so Martin turned straight into an immediate attack. He made two separate runs, approaching from dead astern at 600 feet and dropping one bomb each time, using the newly-introduced hand-held low-level bombsight fitted in the bow hatch. The crippled submarine was so slow-moving that Martin was able to fly each of these bomb runs 'straight and level', thereby delivering each bomb with such accuracy that it burst in the water only yards from the U-boat's hull. As the Sunderland came in on each run, the front gunner exchanged tracer fire with the submarine's 20-mm gunner on the 'bandstand' abaft the conning tower, while the tail gunner, Sgt R. F. 'Mick' Mattner, sprayed the conning tower with .303 from his four guns as he went past. The Sunderland took a 20-mm cannon shell in the port wing on the second run, after which it gained height and circled around, with the crew observing a 'steady jet of grey smoke' coming from the submarine's engine compartment. However, they could only remain for ten minutes before the aircraft's fuel state demanded setting course for base. At 10 a.m., Martin had the wireless operator send a message advising that the aircraft was heading home badly damaged. The second pilot, Plt Off. Geoff Rossiter, thought that W/10 had suffered 'no serious damage'.[34] However, after regaining Mount Batten, the repairs proved extensive enough that she did not fly again until 27 June.

Martin had attacked *U-105*, sailing on her seventh war patrol. Like the *Luigi Torelli*, she was sufficiently damaged by the depth-charge attack as to be rendered unseaworthy, and after the disappearance of the Sunderland, she similarly limped for the refuge of the nearby Spanish port of El Ferrol, which she entered on the 12th. Despite Spain's officially neutral status, the Spanish authorities were in fact collaborating with Germany to the extent that they had allowed El Ferrol to become a covert U-boat repair base: the German navy tanker *Max Albrecht*, moored in the harbour as a *de facto* U-boat depot ship, saw to *U-105*'s repairs.[35] The Spanish authorities also violated the rules of neutrality by permitting the damaged U-boat to remain for more than a fortnight, without suffering internment, while undergoing these repairs; she was allowed to depart unmolested for Lorient on the 28th, safely entering that port two days later.[36] *U-105* had evidently been severely damaged, for despite having already received a fortnight's worth of repairs in Ferrol, she remained in dockyard hands in Lorient until 23 November.[37]

Coastal Command's New Depth-Charges

It might be considered disappointing that not one of these three submarines had been sunk, despite the accurate attacks made. In such matters, timing was everything, for Coastal Command at that very moment was completing the technical development of the U-boat killing weapon that would give it its greatest successes, and which would take it through to the end of the war: the 270-pound Mk XI depth-charge, fitted with a concave nose and a frangible tail to make it sink more slowly, filled with the powerful new Torpex explosive, and equipped with a hydrostatic pistol set to explode at a depth of 25 feet. The new explosive was 50 per cent more powerful than the previous TNT fillings, giving an underwater lethal blast radius 30 per cent greater, and thus a hull-busting effect from 26 feet away from the submarine's side. Moreover, whereas previous depth-charges had sunk too deep before exploding, too far below the submarine's pressure hull to do more than deliver a severe shaking, the new combination exploded reliably at the correct depth.[38]

In early June, at the same time as No. 10 Squadron crews were making their close-but-not-close-enough attacks on *U-71*, *U-105*, and *Luigi Torelli*, No. 172 squadron was trialling this new depth-charge configuration with its Leigh Light Wellingtons.[39] The new depth-charge had been issued to the Sunderland squadrons in May 1942, but the fusing had still not been right: although the depth-charge pistols were billed as having a 25-foot setting, in fact, the depth-charges had plunged so rapidly into the water that the pistol had been slow in firing. It is likely that in No. 10's recent attacks, the depth-charges had suffered from this delayed firing, still exploding too deep in the water to crack the submarines' hulls. Once the new modifications were incorporated, the Mk XI depth-charge at last featured a 'genuine twenty five foot setting', meaning that the underwater detonation would take place shallow enough to bring the destructive radius of the explosion close to the submarine's hull.[40] It was only now, right in the middle of the campaign, that Coastal Command squadrons would finally get a fully fit-for-purpose anti-submarine bomb, fully able to sink a surfaced submarine. The production design for the new depth-charges and fuses was finalised over July–August 1942, and orders placed for the production of 3,000 per month.[41] This was too late for Sam Wood, Tom Egerton, Eddie Yeoman, or Eric Martin to get their first U-boat scalps in June 1942; or alternatively, too late to send the crews of *U-71*, *Luigi Torelli*, or *U-105* to watery deaths that same month.

Despite No. 10's failure to actually sink its submarine victims, the air-sea battle in the Bay of Biscay was turning the Allies' way. In the first five months of 1942, No. 19 Group aircraft had not achieved a single U-boat sinking despite flying 5,041 hours of Bay patrols.[42] Nonetheless, it was the sheer number of RAF air attacks on U-boats transiting the area, both by day and by night, that became a cause of great concern at Admiral Dönitz's U-boat Command HQ in Paris. The rising frequency of such attacks was related to the by-now universal fitment in British patrol aircraft of ASV Mk II radar equipment. A well-tuned set could 'paint' objects as small as motor boats, fighter aircraft, and U-boat conning towers: for example, 10 Squadron operators demonstrated detection ranges of 20 miles or more against submarines. No longer solely dependent upon the 'Mark I eyeball', Coastal Command aircraft could now traverse their patrol area covertly, hidden in cloud or darkness, but nonetheless maintaining an effective radar watch over the sea surface around them. Once the crews' radar operators improved their skills by training and practice, this device was by itself sufficient to change the tactical balance between aircraft and U-boat in the Bay in mid-1942. ASV II radar allowed RAF aircraft to surprise U-boats running on the surface, by making radar-guided approaches through cloud and at night—in other words, in precisely those conditions in which U-boat captains had previously felt themselves to be safe.

As a result, by 11 June 1942, Admiral Dönitz was complaining about the Bay of Biscay being 'the playground of British aircraft', and on 1 July, he confronted *Reichsmarschall* Hermann Göring, head of the Luftwaffe, demanding that air cover be provided over the waters of the Bay during daylight hours. His representations were sufficiently successful for the Luftwaffe to assign to the Atlantic Air Command a new unit, which came to be designated V./KG40, equipped with long-range Ju 88C twin-engined fighters. These aircraft featured a powerful forward-firing armament of three 20-mm cannon, so were a formidable threat to RAF patrol aircraft. In addition, Dönitz was so alarmed by the perplexing ability of RAF aircraft to repeatedly make surprise appearances over his U-boats that he also ordered his U-boat captains to make the passage through the Bay submerged, both by day or by night, surfacing only to recharge the batteries.[43] Previously, the operational norm had been to transit on the surface by night and submerged by day, so Dönitz's change of tactics constituted a significant admission of tactical disadvantage.

Air Combats over the Bay

Although outright sinkings remained frustratingly elusive, 10 Squadron crews had certainly demonstrated a penchant for finding, attacking, and hitting enemy submarines. By contrast, since No. 461 became operational on 1 July, even the barest sighting of enemy submarines seemed at first beyond the capability of the new unit's tyro crews. However, as they flew their first operations, these crews had no difficulty finding enemy fighters; or at least, being found by them. It seems that finding submarines was related to crew proficiency, whereas being found by enemy fighters was largely beyond a crew's control, a random by-product of flying patrol lines across areas patrolled by fighters.

On the second last day of July, Plt Off. Fred Manger's crew took off in C/461 at 1.34 p.m. for a leaflet dropping mission over Spanish fishing boats in the Bay of Biscay. British authorities suspected that these supposedly-neutral vessels were cooperating with U-boats while they made their transits of the Bay. The presence of such vessels in the patrol area was also a profound nuisance to the RAF, as they produced false 'U-boat contacts' on aircraft radar and thus wasted crews' time and effort. The British government therefore issued a proclamation that any boat sailing beyond French or Spanish territorial waters after 24 July would make itself liable to attack. The warning was broadcast by radio and then repeated in leaflet form, in both French and Spanish.[44] After a two-hour transit flight to the northern end of the Bay, Manger made minimum-height, leaflet-dropping passes over each of the fishing vessels sighted, attended by a naval officer who had come along to observe. During these low passes, Sunderland crews and fishing boat crews got to look at one another closely, with the French putting on a good show of their 'very pro-British' sympathies by vigorous waving and the giving of 'V-for-victory' signs. The airmen remained dubious about the fishermen's loyalties, however, amusing themselves with the thought that these same fishermen 'give the Nazi salute when a J.u. or a Kurier [Fw 200] hoves in sight'.[45]

By this laborious process, Manger's Sunderland slowly zig-zagged its way towards the southward end of the Bay and then back again. After four hours of this, having leafleted every fishing boat seen *en route*, C/461 was heading home across the northern reach of the Bay, with a two-hour flight remaining to reach base. By then, with the most challenging and hazardous part of the flight behind them, Manger had changed places with the first pilot, Harry Cooke, who took over the controls in the captain's seat, with Manger himself in the right-hand co-pilot's seat. As the aircraft was not far from the enemy-held coast, and worse still was passing Brest with its German air bases, Manger sought to make a covert exit from the patrol area, flying at the low height of 600 feet to get below the German coastal radar. However, at 7.25 p.m., the British rear gunner, Plt Off. Harry Evans, DFC, suddenly spotted an Arado 196 floatplane, low down against the sea, only 1,000 yards behind. Evans was a gunnery officer from Bomber Command who was visiting the squadron, and who had gone along for the ride in the rear turret; as the Arado drew nearer, the crew might have drawn some comfort from the guest tail gunner's reputation as an 'expert marksman'.[46]

Manger and his crew were keenly aware that a 10 Squadron Sunderland had been shot down by an Arado in a similar position on 21 June, with the deaths of all eleven men of Flt Lt 'Buck' Judell's crew. At that time, Judell's Y/10 had been cooperating with a Whitley from 58 Squadron in a dinghy search, when his crew spotted an Arado approaching. Judell signalled the Whitley to join up for mutual defence, and side by side, the two aircraft had dived away, about a quarter mile apart. Upon levelling out above the sea, the Whitley's captain, Sgt M. W. Randall, RNZAF, was then surprised by a sudden attack from a previously unseen Arado, which exchanged fire with his rear gunner. Both aircraft were hit, with Randall's gunner incapacitated by a wound in the head, and the Arado seen to make an emergency landing on the sea. Looking to his left, Randall realised that the Sunderland too had been hit, for he saw it too land on the sea, with smoke streaming from its starboard inner engine.[47]

The Sunderland made a good landing, but immediately after it came to a halt on the water, it blew up in a great cloud of whitish grey smoke, lit up colourfully by signal cartridges 'cooked off' in the conflagration. By the time Randall flung his Whitley into a turn to evade the next Arado attack, there was nothing visible of the Sunderland above the water.[48] The reasons for Judell's shocking demise seem clear: more than one Arado had attacked; they had attacked from different directions at the same time; at least one of them had attacked without being seen; and had thus fired from within killing range. With rehearsed drills, tactical skills, and determined flying like this, it is unsurprising that one of the German pilots had got good hits on the Sunderland, and some combination of a petrol explosion in the fuel tanks or a fire-induced detonation of the bombload had done the rest. The Arados were not fast aircraft, but with two forward-firing 20-mm cannon, they constituted a much more serious threat than might be supposed. The Luftwaffe's 5./*Bordfliegergruppe* 196 operated about twenty Arados from Brest in order to protect transiting U-boats in the Bay, and from May to September 1942, these otherwise pedestrian aircraft claimed twelve kills against British anti-submarine aircraft.[49] Judell's aircraft would be their first, but not their last Australian Sunderland victim.[50] The loss of this crew was widely felt within the tightly inter-connected Australian Sunderland community: No. 461's Bruce Buls had been second pilot in Judell's crew before transferring to the new unit.

Now, seven weeks after Judell's fiery demise, Manger faced his own Arado attack, and while sitting ineffectually in the co-pilot's seat. He ordered Cooke to dive the aircraft straight down to 50 feet above the waves—this low height, along with the return gunfire from the Sunderland's gun turrets, was intended to discourage the German pilot from pressing home his firing runs too closely. From his position in the astrodome, the second pilot, Plt Off. Phil Davenport, saw that the Sunderland was so low that its propeller wash left a wake on the water, 'a darker blue on the glassy surface astern'. He spotted his first Arado as it emerged from the glare of the sun, by which time it was already 'bigger than a black dot'; when its distinctive twin floats became discernible, enabling it to be recognised as an Arado 196, it was almost within firing range.[51] This Arado made its first attack from the Sunderland's starboard quarter, where, taken under tracer fire from both the tail and midships turrets, it opened fire only cautiously from the long range of 600 yards, and then quickly broke off, turning away past the Sunderland's tail 800 yards behind. It then crossed over to the other side, moved slowly ahead and then repeated the long-range gunnery attack from the port quarter. From that range, the German pilot was wasting his ammunition.

By now, the navigator, 'Wonk' Kennedy, had performed his assigned role of establishing the aircraft's latitude and longitude for the radioed fighter contact report to base, and had handed this over for Davenport to encode. With Kennedy's navigational duties done for now, the two swapped places. Kennedy stepped up on to the wing-spar to get his head within the astrodome, while Davenport sat down to compose an enciphered message to base: 'Emergency. We are being attacked by an Arado. Our position is …' Before he could hand the message to the wireless operator for transmission, he had to encode it, using a 'Syko machine', which was described as 'a gadget that looked like a hybrid of an abacus and an old-time scrubbing board'.[52] This device was like a suitcase that opened out into a portable writing desk, featuring a thirty-two-column, moveable alpha-numerical matrix.[53] The code-of-the-day card was clipped to the inside of the lid, and each letter or number group in the message was converted into its encoded letter group by applying the specified transposition key; the encoded message was then written down, letter group by letter group, on to the message chit clipped to the 'desk', to be handed on to the wireless operator for transmission. This was the painstaking alpha-numerical chore that Davenport had to perform repeatedly during the action, while the aircraft lurched and yawed, banked and turned, the guns hammered, the engines roared, and the intercom buzzed with the crew's fighting talk of targets' ranges and bearings.

Once Kennedy had his head inside the astrodome, he took over as fire control officer, using this position's all-round visibility to keep watch on all enemy aircraft and to provide a running commentary for the benefit of the pilots' manoeuvring and the gunners' firing. While Davenport was performing his numerical transpositions at the plotting desk, the rear gunner, Harry Evans, reported a second Arado, 2,000 yards out on the port quarter. Then Kennedy reported a third one on the same side, working forward to get up-sun for an attack. Meanwhile, Davenport had to compose and encode amplifying signals to base reporting each piece of new information. As he did so, he listened to the action over the intercom, hearing Kennedy's calm controlling of the gunners as the aircraft faced simultaneous attacks.

The reason for the presence of these single-engined floatplanes operating so far from the coast became clear five minutes after the first sighting, when Manger's crew spotted a fully-surfaced U-boat 2,000 yards away. They had to leave it behind as the Sunderland headed north at full throttle, pursued by Arados. C/461 had the standard load of six 270-pound depth-charges aboard, but as Manger later reported, he was unable to make an attack on the submarine 'due to difficulties fighting Arados'. The submarine seemed completely stationary in the water, suggesting that the floatplanes were a defensive patrol to protect a crippled vessel from Allied air attack. Because the German floatplanes had so little speed advantage over the Sunderland, the second Arado was reduced to slowly overhauling the Sunderland from directly astern. This presented Evans in the tail turret with a favourable shot, albeit at extreme range. The tracers arcing out from the tail turret provided sufficient disincentive for this German pilot to open fire from outside cannon range and then break away at 1,000 yards—too far. Then the other two Arados made their attacks in turn, one each from the Sunderland's starboard and port quarters; the first attacked only half-heartedly, breaking off safely at 700 yards, but the second came in to 400 yards, just within practical hitting range. It then made the error of overshooting the target, presenting the Sunderland's tail and midships turrets with clear shots: belatedly alerted to his mistake by .303 tracers, the German pilot banked hard left to get away. Davenport, listening to Kennedy's direction over the intercom, heard, 'Nose and Midships, take the starboard bow attack. Both of you. Nose and Midships, now round to port! Tail, there's one coming down the starboard. Get him, Harold!'[54] Evans fired a five-second burst, then saw the errant Arado continue its left turn and hit the sea with a splash, 3,000 yards behind.

This mishap did not deter the other two German pilots, who laboriously worked their way forward on each side, trying to set up for frontal attacks. The first Arado rolled into its attack from 1,000 yards out on the Sunderland's port bow, but the German pilot had miscalculated by turning in too early; at a combined closing speed of more than 300 knots he was passing over the top of the flying boat only five seconds later, without having had enough time to aim and open fire. He was greeted along his trajectory first by the tracers from the nose gunner and then by those from the midships gunner, as he went past close overhead. When Manger saw the third enemy aircraft turning in from the starboard bow, he finally abandoned any lingering intention of returning to make an attack on the recently-bypassed U-boat, jettisoning C/461's load of depth-charges to get a little more speed and turning right towards the incoming enemy aircraft to ruin its shooting. This Arado broke away to the left over the top of the Sunderland, presenting the midships turret with a shot, then flew away and struck the sea with a big splash 1,000 yards off the starboard beam; but it bounced off the sea, resumed flight, and slowly turned around to resume a parallel course off the Sunderland's rear quarter. The lucky German pilot had evidently attempted to get low over the water to avoid the pursuing return fire, but with such a glassy sea he had misjudged his height and inadvertently kissed the water surface with the bottoms of his aircraft's floats. Meanwhile, with black smoke from full-throttle rich-mixture streaming from his aircraft's four over-wing engine exhausts, Manger was putting as many miles as he could between his aircraft and the German-held coast. After the Arados caught up again, they made two more attacks from the Sunderland's rear, opening fire from a very-optimistic 1,000 yards, and breaking away at a prudent 600 yards. Eventually, at 7.45 p.m., twenty minutes after the first sighting, both remaining Arados gave up and then turned back towards the French coast.

Fred Manger and his crew had performed admirably in this severe test of their professionalism, successfully fighting off nine separate attacks by three cannon-armed enemy fighters. The crew had come through without a scratch, and damage to the aircraft was confined to five bullet holes in the starboard wing outboard of the engines, and one bullet hole in the port tailplane—a very poor result for all the ammunition expended by the German pilots, but entirely typical of the gunnery results from long-range shooting. Besides Manger's manoeuvring, it was the gunners' return fire that was responsible for the gratifying result: the front gunner had fired 400 rounds, the midships gunner 1,200 rounds, and the tail gunner 2,000 rounds. On average, that represented a total of about thirty seconds' firing from each turret.

A fact obscured within Manger's dangerous encounter with the Arados was that his crew had actually seen a U-boat. Even if they had been unable to attack it, this was the first such sighting by a 461 Squadron crew, and was, after all, the reason for the squadron's existence. Aside from this, the immediate thing was that they had come through their first combat alive. Manger's wireless operator, Plt Off. Paul Bird, expressed the crew's reaction to coming into action for the first time as 'high elation': 'It was something we had travelled a long way for, something that we had trained hard to accomplish'.[55]

Importantly for No. 461, this newly-qualified freshman crew had also lived up to the redoubtable standard set by veteran 10 Squadron crews in surviving similar fighter attacks in the contested skies of the Bay of Biscay. Indeed, only two days earlier, on 28 July, Reg Marks's crew from No. 10 had similarly survived an attack by a far more dangerous Me 109 single-engined fighter off the French coast, and then similarly got home safely in a damaged aircraft. The presence of an Me 109 shows how close the Sunderlands were operating to the occupied French coast during their patrol 'beats' on the lookout for German blockade runners and for French and Spanish fishing boats operating in support of transiting U-boats: the Me 109 had an operating radius of only 100 miles, so Marks's Sunderland must have been this close at least to the enemy coast. After Marks's combat, Air Chief Marshal Joubert cabled a congratulatory signal from Coastal Command HQ, praising the crew's performance in surviving the attack and getting home as 'a fine example of co-ordinated effort, resource and flying ability. It is in fact a damn good show'.[56] Something similar could have been said of Manger's greenhorn crew two days later.

Fortunately, not all encounters with Luftwaffe aircraft were as potentially dire as these. Sgt Ed Gallagher, wireless operator/air gunner in Bruce Buls's crew, recorded a wary encounter with a Fw 200 on 13 July, in which both aircraft circled and exchanged fire, after which the German bomber made off, marking its departure by blinking a short English-language message in Morse code by signal lamp: 'So long'. Russ Baird, Buls's first pilot, grabbed a signal lamp and flashed off a 'ruder' signal in reply—something like, 'Fuck off!' Baird's embittered wit and the ultimate harmlessness of the encounter gave the crewmen something to laugh about when they got back to base.[57]

Manger's crew's relief at 'getting away with it' on the 30th was tempered by the sobering news that Flt Lt Eric Martin's crew from 10 Squadron had failed to return from an anti-submarine patrol along the Spanish coast on that same day. No signals were received from Martin's X/10 after its take-off at 2.15 a.m. Next day, George Miedecke conducted a search in U/10, in the hope that the missing Sunderland had force-landed on the water, but nothing was ever found. All twelve men were lost.[58] No. 10's unit history states that the aircraft was shot down, so the likely culprit was an Arado from the Brest-based 5./196.[59] No Sunderland combats were filed by either of the France-based Luftwaffe fighter units, JG 2 or JG 26, so it seems likely that Martin's crew had been ambushed by a flight of Arados as it rounded the Brest Peninsula.[60]

Progress by No. 461 Squadron

No. 461's successful combat by Manger's crew on 30 July capped off a productive month for the new squadron, with a total of thirty-three operations flown by an aircrew cadre that had now grown to four operational crews (captained by Buls, Manger, Smith, and Walker). This was a very respectable achievement, as shown by the comparison with 10 Squadron: with ten crews, this long-established and veteran unit had flown fifty-three operations in the same month. In parallel with this operational performance, 461's flight commander, Colin Lovelock, was meanwhile pressing on with the training commitment so vigorously that within the next month the squadron built itself up to seven operational crews. By the end of July, besides the pilots who had qualified as captains, Lovelock had by then checked-out three more pilots as night-qualified, and hence approaching their captaincy qualification. He had checked out another five pilots as day-qualified only, and thus able to fly within crews as first pilots; there were, in addition, four more pilots under training and hence fit to serve as second pilots. Besides this, there were now also seven qualified navigators, plus four navigators under training. Lovelock and Gillies, the training captains, had been both busy and productive.

By the start of August 1942, after one month of operations, No. 461 had nine aircraft (the same as No. 10), and with a total of 254 personnel on its books. However, only ninety-two of these men were RAAF, the rest being mostly RAF (with a few RCAF and RNZAF as well). The proportion of Australian-manning was higher among the ninety-seven aircrew, fifty-one of whom were RAAF. Within the aircrews, the Australian members were disproportionately represented at the front of the aircraft: as a general pattern, the pilots and navigators were RAAF, while the majority of the 'back-seater' complement of wireless operator/air gunners, fitters and riggers were RAF.

By comparison, 10 Squadron finished the month with 395 personnel, of whom all but seven were RAAF. This divergence in rates of Australian-manning within the two squadrons clearly shows the effect of the demarcation dispute within the RAAF bureaucracy about the employment of RAAF personnel. Right through to the end of 461 Squadron's existence, flight crews continued to rely upon RAF flight engineers and wireless operator mechanic/air gunners, because the RAAF did not include either specialisation in its EATS training syllabus.[61] The mixed manning within No. 461 was thoroughly typical of other Article XV squadrons as well: for example, after the Canadians formed two Sunderland squadrons in 1942, Nos 422 and 423, as direct equivalents to No. 461, both would struggle to attain 50 per cent Canadian manning into 1943.[62]

In August 1942, No. 461's growth in operational maturity was shown by increased technical proficiency in the use of the radar equipment. For example, after flying a patrol on 2 August, Bert Smith specifically pointed out in his patrol report that his aircraft had 'used ASV throughout'. This pointed notation suggests that No. 461's wireless operators were by now gaining sufficient proficiency in the operation of the ASV II radar equipment to make radar surveillance a practical capability for the entire duration of a patrol. Unsurprisingly, however, No. 10 Squadron's more experienced crews were even more skilful in their exploitation of this technology: on 16 May, Reg Marks's crew used the radar to track an unidentified aircraft; on 5 June, Sam Wood's crew used radar to home onto a hitherto-unseen U-boat from 8 miles away; on 6 June, Marks's crew did even better by making an attack upon a surfaced U-boat at night, after homing on to it by radar; on 16 June, Terry Brown's crew used radar to detect and home onto a convoy from 45 miles out; on 16 July, Sam Wood's crew used radar to detect and avoid an incoming Ju 88; on 22 July, Graham Pockley's crew used radar to home onto and investigate surface contacts at night; on 9 August, Kerv Beeton's crew maintained a radar search throughout its patrol despite flying in 10/10th cloud in conditions of nil visibility; and on 23 August, the same crew detected a suspected enemy aircraft on radar and covertly shadowed it by radar for 22 miles.

Coastal Command's investigation of ASV use throughout the command had concluded that radar performance had everything to do with operator skill: the bottom 15 per cent of operators never detected a U-boat even when it was there.[63] Within No. 10, there can be no doubt that by the summer of 1942, the unit's more-experienced and more thoroughly-trained crews had attained considerable technical proficiency and operational sophistication in their use of the ASV II radar equipment, and that No. 461's crews were attaining competency.

Air-Sea Rescues in the Bay

As we have seen, another role that fell to No. 19 Group's pair of Australian Sunderland squadrons was the air-sea rescue of downed crews, for the simple reason that no other squadrons had long range flying boats. Unfortunately, only some dinghy searches ended as happily as, for example, Wg Cdr Halliday's open-sea rescue of the Whitley crew on 8 July. On 5 August, Col Walker took off at 1.30 p.m. in B/461 on an anti-submarine patrol over the Bay, but at 10.10 p.m. received a signal from Group HQ at Plymouth to search for the crew of Whitley S/502, which had ditched at the northern end of the Bay. A visual search like this for such a tiny object as a dinghy was always going to be a difficult task at night, but at 11.15 p.m., Walker received a further signal instructing him to use his aircraft's radio direction finder to home on to another Whitley, U/502, which was reportedly orbiting overhead the downed crew's dinghy. Coastal Command aircraft could home other aircraft to their position by making a continuous transmission on the special homing frequency of 385 KHz; this allowed the homing aircraft to take directional bearings on the signal, using its medium frequency direction finder.[64] In this case, despite homing on to the signal, Walker searched without success until reaching the limit of his fuel at 12.20 a.m., whereupon he headed for home.

The next day, 6 August, two Australian Sunderlands were despatched to resume the same search: 10 Squadron's Flt Lt Yeoman in A/10 and No. 461's Plt Off. Buls in A/461. It seems that the waters of the Bay of Biscay were littered with empty dinghies, for Eddie Yeoman even took the risk of putting his aircraft down on the water to investigate the contents of two dinghies lashed together that he found floating on the sea. The sea was calm that day, so this was a reasonably safe thing to do for such a highly-experienced Sunderland captain, but Yeoman's successful open water landing would contribute to the existing precedent.

Dinghy searches posed not only the inherent hazards of water landings, but also the hazards of extended exposure to enemy fighters when the ditched RAF aircraft had gone down within the Bay. Bruce Buls, who had taken off earlier than Yeoman on that same day, was instructed to home upon Whitley A/502, which had reportedly found the dinghy, and which was now orbiting overhead with its homing transmitter on. Buls reached the stated position at the northern end of the bay and commenced a square search, but only a minute later, a Ju 88 appeared, approaching low over the sea at 500 feet. The German crew appear to have attempted a *ruse de guerre*, for the Junkers fired off red and green signal cartridges, in the hope that these were the RAF 'colours of the day'. This was worth trying, except that, on this occasion, Coastal Command's colours of the day were red and yellow, and that Buls's crew could recognise a Ju 88 when they saw one. Buls turned his aircraft away as rapidly as he could, thus presenting the incoming Junkers with the four .303-inch Brownings of the Sunderland's tail turret—itself a significant deterrent—while also gaining time by presenting the German pilot with the need for a time and distance-consuming chase out on to the flank. Only from there they could deliver a safer beam attack, clear of the tail turret's firing arc.

However, just then, two Arado floatplanes appeared, equally unexpectedly, at close range off the Sunderland's port bow. The startled Buls turned rapidly away from these new arrivals to present them with similarly unattractive attacking options from the rear. The Arados resorted to a stern chase, but these were slow aircraft, and by 7.48 a.m. had given up and headed home, without having got a single hit on A/461. Buls's crew believed their aircraft had been taken under fire by all three German aircraft, and indeed the dorsal turret gunner, Sgt Ed Gallagher, believed he had heard the Germans' cannon fire over the noise of the engines. Despite the happy final result, for Gallagher, it had been a frightening encounter: even as he fired his guns, he had already resigned himself to being shot down and killed, plagued by thoughts that he would never see Molly Thomson, his future wife back in Brisbane, ever again.[65] No matter how 'keen' the pilots in the front of the aircraft might have been to take their aircraft into action, ambiguous responses like Gallagher's provided the reality check for the back-seaters sentenced to sit behind the pilots as they flew their aircraft into danger.

After this alarming encounter with the fighters, and having searched without success for the dinghy in the prescribed area, Buls broke off the search and set course for the Scilly Isles; this was the basic navigational waypoint used by all 19 Group aircraft transiting between south-western England and the Bay of Biscay, as the resultant dogleg course from Cornwall to the Bay put distance between the transiting RAF patrol aircraft and the German airfields around Brest. However, at 9.05 a.m., 19 Group HQ directed Buls's aircraft to commence a new dinghy search in a new position. By 11.07 a.m., he had brought A/461 overhead the stated position in the sea, commencing a square search at 500 feet, on lookout for the specified object of two dinghies lashed together and trailing high-visibility phosphorescent sea dye. This time the stated dinghy position was correct, for at 12.20 p.m., the two dinghies came into view up ahead, and a pass close overhead confirmed that the occupants were still alive. Buls jettisoned his bombload, set himself up for an approach to alight upon the sea, and made a steady engine-on approach at 100 knots. It all went by the book, and by 12.30 p.m., the Sunderland was alongside the dinghies to take the men aboard. Ten minutes later, they were airborne again, heading home, and at 1.15 p.m., a signal was tapped out to base reporting the rescue.

This was a gratifying result, considering the risks attendant upon a Sunderland alighting upon the open sea. These water landings highlighted three considerations that would bear heavily upon the Australian Sunderland crews' operations in the Bay of Biscay. Firstly, when a crew went into the sea, Coastal Command was prepared to divert considerable operational effort away from the core business of hunting U-boats and towards ASR instead. Besides the obvious humanitarian considerations, there can be no doubt that this was done out of concern for crew morale: considering that the men were required to fly twelve-hour sorties with often unreliable engines, at low altitude, in bad weather, at night, and hundreds of miles from land, it meant a lot to know that the resources of the whole command would be bent upon your rescue if you went into 'the drink'. Secondly, the corollary of this was that because the Sunderland was the only aircraft in 19 Group's battle order capable of effecting a water rescue, the responsibility had by necessity fallen upon the Sunderland crews to perform the needed water landings in the open sea, despite the attendant risks. Thirdly, the frequency with which enemy aircraft were being encountered, and the increasing number of air combats resulting, pointed to an increasingly hazardous operating environment over the

Bay of Biscay in daylight. Coastal Command had played its radar card to trump the U-boats, and now the Luftwaffe was playing its fighter card to try to trump the RAF.

The Fighter Threat Escalates

On 9 August came bitter confirmation of the fighter hazard in the operational area: Eddie Yeoman departed Mount Batten in A/10 on a routine anti-submarine patrol along the Spanish coast, and never returned. At 6.24 p.m., the aircraft sent an SOS signal from a position deep in the Bay of Biscay, 100 miles out to sea from Cape Ortegal. Nothing more was heard, nor was any trace ever found of the aircraft or the twelve men in her crew.[66] This was despite searches mounted straightaway by two other 10 Squadron aircraft patrolling the area, those of Ron Gillies's W/10 and Dave Vernon's Z/10. Fate was certainly capricious, for Yeoman's flight engineer, Sgt Grattan Horgan, remained as the only living member of the crew: after returning to Mount Batten from a flight on 31 July, he had been temporarily grounded by the medical officer, Flt Lt Geoff Wilson, for hospital treatment to his right eye. Horgan's stand-in, Aircraftman Lindsay Ogg, thereby unluckily died with Yeoman's crew.[67] This Sunderland was not shot down by a Ju 88 fighter from V./KG40, as there is no indication of a combat having taken place between a Ju 88 and a Sunderland on the day in question, no Ju 88 pilot claimed damage to a Sunderland, and nor was any loss or damage inflicted on the German long-range fighter unit.[68] The Brest-based floatplane unit, 5./196, can also be ruled out: although it claimed a total of twelve kills against Sunderlands, Whitleys, and Wellingtons over May–September 1942, its Arados were too short-ranged to reach this position, 400 miles out to sea from Bordeaux.[69] The reason for the loss therefore remains unclear, although a sudden and catastrophic, in-flight, technical failure seems likely.

Shockingly, No. 10 Squadron had lost one crew per month over June–August 1942. It must have been a bad enough wrench for Wg Cdr Richards to write the eleven condolence letters to the next-of-kin of Buck Judell's crew, for this had been the very first time that any 10 Squadron CO had had to do so for a full crew. Richards would have hated to think that he would have to write two dozen more such letters within two months. Prior to the loss of Judell's crew on 21 June, No. 10 had flown operations for two and a half years without losing a single crew to enemy action.[70] As Dick Cohen put it after completing his tour with 10 Squadron in 1941, 'flying with Coastal Command was not unduly dangerous, unlike in Fighter or Bomber Command'.[71] On the contrary, the arrival of German combat aircraft in the skies over the Bay had now made it quite dangerous. By the summer of 1942, Coastal Command casualty rates were spiking to levels normal in those other frontline RAF commands: No. 10 had had thirty-five men killed in six weeks, in a unit that had perhaps 120 aircrew on strength. Nor had this sequence of losses been a one-off, for 1943 would be worse.

The loss of the unit's first crew, Judell's, had come as such a shock to the tightly-knit and insular community of 10 Squadron as to spur the unit's poet, Sgt Russ Mullins, to pen an elegy for the fallen. He wrote:

Ghost boats will go on flying, those chaps will never die,
For we just can't forget them, we knew them, You and I.[72]

Sadly, Mullins himself was then killed with Eric Martin's crew on 30 July. WO Wilf Granger, an engine fitter with the squadron from 1940 to 1945, and who over that time mixed with the enlisted back-seaters in the airmen's mess and sergeants' mess, would have empathised with the sentiment expressed by Mullins. Granger afterwards recalled that 'one of the things that stands out in your memory was when you had lost a boat and there were those vacant seats in the Mess. There is no truer saying than "They were too young to die"'.[73] Other airmen would react to the coming spate of losses more viscerally than Mullins and Granger: Russ Baird, a pilot who flew with both Australian squadrons, quickly learnt to 'hate' war because of the loss of so many 'young fellows like yourself'.[74]

Besides the emotional shock among squadron members, these losses had set back 10 Squadron by degrading its operational strength and imposing an unwonted degree of urgency in the training of replacement crews—an urgency that would have been quite familiar to Halliday and Lovelock in resource-poor No. 461. Back in May, before the losses, No. 10 had had ten crews on its operations roster. In September, after the impact of the losses, the squadron had only nine crews available, and even this had only been achieved by pushing first pilots through to captaincy status. The names of three newly-qualified captains were thus chalked up on to the squadron's operations board: Fg Offs Kerv Beeton, Wyn Thorpe, and Doug White. All three had joined No. 10 in 1941 and started flying as second pilots, graduating to first pilot in April 1942. Although these men counted as relatively junior pilots by 10 Squadron standards, they were much more experienced pilots than the first tranche of No. 461 captains rushed through the captaincy qualification process back in May and June. Nonetheless, it is significant that even on well-resourced No. 10, the training program had to be expedited to fill the gaps left by the recent losses, with all three new captains checked-out as night-qualified on the same night, 27 August.

Despite the sudden eruption of casualties, these violent encounters with enemy aircraft cannot be considered occurrences 'against the run of play'. Rather, the losses were part of a clear trend towards greater confrontation with German aircraft over the Bay. Instances were plentiful within No. 10 Squadron: on 16 May, Reg Marks's crew survived repeated attacks by an Arado; on 19 May, Sam Wood's crew was chased by two enemy aircraft; on 5 June, his aircraft sustained damage from the 20-mm cannon of a persistent Fw 200, and on 16 July, he used radar to detect and avoid an incoming Ju 88; on 7 June, Eddie Yeoman's crew fought off repeated attacks from an Arado; on 14 June, Tom Egerton's crew survived repeated attacks from an aggressive Ju 88; on 1 August, Terry Brown's crew encountered an Fw 200; and on 9 August, Kerv Beeton's crew survived getting ambushed in cloud by a Ju 88. No. 461 Squadron too had had its encounters: on 6 July, Bert Smith's crew survived repeated attacks from a Ju 88 (as described previously); on 16 July, Col Walker's crew and a Ju 88 warily circled around each other without engaging; on 30 July, Fred Manger's crew fought off attacks by three Arados (as related above); on 6 August, Bruce Buls's crew fought off an attack from one Ju 88 and two Arados (also as described above); and on 11 August, Col Steley avoided attack from an Fw 200 and Ju 88 by climbing into cloud. The skies above the Bay had now become contested skies, and it was yet undecided which side would prevail.

In a Sunderland, survival against fighter attack was a product of some felicitous combination of luck, circumstance, alertness, and skill. In any given encounter, it was the luck of the draw how many German aircraft one ran into, what type of machine they were, what their fuel state was, how aggressive their pilots were, and whether the enemy aircraft had attained an advantageous position from which to attack, such as suddenly out of cloud or out of the sun; while for the Sunderland crew, there was also the happenstance of whether there was or was not cloud cover close enough to reach and to hide in. Crews from both Australian squadrons had repeatedly demonstrated the piloting skills, tactical nous, crew drills, and gunnery necessary to stand a good chance of fighting off an observed attack. However, 10 Squadron's recent losses show that if a Sunderland faced a surprise eruption of adverse tactical factors, it stood a poor chance of survival. It is telling that neither Martin's nor Yeoman's wireless operators had got off a wireless report before hitting the sea, which suggests a sudden, unanticipated and violent demise. By contrast, throughout Reg Marks's combat with the Arado on 16 May, his wireless operator, Cpl Richard Trenberth, had tapped out repeated messages on his transmitter, providing HQ with positional fixes in case his aircraft went into the water; on 6 July, Bert Smith's wireless operator transmitted

'Am being attacked Ju 88' at the commencement of the combat; and on 30 July, Fred Manger's second pilot, Phil Davenport, had time to encode for transmission a series of fighter contact reports during that action. An alerted Sunderland crew stood a good chance of getting away, but a surprised crew was likely to be lost.

The same day as Yeoman's loss, 9 August, Col Steley's crew made No. 461's first attack upon a submarine. Having taken off at 7.53 a.m. in E/461, he received a signal from base at 12.05 p.m., instructing the aircraft to fly to a given position and attack a submarine reported there; after proceeding towards that point, at 2.10 p.m., the rear gunner spotted a surfaced submarine, 5 miles to port. It was a clear day, with 15 miles of visibility beneath a thin layer of scattered cloud. Steley turned to attack, and despite the good visibility, the submarine made no move to submerge, allowing him to drop his load of depth-charges across its track. As he pulled away in a climbing turn, his midships gunner sprayed 200 rounds of .303 across its decks. It was only after this rude wake-up call that the submarine submerged. However, in their haste, the crew evidently mishandled the boat's dive, for it reappeared stern-first thirty seconds later, before restabilising itself on the surface and then submerging again, this time successfully. Steley's crew returned to Mount Batten understandably pleased to have delivered the new squadron's first blow upon the Nazi U-boat force.

After the buzz of excitement in the briefing room and messes afterwards, it came as a letdown when the target 'was later found to be a British submarine'. The error was traced to a 'misunderstanding of the limits of the restricted bombing area'.[75] Charts were marked with 'no bombing' corridors, through which friendly submarines could transit on the surface across the Bay of Biscay, and Steley had evidently made an attack within one of those areas.[76] Bruce Buls was flying a patrol at the same time in A/461, and his wireless operator, Ed Gallagher, who was listening to Steley's sighting reports, noticed that the position given was in a 'prohibited area', and hoped that Steley 'didn't sink one of ours'. From the perspective of his own crew's tight tribalism, Gallagher had a poor opinion of Steley and his inexperienced crew, unsympathetically explaining their mistake as due to them being 'silly bastards'.[77]

An Expensive Rescue Mission

On 12 August came another SOS from yet another crew forced down in the Bay of Biscay by engine failure; this time, it was a Wellington crew from No. 172 Squadron, captained by an Australian, Plt Off. Alan Triggs.

It is worth noting that neither Whitley G.R. VII nor Wellington G.R. VIII aircraft were capable of maintaining level flight on one engine; even in ideal conditions, neither of these under-powered aircraft had satisfactory engine-out performance, and this was made worse by the Coastal Command configuration of protuberant ASV radar posts and aerials, which added drag, steepened the glide angle, and degraded the engine-out performance. Triggs's Wellington ditched at the top of the Bay, only 60 miles from the German naval and air base at Brest, and therefore right under the enemy's nose.[78]

As he had done on 8 July, Wg Cdr Halliday volunteered to take a crew on the impromptu ASR mission, taking off at 3.40 p.m. in B/461. This time Halliday had commandeered Col Walker's aircraft and his regular crew, with Walker himself left behind, perforce ceding his place to the CO. Three and a half hours later, Halliday reached the reported dinghy position, having flown so good a course that almost at once the rear gunner reported two signal flares 2 miles to starboard. Turning to investigate, they found what they were after: a dinghy with live occupants. Inauspiciously, however, there was a 25-knot wind blowing from the west, whipping the sea into white caps and driving spray. Without Triggs's signal flares, the Sunderland crew would have had great difficulty spotting the dinghy even from only 2 miles away when viewed against the backdrop of a sea so heavy that the dinghy was lost from view in the troughs between waves.

Despite the dangerous sea conditions, Halliday decided to alight to rescue the survivors. This was just as he had done a month before—but that time the breeze had been gentle and the sea surface placid. He orbited around the dinghy three times, reducing aircraft weight by jettisoning the bombload and 500 gallons of fuel. After this, he made one low run over the dinghy to take a photograph, and then on a second pass dropped a smoke float to help him line up into the wind for the final approach. In doing so, he faced the seaplane pilot's conundrum: it was conventional good airmanship to alight into the wind, but in the open sea this meant touching down perpendicular to the line of swell, and so striking the thin hull bottom against the steepest water gradient at the top of each wave.

While Halliday was doing his circuits, the navigator, Fg Off. John Watson, was at his desk on the flight-deck, 'sykoeing' a signal to base reporting that the aircraft was over the dinghies. While busy with this task, he overheard Halliday's directions to the crew over the intercom and got the impression that the CO was in a great hurry to land. Watson heard the armourer report that one of the depth-charges had hung up on its rack, and heard Halliday instruct him not to persist with it; he would alight with the depth-charge aboard. With the aircraft by now already on final approach, Watson queried whether the CO wanted him to persist with his enciphering; Halliday did not answer, instead ordering the crew to stand by for landing. Clearly, things were very busy on the flight-deck. At 7.45 p.m., Watson abandoned the enciphering and instead handed the wireless operator a message 'in clear' that they were alighting to rescue the dinghy crew. As the Sunderland descended steadily on final approach, Watson saw to his assigned role of making sure that the crew came up on to the top deck, secured their Mae West life preservers, and assumed their crash positions braced behind the wing spars. Plt Off. David Laurenti, the second pilot, was one of the last up on to the flight-deck, having been operating the camera down below. He wore no 'Mae West', as in the rush to get airborne the crew had taken off with one life vest short.

Once everyone was stowed away at the rear of the flight-deck, Watson stood up underneath the astrodome and looked ahead. He saw that the waves were a daunting 12 feet high, and instinctively unlatched two of the four clips fastening the astrodome escape hatch. Halliday made a normal, powered approach to alight as gently as possible, but the Sunderland's hull struck the top of a big wave before he had fully rotated the aircraft into landing attitude; travelling too fast, the Sunderland bounced back into the air. Watson managed to maintain his stance beneath the astrodome during the aircraft's forceful but momentary arrival but heard a resounding crash of sprung aluminium panelling from the deck below as he did so: it sounded as if the hull's rear step was stoved-in at the point of water impact. Halliday applied power, stabilised the aircraft, and then set up to complete the landing. The Sunderland flew on for another 400 yards before touching down a second time; this time, Halliday managed to pull the aircraft into a nose-high landing attitude before touchdown. This was as gentle an arrival as could possibly be managed; indeed, Watson considered the aircraft to be flying below stalling speed when it touched down on top of another wave. Despite the slower arrival this time, the hull bottom once again struck the water with a heavy crash: Watson heard metallic rending noises from the hull's planing bottom. Almost at once, a large cross wave struck the port side of the bow, tearing off the port outer propeller and the port wing float. This wave impact slewed the aircraft violently to the right, throwing the crewmen huddled behind the spar against the cabin wall. Then the port wing slumped into the water and the sea started pouring into the hull. The aircraft was now irretrievably lost.

Watson stood up at once beneath the astrodome hatch, fumbling with the two remaining securing clips 'with the willing assistance of the two engineers'. Once all four clips were released, the three men found that the hatch would not budge; evidently, the crash impact had so warped the fuselage structure that the hatch opening was no longer square. The two engineers used force to swing the hatch down and were the first out on to the wing. Before following them out, Watson turned back to his navigation desk to fetch a dinghy pack, a signal pistol, and signal cartridges. This was only one pace forward, but by then he already found himself standing in 2 feet of water. Then the water level rose so rapidly within the hull that the outwards air pressure slammed the escape hatch shut. Watson was now trapped, his head jammed under the astrodome. The water rose over his head, and he lost consciousness.

Watson came to with his head out of the somehow reopened hatch. He found himself held up by David Laurenti, who sat on the edge of the hatch clamping Watson's torso between his knees. Others standing on top of the hull pulled him out and helped him on to the wing, which by now was the only part of the aircraft remaining afloat. As Watson regained his wits over the next minutes, he perceived that the aircraft had broken its back, as the rear fuselage and tail were gone; he saw that the waves were 12 feet high from trough to crest; he saw crew members standing on the wing handling a crew dinghy; he saw Halliday and four others in the dinghy; he saw another dinghy, unoccupied, floating 500 yards away from the wreck; and he counted and identified nine of the eleven men in the crew, including three who were swimming individually with their Mae Wests on, up to 100 yards away. These three swimmers were the first pilot, Fg Off. Roger Barker, the tail gunner, Sgt William Ramsey, and an RAF wireless operator/air gunner, FS T. A. Betts.[79]

Besides the CO, the men who had boarded the dinghy by the wing were three sergeants: Charles Bentley, one of the Australian wireless operator/ air gunners; J. Wright, RAF, the flight engineer; and G. Turner, RAF, one of the flight fitters. Together these men manhandled the still-groggy Watson off the wing and into the dinghy, with Sgt Bentley retaining sufficient *sang froid* to maintain a joking commentary on Watson's awkwardly-achieved transfer. Laurenti retained a profound sense of poise, for after helping Watson aboard, he did not himself board the dinghy but settled into the water with one hand on the wing and one on the dinghy. He knew that the dinghy was designed to hold three men, not six, so it was already 100 per cent overloaded, even without him. It was perhaps not coincidental that after about five minutes, a flaw developed in the rubber on the nose of the dinghy. The appalled men watched the flaw swell into a bulge a foot high—and then burst! Bentley ran out of jokes as all six men subsided into the water, reduced to swimming and holding onto the sides of the now-deflated but still-floating dinghy.

The CO uttered a plaintive apology: 'Chaps, I'm awfully sorry about this'. The men did not answer. With night approaching and everybody in the water, they knew that no one could possibly survive the night without a dinghy. Halliday continued: 'Our only hope is for someone to go for the empty dinghy, can anybody swim it?' After a minute of heavy silence, Watson spoke up, 'I can swim alright,' explaining that he had been a lifesaver back in Australia. Given his condition so far as the designated invalid of the group, this offer surprised everyone. Bentley grabbed hold of Watson as he started to swim and said, 'wait a minute until you get over it a bit,' but Watson struck out in the direction of the inflated dinghy anyway, saying, 'I'll get it. Follow me.'[80] Halliday took position at the nose of the deflated dinghy and told the others, 'hang onto the side and paddle towards the dinghy.' In practical terms, Halliday's plan depended for its success upon Watson reaching the good dinghy rapidly and slowing its wind-driven rate of progress downwind by use of a sea anchor. Once that was achieved, the others might just be able to reach it by swimming.

Watson swam side-stroke most of the way to conserve energy, and made it to the drifting dinghy, but estimated that it had taken him forty-five minutes to bridge the necessary 500-yard distance, as the dinghy was being blown downwind almost as fast as he could swim. By then, he was so fatigued that he could not get in, reduced to standing in the water with his feet on the rope ladder, hoping to use his body as a sea anchor to let the others catch up. However, he was so depleted that he almost collapsed back into the water and lost his hold, so decided to board the dinghy, managing to do so only by a 'desperate effort'. Once in the dinghy, Watson looked for the paddles, but there were none, so he had no ability to retard the dinghy's passage downwind and bring it closer to the swimmers. He scanned the horizon, spotted the Wellington's dinghy 6 miles to the north-west, but saw no sign of anyone or anything from his own aircraft—no wing-float, no swimmers, no wreckage, nothing. After a fit of vomiting and a short period of unconsciousness, he recollected himself sufficiently to do a stocktake of the dinghy's survival kit: it included cans of water, but no food. Then the sun went down, leaving him the lonely occupant of the craft. He suffered alone through a rainy night of shivering cold and cramping damp.

Providence did not grant the men in the water even that. Watson never saw them again in the five days and nights he spent afloat. It was so cold at night that he feared he would develop frostbite, and to develop some body warmth in the darkness he resorted to an improvised fitness program, lying on his back in the bottom of the dinghy and pedalling with his legs.[81] With each dawn after each miserable night came the opportunity to bail out, using the rice beaker from the dinghy's survival pack. Daytime also brought the opportunity to get a little drier and warmer, not only by the exercise of bailing out and prone callisthenics, but also by attempting to semaphore messages to passing aircraft. He noted a steady process of aircraft: Beaufighters, Whitleys, and Hudsons, but also Arados, Ju 88s, and

Fw 190s. Sgt Triggs, in the nearby Wellington dinghy, counted seventy-seven aircraft in total, of which twenty were German. The presence of Fw 190 single-engined fighters shows that the dinghies were less than 100 miles from Brest: 8./JG2 had started operating from there in August 1942 with these short-ranged, single-engined aircraft. Watson kept himself alive by following the briefed procedure for surviving in a dinghy: he bailed out, vainly tried to catch fish by hand, rigged, derigged, and re-rigged the sail in response to sea and wind conditions, and religiously rationed his water consumption.[82] However, with no food rations aboard, by the fourth night, he was so ravenous that he was reduced to chewing the leather band of his watch.

Despite the steady procession of RAF aircraft, it appears that no one actually spotted either dinghy until the 16th, when two Hudson crews from No. 279 (ASR) Squadron finally located and reported the positions of both dinghies. Next morning, two further Hudson sorties relocated them and reported their positions so that High Speed Launches from Cornwall could come out and effect a rescue.[83] From here on, RAF aircraft paid such close attention to the two dinghies that they tried supply drops, but Watson was too exhausted to be helped by these: Beaufighters dropped parcels into the water, but the closest one fell 100 yards off. Hudsons dropped packages tied together with ropes, but these too fell into the water 100 yards distant. Watson knew that to leave the dinghy was to die, so swimming for the parcels was out of the question. The bags contained 'water-tight tins of food, drink, cigarettes and first aid equipment', but they were of no use to a man who could not reach them.[84]

By the afternoon of the fourth day, the two dinghies had drifted close enough together for the occupants to wave at each other. Watson flattened out an empty water can, cut holes in it with the dinghy's knife, and used it as an improvised paddle to draw closer to the other craft. He got close enough to confirm that the men in the other life raft were wearing RAF grey-blue, and thus satisfied that they were not enemy, persisted with his paddling. With nightfall approaching, he got close enough to hail them with a little joke, 'I am all for the open air life, how about you?' They shouted back (rather unimaginatively), 'you would be an Australian would you?' It turned out that the British airmen had initially spied Watson's dark blue RAAF uniform and mistaken it for Luftwaffe blue; as he approached, they were hatching plans to overpower him and take him prisoner. His accent now put them at ease, however, and the two dinghies joined up, allowing Watson to go across into their larger dinghy, 'which was dry', unlike his own. The H-type dinghy was designed to hold an entire bomber crew, but even so it was now very snug with the extra man aboard. Triggs's crewmen pepped-up Watson by giving him a Horlicks malted milk tablet—one of the staples of survival rations—and then a rationed half-tin of tomato juice. They painted his cuts with antiseptic, then settled down for the night by exchanging stories of what had happened and how they had got there. Watson asked whether they had seen any sign of his crewmates, but they had not. On the fifth day, despite some menacing low passes from Fw 190s, there was an almost continuous escort of Beaufighters and Hudsons overhead, and the reason became clear when the men spotted four motor launches approaching. The rescue was accomplished while the Beaufighters interposed themselves between the scene of rescue and the German-held coast, allowing the ASR launch, HSL 180, to get the men aboard and to speed from the scene. The boat put them ashore at Newlyn near Penzance in Cornwall late that afternoon. John Watson returned to Mount Batten the next day (the 18th) after a remarkable survival experience, the only survivor from his crew.[85]

Watson was interviewed by the press while convalescing in hospital prior to going on survivor's leave, which he spent with his father, Mr H. R. F. Watson, who lived in Surrey. The Melbourne *Weekly Times* ran an article on Watson's survival story on 26 August, which caused some upset by giving details of his crewmates' fates, which had not yet been released to their next of kin by the RAAF Casualty Section, namely that the dinghy had burst and thrown them into the sea. The journalist described lone survivor Watson as a scarecrow of a man, with 'burst' lips, a nose sunburned 'raw', and skin stretched 'drum-tight' over his 'gaunt' face, who had 'suffered dreadfully' from his 'privations'; he predicted Watson would carry physical scars for weeks afterwards, and mental scars for a lot longer.[86] Indeed, John Watson must have lived the rest of his life in the memory of his brother officer, mess-mate, and crew comrade, David Laurenti, who had saved his life twice but had himself died in the water. Laurenti can be taken as representative of the rest of the lost crew: in his three months with the squadron, he had flown ten operations, all but one of these with Col Walker. He would never get to marry his finance, Miss E. V. Taylor of Caulfield in Melbourne.[87]

While in his dinghy, Watson had seen a searching Whitley get shot down by Arados on the 13th; this was from 77 Squadron RAF, so the rescue of Triggs's Wellington crew had cost the lives of seventeen airmen in total. The RAAF official historian summarised the episode as follows:

The story of this rescue was told and retold in Coastal Command messes, its lessons having a salutary effect on all aircrew. It taught the vital necessity of good crew discipline and emergency drill when an aircraft is forced for any reason to descend on the sea; the value of a prompt and accurate SOS signal; the need for real leadership when faced by solitude and a lingering death; above all, the lesson of never giving up faith in the air sea rescue arrangements.[88]

This was all true, but it applied more to Triggs's Wellington crew than to Halliday's ill-fated men. The incident had exposed serious deficiencies in the crew's pre-flight checking of their emergency survival equipment, having taken off on a hazardous operational flight with an incomplete stock of life preservers and an incomplete dinghy survival kit. In addition, the official historian also chose not to dwell upon the inadvisability of Halliday's water landing, which had wiped out Walker's crew so unnecessarily.

Prior to this disastrous accident, the CO had been an effective officer who led his aircrew from the front, and who had, by his conscientious training and administrative efforts, been instrumental in getting the squadron formed and operational in rapid and effective fashion. The squadron's subsequent success and fine reputation were not unrelated to Halliday's legacy in its formative period. However, No. 461 Squadron's unit historian has rightly pointed out the limitations of Halliday's flying boat experience, implying that the final disaster was attributable to these piloting shortcomings. This may be a fair comment upon Halliday's piloting proficiency, but the rest of No. 461's aircraft captains would have had even less expertise in carrying out an open-water landing. The unit historian emphasised that 'open ocean landings' were 'one of the more difficult manoeuvres in a Sunderland, and one for which it was not designed', and that these should only have been attempted 'in the most favourable of circumstances'.[89] Sqn Ldr Dick Cohen, an experienced flying boat pilot and 10 Squadron veteran from 1940–41, would have agreed: he thought open sea landings to be viable 'only if conditions were perfect—if there was strong chop or a long swell, even a Sunderland would probably break up quickly'.[90] The 25-knot winds and 12-foot waves in which Halliday chose to alight were so far from 'favourable' that it had been extremely foolhardy to attempt an alighting.

The fact that he had made the attempt nonetheless suggests that Halliday had evidently felt under some pressure to do so. Firstly, as we have seen, there was such plentiful precedent for Sunderland mid-ocean rescues within the 10 and 461 Squadron community as to create an unstated expectation that the execution of such water landings lay within the capability of any 'brave and intrepid flying-boat pilot'.[91] Secondly, Halliday himself had successfully performed such a rescue previously, got away with it, and been acclaimed for it; finally, he must have felt the fraternal bonds to his fellow airmen in the water, imposing a certain moral pressure to attempt the rescue. In the event, he showed very poor judgment in persisting with his approach and attempting to alight his aircraft upon a heaving sea.

Within the flight-deck culture of the squadron, the first and second pilots deferred to the captain, and this culture of deference was only heightened by gaps in relative rank: Halliday was the CO, a regular air force officer, and held the rank of wing commander, while the others were hostilities-only junior officers. Watson overheard no objections over the intercom and said nothing himself despite realising during the final approach that the waves were far outside safe parameters, and nor did he report his perception of hull damage at the first water impact. The air force culture of deference to rank and seniority is also evident in the silence attending the CO's remarks in the dinghy. What Halliday had attempted was patently unsafe, but he had persisted in it without consulting the others, those others had not spoken up, and ten men were now dead because of it. Halliday was not forgiven by men in other crews who had had mates in the lost crew. He had not enjoyed everyone's confidence anyway, for upon hearing that the aircraft was lost, Ed Gallagher, in Bruce Buls's crew, initially hoped that, 'that mad bastard Halliday hasn't skittled the boys'. No news was bad news, and by the next day, Gallagher was saying, 'Damn that coot Halliday!'[92] The thoughts and feelings of Col Walker, whose entire crew had been wiped out by his CO, were not recorded.

As was customary in cases where a sole crew member returned alive, Watson was afterwards accorded particularly solicitous treatment, seemingly in an attempt to keep him alive as a talisman of good luck: he was at once promoted to flight lieutenant and appointed to the post of squadron navigation officer. This kept him from flying any more operations for three months. By contrast, Walker resumed operations at once, at first flying with improvised crews composed of men borrowed from other crew combinations. Walker and Watson were reunited in November 1942, forming the kernel of a new crew and flying five operations together before Watson was again taken off operations, sent off to do a Staff Navigators Course at RAF Cranage in December. He flew only a few more operations with various crews thereafter, despite remaining with the squadron as navigation officer until December 1943, when he was posted off to No. 3 School of General Reconnaissance as a navigation instructor. Watson had remarkably survived the disastrous ditching on 12 August 1942, and now he had survived his tour, and the war.

Autumn 1942 Operations

With Halliday dead, his deputy, the well-qualified Colin Lovelock was made CO and promoted to wing commander. Lovelock was now left as the only experienced pilot on the squadron, so without a single properly-qualified internal candidate, his former role as squadron flight commander role would have to be filled by an external appointment. Flt Lt Maurice Raban, RAF, arrived to assume this post on 11 September, fresh from instructing at No. 4 OTU. This British officer was promoted to temporary squadron leader in accordance with his executive role, but after only three months, he was posted out to No. 95 Squadron at Bathurst in West Africa. It seems that No. 461's new command team of Lovelock and Raban had interim status only, in apparent expectation of the belated appointment of suitably-qualified Australians to fill these spots at the head of No. 461. Lovelock had been an effective trainer during his three-month incumbency as squadron flight commander, and would, like Halliday, try to lead his unit from the front as CO. Despite being distracted by the administrative demands of organising the squadron's move from Mount Batten to Hamworthy, he flew on operations with five separate crews and personally captained two sorties, accruing ninety-seven hours of operational flying before getting posted away to No. 119 Squadron at Pembroke Dock in January 1943.[1]

The Lovelock-Raban team drilled the squadron's new pilots as intensively as had the Halliday-Lovelock team before them. One of the new pilots, Sgt Les Baveystock, RAF, left an account of the training process. He was a noteworthy recruit to the squadron's pilot ranks, having rather unusually been an operational bomber pilot. More remarkably, he had been shot down over Belgium on the night of 30 May 1942, during the famous 'Thousand bomber' raid upon Cologne. Baveystock was triply lucky: lucky to survive the shoot-down, lucky to evade capture and get smuggled out to neutral Spain courtesy of the Resistance, and lucky to thus prematurely finish his bomber tour alive.[2] When he joined No. 461 at the end of September 1942, Baveystock was also triply unusual: in arriving at the squadron with operational experience and a DFM; in being a sergeant pilot in a squadron where all the other pilots were officers; and in being the only RAF pilot within a unit where the pilots were otherwise Australians, and where his fellow British airmen were concentrated in subordinate back-seater roles like flight engineer and wireless operator/air gunner.

'Bav' Baveystock was impressed by the Sunderland. The Manchester bombers he had been flying on No. 50 Squadron were large and powerful machines, but even so, he marvelled at the 'huge' size of the Sunderland and the 'tremendous space' inside its hull. As he went aboard one for the first time, he was intrigued to find watertight compartments separated by naval-style hatches, an anchor 'large enough to hold a battleship', a wardroom, a galley, a bomb-room, a workbench, electric bilge pumps, and a petrol-driven auxiliary power unit to run the generator to charge the 24-volt battery. None of these had been evident in the cramped interior of the Manchester. Overall, he was quite taken with the 'robustness and strength' of the Sunderland's structure, the steadiness with which it moved both on the water and in the air, and the excellent visibility from the flight-deck and astrodome; he was 'immensely glad' that he had the 'chance to fly in such a splendid aircraft', and itched to have 'the immense pleasure of flying solo in this superb monster'.[3] Other newly-arrived pilots, lacking Baveystock's experience with large operational types, were intimidated by the big machine, so immense did it seem after the small aeroplanes they had trained on in Australia and Canada: when Russ Baird joined No. 10, he blurted out, 'Well I'll never fly that. I'll never ever fly one of those.' His instructor said, 'Yes, you will but it takes a lot of training.' In his case, as a relatively-inexperienced, new-graduate pilot, it took two months of training before he flew it solo.[4]

On his first training flight, Baveystock flew with the new CO, along with three other trainee pilots who were also working towards Sunderland type qualification. Lovelock had been favourably impressed with Baveystock's previous experience as an operational bomber pilot (and no doubt, with his DFM ribbon), and so had invited him to join the others and start flying right away. With Lovelock instructing from the co-pilot's seat, it took almost three-and-a-half hours of taxiing, take-offs, circuits, landings, and more taxiing to give all three of the other pupils their turns at the controls. By then, the watching Baveystock knew the drill: he had 'already decided that the aircraft looked just too easy to take-off and land'. Now it was his turn, having received no more formal instruction than standing on the flight-deck behind the pilots, watching and listening as the others went through the repetitive cycle of 'circuits and bumps'. Watched by the CO alongside him, he did a good take-off, flew around at 1,000 feet practising turns and controlling speed by nose attitude, and then made a good approach and an excellent landing—a 'beauty'; all this in twenty minutes at the controls.

The CO was satisfied, so after taxiing in, mooring up, and going ashore, he handed Baveystock over to the flight commander, Sqn Ldr Raban, to continue his training. Baveystock repeated the exercise next day, again taking his turn with the other students. After ninety minutes, Raban invited him to take over in the first pilot's seat, talked him through three circuits and landings 'in quick succession', and then said, 'Okay, taxi back to the take-off point and you can have a crack at solo.' Baveystock was 'absolutely astonished' at this, having so far had only two Sunderland flights and a total of only one hour and ten minutes of dual instruction. Raban got out of his seat and went aft, and as was customary ushered the other trainee pilots out of the flight-deck as he went, to minimise the trainee pilot's 'stage fright'. Fortunately, he lived up to the flight commander's expectation, executing a good take-off, circuit, and landing. Once they were safely waterborne again, Raban reappeared from behind, saying 'Good show! Good show!' Baveystock had gone solo.

With this qualification, Baveystock started flying operations as second pilot with operational crews, steadily gaining experience during the twelve-hour-long patrols by taking one-hour turns flying the aircraft from the captain's seat, followed by an hour on lookout duty from the co-pilot's seat. He then became Dudley Marrows's regular first pilot, and Marrows generously gave him plenty of 'stick time', including 'the occasional daylight take-off to keep my hand in', as well as a good share of the practice low-level bombing runs. Through the whole process, Baveystock found all the captains with whom he flew likeable and impressive men, and appreciated that as a 'new boy' and a mere sergeant pilot, he had been treated by his superiors and seniors in a collegial and professional manner.[5] Russ Baird, another trainee co-pilot, likewise found that the training given to him by his captain, Bruce Buls, was 'wonderful'.[6] These experiences suggest that No. 461 was developing a positive and inclusive team culture as it faced the most challenging and costly year of its existence—1943.

Meanwhile, RAF Hamworthy in Poole Harbour was being made ready to receive its first Sunderland squadron, and so No. 461 began its migration to the new base from 5 September 1942. On 10 September, the Australians flew their first operation from there. After Burrage's earlier condemnation of the site, the choice of location evidently remained in dispute, for on the night of 25 September, Lovelock and Raban took Grp Capt. R. L. Ragg, RAF, for demonstration circuits and bumps in Poole harbour, to establish whether the new base was or was not safe for night flying. It seems that there was some organisational pressure to disprove the Australians' earlier negative opinion, judging by the carefully-nuanced, politic conclusion reached after the trial run on the night of the 25th: although Lovelock reported that 'conditions' were 'quite safe', he added that this was only if 'there is not a strong wind, which would constitute a definite hazard in taxying'. This was a telling qualification, for he had, in effect, conceded that in anything but gentle winds, a Sunderland would tend to be blown out of the channel and on to a sandbank while taxiing or taking off. Lovelock himself might have been experienced enough in handling flying boats to cope with this, but his reservation about taxiing in crosswinds would in practice exclude the base from consideration for operational night flying. Indeed, Poole harbour's obstructions and shallows made it difficult to use even in daylight: on his first flight from there, Baveystock saw how much time was wasted in laborious taxiing through the 'narrow channels' in order to get to the end of the runway to start the take-off run. Despite the ambivalence of his conclusions, Lovelock's heavily-qualified statement was taken as confirmation of the basic soundness of this location, so Poole was No. 461's new base.

The CO and flight commander would therefore go ahead and drill their aircraft captains in circuits and bumps at Poole, but as Baveystock recalled, night landings at Poole were 'none too easy because of the harbour's narrow channels', and therefore the base was in practice used for night take-offs only, not night landings.[7] As a result, crews returning at night were diverted to Pembroke Dock or Mount Batten instead, meaning that throughout No. 461's occupancy of RAF Hamworthy, operational night flying was conducted in a triangular circuit: take-off from Poole, alight at Pembroke Dock or Mount Batten, then fly back to Poole next day to prepare the aircraft for its next operation. Operations from the new base thereby exacted a continuous toll of wasted effort by imposing a tedious cycle of transit flights between bases after operations.

The Fighter Threat over the Bay Escalates

Before the move to RAF Hamworthy, No. 461 lost a second crew. On 1 September 1942, Plt Off. Robert Hosband took off in F/461 at 3.13 p.m., tasked with an anti-shipping patrol in the Bay of Biscay. At 8.15 p.m., the aircraft transmitted 'am being attacked by two Ju 88s', followed by 'lost contact' twenty-four minutes later. After another six minutes came an SOS, and then silence.[8] Colin Steley's crew was out at the same time in E/461 and found that the weather was clear in the patrol area, with good visibility and 6/10th cloud at 4,500 feet. For a Sunderland, these were dangerous conditions, and Hosband had evidently found himself exposed in too big a sky when he ran into the Ju 88s, and so had not been able to disengage into cloud. He had been unlucky to run into a flight of

Ju 88s from V./KG40, for two of that unit's pilots made a shared claim for a Sunderland shot down at 9.17 p.m. Berlin time. Hosband's crew had fought back before they died, because one Ju 88 crash landed at Bordeaux-Merignac airfield, having had one engine shot up in combat.[9]

The eruption of powerful Ju 88 twin-engined fighters into the skies over the Bay had come after Dönitz's appeal to *Reichsmarschall* Göring for Luftwaffe air support for his U-boats crossing the Bay. In response, the Bordeaux-based bomber unit, KG40, formed a new fighter squadron in August 1942 at Nantes, about 30 miles from the Atlantic coast, inland from St Nazaire. KG40 initially formed a new 13th Squadron, at first equipped with 13 Ju 88C twin-engined, cannon-armed, long-range fighters, but as the year went on, the unit expanded to twenty-four aircraft in November and to thirty-five by January 1943. In that month, the unit was officially upgraded to group rather than squadron status, becoming V./KG40.[10] This formidable unit would prove to be the nemesis of many Australian Sunderland crews in 1943.

Once these Ju 88s started patrolling, clear weather became dangerous weather for Sunderlands patrolling within the Bay of Biscay, and Steley's own experience that same afternoon suggests how Hosband's crew met their end. At 7.18 p.m., he was heading south in E/461 at 2,000 feet when one Ju 88 was spotted low down over the water, 1½ miles away. While Steley's wireless operator tapped out, 'am being attacked by enemy aircraft', the Junkers duly turned in for an attack from the Sunderland's beam, climbing steeply to get its guns on target. However, it fired from long range, breaking off at 800 yards—beyond effective range. Steley turned away and tried to head for the closest cloud, but just then the gunners called a second 88 coming in, already climbing to attack and only 1,000 yards off. These were late sightings, showing how easy it was for a Sunderland to be ambushed in broad daylight by stealthily but suddenly-arriving Ju 88s—a fact which goes some way to explaining the losses.

The combat ended when Steley reached a layer of cloud sufficiently large and dense to hide a Sunderland in. When Steley's crew took stock of the damage on the way home, they found several small holes in the hull, including four beneath the waterline. The encounter had lasted thirteen minutes. At 7.35 p.m., the anxious listeners back at base received the reassuring message 'lost contact', followed by 'damage slight, no casualties'. It was forty minutes after that when the listeners at Mount Batten received Hosband's first message, but in that case, there was no happy ending; all eleven crewmen were lost. No. 10 Squadron's Terry Brown was also airborne at the time in the same area as Hosband was lost; indeed, he thought he saw Hosband's F/461 flying normally soon after monitoring its first fighter contact report, but later realised it must have been Steley's E/461 he had seen instead. Hosband's final SOS signal was too brief for Brown's wireless operator to obtain a directional bearing, so there was nothing the 10 Squadron crew could do to help their colleagues and countrymen.

Before joining No. 461, Robert Hosband had flown alongside Bruce Buls in Buck Judell's 10 Squadron crew. As we have seen, Judell himself had been shot down and killed in June, and now Hosband had followed his old captain into the deep, unluckily dying on only his third mission in command. He had captained his first sortie as recently as 27 August, and on that occasion, had survived an encounter with an Fw 200; at that time his crew had spotted it at 2 miles off, and so he had enough time to escape. Steley's encounter points to the tactical importance of obtaining the earliest possible visual sightings of incoming enemy aircraft, and also emphasises the much more rapid approach of the faster Ju 88s, compared to the much slower Arados and Fw 200s.

No. 461 had lost two crews in less than three weeks—serious losses for a new unit which had so far relied upon only six operational crews. It was not unusual for a new unit to suffer early heavy losses as its green crews found their feet on operations, and indeed No. 461 had now suffered a loss rate of 3 per cent of operational sorties—similar to that experienced by Bomber Command squadrons in the bombing offensive against Germany. Because of its losses, No. 461 had only four crews left on operational status when the squadron moved into Hamworthy in early September, insufficient to get full utilisation from its eight-remaining aircraft. As it was, during its two months of operations from Mount Batten, the new squadron had produced only sixty-six sorties; by comparison, in the same period, the fully-manned No. 10 had produced 112 operational flights. No. 461's sortie output would deteriorate further after its move to Hamworthy.

This pressure to produce left the squadron's trainee crews on the obligatory steep learning curve under the tutelage of Lovelock and Raban. By this process, four new crews were upgraded to operational status over September–November: those of Cooke, Dods, Weatherlake, and Marrows. The first three had flown as co-pilots in 10 Squadron, had joined No. 461 on the same day in late May 1942, and been fast-tracked to captaincy within Lovelock's training program. Marrows had taken a different route, posted to No. 461 from the Sunderland conversion course at No. 4 OTU, and since then apprenticed as second pilot to Bert Smith. Once the replacements were embodied, No. 461 would end 1942 with nine operational crews and ten aircraft, very similar to No. 10, which ended the year with nine crews and nine aircraft.

Combined Battles against the U-boats by Nos 10 and 461

The growing partnership between the two Australian Sunderland squadrons would be best expressed in combined attacks upon U-boats in the Bay; this was, of course, the *raison d'être* of 19 Group's Sunderland force. However, by the start of September 1942, No. 461 Squadron crews had so far spotted plenty of French and Spanish fishing vessels, a number of dinghies, a British submarine, and a disconcerting succession of German aircraft—but only a single U-boat.

This would change on the first day of that month, when Bruce Buls would see two. This was the same day as Robert Hosband's loss, but it was also a day which saw three Australian Sunderlands combine their efforts in a running action against a U-boat. Bruce Buls took off in A/461 at 6.09 a.m. for an anti-shipping patrol in the Bay of Biscay. In the patrol area, visibility was poor at low altitude due to a hazy blanket of smoke haze blown across the Bay from off the land. These were far from ideal conditions for submarine hunting, but at 10.23 a.m., Buls's aircraft received a submarine sighting report from Graham Pockley's R/10, followed by a similar signal from Sam Wood's U/10.

Wood had been despatched on an extreme-range anti-shipping patrol along the Spanish coast, and as a result of this mission, his aircraft was armed with five 250-pound anti-ship bombs and no depth-charges. He obtained a radar contact at 12-miles range, and then from 5 miles away visually identified it as a motor vessel—exactly the right sort of target for a captain briefed to carry out an anti-shipping patrol. He positioned himself up-sun and then dived from behind a cloud to make a pass over the ship. However, when the Sunderland broke clear of the cloud, Wood saw that the target was in fact a submarine—visibility was poor because of the smog. As he came closer, AA tracers rose up from the submarine's bandstand, arcing around the nose of the Sunderland and then suddenly speeding up and flicking past. As he drew nearer, Wood identified the target as an Italian submarine. He had four 250-pound, semi-armour piercing bombs on his aircraft's bomb racks, their fuses set for a twelve-second delay for a minimum altitude anti-shipping attack; this was the standard fuse-setting for low-level bombing of ships, but it was hardly likely to result in an effective attack on a submarine, as the bombs would detonate too far beneath the water to damage the hull.

Nonetheless, Wood pressed on and made his attack. As he pulled his aircraft into a climbing turn after bombing, his rear gunner reported only a single bomb explosion 30 yards away from the submarine, but also that yellow smoke had spewed out of its engine exhausts for thirty seconds afterwards. The other three bombs had failed to detonate: looking on from a couple of miles away, Pockley's crew also saw only a single bomb explode as they headed in towards the scene. Wood then made a second attack with his one remaining bomb, but it failed to release because he had failed to select the correct setting on the 'Mickey Mouse' automatic bombing switch beside the pilot's seat.[11] He then started signalling the other two aircraft, trying to organise a co-ordinated attack, but base was monitoring the transmissions, and ordered him away to resume his assigned anti-shipping patrol with his single remaining bomb.

Pockley had also been assigned an anti-shipping mission, so also had an unsuitable load of 250-pound bombs aboard. He obtained a radar contact at 10.14 a.m., and after approaching to within 8 miles to investigate, transmitted a submarine sighting report at 10.20 a.m. The submarine captain was clearly intent upon using his boat's AA armament to fight off any air attacks, rather than to submerge, for as Pockley's Sunderland orbited around it at a range of a couple of miles, the heavy gun on the submarine's forward deck tracked the aircraft's progress, marking its circuit with a chain of black shell bursts. After seeing Wood complete his second attack, Pockley turned in to attack, despite receiving a message from base ordering him to proceed on his patrol. HQ's reasoning was evidently this: by expending their bombs on the submarine, both Sunderlands were neutering their offensive potential against ships, their assigned mission.

This target was too enticing to ignore, however, so Pockley dived from 1,500 feet, approaching up the submarine's wake. He ran over the top of the submarine lengthways, dropping two bombs. These splashed into the water 100 yards ahead of the submarine's bow, but like Wood's they failed to explode. Pockley pulled his Sunderland up and around and set up for a second attack; and this time he came in from the beam, flying through 'intense' AA fire fired from every gun on the boat. In reply, his front gunner had only a single .303-inch machine gun, but the pilots on the flight-deck saw the tracers hitting all around the submarine's conning tower. This time Pockley attacked with only a single bomb, and the rear gunner saw it explode 70 yards from the submarine—too far. Like Wood, Pockley was then ordered by base to resume his patrol with his two remaining bombs.

The only aircraft in the vicinity with depth-charges aboard was Bruce Buls's A/461, the third Sunderland to arrive on the scene. Two minutes after receiving Wood's initial sighting report, Buls's radar operator obtained a radar contact at 16 miles off the port bow, and six minutes later, the radar contact was amplified by a sighting of exhaust smoke 8 miles off. Buls approached at 800 feet and saw the U-boat on the surface belching white smoke (after Wood's first attack), with the other two Sunderlands orbiting around it. As he circled and climbed to make his own attack, he saw a second submarine, 4 miles from the first and sailing on a parallel course. Buls flew over to the second submarine and transmitted a sighting report, but while he was orbiting under the cloud base at 3,500 feet, the U-boat disappeared behind a down-hanging tendril of cumulus cloud, then failed to reappear. After descending clear of the murk, Buls could no longer see either boat. More than an hour of further searching delivered no result, despite using radar to extend the search out to each side.

The target submarine was the homeward bound *Reginaldo Giuliano*, and when it ran into the Sunderlands, it had been running on the surface recharging its batteries, only 100 miles away from its base at Bordeaux. Wood's and Pockley's bomb attacks were as ineffective as their crews thought, a result which was virtually guaranteed given the use of unsuitable 250-pound bombs rather than fit-for-purpose depth-charges. However, the Sunderlands' gunners had been highly effective in sweeping the conning tower with .303-inch machine-gun fire: the British intercepted a message from the *Reginaldo Giuliano*, which they deciphered as meaning that the submarine's captain had been killed and others wounded, and requesting immediate air cover.[12] In fact, the captain, Lt-Cdr Giovanni Bruno, had been seriously wounded by being shot through the throat, but was not killed; nonetheless, the Italian crew considered the attack 'extremely violent both due to the volume of fire and the amount of bombs dropped'.

The next day, the damaged *Reginaldo Giuliano* was depth-charged by a Wellington from 304 (Polish) Squadron, which left the submarine so badly damaged that the captain considered it lost. However, like with the *Luigi Torelli* in June, he was able to stabilise his boat enough to limp into the Spanish port of Santander. With the 'acquiescence of the Spanish authorities', the submarine was allowed to undergo two months' worth of repairs and was then permitted to leave; the Spanish government had evidently ceased giving even lip service to the legal requirement to intern vessels of war after twenty-four hours. The *Reginaldo Giuliano* finally departed Santander on 8 November, and under a Luftwaffe aerial escort, she made it safely to the port of Le Verdon the next day.

Considering that four aircraft had attacked her, her survival was an unsatisfactory result for the RAF, and the whole episode had hardly been a display of effective anti-submarine work. Perhaps the most important reason for the failure was the bomb-only armament of the two 10 Squadron machines, which had reduced their attacks to that of symbolic status only, despite the aggressive action taken by both pilots. The only practical chance of delivering an effective attack had lain with Buls's depth-charges, but he had mishandled his approach by getting distracted by the second submarine, thereby losing contact with the first.

Graham Pockley seemed to have a talent for running into Germans, for he contacted a U-boat only eight days later, on 9 September, after detecting it by radar from 18 miles away and homing on to it. He approached covertly inside solid cloud until 5 miles away, when he descended briefly into the clear, saw a white wake in the water dead ahead, then pulled up into cloud again to continue his approach unseen. Then he broke cloud cover 3 miles out, skimming just underneath cloud-base at 2,000 feet. The submarine was still running on the surface, so Pockley commenced his attack dive at a range of 1½ miles. However, seeing men running along its deck, Pockley realised that he would have fully-alerted AA gunners to contend with, so turned aside and circled the submarine, intending to attack it only once it started submerging: before a submarine could commence its dive, the gunners on the upper deck had to scramble below through the conning tower hatch, presenting a thirty-second opportunity for a nearby aircraft to make an attack without suffering any return fire. When the submarine started diving, Pockley immediately dived upon its starboard side, to drop a stick of six depth-charges across its bows from 50 feet. He straddled the submarine so accurately that its forward hull was completely obscured among the heaving pile of white-water detonations. The U-boat had submerged by the time the Sunderland came around again, but Pockley dropped a smoke float upon the patch of disturbed water to mark its position, and then orbited overhead to survey the scene. The submarine seemed to have been seriously damaged, for heavy oil bubbles came to the surface, as well as large air bubbles of 50 feet diameter, which continued for five minutes. In accordance with the standard 'baiting' tactics, as recommended in a recent 19 Group circular, the Sunderland departed the area, then returned half an hour later to see whether the damaged submarine had resurfaced.[13] It had not, and so Pockley's crew had once again to head home without having obtained conclusive evidence of destruction.

Tom Egerton's crew got a similar chance eleven days later, while flying E/10 on an anti-submarine patrol in the afternoon of 20 September. At 4.38 p.m., while heading south just beneath the solid layer of cloud at 5,000 feet, they spotted a submarine, 10 miles off to starboard. Egerton turned and dove on it, but the Germans had spotted the incoming aircraft, and the U-boat began diving when the Sunderland was still 4 miles off. However, the top of the submarine's conning tower had still not disappeared beneath the water by the time the Sunderland arrived overhead, allowing Egerton to drop his six depth-charges across its path. As he pulled the Sunderland around into a climbing turn, the rear gunner saw that the submarine's stern was now sticking out of the water at an acute angle, giving him a clear mark at which he fired his four .303 Brownings. The stern slipped away beneath the water, leaving Egerton to orbit for twelve minutes in hope of seeing proof of the U-boat's death throes, but the water did not stir. He used 'baiting' tactics, departing the area then returning an hour later to see if it had resurfaced. Once again, the submarine did not reappear, leaving Egerton's crew to head home after yet another indecisive encounter.

Nine days later, it was Wyn Thorpe's turn, flying R/10 on only his sixth operation in command. At 11.07 a.m., one of his lookouts spotted a U-boat, 10 miles away through a gap in the cloud. It was heading east on the surface at 12 knots. Thorpe turned in and steered his aircraft for a large cloud, conveniently-placed 2,000 feet lower, to hide his approach from the submarine's lookouts. When he emerged from that cloud, he was only 2½ miles from the still fully-surfaced U-boat, which only belatedly spotted the Sunderland looming up out of the grey sky, commencing its crash dive when the Sunderland was only 1½ miles away. In its haste to hide itself, the submarine dived too steeply and failed to submerge successfully, leaving the rearward one-third of the hull standing steeply out of the water; it hung there poised at a 50-degree angle for thirty seconds before its crew regained control. Thorpe was thus presented with a convenient aiming mark as he headed in to bomb. He got close enough to see the submarine's propellers turning uselessly on their shafts in thin air before the grey hull suddenly lurched and slid beneath the water, just before the Sunderland thundered past overhead. Thorpe dropped his stick of six depth-charges around the swirl left by the steeply plunging U-boat, with the detonations erupting 25 yards from that point. Thorpe circled overhead and climbed, and two and a half minutes after the attack, his crew saw large, 20-foot-diameter air bubbles break the surface, only 75 yards from the disturbed water of the depth-charge explosions. Then came a second and a third outbreak of air bubbles, about 20 yards further along the submarine's track, diminishing in diameter from 15 to 9 feet. Thorpe used standard 'baiting tactics', departing from the scene and then returning two hours later to conduct a square search over the blank ocean.

Despite the encouraging circumstances of Thorpe's attack, he had to abandon the search shortly after that when his starboard inner engine started backfiring, vibrating the airframe so severely that Thorpe closed it down. This obliged a return to base on three engines. The Sunderland shared its Bristol Pegasus engines with other early-war, British, multi-engined types such as the Vickers Wellington and Handley Page Hampden, and in all cases, the de Havilland constant-speed propeller of this power-plant installation was unfit-for-purpose because it lacked a fully-feathering propeller mechanism. Sunderland pilots considered this a 'serious drawback', because in an engine-out situation, the dead engine's stationary, non-feathered propeller blades imposed such massive drag on that side that the power of the remaining engines was barely enough to maintain level flight.[14] This severe performance limitation not only plagued smaller twin-engined machines like Wellingtons, but even a large four-engined machine like the Sunderland. Thorpe sent a signal to base advising that he had abandoned the patrol because of engine failure. Upon recognising that he could not maintain height on three engines, he lightened the aircraft's weight by jettisoning his remaining two bombs; thankfully, the other three engines kept working despite running at increased power settings to compensate, and so he made it back to Mount Batten two hours later after an anxiety-wracked return flight. Thorpe and his crew made it home, but so had their submarine.

More Airborne Encounters

So far, No. 10 Squadron had enjoyed almost a monopoly of the submarine sightings and submarine attacks, but 461 Squadron too got into the action on the last day of September, to make its second ever U-boat attack. Showing the squadron's growth in capability, on that day, the junior squadron had four crews out on anti-submarine patrols in the Bay of Biscay. Fred Manger's patrol in K/461 was enlivened when his crew spotted first a patrolling Fw 200 from 10 miles away, and then half an hour later, three Ju 88s from 6 miles off; in both cases, he avoided them by climbing into cloud-base, which lay close overhead at 2,000 feet. It is significant that the Ju 88s were again flying at minimum altitude, skimming the sea at only 50 feet when spotted. As we have seen, this was their standard tactic, providing a rapid, unobserved approach upon an unsuspecting British patrol aircraft and then a sudden pull-up to open fire. A heavy responsibility thereby fell upon the Sunderland lookouts to obtain early sightings, for the crew's survival depended on it. The coming of the autumn weather had brought thick cloud over the Bay, which was good news for Sunderland crews, offering the prospect of a relatively safe patrol while flying just beneath cloud-base: in such conditions, at the first sighting of any suspicious aircraft, all that was needed was to pull up and hide in cloud. It was while climbing towards the cloud-base to avoid the incoming Ju 88s that Manger spotted a submarine on the surface near two trawlers—the latter were presumably U-boat support vessels. Manger noted their position, gained the cloud, and directed the wireless operator to transmit a sighting report.

Twenty minutes later, Harry Cooke was approaching the patrol area in H/461 when he suddenly saw a submarine dead ahead, less than a mile away, heading west. Although it crash-dived at once, the conning tower was still above the water when the Sunderland arrived overhead only ten seconds after it started submerging. Cooke flew close along the boat's wake, then dropped his stick of depth-charges along its length. As he circled around to look for results, the crew saw a large patch of brown scum in the disturbed water. Cooke dropped a sea marker, but having already reached his minimum fuel state, he was able to circle for only ten minutes before heading for base. The 461 Squadron crews had operated efficiently in this episode; Manger and Cooke had reported their sightings, Manger had deftly avoided unnecessary risk from fighters, Cooke had made a prompt attack to successfully straddle the target.

Fred Manger certainly seems to have had sharp-eyed gunners in his crew, for two days later, on 2 October, he again was able to avoid the unwelcome attentions of a malevolent, rapidly-closing Ju 88 by climbing into cloud, his gunners having spotted it 16 miles away in an open sky. Crews were not always able to obtain usefully-early sightings like this: on 9 October, John Weatherlake's crew survived an encounter with a Ju 88 despite being taken under surprise attack—it dropped out of cloud and closed in to only 150 yards astern before breaking away. The rear gunner fired 500 rounds at it and was adamant that 88 had not fired back; it is not beyond the stretch of possibility that Weatherlake's crew owed its survival to an electrical failure in the Ju 88's gun firing circuits. In any case, K/461 got back into cloud before the German fighter could make a second run.

Only two days later, on 11 October, 10 Squadron's Wyn Thorpe in U/10 also had a close call during an early morning anti-submarine patrol. His gunners spotted an incoming Ju 88 at 5 miles' range, as usual approaching low down at 500 feet. The Sunderland was unable to climb rapidly enough to reach cloud base at 4,000 feet, so Thorpe had to meet the attack with the only means at his disposal: by manoeuvre and .303 gunfire. As the 88 pulled up underneath to fire into the Sunderland's belly, Thorpe rolled the Sunderland into a skidding turn, keeping the wings steeply banked and the nose high to give all three gun-turrets a shot downwards at the enemy fighter. The German pilot did well to get three 20-mm hits in the Sunderland's hull, before climbing away to get up-sun. The 88 came back in from the Sunderland's port quarter, opening fire from 1,000 yards, but Thorpe again used hard evasive manoeuvring to spoil the German's aim, turning and diving underneath the 88's attack path and forcing it to break off its attack early. The enemy fighter gave up, last seen by the tail gunner, Cpl James Challinor, breaking away astern of the Sunderland; it kept on going.

On 11 November, Harry Cooke was lucky to survive a very hazardous confrontation with four Ju 88s in almost cloudless conditions. He was flying H/461, and was less than three hours out of Hamworthy on a search for a crippled British submarine when the gunners reported three Ju 88s coming in. The Sunderland was then flying through 'Ju 88 corner', the navigational datum-point south of the Scilly Isles from which RAF air patrols branched out across the Bay of Biscay to search for U-boats. Through monitoring RAF wireless frequencies and plotting the transmissions, the Germans were aware of the routes by which Coastal Command aircraft tracked into and out of the Bay; from there, it was an elementary precaution to deploy Ju 88s to patrol this RAF air corridor. On this occasion, Cooke's crew spotted the 88s at 5 miles' range, approaching low down at 500 feet; as the enemy drew closer it became evident that there were four Junkers, not three. Once the Sunderland's sudden climb for height betrayed the fact that they had been spotted, the Germans went past without attacking, and then climbed to get up-sun. This gave Cooke's wireless operator plenty of time to transmit a contact report to base.

When the 88s started diving one by one from out of the sun, Cooke turned into each attack, climbing steeply to force the German pilots into rushing their shots at the rapidly looming-up target. To get a better climb rate out of the labouring Sunderland, Cooke jettisoned the whole bomb-load and persisted with his full-throttle climb, heading towards a cloud 15 miles off at 3,000 feet. This distance must have seemed an eternity, but Cooke's crew were fortunate in meeting a particularly risk-averse group of German pilots: the fourth Ju 88 made only a hesitant attack from the climbing Sunderland's port quarter, while the other three stood off cautiously on the starboard beam, evidently deterred by the Sunderland turrets' return fire. The 88s did not attack again, but instead simply watched as the Sunderland gained its cloud cover.

Kerv Beeton's crew survived a similar encounter with three Ju 88s on 24 November. Despite the lateness of the year, this was another day of un-seasonally fine conditions and unlimited visibility. Despite the clear sky, Z/10's lookouts only saw the onrushing enemy fighters at 3 miles off, when they suddenly appeared from the tactically-convenient shadow of a very heavy cloud. The 88s made things very difficult for Beeton's evasive manoeuvring by splitting up to attack, with one coming in from astern, one from the bow and one from the beam. As Beeton turned to evade one fighter, another would come in from another direction, in each case approaching from below and then pulling up to fire. In this way, the 88s delivered attack after attack, but Beeton's manoeuvring seems to have made things so difficult for the German pilots that they only fired from long range—600–900 yards. Indeed, his violent manoeuvring seems to have been positively sick-making for his own crew, for despite the target-rich environment, between them the three turret gunners fired only 200 rounds in total during the whole engagement; presumably, the gunners were sagging in their seats as the Sunderland rolled, turned, yawed, and bunted its way across the sky, edging towards the nearest cloud. After eleven minutes of this, Beeton reached the cloud and circled around inside; the Sunderland had a lot more fuel than the 88s, so could afford to wait for them to go home.

These incidents show that occasional fine days could still bring sharp reminders of the hazards of a contested sky, despite the shorter days, thicker cloud, and deteriorating visibility of the late-season weather over the Bay. In the six months from 1 July 1942—the period during which both Australian Sunderland squadrons were operational—crews from Nos 10 and 461 saw enemy aircraft in the air on thirty-eight occasions, and in twenty of these cases, an airborne engagement had ensued. It is a curious fact that 461 Squadron seemed to attract more than its fair share of the enemy air activity, for despite flying less than two-thirds as many sorties as No. 10, No. 461 ran into enemy aircraft more often than the senior squadron (twenty times rather than eighteen). On average, in the second half of 1942, any given crew from either squadron could expect to encounter enemy aircraft once every nine patrols. The frequency of these encounters shows that in most cases a Sunderland stood a good chance of surviving an encounter with enemy aircraft. However, the chances of disaster were greatly increased by adverse conjunctions of clear weather, late sightings, and adverse numerical odds.

More Inconclusive Submarine Attacks

Despite No. 461's growing capability, 10 Squadron continued to monopolise the submarine sightings. Indeed, from April (the month that 461 Squadron came into being) to December 1942, No. 10 Squadron crews sighted enemy submarines on thirty-four occasions, and in twenty-seven of these cases made attacks upon them. By contrast, on only two occasions had No. 461 Squadron crews encountered enemy submarines. In none of these cases had the encounter resulted in the destruction of the U-boat. On average, in the second half of 1942, each crew would fly thirteen patrols before spotting a U-boat, or put differently, would fly almost 150 operational hours between each sighting.

One of the last U-boat encounters of the year was on 20 October: Sam Wood was cruising in U/10 at the unusually-high height of 8,000 feet when his crew spotted two submarines through the scattered cloud below; they were 12 miles away, sailing about 300 yards apart. Wood turned to get up-sun, exploited the cover of a 'friendly cloud', and commenced his attack from 3,000 feet, about 4 miles away from the targets. When he was 3 miles out, he saw one of the U-boats commence to crash-dive, followed ten seconds later by the other, nearer one. This submarine submerged thirty seconds before the Sunderland reached the spot, which was defined as the absolute maximum time interval within which an effective attack might result.[15] Wood dropped five depth-charges across the submarine's estimated track, 120 yards ahead of the swirl in the water left by the boat's submergence. As the Sunderland circled afterwards, the crew saw two large bubbles break the surface of the area of disturbed water, but that was all. Given the length of time between submarine submergence and bombing, it was very unlikely to have been an effective attack. U/10 had by now reached its minimum fuel, so after orbiting for twelve minutes, Wood took his crew home. With only inconclusive evidence like air bubbles and oil slicks to go on, it is unsurprising that 10 Squadron was not ultimately credited with even a single U-boat 'kill' in 1942. Despite this, Graham Pockley was awarded a DFC in November 1942, among other things, for having destroyed two

U-boats in the previous six months.[16] This shows that there was a pragmatic divergence between the squadron's internal 'kill' tallying for the purposes of award citations, and the Admiralty's far stricter, evidence-based accounting of enemy submarine losses. Neither process referenced the other.

In-Flight Emergencies

The deteriorating autumn weather not only diminished the chances of encountering both enemy aircraft (good news) and enemy submarines (bad news), it also posed direct hazards. In the early morning of 3 September, Fred Manger's crew was setting out on a convoy patrol, flying C/461 in the darkness within unbroken cloud at 4,000 feet. It would be difficult finding the convoy in these conditions, but it rapidly became apparent that there would be higher priorities than that on this flight, like maintaining control of the aircraft. Without weather radar, there was no way of avoiding storm cells, and the aircraft flew straight into a cumulonimbus cloud, suddenly 'crashing through heavy rain and hail with a noise that overwhelmed the roar of the engines'. It was four and a half hours after take-off, and daylight was still an hour away. At that moment when the aircraft entered the cloud, the captain was off the flight-deck, having handed over the controls to Plt Off. Phil Davenport, his first pilot. Manger had taken advantage of the apparent lull in the flight to answer a call of nature, visiting the Sunderland's 'fully flushing dunny' in the toilet compartment on the bottom deck beneath the cockpit. At the controls, Davenport was taken by surprise by a sudden, violent, vertical gust when the aircraft struck the unseen storm turbulence. Sitting next to him in the co-pilot's seat, Fg Off. Allen Shears was a green pilot on only his seventh patrol. Neither of them had seen anything like this before. Davenport disengaged the autopilot, 'pulled off the power and pushed the nose down', but the updraught was so powerful that the Sunderland shot up to 8,000 feet nonetheless.

Down below on the bottom deck, before the aircraft hit the core of the storm cloud, Manger had already plugged his helmet lead into the toilet compartment intercom socket, to monitor developments while he was otherwise engaged. His ablutions were rudely disturbed: first came the violent lurch of the involuntary, lift-like climb, and then he heard Shears yelling over the intercom, 'Freddie you'd better come up here!' Manger must have broken records getting himself out of the toilet and up the ladder to the flight-deck, for seconds later he was jerking at Davenport's flying jacket and yelling, 'Out!' The captain had only just resumed his seat and secured his seat belt when the Sunderland flew out of the cloud's up-rushing core. The wind velocity fell away suddenly, and at once the aircraft stalled, fell over on to one wing, and rolled on to its back. Having just vacated the captain's seat, Davenport was left dangling in space behind the pilots. Under the negative-g of the aircraft's uncommanded nose-down pitch, he found himself floating in the void with his head pressed against the control panel above the pilots' heads. Before either pilot could get their hands on the throttles to power up, Davenport pushed them forward with his feet as he dangled in space. Down in the galley, off-duty wireless operator Sgt Ian Jones likewise floated like an astronaut, surrounded by his kitchen utensils.

Because the Sunderland was, as Davenport recalled, 'a kindly aeroplane', there was no spin, but both pilots had to apply the 'anti-spin treatment' to get it out of the inverted spiral dive: push the control column forward to un-stall the wing, wrench on the control wheels to roll the wings level, and then heave together on the control yoke to pull out of the resultant dive. By the time the Sunderland was stabilised once again in level flight, it was flying in the opposite direction to that in which it had started, and 'much closer to the ocean!' The crewmen were bruised by tumbling against the sharp edges of the interior fittings, and both decks were a 'shambles' from goods spilled out of their stowage places, and with up-ended batteries hazardously dripping acid through the top deck into the galley. Manger abandoned the flight and headed for Mount Batten.[17] C/461's internal damage was put to rights by the station maintenance staff, and she flew back to Hamworthy on the 5th.

On 12 November, Wyn Thorpe's crew was almost undone by a different weather-related hazard: un-forecasted headwinds. They were returning to Mount Batten from Gibraltar in D/10, having earlier flown one of the periodical transport flights between England and the Mediterranean that fell within either squadron's duties at times; as was typical of such transit flights, they were carrying a party of senior officers. Sgt Grattan Horgan, the flight engineer, had composed a passenger manifest by taking the names of each passenger as they came aboard, during which one of the naval officers had quipped, 'You know, we Naval men are a bit superstitious— we should not be taking off on Friday the thirteenth'. The aircraft took off from Gibraltar in the darkness at 6.30 a.m., into worsening lightning, hail, and sleet; for the non-aviator passengers, the flight soon became a nightmare with bumpy conditions and bucking headwinds of 40 knots. For the flight crew, however, the problem of airsick passengers paled into insignificance beside the question of whether the aircraft had enough fuel to make it home against these un-forecast head winds—or not. Gibraltar to Mount Batten was a twelve-hour trip anyway, so any significant reduction in the aircraft's groundspeed would extend the flight beyond the aircraft's maximum airborne endurance. Facing a similar situation a few months later, Fg Off. Kerv Beeton had recalled how on that flight the off-duty crewmen had gathered around the flight engineer at his control panel, 'watching every time he switched on the petrol gauges to see how much juice was left, and asking the navigator, "How far have we got to go? Can we do it?"'[18] Aboard D/10 on Friday the 13th, Thorpe's flight engineer, Sgt Horgan, must have similarly drawn a circle of anxious onlookers crowding around his instrument panel.

D/10's return flight from Gibraltar had been postponed the previous day because of unfavourable winds, and this flight too should have been 'scrubbed' from the ops board. Instead, the Sunderland bucketed slowly northward into the turbulent headwind. By 11.50 a.m., Thorpe had the wireless operator transmit a signal to Plymouth requesting the latest meteorological data, but the weather was causing such severe electrical interference that the message had to be repeated over and over, such that it took until 1.48 p.m. before the answer was received in ungarbled form. By then, D/10 was well past the point of no return. The engines had already burnt so much fuel that Horgan had changed over to the main tanks one and a half hours previously—and these were the last tanks. With the headwinds not abating, the navigator, Plt Off. Bill Moore, calculated that they might not have enough fuel to make Plymouth, so Thorpe dictated a signal to base that he might have to land on the open sea outside the breakwater. However, in the end, the Sunderland had just enough fuel to make it: after signalling base at 7.50 p.m. that he had fifteen minutes' fuel remaining, at 7.56 p.m., he made an approach to the Mount Batten flare-path.

By then, Mount Batten's alighting area was covered in fog; in normal circumstances, a returning Sunderland would be diverted to Pembroke Dock under such conditions, but D/10's parlous fuel state precluded that option: Thorpe would just have to get his aircraft down on the water in fog at night—reportedly in 'almost zero visibility'.[19] After the long, anxiety-wracked flight, and then faced with the alarming necessity of having to make a landing under such extreme conditions, Thorpe misjudged his first approach and overshot the flare-path. He opened the throttles and went around again, turning to the right; but as he turned for his second approach, the aircraft's starboard wing unexpectedly struck the sea, 1½ miles inside the breakwater. Presumably, Thorpe had misjudged his height above the water in the final turn. The impact with the water somersaulted the aircraft violently on to its back. The first pilot, Plt Off. Dick Gray, was flung straight through the Perspex cockpit roof by the sudden deceleration: one second, he was sitting up in the co-pilot's seat, the next he was rolling head over heels across the surface of the water before splashing in. When he pulled his head up out of the water, Gray dimly perceived through the fog the ghostly white form of the Sunderland hull, floating upside down about 100 yards away.

The bottom of the hull had been torn off in the crash, killing all five of the passengers, who had unfortunately been stowed away in the wardroom on the bottom deck. By contrast, the eleven-man flight crew were braced in their landing positions on the upper deck, so they survived the violent water impact, albeit three of them with serious injuries. Luckily, the buoyant empty fuel tanks kept the inverted wing afloat, holding the hull high enough in the water to prevent the complete submergence of the upper deck, and saving the injured men from drowning in an upside-down hull in complete darkness. Although water craft were despatched from RAF Mount Batten to rescue survivors, it must have taken some time, for by the time they were picked up, eight of the crew were suffering from hypothermia.[20] In the violent and unexpected crash, no one had managed to deploy a crew dinghy, leaving the survivors to swim in the bitterly cold water supported only by their Mae Wests. It was a close-run thing, and despite the deaths of the passengers, No. 10 itself had been very lucky to get through to the end of the year without losing a fourth crew. Beeton and his navigator, Fg Off. Bob Bowley, would both be awarded DFCs for getting their aircraft home safely from their own horror flight from Gibraltar in January 1943, but there would be no DFC for the unlucky Thorpe, who had crashed his aircraft.[21]

Winter Convoy Patrols

The deteriorating weather of late autumn 1942 coincided with the heavy Allied convoy traffic between Britain and the Mediterranean associated with Operation Torch, the Anglo-American invasions of French North Africa. The troop convoys for this had started sailing on 19 October, in time for the first landings on 7–8 November. Remarkably, not one ship was lost out of the 350 ships used in these operations, because Allied naval escorts were concentrated on screening these invasions convoys, and because Admiral Dönitz had been successfully deceived by Allied security measures, concentrating his U-boats on the more northerly convoy routes between the US and Britain instead.[22] The way the war seems to have bypassed the Bay of Biscay in this period is shown by some statistics: whereas Coastal Command aircraft were making one U-boat sighting in every twenty-nine flight hours around threatened convoys further out in the Atlantic, in the Bay, the rate of U-boat sightings fell from one per 164 hours flown in the four months up to September 1942, to one per 312 hours in the five months from October.[23] For now, the war seemed to have sidestepped the squadrons of No. 19 Group.

Despite this drop-off in the rate of contact with the enemy, the task of shepherding the troop convoys past the open mouth of the Bay of

Biscay committed both Australian squadrons to a monotonous program of uneventful patrols along the convoy routes between England and Gibraltar. In November 1942, 19 Group's squadrons flew a record number of 10,500 operational hours, despite the poor autumnal weather.[24] This period of operations during October–December 1942 suggested the continuing skill superiority of No. 10 Squadron's crews, as shown by the fact that throughout this period, No. 10 was assigned the more difficult task of night patrolling, which occupied about a third of its operational hours, whereas No. 461 remained for now a day-operations-only unit.

German Radar Warning Receivers Neuter ASV Rradar

Besides the poor weather and the concentration of effort further out on the Atlantic convoy routes, the main reason why so few U-boat contacts were made in the autumn and winter of 1942–43 was that the Germans had now introduced a radar warning receiver in their boats. This was the Metox set, introduced to the U-boat fleet from mid-September 1942; it was a receiver tuned to detect the radar transmissions of Coastal Command's ASV II radar set, giving enough warning to allow the boats to submerge before the aircraft approached. Not all boats were yet equipped with this French-made set, but there were enough Metox sets in U-boats afloat to change the balance of power in the seesawing conflict between aircraft and submarine in the Bay. The newly-acquired ability of U-boats to deftly avoid aircraft contacts by using Metox warnings is shown in the statistic that out of 286 U-boats, which transited through the Bay of Biscay from November 1942 to January 1943, only twenty-two were attacked by aircraft.[25]

Coastal Command's Operational Research Section crunched the data and concluded that after the introduction of Metox, it was more effective for its aircraft to patrol with the radar switched off, as this at least provided some opportunity for making covert approaches. In this new tactical situation, the use of ASV was reduced to a 'scarecrow' tactic, by triggering the U-boats' Metox sets, prompting them to submerge, and hence slowing down their passages through the operational area. In a war of tight margins, even this reduced role was substantive in its knock-on effect: the lengthened transit times reduced U-boat patrol durations out on the convoy routes, and hence reduced the weight of attack against Allied shipping. Nonetheless, until the RAF's centimetric ASV III radar arrived, Dönitz had countered Coastal Command's previous technological advantage.

A New Year and a New Line-up

Over the turn of the year, both squadrons underwent a changeover in their executive officers, forming the leadership line-ups that would take them through the great battles of 1943. Wg Cdr Jim Alexander had arrived from Australia in September 1942, and after three weeks of orientation at Mount Batten, he took over as CO of No. 10 Squadron at the end of that month. A thirty-five-year-old native of Brisbane, Alexander had joined the air force in 1929, and had been appointed to this command role in order to obtain operational experience to add to his professional CV. He had previously commanded the RAAF's No. 11 Squadron (Empire Flying Boats and Catalinas), but this was before the outbreak of the Pacific War. Despite this deficiency of wartime operational experience, Alexander seems to have been in no hurry to add operational flying to his CV, for it was not until January 1943 that he flew his first and only operation, otherwise confining his flying activity to transit flights between Mount Batten and Pembroke Dock. His limited operational exposure did him no harm professionally, for he was promoted to group captain at the start of February 1943, given the plum billet of station commander of RAF Mount Batten.

The RAAF Loosens its Personnel Policy

Although Alexander made little operational impact with No. 10, his appointment to command RAF Mount Batten was significant, as it showed that the RAAF had at last permitted one of its regular career officers to command an RAF unit for the purposes of professional development. This policy change belatedly fulfilled the Australian government's erstwhile intention to allow regular RAAF officers to be appointed to RAF command positions, rather than keeping the two air forces' officers on strictly segregated career paths.[1] The second such appointment of a regular RAAF officer across the previous RAAF/RAF demarcation line was that of Sqn Ldr Des Douglas, who was made CO of No. 461 on 10 January 1943. As an Article XV squadron, No. 461 was more or less regarded by the RAAF as a unit of the RAF, rather than as one of its own, so in the context of the internal politics of the RAAF, it was a considerable breakthrough that Douglas, a permanent RAAF officer, was allowed to command an Article XV squadron.

This overturning of the old restrictive policy was associated with Air Marshal Richard Williams; he had commanded RAAF Overseas HQ in London before returning to Australia in mid-1942, and so was well aware of the political issues associated with officer appointments. Significantly, he made a subsequent visit to England over the turn of the year 1942–43, while on his way from Australia to the United States to take up his new role as RAAF representative in Washington. Williams was therefore in London during the crucial period when appointments such as Douglas's were being decided upon to inaugurate the new policy. As the official historian says, 'Air Marshal Williams had successfully requested that the Air Board review its original policy to segregate the two classes of its units serving overseas'. The new policy of flexible officer appointment between RAAF and RAF units was promulgated by an Air Board directive which arrived in London at the end of December, and which Williams himself seemed to have drafted as far back as June 1942. This document emphasised the principle of Australian-manned units, whether permanent-RAAF like No. 10 or Article XV like No. 461, being commanded by RAAF officers, and of both types of unit drawing their personnel from the common manpower pool. The days of separate streaming of personnel into two segregated air forces were thankfully over.[2]

New Leaders at Both Nos 10 and 461 Squadrons

No. 461's new CO, Des Douglas, was a twenty-five-year-old professional air force officer who had joined the RAAF in 1937; he was also more or less a 10 Squadron 'original', having joined the unit in November 1939. After that he qualified as a Sunderland captain in 1941, and by April 1942 had stepped up to the role of squadron flight commander, as well as winning a DFC for fine airmanship on operations. Prior to his appointment as CO of No. 461, he had been hard at working in training-up No. 10's new crews, just like Colin Lovelock was doing in No. 461. Douglas was glowingly described as, 'a big broad-shouldered fellow with keen eyes, a strong face, and a black moustache.... He was every inch a commanding officer'.[3] While serving with No. 10, he had led from the front as flight commander by flying regularly on operations through the most dangerous time of 1942, August-September. He was excellently qualified for his new role in No. 461, having also had a spell as acting CO of No. 10 while Wg Cdr Richards was on leave. Douglas was duly promoted to the rank of wing commander at the beginning of March 1943, in line with his new responsibilities. He was supported in his new role by another regular RAAF officer from 10 Squadron, Sqn Ldr Sam Wood, DFC, who took over as No. 461's flight commander. By then, the twenty-eight-year-old Wood had accrued 970 Sunderland hours, having joined the RAAF straight after the outbreak of war, in November 1939, and been rushed through his training in time to join No. 10 in 1940. He had become a stalwart of the squadron since graduating to captaincy in 1941, flying forty-nine patrols in the period from April to December 1942. The depth of Wood's operational experience is suggested by the fact that this personal total was almost one-third the number of sorties flown by all 461 Squadron captains in the squadron's whole history up to that point.

With two superbly-qualified RAAF officers belatedly made available to No. 461 in accordance with the convoluted turnings of RAAF personnel policy, the two caretaker British officers, Lovelock and Raban, could now depart to take up their next postings, leaving 461 at last commanded by Australians. No. 461 Squadron's new command team reflected the almost complete Australianisation of the unit's pilots, with FS Baveystock left as the sole RAF pilot on the squadron. On that basis, Baveystock correctly perceived that his days with No. 461 were numbered, so he applied for a commission, was duly promoted to pilot officer, sent to No. 4 OTU for a captain's course, and then posted to a British unit.[4]

Although it had now belatedly embraced its stepchild, No. 461, the Air Board in Melbourne continued to regard 10 Squadron in particular as a vital stepping stone for the career development of selected officers, and so sent out to England another up-and-coming career appointee from the home-based RAAF, Wg Cdr Geoff Hartnell, to succeed Wg Cdr Alexander as CO of the senior squadron. Hartnell was a twenty-six-year-old pre-war professional from Melbourne who had been in the air force since 1936, and had been itching to get into No. 10 ever since the first contingent left Australia back in 1939; his friend, Dick Cohen, had fanned this desire by sending him letters from England detailing his tour of duty with the squadron.[5] During the five weeks of Hartnell's voyage from Australia, Sqn Ldr Reg Marks stood in as acting CO, with the new arrival taking over on 9 March 1943. Hartnell proved to be a success in the role; like his predecessor, Jim Alexander, he had formerly commanded a Catalina squadron, No. 20 Squadron, but unlike Alexander had commanded this unit on war operations in the Southwest Pacific Theatre, and so had some relevant operational experience. Also unlike Alexander, he now led his new unit from the front, flying eleven operational patrols in the most dangerous months of 10 Squadron's war, from May to October 1943, and remaining in his role until the end of that critical year. Adding to the solidity of 10 Squadron's leadership cadre was the newly-appointed flight commander, Reg Marks. Appointed to fill the vacancy left by the departure of Des Douglas to No. 461, the twenty-six-year-old Marks was another of No. 10's veteran professional airmen, having served a lengthy apprenticeship while flying on operations as second pilot through 1941, attaining his own captaincy in June 1942, and then serving as the squadron training officer. This well-credentialed pilot remained in the flight commander role within No. 10 through to September 1943; like Hartwell, he set a good example by flying eleven operational patrols in the danger-year of 1943, before he was returned to Australia as tour-expired, having accumulated a total of 1,346 Sunderland hours over the course of a two-year tour.

The depth of 10 Squadron's personnel riches is further evident in the appointment of some of its officers to the vital squadron training officer roles in both Nos 10 and 461. Within a Sunderland squadron, the training officer took the ceaseless burden of crew training off the shoulders of the squadron flight commander, allowing the latter to concentrate upon planning and supervising the squadron's operational program, directly overseeing the operational crews, and mentoring the captains. Supporting Reg Marks in the role of No. 10's training officer was Flt Lt Ron Gillies, who as we have seen, had fulfilled the same function with No. 461 upon its formation, before returning to No. 10 in June 1942. The hard-working Gillies had flown thirty-nine operational patrols between rejoining No. 10 and taking over that unit's training role. To fill No. 461's training officer position, twenty-eight-year-old Flt Lt Tom Egerton was transferred from No. 10 in January 1943, having flown fifty operational patrols as aircraft captain with the senior unit during 1942. He had originally joined 10 Squadron as a sergeant pilot, served his apprenticeship as first pilot through 1941, attained his captaincy, and by the end of 1942 had effectively become tour-expired: screened from operations, he stayed on with No. 461 to perform a training-only role, and would be posted back to Australia in December 1943 after a three-year tour of duty.

No. 10 hit the 1943 campaigning season led by the experienced team of Hartnell, Marks, and Gilles, while No. 461 was similarly led by the solid ex-10 Squadron trio of Wg Cdr Douglas, Sqn Ldr Wood, and Flt Lt Egerton. Both Australian Sunderland squadrons thereby obtained a solid and secure line-up of operationally-experienced leaders to guide their crews through the most difficult, dangerous, and decisive year of campaigning—1943.

Besides the accession of talent and experience represented by the transfer into No. 461 of Des Douglas, Sam Wood, and Tom Egerton, the junior squadron was beefed up further by the transfer from 10 Squadron of two other highly-experienced officers: Fg Off. Eric 'Lucky' Long, as the new armament officer, and Plt Off. Alan Petherick, as the new gunnery officer. Petherick had started off in No. 10 as a ground crewmember in the lowly rank of aircraftman, and by March of 1941 had commenced his career as aircrew, promoted to corporal and flying operations as a wireless operator/air gunner. As a newly-commissioned ex-ranker with two years' operational experience handling Sunderland guns and turrets in action, he was exceedingly well-qualified to supervise and mentor No. 461's air gunners. Similarly, Long was an ex-ranker with an impressive professional pedigree, having been handling Sunderland bombs, depth-charges, fuses, and bomb racks since he was a sergeant armourer back in 1940. Guided by a new, more generous, inclusive, and rational personnel policy, the RAAF had belatedly put things to rights within No. 461, giving the unit for the first time a cadre of expert Australian leaders who would bring the squadron up alongside its senior sister unit, just in time for the most critical fighting of its life.

Official Recognition and 'Gongs'

As 1942 turned to 1943, both Australian squadrons found themselves the objects of official recognition. Although Coastal Command often found itself eclipsed by other, more glamorous frontline commands – of which the 'fighter boys' of RAF Fighter Command were the most iconic example—it nonetheless competed with some success for media attention, getting its 'story' into the public eye alongside the competing claims of other RAF commands, other services, and other theatres. Of course, Britain's Air Ministry did not leave this to chance: as early as 1941, the RAF's Directorate of Public Relations had built up a staff of 230, including editors, feature writers, and photographers, and both the Canadians and the Australians followed suit by creating their own publicity organisations.[6] As a typical example of the process by which stories were created, No. 10 was visited on 29 August 1942 by Sqn Ldr Cawthorne, an RAF Press Relations Officer, with two journalists in tow— Messrs A. Narracott and R. Walker of the London *Times* and the *News Chronicle*—to research their stories on anti-U-boat operations. Two days later, Cawthorne reappeared on a similar errand, this time bringing Messrs Sale and Fairhall, representing the London *Telegraph* and a news agency;

followed by a third visitation on 2 September, with Mr. W. Stoneman of the *Chicago Daily News* and Jerome Wills of the *Evening Standard*. On 3 October came another public relations officer, Flt Lt Elliott, escorting Mr Hodson from the BBC.

Besides securing a share of news coverage, long form print formats were another means of keeping the public on-message. By the end of 1942, Britain's Ministry of Information was working closely with the service propaganda arms to publish for the public's edification books about Britain's various frontline commands. Aiming their message at the voracious readership of the mid-twentieth century, they did this by publishing popular narratives of each command's war operations to date: for example, *Bomber Command Continues*, *The Mediterranean Fleet*, and *Libyan Log*. There was also *Coastal Command* and *Coastal Command at War*.[7] All these works were, of course, propagandistic, but subtly so, relying for their impact upon cultivating a plausible and restrained tone of authentic detail, and disarming candour. There was nothing shrill about this type of clever propaganda, which imparted a largely-justified impression of veracity through laying down layer after layer of factually-correct detail. For example, in *Coastal Command*, the reader was given an illustrated tour of Coastal Command's command structure and operations room, and interesting expositions of how photographic reconnaissance was used to track enemy ship movements, or of the navigational techniques used to effect rendezvous with convoys at sea.[8] *Coastal Command at War* was a little more popular in tone and style, by providing vivid word portraits of the men themselves, and by framing their personally-told, first-hand stories; significantly, the Australians of No. 10 were given special emphasis in the chapter on Sunderland operations.[9]

The equivalent propaganda publication for the Australian public in this period was *These Eagles*, a nicely illustrated, larger format, hard cover collector's item, produced by the RAAF Directorate of Public Relations.[10] This similarly relied for its propaganda effect upon creating an impression of veracity through the provision of plausible detail, which in this case was established by layer after layer of first-hand stories and impressions by specific Australian airmen, whose exploits were rendered more impactful by the added personal touches of names and home towns. In this manner, for example, the reader discovered how the original band of 10 Squadron airmen came to be awarded their DFCs, thereby gaining some insight into the nature of No. 10's operations.[11] Publications like these, both in Britain and Australia, were furthermore lent the cachet of authenticity by being published under the imprimatur of the fighting services themselves.

Primed by this kind of detailed reportage, once the media noticed the work of the Sunderland squadrons, it was inevitable that the more senior, more expert, and more illustrious No. 10 Squadron hogged most of the resultant attention. Such attention was not only from Australian, or even British media outlets: on 4 November, US interest was signalled by the visit to Mount Batten of Col. Morrow Krum, the director of Public Relations for US Forces in Britain. This visit might have been triggered by the Ministry of Information's documentary feature film *Coastal Command*, which was filmed and released in late 1942, and which gave a starring role to an anonymous RAF Sunderland crew, but which also included the highly complementary appearance of a second, unnamed Sunderland crew from 10 Squadron, with deliberate emphasis given to their Australian identity as a sign of international solidarity in the war against Hitler's Germany. The film was released in the USA, making an implicit appeal for American support for Britain—with Sunderland operations and 10 Squadron's Australian airmen forming part of the appeal.[12] The transatlantic attention continued into 1943, with the visit on 4 March by Miss Dixie Tighe of the US International News Service—as always, No. 10 attracted the best talent. She stayed for several days, flew an uneventful operation with Fg Off. Dave Griffiths's crew on the 7th, and returned to London to write her story, emphasising the RAAF identity of the crew of R/10—'Australia's crack flyers'.[13]

Official approbation and thereby public recognition were also shown by the slew of DFCs awarded to representatives of the senior unit during 1942. As usual, the unit's more senior pilots took the lion's share of these: in November, Flt Lt Graham Pockley was awarded his second DFC for purportedly sinking two U-boats; other recipients from 10 Squadron were Flt Lt Sam Wood, for surviving fighter attack and getting home safely; and Sqn Ldr Des Douglas, for effective leadership as No. 10's flight commander. For the sake of inclusivity, one of the squadron's senior navigators was also so honoured: this was Fg Off. 'John' Jewell, who was singled out for his extensive operational experience and his mentoring role over the junior navigators.[14] Jewell was one of the unit's 1939 originals, having joined as a sergeant navigator, and risen by longevity and proficiency to commissioned rank. DFCs conferred a 'leg-up' in promotion, so Jewell would soon be promoted to flight lieutenant to take over the role of squadron navigation officer, before finally finishing his tour in September 1943 with the impressive total of 1662 flying hours on Sunderlands.

DFC citations typically came towards the end of an officer's tour, in conjunction with the recipient either becoming tour-expired and/or taking up a command position: examples include Des Douglas, who took over the command of No. 461; Sam Wood, who took over the role of 461's flight commander; Jewell, who was groomed to assume the role of No. 10's navigation officer; and Graham Pockley, who finished his tour in December

1942 and returned to Australia. Besides the basic prerequisites of sheer survival to become tour-expired, these gongs also required the recipient to have demonstrated operational proficiency, and moral example in action. Nonetheless, the awarding of DFCs was also to a considerable extent a formulaic rite of passage to crown the end of an officer's operational tour and was also instrumental in facilitating the advancement of favoured officers into executive roles.

It is noteworthy that this slew of DFCs went to 10 Squadron officers rather than to those of No. 461. Because DFC recipients tended to be senior men on the cusp both of tour-expiry and of promotion to flight lieutenant, No. 461 Squadron got none because it had simply not existed long enough for any of its officers to have attained the requisite rank, seniority, and experience to qualify for this award. Indeed, when one of its junior pilots was thus recognised, it was awarded for his exploits while previously serving with No. 10: Plt Off. Harry Winstanley, who was one of the crop of navigators transferred from No. 10 to No. 461 in mid-1942, had his DFC gazetted at the end of October.[15]

Winstanley's DFC is noteworthy in showing that the awards process could be influenced by personal connections, conjunctions of circumstance, and the whim of commanders' impressions. He had come to the personal notice of the commander of 19 Group, Air Vice-Marshal Bromet, when the latter had accompanied Reg Marks's crew on an anti-shipping reconnaissance patrol on 16 April 1942. During this flight, Marks had made a determined bombing attack upon an armed trawler in the face of such intense and accurate AA fire that the Sunderland was hit: a 6-inch hole was punched through the bottom of the hull, and minor shrapnel wounds inflicted upon the second pilot, Plt Off. Max Mainprize, as well as to the navigator, Winstanley. Although the wounding no doubt played a role in advancing the latter's DFC citation, this was not the only consideration, for Mainprize too was wounded, yet he had to wait until October 1943 before receiving a DFC—and that for a later incident as a senior captain with No. 10.[16] Similarly, although it was normally the captain who got the DFC, Marks would never be so awarded, despite his excellent operational record, and despite being the command pilot who personally pressed home the attack that prompted the 'gong'. Winstanley won the DFC as a result of that action, and not Marks or Mainprize, because it was the former who had impressed the watching air vice-marshal with his coolness under fire and navigational proficiency under duress. On the strength of such qualities, but also of his gong, and hence qualification for promotion, he would be appointed No. 461's navigation officer in 1944.

Bromet's singling-out of Winstanley for the DFC also suggests a deliberate policy of dispensing awards beyond the privileged inner circle of pilots; this was done to provide symbolical encouragement to aircrew back-seaters in a service organisation that was heavily dominated by pilots. Indeed, within No. 10, the two navigator DFCs were not the only exceptions to the air force's habitual privileging of pilots in the awarding of gongs, for four enlisted back-seaters were awarded DFMs for their services to the squadron through 1942 (the DFM being the enlisted man's equivalent to the officers' DFC). The lucky recipients were LAC Bob Scott, FS 'John' Burnham, and Sgts Arthur 'Snowy' Couldrey and John Keily.[17] These men were recognised for long service to the squadron, operational proficiency, courage in action, and setting the highest example for the emulation of the other enlisted aircrew.

Civic Diplomacy in the Flying Boat Base Communities

By now, it was three years since No. 10 commenced its residency of Mount Batten, and as a result of this extended incumbency the unit had acquired a considerable public relations profile within the municipality of Plymouth. The official relationship between the squadron and the town was deliberately cultivated on both sides, with 'all ranks' (the phrase meaning 'even the enlisted men!') 'invited to visit magnificent mansions and castles … and often provided with afternoon tea and sometimes dinner'.[18] No. 10's status as the resident flying boat unit gave the squadron considerable 'pulling power' in social events. On 20 July 1942, when the squadron hosted a ball at the Continental Hotel, the event was attended by a bevy of VIPs, including Plymouth's Lady Mayoress, Lady Astor, and Air Vice-Marshal Bromet and his wife. By contrast, when No. 461—then a transient guest unit at Mount Batten—held its own dance in the same hotel on 6 August, there were no VIPs in attendance. The same VIP pulling power was still evident a year later, when Australia's foreign minister, Mr Evatt, chose to make a visit to 10 Squadron, accompanied not only by Air Vice-Marshal Wrigley of the RAAF and Mr Smart of the Australian government's Department of Information, but by both Lord and Lady Astor, who gave speeches in their capacities as the Lord Mayor and Lady Mayoress of Plymouth. No. 10 also performed a representative role in providing ceremonial guards of honour at the funerals of Luftwaffe airmen killed during air raids on Plymouth: the squadron provided a party of six officers and six enlisted men to honour a German fighter pilot buried on 19 May 1942, and a similar party for the funeral of three German bomber crewmen who were ceremonially interred in St Budeaux cemetery on 16 June 1943.

In accordance with its special relationship with the town, No. 10 sent a delegation of twenty-five men into Plymouth to participate in the

RAF Mountbatten, centre left, from the midships gunner's position of a Sunderland, showing 10 Squadron aircraft at their moorings in the Cattewater. Plymouth at upper right and Plymouth Sound upper left. (*AWM 044906*)

U-71 on 5 June 1942, damaged by depth-charge attack from Flt Lt Wood's U/10, down by the bows from flooding forward, under strafing attack from the Sunderland's gunners. (*AWM 128198*)

The flight engineer's station at the rear of the flight deck, manned by Sgt Keily, DFM, a 10 Squadron stalwart. The engineer position faces aft, so that the photograph shows the starboard side of the flight deck. The photographer stood on the ladder descending to the bomb-room on the bottom deck. (*AWM SUK10676*)

Depth-charge bursts from Flt Lt Martin's W/10, exploding around *U-105* (out of picture at top) on 11 June 1942. Although damaged, the U-boat survived to make port. (*AWM SUK10562*)

No. 10 Squadron engine fitters on their exposed workplace atop a Sunderland parked for a maintenance inspection in front of one of the hangars at Mount Batten. The engine's flame-damping exhaust shroud is evident, to make the exhaust flames less visible on night patrols. As was typical on RAAF squadrons in Britain, the men wear overalls rather than subjecting their service dress to wear and tear, and a mix of berets and forage caps. (*AWM SUK11737*)

The astrodome (top) and navigator's position (left), just aft of the co-pilot's seat. The navigator bends over his chart table—no seat was provided. At right, the second pilot, standing on top of the wing spar, takes up fighter lookout position, with his headset plugged into the intercom. The Perspex astrodome is set within the rectangular crew escape hatch, which hinges downward into the hull. (*AWM SUK15161*)

No. 10 Squadron navigators in the Mount Batten Ops Room, preparing the flight-plans before boarding their aircraft for an operation, assisted by squadron navigation officer, Flt Lt Jewell, DFC, second from right. The wartime censor has deleted from the image confidential material posted on the wall behind Jewell. (*AWM UK0015*)

Two 461 Squadron Sunderland Mk III's, near Milford Haven, showing precisely the configuration of the aircraft in which the crews of Nos 10 and 461 flew and fought in 1943. Note the ASV II radar aerials atop the fuselage and beneath the outer wings, the midships turrets (traversed to starboard in the nearer aircraft), and the open galley hatches for the .303-inch 'galley guns'. (*AWM P01520.005*)

The view from the galley hatch, showing the obstructed firing arc of the galley gun, the port float and its vulnerable struts and bracing wires, and the ASV II radar aerial further out. Evident is the white camouflage paint used throughout Coastal Command from 1941 onwards, proven in trials to make the aircraft harder to spot against the sky from a U-boat. (*AWM P00687.167*)

No. 461 Squadron navigator Fg Off. Rolland working at his chart table, perched on the wing spar. At left is the black-out curtain to close off the radar operator's position, which was squeezed between the chart table and the co-pilot's seat. The flight engineer is evident behind Rolland's right arm, wearing headphones and a sheepskin flying jacket and hunched in his enclosed position on the rear side of the wing spar. Visible past Rolland's helmet is an off-duty crewman, sitting on the edge of the hatch leading to the bomb-room below, while visible on the aft cabin bulkhead is the pentagon-shaped hatch leading aft to the midships turret and the rear hull. (*AWM UK1083*)

The crew of E/461, captained by Plt Off. Colin Steley (fifth from right, back row). Steley, a former sergeant pilot, finished his tour in March 1943, handing over 'E-Emu' and her crew to his first pilot, Plt Off. Gordon Singleton (back row right), who would complete his tour with this crew in September 1943. Visible on the flank of the Sunderland's rear fuselage are the stubby radar transmission aerials for the ASV II set; this particular array was used to scan the sea and sky on the aircraft's port side. (*AWM SUK10386*)

Pembroke Dock's busy hard-standing on 6 May 1943, photographed from the top of the hangar, showing six aircraft out of the water undergoing maintenance inspections, six aircraft at their moorings in Milford Sound, the flying-boat slipway centre right, and the workshops at left. The newly-delivered, brand-new aircraft in the foreground shows the then-current Coastal Command camouflage scheme of white sides with dark grey upper surfaces. (*AWM UK0119*)

No. 461 Squadron CO and former 10 Squadron stalwart, twenty-five-year-old Wg Cdr Douglas, accompanied by his wife, the former Joan Hunter (from Neutral Bay in Sydney), at Buckingham Palace on 11 May 1943, after the investiture for Douglas's DFC, which he won for his service with No. 10 in 1942. (*AWM UK0115*)

Z/10 on the slipway at Mount Batten, in the process of being returned to the water after undergoing a maintenance inspection on 10 Squadron's busy hard-standing at right, where two other aircraft are also visible, undergoing work by No. 10's Maintenance Flight. Noteworthy on 'Z' are the beaching gear used to move the flying-boat out of the water, the bow turret retracted to give the crewmen access to the mooring gear, the open crew entry door below the cockpit, the open galley hatch further aft, the partly-open port bomb-door below the wing, the ASV II radar aerials mounted on wing and fuselage, and the weathered coat of white over-paint, exposing patches of the previous grey-green camouflage scheme underneath. This aircraft was shot down on 17 May 1943. (*AWM SUK14699*)

No. 10 Squadron's Christmas party on 22 December 1942 in the station gym at Mount Batten. The men in the photo are all enlisted men, and mostly ground-crew, with a couple of exceptions identifiable by the half-wing aircrew brevet above their left jacket pocket. (*AWM SUK10737*)

Two survivors from a 224 Squadron Liberator crew, about to be rescued on 19 May 1943 by Flt Lt Rossiter's crew in Sunderland S/10. The two men had been on the water for six days, and despite Rossiter's alacrity in getting them back to Mount Batten, the badly-wounded air gunner, Plt Off. Barham, died in Plymouth Hospital. The sole survivor was Plt Off. Willerton, the captain—evident in the photo as the man wielding the paddle. (*AWM SUK10840A*)

The tired crew of Flt Lt Rossiter's S/10, photographed after dumping their gear upon coming ashore from their twelve-hour flight on 19 May 1943, during which Rossiter successfully landed to rescue two survivors from a shot-down Liberator, and then successfully took-off from the open sea to get them to medical help at Plymouth. Rossiter is sixth from right, wearing a white scarf. Note the binocular cases on the ground at left, the dinghy paddles, the two carrier-pigeon transport-cases at right, and under the pile of sheepskin flying jackets the two suitcases and flight-bag necessary to contain the navigator's and pilots' logs, manuals, instruments, charts, and equipment. (*AWM SUK10944*)

Two crews in their dinghies in the early morning of 29 May 1943, taken from Fg Off. Singleton's E/461, which had alighted upon the water to effect a rescue. The survivors from Sunderland O/461 and from a Whitley from 10 OTU had tied their dinghies together to stay together during the night, and soon after dawn, all sixteen men were taken aboard 'E-Emu'. (*AWM 045298*)

Plt Off. Singleton's E/461 after alighting to rescue from their dinghies sixteen men from two aircrews; the whaleboat from the Free French destroyer, *La Combattante*, has come alongside the Sunderland's aft hatch, transferring the survivors to the ship, and leaving Singleton with the challenge of getting his aircraft safely off the water afterwards. The sea might look moderate in the photo, but was already beyond safe parameters for a Sunderland take-off. Between the two men standing upright atop the Sunderland's wing, note the open astrodome hatch—this was the only escape hatch available for most crew members in a crash. (*AWM UK1126*)

E/461 in an unnatural posture on the grass runway at RAF Angle, after Plt Off. Singleton's crash-landing on 29 May 1943. Visible to the right of the car is the wide breach in the hull caused by his take-off from the open sea, after alighting to rescue sixteen survivors. Evident are the extended flaps, the fold-out engine access platforms on the starboard wing leading edge, the galley hatch swung half open on the side of the hull, the hull's grimy waterline, the portable gantries visible above the port wing, being used for engine removal, and the fact that the radar array has already been removed from the V-shaped mount above the cockpit. This aircraft never flew again, but was scrapped *in situ*, stripped of spare parts for reuse. (*AWM 045299*)

U-518 under attack from Flt Lt Skinner's T/10 on 30 June 1943. Evident are the gunners on the U-boat bandstands, each swinging their 20-mm guns around on to the Sunderland. Further crewmen can be seen hunched down on the bridge and on the after-bandstand, either to get out of the line of fire from the Sunderland's machine guns or to fetch more ammunition from the ready-use lockers. (*AWM SUK11049*)

Opposite above: Flt Lt Walker, right, and his navigator, Fg Off. Simpson, both instrumental in N/461's iconic air battle on 2 June 1943 against a squadron of Ju 88s. Walker, looking very old here for his twenty-five years, got the DSO, and Simpson the DFC. Note Simpson's 'winged-O' observer's brevet. Although the terminology was changed to 'navigator' in 1942, and the corresponding aircrew brevet to 'N', the earlier-trained observers continued to wear their 'flying arseholes' with pride. (*AWM SUK10580*)

Opposite below: Left to right: Flt Lt Walker, Fg Off. Dowling, and the two decorated air gunners, Sgts Watson and Fuller, making a recording at the BBC studios on 3 June 1943, the day after their famous combat against eight Ju 88s. This shows how rapidly the crew's feat of survival was turned into grist for the propaganda mill. Mr Loch of the BBC is prompting the evidently-reluctant 'talent' as they go through their lines. (*AWM UK0194*)

In the process of fending off air attack from Liberators and Halifaxes, *U-461* and *U-462* take evasive action on 30 July 1943; the photo was taken from Flt Lt Marrows's Sunderland 'U/461' before he made his own attack. (*AWM P02184.006*)

Opposite above: Two veteran 10 Squadron air-crewmen, FS Couldrey (left) and Sgt Keily, at Buckingham Palace on 20 July 1943 after the investiture in which they received their DFMs. Both were so awarded for the excellent example they set for the other NCO airmen. (*AWM UK0281*)

Opposite below: Fg Off. Humble's crew (he is fourth from right), pleased to be alive after fighting off an attack by four Ju 88s on 27 July 1943. Their aircraft, E/10, was so severely damaged that she had to be sent away for repairs, and here is the crew on 6 August, in front of their replacement aircraft, 'K'. Note the partly-open galley hatch in the centre of the photo, the weathered state of the heavily-used aircraft's exterior, the partly-open bomb-door at top left, and just visible at top left beneath the wing are the rails along which the electrically-operated bomb trolley was winched outboard from the bomb-room. (*AWM UK0363*)

The fatally-damaged *U-461* emerging from the depth-charge detonations left by Flt Lt Marrows's attack in Sunderland 'U/461', on 30 July 1943. The U-boat's hull is now severely breached, and she is already sinking away beneath her captain's feet. (*AWM P02184.007*)

Survivors from Flt Lt Fry's B/10 on 1 August 1943, using the snapped-off stump of the Sunderland's starboard wing as an improvised life-raft, about to be rescued by HMS *Wren*, alongside. The Sunderland had just sunk *U-454* but was itself shot down by the U-boat's flak gunners. Only half the crew survived B/10's violent crash. The indistinct shape in the water in front of the stump appears to be a man, FS Conacher, whose broken ankle was so painful that he could not get on to the wing. (*AWM SUK11307*)

Photographed from the port galley hatch of Flt Lt Clarke's M/461, this is *U-106* just after getting straddled by a salvo of depth-charges on 2 August 1943; she was fatally damaged. Evident are the splash marks left by the depth charge detonations, and the tight zooming turn executed by Clarke after bomb-release, providing the dorsal turret gunner with a clear shot to keep the U-boat gunners' heads down as the Sunderland extended the range. (*AWM 128221*)

Photographed from the starboard galley hatch of Flt Lt Clarke's M/461, *U-106* under machine-gun fire from the Sunderland's midships turret on 2 August 1943, as the Sunderland banks to starboard in the course of her second attack. Splashes from the aircraft's .303 machine guns are evident, aimed at the conning tower to suppress AA return fire from the gunners on the bandstands, aft of the bridge. The U-boat is trailing smoke from her machinery compartments aft, from the damage inflicted in Clarke's first attack. (*AWM SUK11508*)

A crippled *U-106*, wreathed in smoke and with poisonous chlorine gas escaping from the conning tower hatch, after repeated depth charging from Sunderlands N/228 and M/461. Her crew have abandoned ship, as seen by the heads of her crew evident in her wake. Thirty-five men survived the sinking, rescued that evening by a German destroyer. (*AWM SUK11511*)

The funeral of FS Woolhouse at Llanion Barracks at Pembroke Dock on 19 August 1943. X/461's midships turret gunner was killed on 15 August when the aircraft was attacked by a flight of Ju 88s. The second officer in the procession is Fg Off. Davenport, Woolhouse's skipper in the fatal combat. (*AWM SUK11404C*)

Opposite: Airmen from Flt Lt Williams's crew inspect the damage to their aircraft, J/10, inflicted during attacks by seven Ju 88s on 3 August 1943. With their 'J-Johnny' up on the hard-standing at Mount Batten for repairs, on 6 August, Sgt Guy points at the hole made by a 20-mm cannon shell, watched by crewmates, Sgts Simon and McVinish at left, and Sgt Moser at right. The open astrodome escape hatch is clearly seen. (*AWM UK0359*)

Photographed from a Ju 88, this is Flt Lt Marrows's E/461 after being shot down on 16 September 1943, with the port wing sinking after the collapse of the wing float. The crew have emerged from the escape hatch just aft of the cockpit, and have deployed two six-man dinghies on top of the wing before the aircraft sinks. From this point on the victorious German pilots chivalrously left them alone. (*AWM P02184.001*)

Flt Lt Marrows (centre rear) and crew photographed at Pembroke Dock, safe and sound having been rescued from the sea after being shot down on 16 September 1943, posing to show how crowded it was with eleven men in one six-man dinghy. (*AWM P02184.003*)

Right: Flt Lt Dick Lucas, captain of D/461, after sinking *U-571* on 28 January 1944. Typical of the pilots trained up on the unit through 1943, the twenty-year-old Lucas joined No. 461 in March 1943, became a captain in October, and went on to finish his tour in July 1944. (*AWM SUK11729*)

Below: The object of the whole business—an enemy submarine going down stern first. It is evidently an Italian submarine, not a German U-boat. Crews from No. 10 made several attacks upon Italian submarines in the Atlantic, including sinking the *Alessandro Malaspina* on 7 September 1941, with all sixty souls aboard lost. (*AWM 304943*)

A staged press-shot of a 10 Squadron crew coming ashore up the slipway at Mount Batten. The photo was taken in 1944–45, showing the Sunderland secured to her (red) buoy, as well as the tender from the RAF Marine Section, which shuttled men between shore and aircraft. (*Ross McMurtrie via Neil McMurtrie*)

Thanksgiving Day celebrations on 26 November 1942. The party was led by Plt Off. Tom Jensen, a wireless operator/air gunner who had joined the unit in 1940 as a corporal, been commissioned, and was now virtually tour-expired (he would soon go on staff as the squadron gunnery leader, staying with the unit until November 1943, but only flying two operations that year, both in February). The American custom of Thanksgiving was celebrated in Plymouth because it was from that port that the 'Pilgrim Fathers' had sailed for America in the *Mayflower* in 1620, which fact gave rise to the local tradition of observing the day with official speeches and festivities at the Mayflower Stairs on Plymouth's Barbican waterfront. This theme was never more apposite than in 1942, given that since the previous Thanksgiving Day, the USA had joined the war on Britain's side, and that this accession of strength meant that, as Prime Minister Churchill put it, 'We had won after all.'[19] By November 1942, with Operation Torch successfully launched in French North Africa, Hitler's 6th Army fatally encircled at Stalingrad, Rommel's *Afrika Korps* defeated at El Alamein, Malta made secure, the Imperial Japanese Navy defeated at Midway, and Japanese forces locked in a losing battle at Guadalcanal, there was indeed much for the Allies to be thankful for.

No. 10 celebrated Christmas on 22 December with a party in the base gymnasium attended by VIPs., including Air Marshal Richard Williams, the 'Father of the RAAF', who was *en route* to Washington; accompanied by his senior staff officer, Grp Capt. Ern Knox-Knight, formerly CO of No. 10; and Grp Capt. L. Martin, RAF, the then-commander of RAF Station Mount Batten. After their visit to No. 10, Williams and Knox-Knight went on to Poole to visit No. 461, but this visit was less festive and less convivial: the squadron's RAAF members were paraded for the senior officers, but made only a small 'show', as three crews were away flying patrols and two others were detached or on leave—thus no more than about fifty of the squadron's 100 or so RAAF members could have been present. No. 10 continued to hog the VIP attention, with a visit on 8 February from Air Chief Marshal Joubert, the commander of Coastal Command.

Heavy Training Commitments over Winter

Other than these token festivities, it was business as usual for both squadrons over the Christmas–New Year period, with operational patrols despatched as frequently as the winter weather permitted, irrespective of the calendar: No. 10 flew two patrols on Christmas Eve, seven patrols from the 28th to the 30th, and three on New Year's Day. The weather forced No. 461 into a very similar pattern, flying four operations on Christmas Eve, one on Boxing Day, one on the 29th, and two on New Year's Day. On top of maintaining the normal operational output (weather permitting), Coastal Command's training tempo also did not slacken over the festive season, with personnel sent away repeatedly on the by-now routine cycle of training courses: on 29 November, 10 Squadron's armament officer, Flt Lt Tom Patrick, departed for a fortnight-long course on the Sunderland's FN gun turrets, and on the same day, No. 461 crews received a lecture program on submarine warfare from Commander Claude Brooks, RAN, an experienced Australian destroyer captain serving with the Royal Navy. Harry Winstanley from the same squadron was meanwhile attending a three-week-long Bombing Leaders' Course at No. 1 Air Armament School at RAF Manby, while Plt Off. A. C. Hennessey, RAF, the squadron's gunnery leader-designate, departed to RAF Stormy Down in Wales for a week-long gun sighting course with No. 7 Air Gunnery School. He would soon be promoted two ranks to flight lieutenant, in keeping with his new responsibilities.

The training load on the squadrons themselves was relentless, because most of the new airmen posted-in from Australia, whether via the personnel reception centre at Bournemouth, or straight from the new-arrivals' reception centre at Blackpool, were still joining the squadron without having completed the Sunderland conversion course at No. 4 OTU. The training burden thus fell upon the squadrons themselves to convert each newly-arrived cohort of aircrew to the Sunderland and to qualify each member for their assigned operational duties. On 13 December, No. 461 sent away two trainee pilots, Russ Baird and Raleigh Gipps, to undertake a captain's course at No. 4 OTU, but this was an exception—most captains continued to be trained on-unit. For example, Tom Egerton fulfilled his role as No. 10's training captain by taking trainee captains on navigation exercises between Mount Batten and Lough Erne in Northern Ireland; also taking trainee captains to Pembroke Dock for night circuits and bumps. No. 461 also gave its new pilots some captaincy experience with triangular training flights between Poole, Mount Batten, and Pembroke Dock, practising alighting and taking off at each base.

Such a forced tempo had to exact a toll, and it was on such a practice flight that one of 10 Squadron's trainee captains, Plt Off. Dick Gray, made a heavy landing in F/10 at Pembroke Dock on 17 January 1943: he failed to keep the wings level as he held-off before touchdown, and the port wingtip float struck the water first. The heavy impact damaged the float itself, as well as its struts and attachments. Gray opened the throttles and went around again, and on the second attempt, he got down safely, holding the port float out of the water with opposite aileron and taxiing to the slipway with his crew out on the starboard wing to keep the damaged float out of the water.

Gray had at least saved F/10 for another day: she survived on No. 10 until August 1943, when she was shot down in the Bay of Biscay. Of course, for every such flying mishap involving damage to the aircraft, there were many more near misses, and so it was a dubious honour for the duty wireless operators and flight engineers to fly on these training hops with sprog pilots, forced to share the risks from their work stations at the rear of the flight-deck. Ed Gallagher, a 461 Squadron wireless operator, flew with both good pilots and bad pilots, and the latter gave him many frights: 'Some of these new pilots are more dangerous than any Jerry could be. They'll break their silly necks and ours too, one of these days. One chap today, in attempting a landing bounced her about fifty feet into the air first go'.[20]

To meet the demand for trained aircrew, the Coastal Command organisation gave increasing attention to the task of training the trainers. On 28 December, 461's navigation officer, Flt Lt John Watson, departed to RAF Cranage in Cheshire for a Staff Navigator's Course at No. 2 School of Air Navigation, and on the same day No. 10's Fg Off. John Lanyon returned to Mount Batten from the same course, now qualified for the same role in the senior squadron. In the first half of January, No. 461's Pete Jensen left for RAF Yate in Gloucestershire to attend a course on gun turrets at the Parnell Armament School, and Harry Cooke was sent off to RAF Leuchars in Scotland on a Beam Approach Training course. The ground staff officers were not exempt from the training demands either: for example, No. 10's Engineering Officer, Sqn Ldr Ray Rice, went to Bristol for a course on Pegasus engines with the manufacturer, the Bristol Engine Company.

The above sampling of activity represents a typical training tempo for both squadrons through the winter of 1942–43, showing the extent to which RAF Coastal Command was intent upon professionalising its organisation, by progressively extending an in-service training program, and by formally qualifying its officers for their departmental roles. In this process, the RAF recognised the professional expertise of the Australian airmen by taking them on staff at its training schools: for example, two of the Australian squadrons' tour-expired navigation leaders were appointed as staff navigation instructors at No. 3 School of General Reconnaissance, namely John Lanyon from No. 10 in April 1943, and No. 461's John Watson that December. Lanyon would finish his tour with the epic total of 2,023 Sunderland flying hours, accrued over a three-year tour of duty.

No. 461's Problems with Poole

Despite a new leadership team and an improved training system, 461 Squadron remained unhappy at RAF Hamworthy. It was said of Poole

Harbour and its surroundings that they were 'probably rather pleasant, but it wasn't flying boat country'.[21] The 'harbour was small and dotted with sandbanks'.[22] This was a significant operational handicap, because as even loyal Sunderland crews admitted, 'It's the hardest thing in the world to taxy Sunderlands' because they weathercocked almost uncontrollably in a crosswind.[23] As a result, going aground while taxiing was a hazard at Hamworthy even in normal conditions. Moreover, all crews got sick of the long boat trips to and from the aircraft moorings, with the squadron's Sunderlands moored at buoys spread over 'the unbelievable distance of seven miles'.[24] These were dotted along two widely separated channels.[25] The squadron's facilities on land were unimpressive as well, with Harry Winstanley finding them 'hopelessly dispersed round the shore of Poole Harbour': the Officers' Mess was at the Harbour Heights Hotel at Sandbanks; the Squadron Headquarters and the Marine Craft Section were at Parkstone Yacht Club; the Station HQ was in Parkstone half a mile away; the Sergeants' Mess was at Poole; the technical sections, pilots' room, and airmen's mess at Hamworthy; and the airmen's accommodation spread throughout town in civilian billets. Officers and men got from one location to another, depending on distance, either by riding service bicycles or by using the RAF shuttle lorry, which went on its rounds morning, midday, and evening.[26] The latter form of commuting may not exactly have enhanced community relations, for as the lorry went on its rounds, the men gave 'the local girls the benefit of our gentlemanly remarks from the back of a truck'.

One of No. 461's RAF armourers, LAC Reg Wheaton, provided a negative perspective of working at Hamworthy, despite the relatively upmarket (by wartime RAF standards) accommodation he enjoyed: he and his colleagues were billeted in a large, modern house outside Poole called the 'White House', dining at 'a peace-time swimming and pleasure spot' called the 'Blue Lagoon', at Salterns Marsh. The morale problems were evidently not attributable to the accommodation, but seem to have started at work, for Wheaton and his fellow armourers worked shifts in a makeshift armoury located in a private house opposite the slipway; there were no comforts provided at this improvised work station during the cold winter months, and the work was done in social isolation from the rest of the unit: 'We never saw an officer, and none seemed to be very bothered about our welfare. There was never that feeling of belonging that comes from being in a squadron'.[27]

However, it seems that different men experienced the squadron differently, and one's impressions also seem to have depended upon whether one was aircrew or ground crew. By contrast with Wheaton's experience, an aircrew NCO, Sgt Ed Gallagher, seems to have enjoyed congenial relationships with aircrew officers, referring to them habitually in his diary in familiar and informal terms, such as 'Bullsie' (Flt Lt Buls), 'Woodsie' (Sqn Ldr Wood), and 'Tommy' (Plt Off. Egerton).[28] In any case, things became a little more cohesive for squadron ground-staff members in mid-January, when the squadron headquarters moved into the Harbour Club Building at Salterns Pier, where it was helpfully co-located with the flying control station.

Irrespective of individual members' state of morale, No. 461 was not an efficient unit while residing at Poole. Harry Winstanley recalled: 'Because of the dispersal and unreadiness of facilities, serviceability was of a poor standard. Many frustrating days were spent at primitive Hamworthy'.[29] This assessment of 461 Squadron's serviceability problem is borne out by statistics, for the proportion of squadron aircraft available for flying operations declined steadily after moving to Poole: the squadron had six aircraft out of nine available to fly over August-September 1942, dropping to four out of nine in October–November, after the move to Hamworthy, and then to only one in nine by the end of January, after four months' occupancy. One reason for the precipitous decline in the serviceability rate through the final months of 1942 was that the major inspections on a number of squadron aircraft fell due in those months, requiring those aircraft to be taken offline and sent away to maintenance units for the schedule of work entailed in each aircraft's particular maintenance inspection.

A sample of the squadron's serviceability state can be provided from 29 January, when out of the nine aircraft on squadron strength, only aircraft 'I' was serviceable. Of the rest, three were 'up-slip' on Hamworthy's hard-standing—'D' was awaiting spares, while 'E' and 'K' had unrectified engine trouble; and there were another three at their moorings but unairworthy—'M' was undergoing a 'special inspection', while another two aircraft were waiting to be slipped once the logjam on the hard-standing was cleared, with 'N' needing to have its compass calibrated, and 'L' to have a propeller change. Besides these six unserviceable aircraft, there was also 'H' away at a maintenance unit for a major inspection, and 'C', which had been bombed up and fuelled up for an operation, but then gone unserviceable.[30]

No. 461's poor maintenance outcomes can be shown by a comparison of flying hours with 10 Squadron, which had a comparable number of aircraft on strength: in October 1942, No. 10 produced 468 hours of operational flying, compared to 461's 250 hours; while in November, the figures were 531 hours compared to 285.[31] Similar deficits would continue until August 1943, when 461 finally caught up with the senior squadron.

Hazardous Winter Operations

Once aircraft became serviceable and got airborne on operations, the severe winter weather posed a hazard for all crews, however experienced they might have been. On 21 January 1943, both squadrons despatched two aircraft on operational patrols, despite the forecasted frontal conditions. As a result, the four crews found themselves flying over a rough sea, buffeted about in a shallow layer of bumpy air beneath 10/10th cloud, with rain at times reducing visibility to three miles. The weather was forecasted to deteriorate, so at 6 p.m. base signalled all aircraft to abort the mission and divert to Pembroke Dock, where the weather was clearer than at Mount Batten and Poole. In conditions like this, captains would need to apply all the blind approach skills they had been trained to use, and three of the Australian Sunderlands duly made night landings in Milford Haven for an overnight stop at 'PD'.

However, neither Bruce Buls nor his aircraft, A/461, ever returned. At 3 p.m., this aircraft transmitted an SOS, less than three hours after taking off. This gave only an approximate position, suggesting that the aircraft had been flying in cloud and that the navigator, Plt Off. Hal Dent, had not been able to fix its position for some time. RAF ground stations tried to obtain a bearing upon the transmission but obtained only a poor-quality fix indicating that the aircraft was somewhere in the Bay of Biscay area.[32] No. 19 Group despatched two ASR Hudsons from No. 279 Squadron at Bircham Newton to conduct a search, but the sea was very rough and the visibility too poor to see much. Indeed, flying conditions were so bad that the crew of Hudson F/279 failed to find base upon their return, having suffered the failure of both their radio sets and hence unable to obtain homing bearings; the crew baled out, and luckily all came to earth safely near Swansea in Wales. Nightfall and the awful weather quickly condemned the afternoon search to impotence, but No. 279 launched another two ASR Hudsons the next morning. No. 19 Group also tasked five Whitleys and two Sunderlands to search the deduced crash area while *en route* to their patrol areas further south. Again, the weather was so bad that another one of the searching Hudsons was lost, again through suffering radio failure. Again deprived of a homing bearing, this crew was obliged to bale out after failing to find an airfield; again, luckily, all four men came to earth safely near Bodmin in Cornwall.[33] But no trace of the lost Sunderland was ever located, and all eleven men were lost.[34] Bruce Buls was one of the squadron's originals, having flown his first operation as captain in July 1942, and flying twenty-one operational patrols before his final, fatal flight.

Of the lost crew, Dent had been flying with Buls since November; the second pilot, Plt Off. Jack Moore, had flown only four patrols with him previously; while the first pilot, Henry Osborne, was especially unlucky, dying on only his first trip with this crew, having previously flown thirteen operations with Harry Cooke. Luck went both ways, of course: FS Ed Gallagher had been wireless operator on Buls's crew, but was grounded by the MO for medical reasons, and so missed the fatal flight. While on leave in London, he heard the news that Buls was missing from his squadron mate, Sgt 'Paddy' Druhan. Gallagher was appalled to think that 'Bulsie and his merry men' were gone, realising that were it were not for his medical condition, he would have gone with them. To deal with it all, Gallagher went on a pub crawl through Leicester Square with two squadron mates, Druhan and Ron Mackie. The next day, upon meeting another squadron mate at Australia House in the Strand, Gallagher received an update as to who had been aboard the fatal flight, and was relieved to hear that 'Bulsie had almost a new crew with him', and that most of his old crew were 'OK'.[35] Within the exclusive circle of a crew, it was instinctively preferable for strangers to do the dying, rather than one's own mates.

Buls's father, Mr E. H. Buls of East Balmain, Sydney, wrote to the Air Board after receiving the official notification that his son was missing: Mr Buls felt a 'double burden' of anxiety about his son's fate, out of recognition of Bruce's extra responsibilities as captain of 'this expensive aircraft with its numerous crew'. His only consolation was his knowledge that Bruce 'fully realised and was so proud of the trust that had been placed in him by the Chiefs of Coastal Command, and his whole heart and soul was in his work'. Buls senior explained that his son had 'idolized' his Sunderland, and had felt himself so 'fully occupied' looking after both it and his crew that he had neglected his correspondence with friends back home, and so had asked his father to apologise to them on his behalf on that basis.[36] Bruce Buls would never get to renew those relationships after the war.

High Command Changes

Not only did the New Year bring bad flying weather and this sad loss, as well as a change of leadership cadre in both squadrons, but it also brought an upheaval in high places: starting on 14 January 1943, the US and British leaders met together to plot their combined war strategy at the 'Arcadia' conference in Casablanca. With the Battle of Stalingrad heading towards its triumphant climax, Stalin had decided not to attend, but beforehand he had reminded President Roosevelt and Prime Minister Churchill of their promise to open a 'Second Front' in the West by the spring of 1943, in order to take some pressure off the hard-fighting Soviet forces. In the event, D-Day would not in fact take place until June 1944, but the strategic priority for the Anglo-American leaders was nonetheless clear: any descent upon German-occupied Europe by the American, British, and Canadian Armies was dependent upon transatlantic shipping, which formed a multi-channelled super-highway from the resource-rich United States to the Allies' forward operational base in Britain.[37] November 1942 saw the highest shipping losses of any month of the war so far: 134 ships sunk, or 807,000 tons. With U-boats responsible for 730,000 tons of these losses, it was self-evident that the defeat of the U-boat menace was a precondition for D-Day, irrespective of when the invasion was launched.[38]

The groundwork for a change in policy settings had been set in November 1942, when London's Cabinet Anti-U-boat Warfare Committee met for the first time, having been formed at the urging of Australian High Commissioner Stanley Bruce in response to the severe shipping losses to U-boats suffered that year. The committee noted that Germany's production of U-boats was far outstripping the rate at which Allied forces were destroying them, and responded with a call for 'more and longer-range air patrols in the Bay of Biscay'.[39] Impelled by the force of this strategic logic, the British and American delegations at Casablanca put the defeat of the U-boat threat at the 'top of the agenda', jointly prioritising this task as having 'first charge on the resources of the United Nations'.[40] Thus Nos 10 and 461 Squadrons, as they pursued their program of anti-submarine patrols over the Bay, found themselves at the leading edge of Anglo-American strategy for 1943.

Besides this reordering of priorities at the highest level of the Allies' combined command structure, Coastal Command got a new commander in February 1943, with the departure of Air Chief Marshal Joubert. The latter was justifiably disappointed at being relieved from his post, for during his tenure, he had set in place an array of technological, tactical, and procedural innovations that would bring new success to Coastal Command's air-sea warfare in 1943: new airborne radar, new depth-charges with new depth-setting fuses, new aircraft, a new maintenance program to maximise aircraft availability, new scientifically-based search patterns, new scientifically-based attack methods, and popular new training approaches for propagating these doctrinal developments throughout his command.[41] After having made himself unpopular with his superiors by too-forthrightly complaining to them of the numerical weakness of his command, they had in effect retrospectively conceded the validity of his complaints by now strengthening his command with large reinforcements. As a result, his successor obtained command over a rejuvenated force of sixty squadrons and more than 800 aircraft.[42] This force included not only legacy aircraft types like Whitleys, Wellingtons, and Sunderlands, but also modern Liberator and Halifax four-engined bombers and formidable twin-engined Beaufighter long-range fighters to take on the Ju 88s. In short, after years of being the poor cousin to Bomber Command and with its aircraft reduced to the role of airborne 'scarecrows' over U-boats, Coastal Command would fight its 1943 campaign as the largest anti-submarine air force in the world, with the aircraft, weapons, techniques, training, and tactics to find and kill U-boats with unprecedented effectiveness.

This was fortunate for the Allies, for by February 1943, Admiral Dönitz had also built up his U-boat force to a total of 409 boats, of which about 170 would be at sea in the Atlantic.[43] As these headed out on patrol or returned home afterwards, most of these boats sailed to or from one of the five U-boat bases in the Bay of Biscay. To provide these transiting U-boats with air support, the Luftwaffe's Atlantic Air Command now had about eighty patrol aircraft at air bases similarly stretching from Brest to Bordeaux, comprising about twenty Fw 200 long-range patrol aircraft, about twenty Ar 196 short-range attack floatplanes, and about forty Ju 88C long-range fighters.[44] To oppose this German air-sea concentration in the Bay, Coastal Command's No. 19 Group, concentrated in southwest Britain, now had 244 aircraft with the range to operate over the Bay, organised in sixteen squadrons.[45] The two Australian squadrons went through 1943 as two out of the three Sunderland units operating over these waters, sharing the role first with the RAF's No. 119 Squadron and then with No. 228. Moreover, the Casablanca conference had also specified the need to extend the reach of Coastal Command patrols through the provision of long-range aircraft like Liberators, which could fly patrols out to an 800-mile radius, and so No. 19 Group now obtained three squadrons of these excellent aircraft. [46] There were also now three squadrons of Halifaxes or Fortresses to support the Sunderlands in their long-range patrols to the south-western reaches of the Bay. Thus, whereas 1942 had started with No. 10 as the sole unit of long-range, four-engined patrol aircraft operating over the Bay, a year later there would be nine such squadrons, making a total of 108 four-engined patrol aircraft.[47]

Coastal Command's new commander was Air Marshal John Slessor, who assumed his role very well-informed about the role of his command within Allied war strategy, thanks to having been part of the British delegation at Casablanca, and before that as part of the RAF delegation to Washington. Slessor was an effective officer, who like in his previous command role with No. 5 Bomber Group, learnt rapidly, collaborated with his specialist teams, and led men with considerable inter-personal aplomb.[48] In the course of his earlier command role, he had favourably impressed the officers building the first Australian bomber squadron in Britain, No. 455, and he would similarly prove a success at Coastal Command.[49] Slessor got off to a good start with No. 461, making an early visit to the new unit during its troubled time at Poole, on 13 February. The new commander of Coastal Command retained an interest in No. 461, visiting again on 10 July, in company with Air Chief Marshal E. R. Ludlow-Hewitt, the inspector-general of the RAF. Not only was Slessor good at jollying-up the troops, he was also good at 'upwards management', for compared with the abrasive Joubert, he was a smooth political operator with the ability to influence his superiors, win the confidence of his subordinates, keep people on-side, and charm the Americans. In addition, he was also lucky in his timing, taking over Coastal Command at an auspicious juncture, thanks to the aforementioned accession of new squadrons, as well as the suite of new technological capabilities instituted under Joubert's stewardship.[50]

Night Operations

While these changes were going on at the top, and despite the continued growth in operational capability by No. 461's crews, the junior squadron's proficiency-gap behind No. 10 persisted: up until the 1943 New Year, No. 461 had been, in effect, No. 19 Group's daylight-patrolling Sunderland squadron, with the more experienced and proficient No. 10 as the nocturnal patrol specialists. This started to change in February 1943, when 461 Squadron took its place on the night operational program. These night patrols by Sunderlands were disruptive only, as the flying boats lacked any means of reliably sighting, tracking, and attacking in the darkness any U-boat they detected on radar; nonetheless, the night patrols had a valid, if prosaic purpose, namely to so swamp the Bay transit area with radar transmissions that any U-boat travelling on the surface would detect the transmissions on its Metox receiver, and so submerge to avoid attack. This would oblige the enemy submarines to surface again to recharge their batteries, hopefully during daytime, when they might be exposed to deadly attack. Slower passages through the Bay also meant reduced patrol times out in the Atlantic, and thus reduced U-boat numbers in the convoy battles. It all helped.

While No. 10's Sunderlands were fulfilling this nocturnal scarecrow role, the RAF's nocturnal attack specialists, No. 172 Squadron, were turning night-time into a hunting time, thanks to two items of equipment that transformed the state-of-play at night, both of which had been developed under the aegis of the now-deposed Air Chief Marshal Joubert: firstly, No. 172's Wellingtons were equipped with the new ASV III centimetric radar, which besides being longer-ranged and more accurate, could not be detected by the U-boats' Metox radar-warning receivers; secondly, they introduced the new Leigh Light spotlights, which enabled the Wellingtons to mount a blinding, surprise attack on a surfaced submarine from out of the black night. No. 172 had started operating with Leigh Light Wellingtons back in June 1942, so by Spring 1943 was very well-practised in the new equipment, such that during February–April 1943, No. 19 Group aircraft would make seven effective night-time attacks upon U-boats in the Bay, all by 172 Squadron Wellingtons.[51]

More In-Flight Emergencies

By contrast to the Wellington crews' comparatively action-packed night operations, the Sunderlands' night patrols lacked the stimulation of combat, but things could get very exciting indeed if an aircraft suffered an in-flight emergency. Such happened on the night of 22 February, on only the seventh night patrol by No. 461: Bill Dods took off in K/461 at 3.17 a.m., tasked with searching for a dinghy, but at 5.35 a.m., the fuel pressure on the starboard inner engine started dropping. Given the engine-out performance limitations imposed by the Sunderland's non-feathering propellers, engine failure over the ocean at night was a real emergency. Two minutes later, the misbehaving engine exploded, disassembling itself in violent fashion: the explosion ripped its cowling panels away, and these crashed against the wing in a 'spectacular' display of sparks and smoke. Dods cut the fuel to the damaged engine to strangle the fire, turned back towards England, and proceeded to reduce aircraft weight by jettisoning all depth-charges and 800 gallons of fuel. He ordered the wireless operator to advise base of the emergency, meanwhile wrestling with his crippled machine, which on three engines would fly only an erratic course and would not maintain height. Then he ordered the crew to start throwing out equipment to save weight, and after losing more than 2,500 feet of height, he finally stabilised the aircraft in level flight at only 800 feet. Dods asked the wireless operator to signal base again and request direction-finding fixes, but there was such 'severe jamming' on the frequency that he could not obtain a bearing.

After a nail-biting one-and-a-half-hour transit flight, at 7.08 a.m., the cockpit crew were much relieved to see the rotating beacon of the Eddystone Lighthouse appear ahead—this was only 13 miles south-west of Plymouth. However, the relief was short lived, for one minute after the beacon was sighted, the port inner exploded into 'a sheet of flame and great lumps of white-hot metal'. After the initial engine failure, the remaining three engines had been run continuously at high power settings to maintain height, and this appears to have had a deleterious effect upon the port inner. The ruined engine evidently displaced itself from its mountings, shaking the airframe so violently that the radar stopped working, and juddering the pilots' control panels so severely that Dods and the second pilot, Plt Off. Jack Nicholls, could no longer read the blurred instruments right in front of them. Dods ordered the wireless operator to transit an SOS and put the nose down to alight at once.

With nothing visible in the darkness ahead when looking through the Perspex windscreen panes, Nicholls stuck his head out of the side window 'into the tearing slipstream', yelling to Dods as soon as he discerned the water surface below. Dods then applied the prescribed piloting drill for landing at night: he pulled the power off, pulled back the control wheel to attain the correct landing attitude, and then held that attitude with wings level. With its nose high, the aircraft slowed, gently descended, and made water contact. Dods 'thumped the aircraft down on the open sea and held it there straight and level'.[52] This successful landing in a barely controllable aircraft on the open sea at night was a remarkable achievement. Using his two remaining engines, he started taxiing towards the sheltered waters of Plymouth Sound, but after forty-five minutes had to turn both remaining engines off (presumably they were overheating from all the taxiing). The Sunderland was now left drifting with the tide, but the water was too deep below the keel to drop the anchor. Three launches came out from Plymouth to look for the stranded flying boat, and by 8.50 a.m., one of them had 'K' under tow, so that she was moored to a buoy off Mount Batten at 11.27 a.m. With two engine changes on the job list, the Sunderland was repaired commendably rapidly at RAF Mount Batten, allowing Fred Manger to fly her back to her unit on 1 March.

Improved Maintenance Efficiency

Despite improvement in No. 461 Squadron's operational capability, there was no denying the evidently intractable nature of its maintenance shortfalls while operating from Poole. At the end of January 1943, the squadron had only one aircraft out of nine serviceable, and by the last day of March, not one of its eight aircraft were available for operations. The problem was shown in the divergent sortie outputs of the two Australian Sunderland squadrons: in January, No. 461 produced only eighteen operational patrols, compared to No. 10's forty-five; the pattern was sustained in February, with nineteen patrols compared to forty-nine; and in March, with twenty-eight patrols compared to fifty-four. It would not be until May–June that No. 461 significantly improved its sortie output, when it flew about fifty operational patrols each month, comparable to

No. 10. The situation was exacerbated by Coastal Command's decision to increase the aircraft establishment of its flying boat squadrons from nine to twelve aircraft: with one-third more aircraft to deal with, this was bound to overtax Poole's facilities even more.

Luckily for the careers of No. 461's executive officers, the serviceability problem was not confined to that squadron, but was characteristic of Coastal Command as a whole. Indeed, Air Chief Marshal Joubert's repeated complaints to the Air Staff about his command's inadequate aircraft strength had been countered with the valid observation that, even if he were given the extra aircraft he demanded, his command should make its own contribution by addressing the unsatisfactory rates of daily aircraft availability that were evident within its squadrons. The logic of this was inescapable, so Joubert had turned to Coastal Command's Operational Research Section for a solution. This section's brief was to 'define the problem (reviewing data to inquire what the problem is), attack the problem using various methods, and produce reports with actionable recommendations'. That is exactly what it did in this case: it 'analyzed the inputs required to generate combat power'.[53] From that, it developed a new system of 'Planned Flying and Maintenance' for implementation throughout the command.[54]

In essence, this constituted an adoption by the RAF of established civil airline practice, whereby each aircraft's flying hours were used-up at a planned rate per month. This allowed the aircraft's scheduled 45, 90, 180, and 270-hourly inspections to be pre-planned on the unit's work calendar. With its aircraft thereby rotated offline one by one in predictable fashion, the squadron could organise itself to produce a guaranteed minimum-output of flying hours per month, every month. It did this by counting down the remaining flying hours to each aircraft's next inspection, on a daily basis, thereby metering-out each particular aircraft's allocation to operations.[55] From the perspective of the squadron's Maintenance Flight, the engineering officer could mark on the calendar in advance when each particular aircraft was due to be beached and brought up on to the hard-standing for a scheduled inspection, or booked-into a maintenance unit for deep maintenance. This practice contrasted with air force methods used hitherto, according to which squadrons used up the flying hours on their aircraft on an as-available basis, with the result that aircraft were taken offline for inspections and maintenance whenever they ran out of hours. The result was that half or more of a squadron's aircraft could be offline at one time, as had happened repeatedly to No. 461 from late 1942.

It did not help that some of the rear-area servicing units did not provide as rapid a service as squadrons desired. When Fred Manger's crew dropped off their aircraft, C/461, on 21 October 1942 for a 270-hourly inspection by the flying boat service unit at RAF Wig Bay (near Stranraer on the western coast of Scotland), they found the base to be 'impressive for lousy weather, low morale and inefficiency'. When Manger returned on 6 December with a skeleton crew, ostensibly to bring 'C-Charlie' home, the aircraft was not ready, obliging the men to kick their heels at the base until 3 January. They did not get back to Poole until 6 January. In the enforced protraction of this second sojourn at Wig Bay, Manger's second pilot, Phil Davenport, again found the place 'an inefficient, unhappy station'. Perceiving themselves as 'alien new arrivals', the 461 Squadron men thought they were 'resented' in the base officers' mess and complained that the canteen staff withheld from them the supply of rationed chocolates or cigarettes, and that the bar staff hid away the 'better Scotch whiskey' whenever they wanted to order a drink. While waiting for their aircraft to be made ready, Manger, Davenport, and Kennedy were obliged to 'celebrate' Christmas in this glum mess as exiles from their squadron community, amongst Wig Bay 'die-hards' who 'drank their grog in little groups, looking inward'. Davenport dryly conceded that by 'Hogmanay' (New Year's Eve), 'the locals learnt that at least one of our crew spoke English'.[56] Manger's crew was not alone in hating Wig Bay. After an earlier visit there with Bruce Buls's crew, FS Ed Gallagher agreed with Davenport's assessment: he noted that his crew had to walk 3 miles from their billets to the mess, where 'we get nothing to eat', then another 3 miles to the slipway to check on their aircraft; he evidently accepted a rumour that the station CO was 'the biggest bastard in the world', and that as a result 'two blokes have committed suicide here already'. Although their aircraft was not quite finished, Buls's crew was 'in such a hell of a hurry to get away' from the place that Gallagher claimed to have 'kicked the two so-called wireless mechanics off the kite, told Bullsie to take off', and then himself finished the overhaul of the wireless set after take-off.[57]

 Fred Manger's C/461 had been away from the squadron for two and a half months getting its overhaul. Although this seems a long interval, it was in fact not far outside normal expectations, which ranged from six to ten weeks.[58] During this time, its crew had not flown a single mission, with Manger's skeleton crew instead spending six weeks unproductively waiting for their aircraft.[59] This experience at Wig Bay points to systemic inefficiency in the time-honoured Sunderland squadron norm of each crew 'owning' their allocated aircraft, which meant that when that particular aircraft was 'down', the crew was also 'down'—rather than them simply taking the next available aircraft from the squadron 'pool'. Of course, by October 1942, Manger probably deserved a break from operations, and whether intentionally or not, his aircraft's protracted maintenance inspection certainly delivered this as a by-product of its own inefficiency.

Up to that point, Manger had flown nineteen often-too-eventful operations (as we have seen) over four months, and after this break he would go on to fly another twenty-two before becoming tour-expired in September 1943.

The subject of this protracted refurbishment, C/461, failed to live up to expectations as a supposedly refurbished aircraft once Manger returned her to Poole in January. In fact, after returning from Wig Bay, the aircraft 'was never the same again', and she was again up on the hard-standing all day on 21 March, while Maintenance Flight worked to make her serviceable in time for a scheduled night operation. The work was not finished by nightfall, so the fitters continued to work on one of the engines after the aircraft was returned to the water, while she floated at her mooring. With the job done 'just in time', the aircrew then came out on the tender, went aboard, stowed their equipment, took their stations, conducted their checks, and started engines to slip the mooring and taxi. Visibility was poor with haze and patches of fog, and with no wind and a glassy sea, it was going to be a very long take-off run: a flying boat needed a bit of chop on the surface of the water to help its planing hull 'break the suction' and unstick from the water, as well as a bit of head-wind to shorten its take-off run. Neither of these favourable factors was present on this murky night.

To compensate for the still conditions, Manger taxied right to the far end of the flare-path to maximise the length of his run; in fact, he went so far to the downwind end of the runway that the third and last flare-float was out of sight by the time he turned around for take-off. At 8.25 p.m., he lined up on the other two flares that were still visible. Take-off was always an anxious time, a fact betrayed by Manger's old habit of lighting a cigarette and having a few calming drags in the pilot's seat before opening the throttles—until the crew had remonstrated with him that this was an unacceptable fire hazard in a just-fuelled-up aircraft! Night take-offs were even worse, when the aircraft could drift imperceptibly off the flare-path axis, and when the pilots were unable to see and avoid floating obstacles on the water ahead.

When the duty pilot in the flight control launch flashed the green light, Manger advanced the throttles and peered ahead through the windscreen, keeping the aircraft running straight by reference to the incomplete line of dimly-glimmering flare-pots. As the engines bellowed out their power, the nose rose up, the hull heaved itself up in the water, and then the aircraft sat up, skimming along the surface of the water, planing on its step. But Davenport, in the co-pilot's seat, could see that Manger was having difficulty keeping the aircraft straight and wings-level; by the way the captain was holding the wheel over and pushing on the rudder pedal, it looked as though one of the engines was surging in power and wanting to turn the aircraft off the flare-path.

Davenport's attention had to be focussed upon the air speed indicator, calling the speeds for the pilot at the controls: '90 ... 100 ... 110'. Just after that Davenport felt the aircraft become airborne. He looked up from the ASI just in time to see Manger hurled from his seat. The aircraft slewed violently around, with Davenport glimpsing a 'kaleidoscope of colours' through his open side windows. Then in an instant, 'it was dark: outside and inside'. In the sudden, deafening, engine-less silence he heard 'hissing as hot metal changed seawater into steam'. Soon after, a bright light illuminated the water close around him, allowing Davenport to see that the surface of the sea in front of the cockpit windows was coloured green from a spreading pool of spilled 100-octane. The duty pilot, Plt Off. Jack Nicholls, had arrived in his launch and was shining a bright spotlight upon the sorry scene. As the shocked-but-alive crewmen pulled themselves out of the astrodome hatch atop the half-sunken hull, Nicholls called out, 'You alright, Freddie?' Manger had enough *sang-froid* to reply sardonically, 'Come here, Nichols, you bastard, and get us off this boat!'

The aircraft had crashed on to a sandbar, leaving the tall hull sitting so high out of the water that the top deck remained above the waterline; this enabled the men to avoid drowning in the breached hull and to escape the wreck in the pitch darkness. When Davenport and Manger returned to the scene in daylight, they saw that the port wing was completely gone, torn off at the root. In the subsequent recovery of the wreckage, only three of the four propellers were found, suggesting that the fourth prop (on the port side) had over-sped, and that it had then sheared from its shaft, spun away from its engine, and induced the just-airborne aircraft to make an instantaneous and violent yaw to the left. The imperceptibly over-speeding engine would have caused the yawing to starboard against which Manger had been struggling during the take-off run, and because the failure had occurred in the second or so after 'unstick', Manger had momentarily lost visual reference as he moved his eyes from the flare-path to the blind flying instrument panel; in that interval, the aircraft had rolled and yawed in the opposite direction, too rapidly for Manger to respond. With the aircraft yawing and rolling uncontrollably just after getting airborne, the port wingtip had dug into the water and the sudden deceleration had snapped the port wing off. The aircraft had then cartwheeled, coming to rest on a sandbar only 50 yards from a stone jetty. If it had hit that immovable barrier, things must have gone much worse for the crew.

'C-Charlie' was a write-off, and as was the custom, the crewmen were sent away on 'survivor's leave'.[60] Manger did not fly his next operation until 4 May. Because the crash was diagnosed as due to a runaway propeller, it did no harm to anyone's career: Davenport was promoted to flying officer two days after the crash and flew only one more operation (with Bill Dods) as first pilot before achieving his own captaincy in July, after flying twenty-eight missions as a co-pilot. A month after the accident, Manger was promoted straight from pilot officer to acting flight lieutenant, in recognition of his stature as one of the squadron's most senior and most experienced captains.

No. 461 Relocates to Pembroke Dock

If No. 461 was to pull its weight in the coming decisive campaign against the U-boats, it would need to improve its serviceability rate, and hence sortie output. The solution proved to be twofold: to adopt Coastal Command's new, command-wide planned-maintenance system, and to shift the squadron out of the inefficient Poole base. The changes were made during a period of organisational upheaval caused by Coastal Command's decision to increase the establishment of its flying boat squadrons from nine aircraft to twelve. Considering the RAF's limited inventory of Sunderlands, this could only be achieved by disbanding some squadrons and redistributing their aircraft to the others. No. 119 Squadron at Pembroke Dock was thus disbanded in April 1943, with both Australian squadrons benefitting from its demise: No. 10 obtained three of its aircraft, while 461 Squadron moved into No. 119's vacated base facilities at Pembroke Dock, commencing its relocation from Poole on 21 April, after receiving 'very short notice' of the move. The same applied in reverse to No. 210 Squadron, which had been flying Catalinas out of Pembroke Dock on very-long-range patrols out over the convoy routes; this unit drew the short straw in this reorganisation, forced to swap places with No. 461, and move into Hamworthy.

After three days of organisational upheaval and a laborious road trip, and almost one year after the squadron's formation the previous Anzac Day, on 24 April came 461's first sortie from its new base, when Col Walker took off from Pembroke Dock in N/461. By 1 May, the squadron had completed its translocation from Poole to 'PD', although the newly ensconced Australians would not have the place to themselves, for No. 228 Squadron also moved into the Welsh base later the same month. In the complicated rearrangement of units, No. 210 had swapped places with No. 461, and No. 228 had replaced the disbanded No. 119. Like 10 Squadron, No. 228 was a veteran outfit, having been flying Sunderlands since 1938: it had been part of 15 Group since October 1941, based most recently at RAF Castle Archdale on Lough Erne in Northern Ireland, but was now redeployed to 19 Group to further strengthen the force available for long-range patrols across the Bay of Biscay.

Pembroke Dock had been an active RAF flying boat base since 1931, and although No. 461 had to share the dockyard precinct with No. 228, with the Royal Navy, and with civilian dockyards, it had finally obtained purpose-built flying boat facilities, with conveniently co-located slipway, hard-standing, workshops and hangars.[61] The base was a hive of flying boat activity, with aircraft and crews coming and going, not only those of the two resident Sunderland squadrons; but also from No. 308 Ferry Training Unit; Nos 11 and 12 Flying Boat Fitting Units, which modified aircraft to the latest operational configuration and then flight-tested them; and No. 3 Flying Boat Servicing Unit, which put aircraft through their maintenance inspections and then flight-tested them before returning them to their units. The rolling hills, farmland and villages surrounding the harbour gave the base a pleasing outward aspect, while the town of Pembroke and the ruins of Pembroke castle lay only a few miles inland for the visitation of off-duty personnel. However, having suffered the double catastrophe of pre-war economic dislocation followed by wartime bombing (the German bombers had been attracted by the docks), Sgt Gallagher considered the town surrounding the docks a 'bleak place', 'the end of the earth'. Indeed, having been there previously with 10 Squadron in 1942, he was appalled to be told they were going back, exclaiming, 'Lord preserve us from that!'[62] Indeed, some of the accommodation at Pembroke Dock was positively revolting: one of the ground crew NCOs, Ken Field, was billeted with other newly-arrived squadron men in one of the wards of the bombed-out Naval Hospital, which lay open to the elements at the bombed-out end.[63]

Despite the aesthetic unattractiveness of the town itself, once clear of the busy water traffic around the docks, the 11-mile-long reach of Milford Haven provided a superb waterway for flying boat take-offs and landings. Compared to the cramped obstacle course that was Poole harbour, this generous expanse of sheltered water made 'PD' 'a flying-boat Utopia', 'one of the best areas in the country for flying-boat operations'.[64] Moreover, RAF Pembroke Dock was a base in the full sense of the word, referring not only to the physical location, but also to the provision of deep administrative, logistical, and technical support to its resident squadrons. Standing behind Nos 228 and 461 Squadrons stood a base unit of nearly 1,000 officers and men, including the 300-strong flying boat servicing unit.[65] With all these facilities, once settled into Pembroke Dock, No. 461 showed the improvement in its aircraft availability that was the intended objective of the move, increasing its monthly sortie output by about 60 per cent, to the figure of fifty sorties per month. Thanks to the support of the co-located base unit, to the new system of planning flying and maintenance, and to its own growing organisational maturity, No.

461 would soon show that it was able to shrug off the impact of what could easily have been destabilising losses of aircraft and crews through the summer and autumn of 1943.

No. 461 Comes of Age

No. 461 began the prime U-boat hunting season of 1943 in good shape, having addressed its serviceability problems and having had half a year of substantial crew continuity despite the loss of Buls's crew in January. By now, two of the founding captains had been killed: Buls and Hosband. Another captain who was no longer available on the flight roster was Plt Off. Colin Steley, but for a happier reason: he had finished his tour in March after captaining twenty-eight operations with No. 461, having previously served an operational apprenticeship as second pilot with 10 Squadron.

No. 461 thus commenced the pivotal month of May 1943 with seven surviving captains who had been trained up in the early months of the unit's existence, and who had since grown in operational stature to something comparable to the veterans of No. 10. The promotion to flight lieutenant rank of six of these pilots suggests their senior status within the squadron, as well as the fact that obtaining a captaincy was a good way to speed up the tempo of wartime promotion: Smith had by then led thirty-eight operations as captain, while Dods had thirty-four, Manger thirty-one, Cooke and Walker twenty-seven each, and Marrows twenty-one; besides these newly-minted flight lieutenants, there was also Fg Off. John Weatherlake, who had flown sixteen operations since gaining captaincy status in October 1942.

In addition to the seven experienced captains still flying with the unit in May 1943 (as above), the flight roster was being filled out progressively by newly-qualified captains as each one completed their apprenticeships as co-pilots. For example, Plt Off. Gordon Singleton had joined the squadron as a sergeant pilot, been commissioned, and flown twenty-two operations as second pilot to Col Steley; he then went on to captain his first missions in March 1943. Another two new captains commenced operations in May: Fg Offs Russ Baird and Irwin 'Chic' Clarke. Baird had started with No. 10, been posted to No. 461 in May 1942, flown twenty operations as second pilot to Bruce Buls, then been sent on a four-month captain's course at No. 4 OTU, thereby avoiding being lost with Buls's crew in January. Similarly, Clarke had joined No. 461 in October 1942 and since then had flown twenty operations as second pilot, apprenticed to Bert Smith. The substantial operational experience of these pilots suggests the growth in operational maturity and experience within No. 461, compared to the earlier days.

No. 10's Enviable Maintenance Capability

Despite No. 461's growth in maturity, the veteran No. 10 continued to set the standard. Because it was a unit of the RAAF, rather than part of the RAF like No. 461, the senior Australian unit had not adopted Coastal Command's new 'Planned Flying' system. This was permissible because although its operations were directed by the RAF, its internal procedures were autonomous, directed by the RAAF. Whereas No. 461's aircraft were on charge to the RAF, No. 10's aircraft were 'owned' by the unit itself; whereas No. 461 sent its aircraft away to RAF maintenance units for major inspections and repairs, No. 10 carried out these tasks itself. It helped that No. 10 had long been producing monthly sortie outputs which were the envy of No. 461, thereby accruing considerable credibility in the eyes of the RAF commanders at both 19 Group HQ and Coastal Command HQ. The unit's greater autonomous capability was the result of its being more liberally staffed, with 465 personnel on strength at the beginning of May 1943, rather than No. 461's complement of 324. The RAAF had manned No. 10 on this fuller basis because it was an independent unit a long way from home. This greater level of staffing enabled No. 10 to be a more vertically-integrated organisation, with the internal resources to accomplish repair and overhaul tasks that were beyond RAF-administered squadrons like 461. Unlike No. 10, No. 461's maintenance flight performed only minor inspections and repairs, passing on anything bigger to one of the servicing units run by the RAF's No. 43 (Maintenance) Group.

Organisationally, Coastal Command achieved its targeted 'planned flying' outcomes by downsizing each squadron's organic maintenance flight, the duties of which were now reduced to that of a servicing echelon; this enabled maintenance personnel to be skimmed off from the squadrons and redeployed to the supporting maintenance units—the same men would be working at the same base, but now as members of a base servicing unit rather than the squadron. These supporting units assumed responsibility for overhaul and repair tasks formerly done by squadrons' maintenance flights. Although this restructuring would deliver a gain in efficiency, seen in improved serviceability rates and sortie outputs, a side effect was a diminution in the personnel strength of RAF squadrons like No. 461: after expanding its ground staff component by twenty-nine men in May 1943, achieving in that month a total squadron strength of 379, after the down-sizing, by mid-October the unit's ground staff establishment had been reduced to only 119 personnel. By then there were more aircrew (145) than ground crew in the unit. By contrast, the independently-organised No. 10 retained full staffing, ending the month with a total of 429 personnel.

With this extra in-house resourcing, No. 10's Maintenance Flight prided itself on the rapid turnarounds it achieved for both sub-assembly replacements and aircraft inspections and overhauls. An example was Sunderland 'F', which was damaged in a heavy landing at Pembroke Dock on 17 January 1943, with its port wing-float torn off. On the following day, a squadron maintenance party arrived from Mount Batten, and on the 21st, 'F' was flown back to base, repaired in time to depart on its next patrol on the 22nd. On 3 March, the same aircraft again alighted heavily at Pembroke Dock in gusty conditions, damaging the starboard float and the trailing edge of that wing. A squadron servicing party arrived on the 5th, the aircraft was flown home repaired on the 8th and resumed patrolling on the 10th. No. 10 had the internal resources to make expeditious repairs, without out-sourcing the job to a relatively slow-moving maintenance unit as No. 461 would have to do.

No. 10's more autonomous maintenance system might have looked old-fashioned after the introduction of the modern system of 'Planned Flying and Maintenance' within RAF squadrons like No. 461, but under a succession of vigorous engineering officers it had innovated internal procedures which delivered a similar result. The senior unit gave each newly-arriving aircraft an 'arrival overhaul' to bring it to a standardised squadron specification, allowing all sub-assemblies to be interchangeable between its aircraft. The squadron's Maintenance Flight evolved a 'garage system', whereby aircraft which had become unserviceable would be made serviceable by the replacement of the defective sub-assembly, rather than by subjecting the component to more time-consuming repair *in situ* within the aircraft. No. 10 delivered the guaranteed aircraft availability demanded by Coastal Command without needing to change its maintenance procedures to accord exactly with the command's new system.[66] When No. 19 Group launched its Bay offensive starting in April 1943, both squadrons were configured to reliably deliver the 'constant minimum daily effort' required of them by HQ: No. 10 was committed to providing two patrols per day, while No. 461 was allotted a quota of 1.5 patrols on average. If all squadrons met their minimum requirement, then there would be no gaps in the resultant anti-submarine search program.

Despite 461's progress, No. 10 remained the standard bearer for the RAAF in Britain: its special status as the RAAF's 'own' squadron was reflected in the visit on 24 April by Air Vice-Marshal H. N. Wrigley, the newly-appointed commander of RAAF Overseas HQ. He attended the squadron's Anzac Day ceremony in the base gymnasium at RAF Mount Batten, accompanied by two former squadron COs, Grp Capt. Jim Alexander, who was now the base commander at Mount Batten, and Wg Cdr 'Axle' Richards, who was now senior staff officer at RAAF HQ in

London. Afterwards, all ranks gathered for 'smoko' in the gym, with the visiting VIPs served beer in capacious pewter tankards. There was always more than a hint of an 'old boys' club' amongst 10 Squadron veterans.

After No. 461's move to the new base, it sought to establish its own credentials as a good citizen of the Pembrokeshire community, engaging in the same kind of civic diplomacy as No. 10 had long practised at Plymouth. On 15 May, Sqn Ldr Wood led a party of twenty-seven squadron members for a 'Wings for Victory' parade in Pembroke, in support of popular fund-raising for air armaments. As Wood took the salute in the march-past, Flt Lt Egerton led two Sunderlands overhead in a low flypast. While no doubt appreciated by the local civic leaders, public events in 'end of the earth' Pembrokeshire could not compete with those in Plymouth. No. 10 performed a similar role in that city's Wings for Victory parade on the 29th, and put on an even better show than No. 461 had managed: the adjutant, Flt Lt Col Brigstock (one of the squadron's originals), led a party of seventy-five men in a massed inter-service march-past led by the CO, Wg Cdr Alexander, with Stanley Bruce, the Australian High Commissioner, taking the salute.

New Operational Techniques within Coastal Command

While Coastal Command was undergoing its reorganisation, both Australian Sunderland squadrons had maintained their relentless but monotonous patrol commitments through the winter. This operational drudgery proved as unrewarding as winter operations usually did. However, the new year of 1943 would bring new tactics which would soon change 19 Group's fortunes. Coastal Command's new commander, Air Marshal Slessor, had served as a bomber group commander during a critical period for Bomber Command, when its staff organisation was transitioning to an evidence-based targeting methodology, led by the research and analysis skills of civilian academics. This progress was reflected in the creation of Bomber Command's Operational Research Section in September 1941, and in the command's subsequent and substantive response to adverse operational evidence.[67] After this formative experience in a time of transition, Slessor wasted no time in embracing a similar operational research process within Coastal Command: he ordered the command's own Operational Research Section to undertake a statistical analysis of operations from June 1942 to February 1943.

The ORS's review of the data drove a purposeful reconfiguration of 19 Group's search patterns over the Bay of Biscay through 1943: aircraft searches would now be concentrated in calculated 'probability' areas—

those predicted to have the highest chance of U-boat sightings. A new program of experimental search patterns was initiated, to test whether these projected statistical probabilities could be converted in practice into increased rates of U-boat sightings and sinkings. This started with 'GONDOLA' searches, under which aircraft searched within patrol areas lying athwart the U-boats' east–west transit routes; this program produced only a moderate improvement in results, with nineteen submarine sightings in 312 sorties. In March, 19 Group implemented the second experimental search program, the 'ENCLOSE' patrols, which directed sorties into defined search areas between 7 degrees and 10 degrees 30 minutes west. This delivered better results, with twenty-seven submarine sightings in 182 patrols. This was one sighting per sixty-six patrol hours, which for the first time in the long history of Bay of Biscay air operations was an air search efficiency comparable to that around threatened convoys out in the Atlantic. In April came the third iteration, 'DERANGE', which focussed on the area between 8 degrees and 12 degrees west. This area was so far offshore that aircraft did not even enter the patrol area until they were more than 300 miles off the Biscay coast, from which point Sunderland aircraft patrolled to a corner of the Bay 600 or more miles from Plymouth. The even longer-ranged Liberators were patrolling yet further out on the extreme fringes of the Bay patrol zone, out to an 800-mile radius.[68] These Liberator patrols proved particularly effective, for although 19 Group aircraft made only four effective daylight attacks on U-boats in the Bay area during February–April 1943, all of these were made by Liberators.[69] The further an RAF aircraft could extend its patrol towards the south-western extremities of the Bay, the greater its chances of finding a surfaced U-boat, as the U-boats tended to hug the Spanish coast during their Bay transits, in an attempt to distance themselves from RAF patrols and to mask their radar returns against the high ground beyond; by using this route, they entered the open ocean off Cape Ortegal, at the furthest south-western corner of the Bay.[70] This focal area, 600 miles from Plymouth and beyond, became the location for repeated confrontations between 19 Group aircraft and U-boats.

With the Liberators hogging the trade by day and the Leigh Light Wellingtons hogging it by night, No. 10's Flt Lt George Miedecke was one of the few Australian Sunderland captains to get a sighting of a U-boat during these winter patrols: on 3 February, flying F/10, his crew spotted a submarine, 12 miles away, but despite setting up for a stealthy approach from out of the sun, he saw the boat start to submerge at 2 miles; by the time he went overhead, it had been submerged for fifty seconds. This was outside attack parameters, but for good luck he dropped two depth-charges across its track, but the submarine did not reappear. Sam Wood's crew from No. 461 got their turn on the 15th, having spotted a submarine at 7 miles away: Wood made a tactically-astute, cloud-obscured approach and caught the U-boat on the surface, but a fault in the aircraft's electrical bomb distributor meant that he had to salvo his depth-charges manually, with the result that they overshot the target. The chagrined crew of A/461 was reduced to circling around the submarine, watching it submerge.

Despite 461 Squadron's growth in capability, it had not quite closed the gap behind No. 10, as shown by the continuing role differentiation evident during this period, with No. 10 deployed on extreme range U-boat-hunting patrols to the outer south-western fringes of the bay, while No. 461 was assigned the easier task of patrolling Allied convoys as they trailed across the mouth of the Bay *en route* between Gibraltar and England, as well as on anti-shipping patrols closer in towards shore, looking for German blockade runners, as well as French and Spanish fishing boats operating in support of the transiting U-boats. Such inshore operations were less navigationally challenging than 10 Squadron's extreme range patrols further out to sea, but on the other hand, these shorter-range operations brought the squadron's crews much closer to the German fighters: on 4 February, a Ju 88 got within a couple of miles of Fred Manger's crew before he got his Sunderland into cloud, and on 8 February, Bill Dods's crew was chased by two Ju 88s, which exchanged fire with his rear gunner before the Sunderland made cloud cover.

Colin Walker's crew was lucky to survive a more severe encounter on 13 February: N/461 was more than two hours into an anti-submarine patrol, flying a beat parallel to the French coast, when the Sunderland was suddenly bounced from out of the sun by two Ju 88s. The enemy aircraft were only spotted in the instant they opened fire, and firing from as close as 250 yards, they got hits on the cavernous hull of the Sunderland. Walker made a diving turn into a conveniently placed cloud, but upon re-emerging saw two Fw 190s coming in from head-on, 800 yards off. Walker tried to edge his way out of trouble, going from cloud to cloud, and navigating 'blind' with the help of radar: this could 'paint' the promontories and islands of the French coast on its tiny cathode ray screen. As the ASV II radar could detect high landforms at a maximum range of 75 miles, this shows how dangerously close to the enemy-held coast the Sunderland's patrol line had taken it.[71] This proximity was confirmed by the presence of the short-ranged enemy single-seat fighters. After an hour of laborious but purposeful manoeuvring, Walker found solid cloud, hid in it, and headed home safe at last. He landed at Mount Batten more than two hours later in a badly-damaged aircraft, the hull, wings, and tail unit of which had been perforated by cannon and machine-gun hits. The crew's fitters had spent the return trip plugging the holes below the waterline so that the 'boat would not sink while taxiing to the slipway'. This worked well enough for her to be kept afloat, but only long enough to be towed to the slipway and then hurriedly beached. Walker's crew had been lucky, for despite all the gunfire passing through the hull, only two men had suffered 'slight, superficial' wounds. Moreover, the shots had only come close to the aircraft's vitals without actually hitting them: the port outer propeller was chipped by gunfire, and cannon shells had struck the leading edge of the port wing without hitting the engines. It took a month for RAF Mount Batten to finish the repairs to N/461, allowing Walker to fly her back to her unit on 15 March.

Rising Action in the Bay, Spring 1943

By April 1943, one year after the squadron's formation, No. 461's coming-of-age was shown by 19 Group HQ's readiness to now employ it on long-range 'Enclose' and 'Derange' anti-submarine patrols. This was precisely the same duty upon which No. 10 was deployed. However, because of the organisational disruption caused by No. 461's relocation from Poole to Pembroke Dock in late April 1943, the squadron's operational output that month was only twenty-five patrols—meanwhile No. 10 flew forty-nine. Despite such concentration of effort on Bay patrols, and these within high probability areas, outright success remained elusive during April, with only a single U-boat sunk in Bay of Biscay waters by Coastal Command—and that by a Wellington of 172 Squadron, at night.[1] The limited success was not for want of trying, as shown by the increasing frequency with which Sunderland crews encountered surfaced U-boats during the new program of nocturnal 'Enclose' patrols. Lacking the equipment for effective night attacks, the Sunderland night patrols were in fact 'scarecrow' flights intended to swamp the area with radar transmissions, prompting the U-boats to submerge.

For example, on the night of 5–6 April, Dave Griffiths was flying U/10 on a nocturnal 'Enclose' patrol 500 miles off Bordeaux, when his radar operator reported a radar contact. Griffiths homed upon the radar return and then spotted the submarine's wake against the dark sea below; it was heading for Bordeaux at 10 knots. Griffiths began a gentle descending turn to make an attack, but despite descending to as low as 100 feet, his crew lost visual contact with the submarine during the turn. After that radar contact too was lost—the U-boat lookouts had evidently spotted the aircraft, and the submarine had dived. Griffiths was a well-experienced airman, having flown twenty-five operational patrols since attaining his captaincy in November 1942, and before that having served an apprenticeship as first pilot to Sam Wood. Such experience could not make up for fundamental technological shortcomings, however: losing the target was entirely what would be expected in a radar-homed approach at night using the Sunderland's ASV II, the radar scope of which was swamped by sea returns inside 3–4 miles range; the set was moreover too imprecise in azimuth to permit an accurate radar-guided approach upon a moving target. A successful night-time attack required the more accurate ASV III to track the target down to minimum range, and a Leigh Light to illuminate it—in other words, it required one of 172 Squadron's Wellingtons, not a Sunderland.

The following night, on the evening of 6 April, Fg Off. Geoff Rossiter was flying W/10 on a similar Enclose patrol when his ASV operator obtained a radar contact, 6 miles off the port beam. He turned towards it and five minutes later flew over it at 2,000 feet. Again, the crew succeeded in spotting a surfaced sub, this one heading for St Nazaire at 6 knots, but again lost visual contact in the descending turn to attack; this submarine too disappeared, hidden somewhere nearby in the darkness or already submerged.

Despite being unable to make attacks, most crews were doing exactly what the nocturnal Enclose patrols were intended to do: by flooding the transit area with ASV II radar transmissions, they were triggering the U-boats' Metox receivers and thereby prompting the boats to submerge. Although not decisive in itself, this was useful service, as it slowed the U-boats' passages through the Bay and thereby increased their exposure to air attack—perhaps by a Wellington with up-to-date radar and searchlight equipment. Continuous radar transmissions were so integral to Enclose patrols that when, on the night of the 8th, Fg Off. Norm Gerrard suffered a radar failure in F/10, he aborted the flight at once and headed for base. By now, moreover, it may be that the U-boat crews were starting to turn off their Metox sets, influenced by the mistaken belief that the troublesome Leigh Light Wellingtons were homing on their Metox emissions. This might explain why crews from Nos 10 and 461 made close submarine contacts every night from 5 to 11 April, sometimes several per night. For example, on the same night as Rossiter's contact (as above) on the night of 6–7 April, No. 461's Harry Cooke's aircraft obtained a radar contact, but the submarine disappeared when the Sunderland approached. The following night, something similar happened both to No. 10's Max Mainprize and 461's Dudley Marrows: both got close enough to drop a flare over their target submarine's position, but by then all there was to see was the swirl of disturbed water left by the boat's submergence.

On the night of 10–11 April, No. 10's Fg Off. Keith McKenzie actually managed to get so close to his submarine that he made an attack on it.

Z/10's ASV operator obtained a radar contact at 7 miles off the port beam, at which McKenzie turned towards it and commenced a descent to 500 feet. Pre-centimetric radar sets like ASV II were not particularly precise in azimuth, and despite homing on the radar contact, the Sunderland flew straight past the U-boat: his crew spotted it 250 yards away off the port beam, which gives a rough measure of the radar's inaccuracy in the terminal stage of a radar-directed approach. The boat was motoring on the surface at 15 knots, heading due east for the Biscay ports. With a waxing crescent moon, there was enough visibility beneath the broken cloud at 3,000 feet to see the phosphorescence of the submarine's wake, and to discern the darker form of the low hull against the water. After Z/10's initial miscued approach, the submarine was now too close to attack, so McKenzie had to go around again to give himself enough room to set up for another pass. He turned across its track to come in from the far side, and then lined up to make his attack run across the submarine's starboard quarter from 600 feet. By now, however, the U-boat's lookouts had got wind of the Sunderland's approach and the submarine started to dive. Against the luminescence of the submarine's wake, McKenzie thought he saw the dark shape of the U-boat's hull still breaking the surface as he went over the top and bombed. His six depth-charges exploded 100 yards ahead of the visible wake, after which he orbited overhead, dropped a flame float and tried baiting tactics, but the submarine was gone.

Another Changing of the Guard at No. 10

The 10 Squadron captains who feature in the actions above represent the fourth generation of captains who by now had grown to captaincy status within the senior squadron. These were the men who would lead the squadron's battles against the U-boats in 1943, who would have to carry on the fight without the guidance and example of squadron stalwarts who in this period began to leave the unit upon completing their tours. Besides the transfer to No. 461 of Sam Wood and Des Douglas at the start of 1943, No. 10 lost five captains tour-expired in March–April, including Flt Lts Kerv Beeton, Wyn Thorpe, George Miedecke, and Doug White and Fg Off. Gerald Roberts. The quota set for the crews of long-range patrol aircraft to complete their tours was 800 operational hours, the equivalent of about seventy patrols, or eighteen months on operations.[2] These norms had been more than fulfilled in these cases: for example, Kerv Beeton had flown thirty operations as captain after flying through 1942 as first pilot to Dave Vernon, accruing 1,291 Sunderland hours in the process. About 80 per cent of No. 10's total flying hours were devoted to operational flying, so Beeton must have been comfortably in excess of the 800-hour benchmark.[3] The others were too: Wyn Thorpe had flown only thirteen operations as captain, but he had been flying in co-pilot roles since April 1941, amassing 1,143 hours; Doug White had flown his first operation as a co-pilot back in July 1941, going on to captain twenty-nine operations, and chalking up 1,472 Sunderland hours; Miedecke had similarly flown 1,359 hours on Sunderlands since commencing operations in 1941, and had captained thirty-four operations.

There can be no doubt that the experience accumulated by these men was a loss to the rest of the unit, and particularly to the newer crews. However, it must be emphasised that by the time an airman qualified for tour-expiry, he was profoundly tired and strung-out from the mental and moral 'strain' of flying operations; he needed to be relieved from his duties for everyone's safety, including his own.[4]

Another three veteran 10 Squadron captains departed the unit over June–July 1943, just in time to miss the coming crisis of combat. When an aircrew member finished his tour was an accident of timing, randomly determined by their time of commencement. Sometimes the timing proved to be auspicious, such as when it permitted the member to go off operations in time to miss a spike in losses, like that which was soon to hit the unit in August 1943. An example was Flt Lt Dave Griffiths, who finished his tour in June 1943, having flown through 1942 as a co-pilot, graduated to captain towards the end of that year, and completed another thirty-four ops in command, accruing 944 hours in Sunderlands in the process. Other 10 Squadron stalwarts who luckily became tour-expired before the coming carnage were Flt Lts Geoff Rossiter and Max Mainprize. The latter became tour-expired in July 1943, having flown 979 Sunderland hours in a year-and-a-half-long tour of duty that culminated in thirty-five operations as captain. He was posted out to 'fly a desk' as base commander at RAF Roborough. By contrast, Rossiter flew his last operation in June 1943, but stayed on the unit in a non-operational role as training officer, having flown operations through 1942 in co-pilot roles, finishing his tour after thirty-four operations as captain.

Compared to the extended pilot apprenticeships of the earlier captains, the pathway to captaincy of the latest generation was quite short. Norm Gerrard is an example, having arrived from Australia as recently as August 1942: he flew only five operations as first pilot before commencing his training for captaincy qualification, captaining his first operational flight on 20 March 1943. McKenzie was similar, having joined the squadron from Australia in July 1942, flown a mere two operations as first pilot, and graduated as captain in January 1943. The rapidity of these pilots' transition to command qualifications compared to that of the earlier generations suggests that pilots were now arriving from Australia much more thoroughly trained than in the earlier days. Those earlier cohorts of co-pilots sent out from Australia in 1940–41 had arrived on the unit trained only to 'wings' standard at a Service Flying School, whereas these newer arrivals came trained to a post-graduate standard, having graduated from one of the General Reconnaissance Schools, or from the Sunderland conversion unit, No. 4 OTU.

Increasing U-boat Contacts

After No. 10's monopolisation of earlier opportunities, No. 461 Squadron got into the U-boat action on the night of 11–12 April, when Col Walker in N/461 obtained a radar contact from 8 miles away while on an Enclose patrol. Walker turned in at once, circling around behind the target to put the U-boat 'up-moon': this enabled the Sunderland to make its approach covertly out of the gloom, while the submarine itself was visible ahead, silhouetted by the moonlight behind it. Walker levelled out at 400 feet to make his attack run, but by now could see that the U-boat was diving, with its decks already half awash. By the time the Sunderland arrived overhead, the submarine had been submerged for forty-eight seconds. The Coastal Command norm was thirty seconds maximum time delay, so Walker kept his depth-charges aboard and circled. As in all such cases, the submarine did not reappear.

Fortunately, from mid-April, 19 Group began tasking its Sunderland squadrons with daytime 'Derange' patrols. These were better suited to the aircraft's technological capabilities, and it was in one of these on 14 April that Geoff Rossiter from No. 10 got his next opportunity. Patrolling in W/10, flying at 4,000 feet through a perfectly clear sky, he was 500 miles out to sea from Land's End, in the furthest south-west corner of the Bay patrol area, when at 1.28 p.m. the crew saw a submarine, 12 miles away. Rossiter turned towards it at once and started his descent, approaching from out of the sun. Through their binoculars, the pilots on the flight-deck could see that the boat's decks were awash; it was trimmed to run with only the conning tower above the waterline. Despite Rossiter's down-sun approach, the U-boat's lookouts evidently spotted the incoming aircraft, for the submarine started diving when the Sunderland was still 2½ miles off. It was submerged by the time the flying boat was 1½ miles off, and the pilots' stopwatch showed that it had been submerged for thirty-eight seconds by the time the Sunderland swept overhead. Although this delay was outside of Coastal Command's prescribed parameters, Rossiter dropped his stick of six depth-charges anyway, straddling the submarine's track, with the depth-charges detonating 100 yards ahead of the swirl of its submergence. As usual, he circled overhead, dropped his marine marker, and tried the usual baiting tactics by flying away and then coming back again, but this U-boat too had got away.

Four days later, another Australian Sunderland on a Derange patrol got even closer to scoring a kill. This time it was Plt Off. Ted Farmer, who had the luck to do this while flying his debut operation as captain. He was another one of 10 Squadron's newly-minted captains, having commenced his apprenticeship as co-pilot at the end of September 1942, and then commenced training for captaincy in February 1943. By 8.55 a.m. on 18 April, he was cruising in E/10 in a near cloudless sky at 3,500 feet when his lookouts spotted a submarine on the surface, 8 miles to port. Farmer dived towards it at once, but after levelling out at 500 feet altitude and 1,000 yards range, ran into such heavy AA fire that he turned away to avoid it. This was in accordance with Coastal Command instructions: the recommendation was to wait until the U-boat started submerging, and only then to attack. He had aboard two 250-pound bombs as well as six depth-charges, and in view of the AA threat decided to make a bomb attack first, from a safer altitude. Farmer climbed away and then made a second approach from out of the sun, setting up for a bomb run at 1,600 feet, with his two bombs fused for a 0.025-second delay. This near-instantaneous fusing would hopefully allow them to detonate shallowly enough to damage the submarine's hull, while the 1,600 feet height was the minimum permissible to keep the aircraft safe from bomb splinters. Farmer flew his Sunderland up the wake of the submarine and made a good drop upon the boat despite its going into a hard, evasive turn; the bombs splashed into the water 30 yards off the submarine's stern, but they failed to explode, as had happened in previous 10 Squadron attacks upon submarines using bombs rather than depth-charges.

Farmer prudently climbed to 2,000 feet and circled, still hoping the submarine might submerge, but it did not, and so at 9.22 a.m., he made his third run. He dived upon it from astern, from out of the sun, in order to blind the German gunners. The downside was that U-boats' 20-mm automatic AA guns were mounted on the 'bandstand' gun platforms abaft the conning tower, and so by sailing down-sun, the submarine captain was placing his guns where they could best engage the attacking aircraft. The Sunderland's nose gunner, Sgt Hugh Burbidge, opened fire with his .303 Vickers K-gun at 1,000 yards, to keep the U-boat's flak gunners' heads down. He fired a five-second burst, expending all 100 rounds in the magazine. Awkwardly, this obliged him to change ammunition pans at only 500 yards range, by which time the Sunderland was down to 800 feet altitude.

The U-boat's gunners took advantage of the lull in .303 fire by opening up with their 20-mm guns: two explosive shells struck, one on the nose compartment and one on the starboard wingtip. By this time, Farmer was committed, so pressed on, descending to 100 feet to bomb. The U-boat turned hard a-port, presenting its beam to the on-rushing Sunderland in order to present a narrower bombing target. Farmer held his dive and dropped his stick of six depth-charges across the target, fused to explode at a killing depth of 25 feet. He turned so hard straight after bombing that no one even saw the depth-charges explode; the tail and dorsal gunners were in good positions to observe but must have been disorientated by the steep bank angle and hard turn. By the time Farmer eased the turn, the submarine was still afloat, on an even keel, right in the middle of the patch of disturbed water left by the depth-charge detonations. Farmer continued a wide turn around the U-boat, but by the time the Sunderland was in-bound for a fourth run, the submarine had submerged. The crew reported a 'large brown circular patch thought to be oil' on the surface, but nothing more.

With the U-boat gone, aboard E/10 it was time to take stock. Hugh Burbidge, the nose gunner, had been struck with shrapnel in both legs, while the wireless operator, Sgt Ron Gibbs, had been 'slightly injured above one eye'. The pilots on the flight-deck thought that Burbidge's suppressive fire had 'restricted the enemy gunners' aim and enabled the aircraft to 'escape fairly lightly'. They were probably right, but with holes in her hull, 'E' had to be slipped immediately upon arrival back at Mount Batten, lest she sink. She was towed up on to the hard-standing for repair and made ready to fly her next operation on 1 May. Ironically, it had been Ted Farmer, the greenest captain in the squadron, who had come closer than anybody to killing a U-boat since the autumn of the previous year. Burbidge and Gibbs were admitted to the Royal Navy Hospital at Plymouth, thankfully on the 'not serious' list.[5]

On the very next day, 19 April, another 10 Squadron crew ran into a U-boat. As we have seen, most U-boat contacts were occurring in the Enclose and Derange submarine-hunting patrols further out to sea, but unusually, this contact was made during a patrol over a convoy on passage between Gibraltar and England. This opportunity fell to another one of the squadron's newly-qualified captains, Fg Off. Hec Skinner, who had joined the unit on the same day as Norm Gerrard, in August 1942, and similarly been pushed through to captaincy status after flying only three operations in co-pilot roles before commencing his captaincy training. He had led his first mission as recently as 14 April, and now ran into his first submarine on only his fourth patrol in command. Flying conditions were poor in the late afternoon, with frontal conditions prevailing across the patrol area, and while heading south to meet the convoy, Skinner was flying T/10 through bumpy, hazy air beneath a solid overcast at an altitude of less than 500 feet. The poor visibility was hardly conducive to U-boat hunting, but his gunners suddenly spotted a submarine, only 4 miles away, behind and to starboard. Skinner turned to attack, but the Germans had spotted the Sunderland: the submarine turned away to present its stern to the incoming flying boat, giving its AA gunners the best arc of fire. Skinner held his line, and at 600 yards the nose gunner opened fire, firing away his pan of 100 rounds at the submarine's conning tower. As the Sunderland roared overhead at 70 feet, Skinner dropped a stick of four depth-charges. These straddled the submarine nicely but splashed in without exploding. In the rush to attack, he had forgotten to fuse them. His tail gunner sprayed the conning tower with .303 as the Sunderland pulled away, but the submarine commenced diving, and was submerged forty seconds after the attack. Skinner hung around for six minutes in the hope that it might resurface, but he had his assigned duty to attend to, so resumed his flight to meet the convoy. Skinner had flown a great attack, except for his one, critical mistake.

Farmer's and Skinner's attacks show that the Sunderland crews' task of delivering depth-charge attacks upon U-boats had been unwittingly facilitated by the German commanders' decisions to stay on the surface and fight off the air attacks with AA. In neither case had it worked to the Germans' advantage, and both boats were lucky to escape damage or destruction. Despite the evident ineffectiveness and counter-productivity of the fight-it-out-on-the-surface tactic, Admiral Dönitz would only a week later, on 27 April, issue an instruction to his crews requiring them to fight back on the surface when under air attack, rather than to submerge as formerly.[6] Although Skinner and Farmer had unluckily missed their chances, the new German tactic would give other Australian Sunderland crews exactly the killing opportunity they had been hoping for.

With heavy frontal conditions persisting in the patrol area, flying conditions remained challenging, even dangerous. On the morning of the 23rd, Dave Griffiths was flying a Derange patrol in R/10 when he almost put the aircraft into the water by accident. By 9.20 a.m., the crew had been bumping and jolting about in nauseating fashion for three hours inside 10/10th cloud, without a glimpse of the sea beneath. Suddenly, while still inside the cloud at only 700 feet, the Sunderland was struck by a violent gust. With the airflow over the wing disturbed, the aircraft stalled. It was at dangerously low altitude, Griffiths had no visual references outside the cockpit, and had only the blind flying instruments on the panel in front of him to refer to. With the turbulent sea unseen below, he applied the stall recovery drill: ease the control column forward, regain control effectiveness, roll wings level, and pull back to regain level flight. He did this quickly enough to pull out at 200 feet. Shaken by the close call, Griffiths concluded that the conditions were too dangerous to persist with the operation, so abandoned the patrol and headed home, landing back at Mount Batten after an unusually short seven-hour flight. This close call might suggest one manner in which other crews were lost while out on patrol, in circumstances where no radio signal was made.

As was normal, Griffiths escaped censure for aborting the mission, but 19 Group HQ judged that flying conditions were acceptable after all, continuing to schedule patrols despite the persistently poor frontal conditions over the Bay. Australian Sunderlands thus bumped, shook, and lurched their way through three to four missions per day over the following days. However, as always, the Met officers at HQ continued to monitor the meteorological data, and when the latest weather updates suggested unacceptably dangerous conditions, base would recall its aircraft. For example, Ted Farmer was recalled on 24 April soon after taking off, and had B/10 back on the water less than an hour after getting airborne. Technical failures in the aircraft were doubly alarming in such poor flying conditions, and during a patrol on 28 April, Farmer had trouble with both of U/10's inner engines, neither of which would hold their revs, and so abandoned the mission after three hours in the air. On the following day, Keith McKenzie had the oil pressure on his port outer engine drop to zero after three and a half hours in the air, so abandoned the mission at once and headed home, dumping hundreds of gallons of fuel, jettisoning the depth-charges, and tossing 'heavy gear' overboard to lighten the aircraft and thus maintain height. The extremity of the action taken after the shut-down of a single engine shows how dire the Sunderland's engine-out performance was.

Days of solid cloud and low overcasts persisted until the end of April, but the weather was good enough for crews from both Australian squadrons to combine for an attack upon a U-boat on the 29th. No. 10's Norm Gerrard was first away, in the darkness getting F/10 airborne from Mount Batten at 3.10 a.m., tasked with making an east-to-west sweep along the north coast of Spain. Two hours later, P/461 departed Pembroke Dock in the hands of Fg Off. Raleigh Gipps, tasked with undertaking a Derange anti-submarine patrol further out. Although assigned different patrols, both aircraft were converging on the outer south-western corner of the Bay of Biscay, the area which was bringing much contact between U-boats and aircraft.

Gipps was a trainee captain recently returned from a Sunderland captain's course at 4 OTU, having initially joined No. 10 back in April 1942 and done thirteen trips as co-pilot, before getting posted to No. 461

and becoming apprenticed to Bill Dods. After completed his captain's course, Dods had taken his former co-pilot under his wing to get him up to captaincy status, and now accompanied him on his first operation in command. As a just-qualified captain, Gipps did not yet have his own crew, and because Fred Manger's crew had been temporarily off operations because Manger was ill, Gipps was given this crew to command for his first operation as captain—albeit under supervision.

Given the superstitious hyper-sensitivity that operational crews had about flying with 'unlucky' outsiders, Manger's crew can hardly have been happy to have their lives put in the hands of a sprog captain like Gipps. However, there was some reassurance in the presence of Bill Dods, a squadron stalwart, sitting up beside him in the co-pilot's seat. Dods was on-board ostensibly as 'second pilot', but also as a check captain to observe his trainee.[7] The crew was also accompanied by Air Vice-Marshal George Baker, RAF, the former 'chief of Coastal Command's anti-U-boat campaign', to observe first-hand what Coastal Command crews were experiencing over the Bay.[8] With two supernumerary pilots along for the ride, standing room behind the pilots' seats must have been crowded. Manger's regular first pilot, Phil Davenport, nonetheless found space to stand at the back of the flight-deck alongside the air vice-marshal, finding the forty-eight-year-old senior officer to be 'a thoroughly nice bloke'. Gipps certainly had reason to be nervous with all these extra eyes burning upon the back of his neck, but as things turned out, he proved to be anything but an unlucky charm to Manger's borrowed crew.

Off the Spanish coast, the two Sunderlands passed one another on reciprocal courses as they went about their respective patrols. Gipps was first into contact soon after: at 10.35 a.m., his radar operator reported a contact at 12 miles dead ahead. The Sunderland approached, and at 10.40 a.m., the excited flight-deck party saw a submarine conning tower visible ahead, in the very act of submerging. The Sunderland arrived overhead too late to make an attack, so Gipps dropped a flame float, an aluminium sea-marker and a marine marker to 'mark the spot', orbited for a few minutes, then flew away, applying Coastal Command's standard baiting tactics.

As luck would have it, Gerrard was just then heading for home, about to pass through the same area. His navigator, Fg Off. Corbet Gore, spotted Gipps's smoke float, 6 miles to starboard, and as Gerrard turned the Sunderland to investigate, the pilots used their binoculars to scan the sea surface around the smoke float. Immediately, a periscope wake became visible, and as the Sunderland came closer, the periscope turned into a surfacing submarine. Once again, the Germans had sharp eyes and quick responses, for as quickly as Gerrard could go straight at the surfacing submarine, the U-boat's AA guns were manned and firing before he could bomb. As the Sunderland dived through the tracers, it took hits in the port inner engine cowling and propeller, and in both wings. With the nose gunner spraying his 100 rounds of .303 over the conning tower to put the gunners off their aim, Gerrard dropped his stick of six depth-charges across the submarine's back, from a bombing height of 70 feet. They detonated in a perfect straddle, and as the spray subsided, the crew saw an oil streak in the disturbed water. There was also blue and black smoke coming from the engine compartment aft, but this was evidently exhaust smoke from the diesel engines, as the U-boat remained in fighting trim, motoring briskly through a series of evasive turns and with its AA tracers following the Sunderland around its orbit whenever it strayed too close.

Just then, Gipps's Sunderland reapproached, initially unseen by either the U-boat's or Gerrard's crew, both of whose bridge parties evidently had their binoculars fixated upon each other. It was now thirty-five minutes after Gipps had departed the scene following his first sighting: he was now returning to the area in accordance with the usual 'baiting' routine, in the hope of finding his U-boat resurfaced. For once, it was. Gipps's crowded flight-deck party saw the submarine 5 miles ahead, and two minutes later, Gipps started his attack.

The Germans spotted the second aircraft coming in and refocussed their AA fire upon it, but too late, for the Sunderland went past close overhead without taking a hit, straddling the submarine with a stick of six depth-charges. Aboard Gerrard's aircraft, the flight engineer, Sgt Grattan Horgan, saw the U-boat 'start to sink horizontally': the decks were awash, but the conning tower remained above the surface, floating on an even keel. 'A few seconds later the stern emerged and then disappeared at a very steep angle'. After that came a display of large air bubbles, 'churning the sunlit sea into vivid green and ultramarine, bubbling and boiling, until the disturbance was eighty yards long'. Understandably, and not without empathy, the watching Sunderland crewmen interpreted this to mean that the crippled U-boat crew were 'at the climax of despair, trying to blow the tanks, trying to get back to the surface'.[9] They even reported seeing sailors in the water. On the strength of this, Gipps and his borrowed crew believed they had sunk their U-boat, but as they winged their way home to Pembroke Dock afterwards, Davenport recalls that 'there was no jubilation on board', out of anxiety about getting home safely in deteriorating weather, with 'dwindling fuel reserves'.

Base reported cloud-base down to 300 feet at Pembroke Dock, so diverted both Sunderlands to Poole further south, where the English Channel weather was still clear. However, Gipps was so keen to get back to his own squadron that he attempted to sneak into Pembroke Dock nonetheless, by squeezing in below the cloud base. The crew's regular first pilot, Phil Davenport, looked on with some disquiet from the rear of the flight-deck, considering the minimum height approach to be 'a procedure which has the odds heavily loaded against success'. It is significant, however, that he himself said nothing, unable to challenge the authority even of a sprog, first-trip captain under training; moreover, neither Dods nor the air vice-marshal spoke up either, likewise deferring to Gipps's power-of-command as captain. The flight-decks of RAF aircraft during the Second World War could be very hierarchical places, despite the superficial impression of good-natured camaraderie across the ranks. Davenport's unease heightened as they approached the landing area, when he saw the cloud-base lowering further, and turning into fog. Only now did Gipps abort the approach: he called for full power and pulled up to climb away above the high ground surrounding Milford Haven. It was a close thing, as Davenport recalled: 'full power was barely enough to clear the cliffs. A glimpse of the rock ledge was much too close to our keel as we climbed'. Gipps would have to land at Poole after all. Although it was a desire no doubt shared with the whole crew, his impatience to get home and celebrate with his squadron mates had endangered Bill Dods, Fred Manger's crew, and Air Vice-Marshal Baker. This did not seem to hurt his career prospects as a captain: the air marshal 'was delighted with the trip' and wrote a letter of appreciation to Gipps.[10]

With both Sunderlands moored up in Poole Harbour by late afternoon, the tired crews could compare notes during the debriefing. Afterwards, the officers and the other ranks respectively were able to conduct the '*post-mortem*' more informally and in more convivial fashion around the bars of the messes at RAF Hamworthy. Next day, both crews flew their Sunderlands back to their respective bases, for proper celebrations in their home messes. The 461 Squadron crew was particularly buoyant, having made a 'brilliant attack', as confirmed by their watching 10 Squadron comrades. Gipps modestly put the U-boat down as 'seriously damaged', but squadron officers hoped the staff officers at HQ would credit it to them as No. 461's first 'definite' kill. The Admiralty Assessment Committee would at length duly categorise the submarine as 'known sunk', and thus it would go down in 461's annals. This was a mistake, however; in fact, the boat was *U-119*, a Type XB minelaying submarine, and she was not even damaged, although one of her sailors had been killed by the Sunderland's gunfire.[11] The submarine's steeply diving departure and the protruding stern witnessed by the Sunderland crews was consistent with a precipitate crash-dive manoeuvre, of which we have seen other instances. After escaping the attack, the submarine proceeded on passage to her patrol area off Halifax, where she laid her mines as tasked. *U-119* did not have long to live, however, for on her return voyage only two months later, she was sunk while crossing the Bay of Biscay by HMS *Starling*, with the entire crew of fifty-seven lost.[12]

Despite the failure to sink the submarine, trainee captain Gipps had carried out a 'textbook anti-U-boat patrol', effectively executing the prescribed Coastal Command tactics: he had withheld his depth-charges when the submarine submerged too early for him to make a good attack, marked the spot with buoys, applied 'baiting tactics', returned accurately to the spot, made a rapid attack, bombed accurately, and successfully straddled the target with his depth-charges. Gipps had had the luck to find and 'sink' a U-boat on the one and only occasion he flew with Manger's crew. Dods, too, had had to look on while his pupil made the 'kill', whereas both he and the crew's regular captain, Fred Manger, although founding 461 Squadron pilots who had been captaining operations continuously since July 1942, had neither of them even attacked a submarine before, let alone sunk one. Dods had little time left in which to get his own submarine kill, with only half a dozen trips still to go before becoming tour-expired.[13]

During April 1943, the Sunderland crews had encountered U-boats remarkably frequently, compared to the long, unrewarding operations over the winter months: through January–March 1943, the Australian Sunderland squadrons had flown 213 patrols and seen a U-boat on only three occasions; whereas, in the course of 122 operations in April, they encountered U-boats twelve times and made seven attacks. Things were building up to a crisis, and May 1943 would be the biggest month ever, during which the Australian Sunderlands would obtain twenty-two sightings and make eight attacks.[14] At this time, U-boats were appearing so frequently in the Bay that the Australian aircrews could almost expect to obtain a U-boat contact on most patrols.

Up to now, No. 10 had continued to hog the lion's share of the action: of all the U-boat attacks so far, only one featured a 461 Squadron crew. This one-sided pattern would soon change, however. On 1 May, the two squadrons combined despatched four crews on Derange anti-submarine patrols, and it was a crew from No. 461 that found the passing trade: at 11.36 a.m., Bert Smith was flying M/461 underneath cloud base at 3,000 feet when the crew spotted a U-boat, 6 miles away off the starboard bow. The latest tactical recommendation from Coastal Command was that 'the pilot should go straight for his objective from whatever direction presented itself and waste no time jockeying for position'.[15] This was because previous attacking opportunities had been lost through the U-boat submerging while the attacking aircraft manoeuvred for advantage (examples of which we have seen). Smith applied the lesson by heading straight in to attack, but despite his alacrity, the U-boat submerged before he reached its position. He dropped a stick of four depth-charges ahead of the swirl of its submergence, but without any visible result. The boat he had attacked was *U-415*, which had been damaged the previous night by a Leigh Light Wellington from 172 Squadron, and evidently sustained further damage from Smith's attack.[16] Later that afternoon she was caught on the surface a third time, this time by a 612 Squadron Whitley. However, *U-415* led a charmed life (for now), making it home to Brest on 5 May.

The momentum was sustained next day, 2 May, when out of four Australian Sunderlands despatched on Derange patrols over the Bay, two found and attacked U-boats. The first was No. 10's newly-promoted Flt Lt Dave Griffiths, who by 8.08 a.m. was 260 miles south-west of the Scillies, cruising in R/10 just underneath cloud-base at 2,500 feet. The first pilot, Fg Off. John McCulloch, was taking a spell away from the controls, standing on the flight-deck behind the two pilots' seats, when he spotted a submarine, 7 miles away off the port bow. Griffiths pulled up into the cloud, turned to get up-sun, and then broke cloud 3 miles from the U-boat to begin his attack dive from its starboard quarter. The submarine, remaining on the surface, was completely surprised by the attack, for the Sunderland arrived overhead without having to endure AA fire. Griffiths's nose gunner started firing his tracers at the U-boat's conning tower from 800 yards out, and none of the Sunderland's crew saw anyone on the upper decks as they passed overhead. However, after all this, Griffiths failed to bomb accurately: he dropped his stick of four depth-charges from 150 feet, and they overshot by 100 yards, exploding uselessly beyond the target.

Griffiths's squadron superiors afterwards critiqued his attack on the basis that he had manoeuvred too long getting up-sun, and that this had resulted in the inaccurate depth-charge salvo: it seems that in his keenness to avoid detection by the U-boat lookouts by remaining within cloud cover for as long as possible, he had commenced his attack dive from too close to the target, and as a result had been unable to lose that last bit of height—attacking from 50 feet was the prescribed norm, not 150. The Admiralty assessment of the attack agreed, concluding that 'the DCs were released from too high'.[17] Having missed with his salvo, Griffiths pulled his aircraft into a steep climbing turn to set up for a second attack, while the tail gunner, Sgt Bill Gleeson, enthusiastically sprayed 1,600 rounds from his four .303 Brownings at the submarine's conning tower. However, the U-boat was already diving, and was fully submerged by the time the Sunderland had doubled back to reattack, leaving Griffiths to release his second stick of four depth-charges ahead of the swirl it left on the surface. The U-boat gave no sign of destruction, nor did she reappear to be reattacked, despite the Sunderland orbiting the area for twelve minutes, and then returning two hours later.

It was Bert Smith from 461 Squadron who got the next chance that same afternoon, while patrolling along the northern coastline of Spain. Again flying M-Mabel, his crew spotted a submarine, 10 miles off, at which Smith immediately manoeuvred into cloud to draw closer without betraying his approach, as Griffiths had done. Dropping out of the cloud at 4 miles range, he dived straight at his target, but this U-boat's lookouts spotted the incoming Sunderland: at 1-mile range, the flying boat was greeted by the sudden black smoke puffs of exploding flak shells. Sgt MacDonald, the British nose gunner, returned fire with his single .303-inch Vickers gun to put the submarine's gunners off their aim, and then Smith roared close overhead to drop a stick of four depth-charges. These exploded close in a good straddle, and as the Sunderland swung around in a turn, Smith's tail and dorsal gunners saw brown vapour streaming out of the submarine, a gout of whitish vapour from its port quarter, and a heavy slick of oil flowing from the same side of the hull. The U-boat went around in a circle, and then stopped with a heavy list to port.

As Smith came back in for his second run, the U-boat was down by the stern, with German crewmen emerging from the conning tower, but failing to operate their AA guns. It seemed they were abandoning ship, to escape the fire and fumes down below. Smith's second salvo achieved as good a straddle as the first, and then as the Sunderland came back around in another turn, Smith's crew saw the U-boat start to sink, sliding away stern first at a steep angle. One of the wireless operators, Sgt John Barrow, was supernumerary, and without a battle station to man was able to watch the action from out of a porthole. He remembered the shocking suddenness with which the submarine disappeared: 'I wondered if we had done enough to sink it, when one end went up in the air and then the whole thing vanished'.[18] As the U-boat's conning tower disappeared, men were seen jumping for their lives into the water. All that remained was 'a great bubbling pool of oil, air, wreckage and survivors'.[19] As the Sunderland circled around the dire scene, the crew counted at least fifteen men in the water. The boat was *U-465*. Sadly, none of the men in the water were rescued; all forty-eight crewmen were lost.[20]

Bert Smith had scored No. 461's first U-boat sinking, the first of the squadron's submarine kills. Although no one knew it at the time, it was only the second submarine actually sunk by either Australian squadron, putting No. 461 on par with the more-fancied No. 10. This outcome went much against the run of play so far, No. 10 having hogged the lion's share of the previous U-boat sightings and U-boat attacks. Smith's efficient kill shows that senior 461 Squadron captains like himself now possessed a similar level of operational proficiency to captains from No. 10. This successful sinking also symbolises No. 461's coming of age after its long adolescence, finally emerging from No. 10's shadow.

The rate at which U-boats were now being detected and attacked in the Bay of Biscay meant that Coastal Command's 19 Group was getting tantalisingly close to its goal of turning the Bay submarine transit area into a no-go zone for Dönitz's U-boat force, and so setting the seal on the Allies' victory in the Battle of the Atlantic. By now, Coastal command's air blockade of the U-boat bases along the French coast was so tightly drawn that the Biscay approaches to those harbours had become 'a most hazardous area' for U-boats.[21]

With May 1943 building to be the climax of the campaign, at Plymouth HQ, Air Marshal Bromet had the task of extracting sustained, high-intensity sortie rates from all his squadrons in order to apply maximum pressure on the enemy. The increased operational tempo exacted by 19 Group's Bay offensive from May 1943 was reflected in the lift in the Australian squadrons' sortie rates: both squadrons now stepped up their operational intensity to three and two sorties per day respectively. The effort of achieving this rate of output is evident from a consideration of both squadrons' aircraft utilisation during May: in the course of that month, each of the Sunderland aircraft within the Australian squadrons flew on average one operational patrol every five days, and because each crew was usually tied to its 'own' aircraft, this tempo typically applied to the aircrew as well. However, this overall average is misleading, for during May, out of the eleven aircraft on No. 10's charge, four were offline at any one time on scheduled maintenance, leaving the remaining seven aircraft, along with the crews who 'owned' them, to fly an average of one operational patrol every third or fourth day. In broad terms, this was a three-day work cycle for each aircraft/crew combination: one day to make the aircraft flight-ready, including bombing up and fuelling up; one day to brief the crew, fly the operation, and debrief; followed by a day of cleaning up and fault rectification by Maintenance Flight—and some rest for the aircrew. Then the cycle resumed. At times, individual Sunderlands were worked harder than this if their state of serviceability allowed, in which case they might even fly operations on consecutive days, or at least every second day. From the crews' perspective, flying a twelve-hour patrol every third day was just about sustainable, but flying back-to-back operations could only be essayed once, before the urgent need for crew rest interposed itself.

Coastal Command's recently introduced Planned Flying and Maintenance system was designed to deliver just the sort of sustained flying output that the emerging crisis called for, and it is no coincidence that after No. 461's move to Pembroke Dock and the reconfiguration of its maintenance procedures, the squadron was by May 1943 finally showing greatly improved sortie outputs: in that month, the squadron delivered fifty operational sorties, the rate it would sustain throughout the rest of the year. No. 461 had undoubtedly improved its efficiency just in time for the sustained maximum effort of May 1943.

To fulfil a maximum effort push by 19 Group, on 3 May, the day after Smith's U-boat kill, the two Australian squadrons despatched three patrols each over the Bay. One of No. 461's brand new captains, Fg Off. Russ Baird, was lucky enough to see not one but two U-boats on his very first operation in command. He was flying S/461 on a Derange patrol out along the western fringes of the Bay, flying underneath a layer of low cloud at 2,000 feet, when at 9.22 a.m. two submarines appeared ahead. They saw him coming and submerged, so he dropped sea markers and commenced baiting tactics, flying away from the scene and then returning an hour later. This time, the tactic worked, for upon returning to the area to resume the search, the two submarines were again sighted, running on the surface. They submerged again, but Baird arrived overhead the nearest one only twenty-two seconds after its submergence. This interval was within attack parameters, so he dropped a stick of four depth-charges ahead of the swirl. With no sign of damage evident in the water, he now initiated baiting tactics for a second time. S/461 received a message from base instructing her to head for home, but Baird signalled that he was 'unable to carry out orders'.

In his zeal to pursue his U-boat contacts, Baird had already ignored an earlier signal from base ordering him to abandon the patrol. Within RAF culture, 'keenness to attack the enemy' was a good excuse for 'turning a blind eye', and Baird remained in the area for more than an hour in hope of the U-boats reappearing; indeed, he stayed so long that a Ju 88 appeared, probably homed to the area of the U-boats' transmission of an enemy contact report. When it came in to attack, Baird pulled up to climb into cloud, and reached it in time to give the German pilot opportunity for only a single burst from the extreme range of 1,000 yards. By now Baird had cut into his aircraft's fuel reserves as far as he could, so he headed for home, and landed back at Pembroke Dock at the end of a twelve and a half-hour flight. That same afternoon, while *en route* to meet a convoy steaming off the western coast of Spain, No. 10's Ted Farmer also spotted a submarine, but it had been submerged for thirty-five seconds by the time he reached its position. He dropped one depth-charge along its track just for moral effect but was then obliged to proceed with his mission and search for his convoy.

On the following days, No. 19 Group's offensive against U-boat transits of the Bay was hindered by frontal conditions that passed across the operational area, bringing low cloud, haze, and rain showers, as well as rough seas whipped up by 25-knot winds. The winds became so severe by 6 May that base ordered Farmer to abandon his patrol while still outbound, only 260 miles past the Scilly Islands. On the 7th, Keith McKenzie, also from No. 10, was similarly ordered to cut short his Derange patrol due to worsening weather. These were hardly ideal conditions under which to maintain visual searches for small, low-lying objects like submarines. Despite this, crews still managed to produce U-boat sightings during these bad weather days: for example, on 5 May, No. 10's Plt Off. Gordon Strath was flying a Derange patrol in S/10 when he made his first sighting of a U-boat—but it submerged at once. Despite his lowly rank, Strath was an experienced pilot, having only just been commissioned after flying his previous eighteen patrols as a sergeant pilot; before getting commissioned, he was an aberration, the only sergeant pilot in the officer-dominated 10 Squadron.

Coastal Command lookouts used a visual search technique, scanning from left to right or *vice versa* across an allocated search arc, for example, the starboard bow or the port quarter. Within their allocated arc, the men examined the span of sea below the horizon, to a depth of three or four fingers on an outstretched hand, looking within each segment to decide whether or not there was something there, before moving their gaze to the next segment of search arc.[22] Usually there was nothing, making lookout duty into attention-sapping, monotonous drudgery. Flt Lt Ivan Southall, a captain with No. 461 in 1944, admitted that he resorted to self-medication with stimulants to resist the monotony and keep awake. With or without chemical help, the endless looking at sea and waves could be hallucinogenic in effect: the same squadron's WO William Darcey recalled seeing 'little men riding bicycles' and 'tram cars' travelling over the tops of the waves.[23] With the crewmen rotated through a sequence of duties to keep them as fresh as possible in each role, the pressure was hopefully relieved by rejuvenating tea breaks in the galley, or even occasional kips on the rest-bunk. Off-duty crewmen could wake themselves up a bit by doing the rounds of the watch positions, distributing hot, sweet coffee, cocoa, or tea to the isolated turret gunners.

The captain was responsible for rotating the crewmen through their duties in such a manner as to foster alert lookout. Such rostering required substantial multi-skilling within the crew roles, such that the fitters, riggers, and wireless operators took turns at the lookout positions in the three gun-turrets. Out over the Bay, in all weathers, it was a battle between crews, U-boat or aircraft, for who sees whom first: by September 1943, Coastal Command knew that in two out of three cases, on average, it was the U-boat lookouts who saw the aircraft first, enabling their submarine to submerge before it could be attacked.

Despite the head-sagging drudgery for the lookouts, crew routines like these seem to have enabled the watch-keepers to maintain a good degree of

alertness, judging by results. For example, on the morning of 7 May when
10 Squadron's Flt Lt Geoff Rossiter was flying a Derange patrol in W/10,
out over the Atlantic 400 miles west of St Nazaire, his lookouts spotted a
submarine wake 10 miles off the starboard beam. Upon investigating the
contact through binoculars, the flight-deck crew ascertained that it was
a submarine running trimmed with only its conning tower above water,
heading west into the Atlantic at 6 knots. Rossiter headed towards it, but
the U-boat submerged when the Sunderland was still 6 miles off. Rossiter
headed away to carry out baiting tactics, but upon returning to the area
found nothing, so resumed his Derange patrol pattern. At 12.20 p.m.,
nearly two hours after the previous sighting, and right in the middle of
his allocated search area, he was cruising underneath cloud-base at 2,000
feet when his first pilot, Fg Off. Merv Jones, spotted another submarine,
17 miles off the Sunderland's starboard bow. Jones was known on the
crew as 'Hawk-eye', evidently for good reason. This submarine was
homeward bound, sailing east. Rossiter pulled up into cloud to hide his
approach, then descended into the clear when 4 miles out to make his
attack. The U-boat seems to have seen the incoming aircraft, for instead of
submerging, it turned to the right, presenting its starboard quarter to the
Sunderland, seemingly intent on fighting off the attack with its guns.

Rossiter's nose gunner performed his role well, opening fire at the
submarine's conning tower from 800 yards range and firing off his pan of
100 rounds. Unexpectedly, the submarine's AA guns were still unmanned
or unready when the nose gunner opened fire, for Rossiter reported 'no
return fire whatever'.[24] As the Sunderland swept over the U-boat at 100
feet to bomb, two men were visible, standing in the submarine's conning
tower. The undisturbed run-in enabled Rossiter to aim and bomb under
ideal conditions, laying a stick of four depth-charges across the submarine's
forward hull in a perfect straddle. Two watery explosions rose up to each
side of the U-boat, the closest ones only 50 feet away from the hull. The
Sunderland banked around tightly to set up for a second run, giving the
tail gunner, Sgt Mick Mattner, a chance to spray 600 rounds of .303 at the
submarine's conning tower as he went. After the tight turn, Rossiter rolled
out to make his second attack run from the submarine's port quarter.
The U-boat's AA gunners appear to have been effectively suppressed by
the Sunderland's strafing fire, for the flying boat again arrived overhead
unscathed to deliver another salvo of four depth-charges. In another
perfect straddle, one exploded only 20 feet from the submarine's port
side—within killing distance of its hull.

As the Sunderland zoomed away into a wide turn, Mattner fired another
600 rounds at the U-boat as it turned in tight circles beneath, evidently
severely damaged, losing speed and trailing a slick of diesel oil. Then it

came to a stop, lying dead in the water with its rear deck awash; settling deeper into the water, it then slowly slipped beneath the waves, stern first, at 1 p.m. Once the submarine had sunk away, Rossiter continued to orbit overhead, watching the resultant oil slick grow into a dirty, crescent-shaped patch 250 yards across. Six weeks later, the squadron duly received advice from HQ confirming that the U-boat was 'known sunk', based on the interception and decoding of German wireless transmissions. The boat was *U-663*, and although severely damaged by Rossiter's depth-charges, she had in fact survived the attack, for she was somehow able to surface again and send a signal to base three days later.[25] However, she had evidently been so severely damaged that she did subsequently sink, lost with all forty-nine hands before she could make port.[26] This was 10 Squadron's second actual U-boat kill, after a frustrating series of close-but-not-close-enough attacks through 1942.

More mid-Ocean Dinghy Rescues

The evidently deadly result must have been gratifying to Rossiter and his crew, as it was their fourth attack on a submarine over almost a year of operations. The crew was not given the chance to dwell upon the achievement, however, flying nine operations in the course of the month at the punishing tempo of one every three days. On a Derange patrol on 17 May, Rossiter made three separate submarine sightings, but in each case, the U-boat submerged before he could reach it. Two days later, Rossiter was flying S/10 on another Derange patrol. He had earlier attempted to take-off in his regular aircraft, W/10, but had swung off the flare-path during the night take-off, bashed the port float against a flare-boat, damaged his aircraft and abandoned the attempt. This had necessitated a change of aircraft and hence a delayed take-off.[27] By the time he took-off again in aircraft 'S', base advised of an amended search area a few degrees further west than that originally briefed. Having reached the new area, further out to sea, the crew spotted a sea marker at 10.30 a.m. During the visual search for the U-boat, one of the off-duty crewmen in the galley spotted a dinghy, 8 miles away from the marker.

Rossiter made a low pass over the dinghy, ascertaining that there were two live occupants, but that one of them was in a bad way. The Sunderland's first pilot, Merv Jones, recalled that the flight-deck crew 'could see that one chap was very badly injured. The other chap was frantically waving for us to land'. They were 300 miles out to sea from enemy-held Brest. A debate ensued among the officers on the flight-deck: Jones recalled that they 'weighed the question of landing and picking the poor devils up'.[28] With 'a fair sea running with about an eight-foot swell', they rightfully felt 'very cautious' about making a sea landing, knowing that the Sunderland's bottom plating was not built to withstand a hard arrival on open water. Nonetheless, Rossiter dictated a message for his wireless operator to transmit, advising base of the location of the dinghy, and requesting permission to alight on the sea to make a rescue. He also contacted a nearby Whitley on voice radio, advising that he was going to land.

Rossiter then made a low pass over the dinghy to drop a Thornaby bag: this was Coastal Command's standard survival pack, consisting of watertight tins of food, water, cigarettes, and first-aid equipment, packed into a parachute bag with buoyant kapok pads.[29] The bag splashed into the water 50 yards from the dinghy, and it was a good sign when the healthy survivor paddled the dinghy over to it and recovered the bag. Soon after 1 p.m., the Whitley had to depart for home because of fuel, leaving Rossiter to orbit around the dinghy for two and a half hours awaiting permission from base to alight. After a lot of 'messing about' by wireless, the crew finally received a signal from base approving the sea landing. With no further official impediment, Jones recalled that 'the skipper asked everyone if they were game'. Although Jones reported that 'Everyone seemed keen enough', it must have been some very apprehensive crewmen who took up their crash positions behind the wing spar on the upper deck. According to the crew's new second pilot, Plt Off. John Roberts, they consented to the landing 'because Geoff was such an excellent pilot and because it was one of the few days of the year when the swell was light enough to make it possible'.[30] Rossiter advised base of the dinghy's latest position and of his intention to land. At 2.42 p.m., he made a 'beautiful landing' on the sea 2 miles from the dinghy, then taxied over to pick up the two survivors.

Despite Roberts's impression of favourable sea conditions, once they were on the water, the swell was so 'marked' that the Sunderland 'shuddered a lot' as it taxied over each wave and down into the next trough, such that the dinghy kept disappearing from view and then reappearing, as both craft rose and fell on the swell. As the Sunderland taxied closer, Jones went aft to the entry hatch on the starboard side of the hull; his job was to hook the dinghy with a gaff, but as the Sunderland came alongside, he could not gain a secure purchase on the bobbing craft. Rossiter had to make three passes before Jones could obtain a positive hold upon the slippery dinghy, only achieving this by cutting the engines on the final attempt. Jones and the others manhandled the two survivors out of the pneumatic craft and through the rear hatch. They proved to be crewmen from a 224 Squadron Liberator, Plt Off. G. B. Willerton, the captain, and Plt Off. R. G. Barnam, one of the air gunners, whose aircraft had been shot down by

Ju 88s six days earlier.[31] By now, Barnam was in a bad way: Jones found him 'badly wounded in several places', and 'just about done'. After almost a week of exposure to the elements, it was hardly surprising that even the unwounded Willerton was found to be 'very weak and badly burnt'.[32]

With the survivors aboard, there was nothing for it but to take-off again, but the crew knew that this would be harder than the landing. Jones felt scared by the impending take-off as he went about the well-practised routine of starting each of the engines for the captain. Once everyone had assumed their crash positions to the rear of the flight-deck, Rossiter lined up the aircraft along the swell.[33] He had thereby accepted a crosswind take-off, which was hardly ideal, but it was meant to minimise wave impacts on the fragile hull bottom during the take-off run. However, once he opened the throttles and got the take-off run underway, the aircraft weathercocked into the wind and off the line of the swell, involuntarily running down into the trough and then up over each swell as it accelerated for airspeed. Rossiter was now committed to exactly the sort of take-off run he had tried to avoid: Jones recalled that the Sunderland 'reared up and bounced from the top of one swell to the other at an alarmingly low speed'. After a long, bucketing take-off run, she bounced like this across the tops of three or four swells before staggering into the air and shrugging herself free of the waves so close below. After almost an hour on the water, Rossiter had got his aircraft airborne again at nearly 3.30 p.m. His wireless operator reported the rescue to base, requesting 'urgent medical attention' for Barnam once he landed.

Despite Rossiter's alacrity in making the rescue and getting him to shore, Barnam died that evening in Plymouth hospital, leaving Willerton as the sole survivor of his nine-man crew.[34] However, in a pleasing sequel to the rescue, when Jones was flying for the British airline BOAC after the war, he ran into Willerton, another BOAC pilot, during an overnight stop in Cairo. Upon mentioning their wartime flying, and upon recognising Jones's Australian accent, Willerton asked him if he had flown with 10 Squadron, and if he had rescued 'two RAF bods from the Bay'. He had.[35]

Rossiter and his crew had made great exertions through May, having flown twenty operations in two months, so they were sent off on a well-deserved leave on 2 June, stopping only to visit Coastal Command HQ to debrief their experiences with their senior commanders and staff officers. Rossiter was now tour-expired, so would fly no more operations; but he stayed on as an instructor pilot, acting as assistant training officer to Ron Gillies.

Despite the happy ending to Rossiter's sea rescue for Willerton, the fate of the other members of Willerton's crew attests that not every story ended as well. For example, on 9 May, ten days before Rossiter's successful rescue, No. 10's Fg Off. Ted Farmer was on a Derange patrol when he encountered another dinghy with two live occupants. The dinghy appeared not to have been in the water for long, as close nearby lay a large oil slick on the surface of the water, with floating wreckage within, including an aircraft wheel. It was 2.55 p.m., and these two survivors were 400 miles out in the Atlantic, south-west from Land's End. Making a low pass overhead to ascertain the situation, Farmer considered that 'The men appeared to be in good spirits, as they both waved'. Unfortunately, the weather was worsening due to the passage through the area of another frontal system, and the sea was too rough to land, so Farmer lined up for another pass, this time dropping a Thornaby Bag. It splashed into the water 100 feet upwind, which meant that the dinghy would be blown downwind away from it, so the two men made no attempt to paddle towards the floating survival pack. Thwarted, Farmer's crew made up an improvised survival kit from the rations and stores in the aircraft, secured these in a bag, lashed it closed with a rope, and made a third low pass. This bag fell closer, and the crew saw the marooned airmen grab the rope and haul the bag aboard the dinghy. Farmer made a fourth pass, marking the spot with a marine marker, then climbed and circled, transmitting the dinghy's position to base and making homing transmissions for other aircraft.

By 3.40 p.m., Farmer too had to leave, prompted by his own aircraft's fuel state: he dropped a fresh marine marker, waggled his wings in farewell at the two airmen, and disappeared into the hazy air beneath cloud-base. Gordon Strath was also on patrol, receiving Farmer's position report, but despite flying a search pattern in the indicated location, did not spot the dinghy in the deteriorating conditions. The men in the dinghy, evidently survivors from Halifax N/58, which was shot down that day, had the bad luck to go into the water in a period of deteriorating weather.[36] In fact, conditions got so bad that Norm Gerrard, flying No. 10's third sortie that day, was recalled by base while outbound to his assigned patrol area; the weather was worse still the next day, such that all flying was scrubbed. Flying was resumed on the 11th, when 19 Group's air-sea rescue operations room despatched Farmer on a creeping line ahead search to look for the dinghy he had found, but it was now two days after his original sighting, and despite searching the area for more than five hours, he had no joy. The two men in the dinghy had disappeared, so that all eight crew members of the Halifax were lost.[37]

On 28 May, crews from both No. 10 and No. 461 became involved in what turned out to be a particularly complex rescue operation. That day, the two Australian squadrons each despatched two crews on Derange patrols along the western fringes of the Bay, and in mid-afternoon, Bill Dods's crew in O/461 received a signal from base to search for a dinghy containing six survivors of a Whitley crew from 10 OTU (No. 10 OTU was a bomber training unit that had been seconded from Bomber Command to reinforce Coastal Command's No. 19 Group in February 1943).[38] This was Plt Off. W. Hugh's aircraft, which had sent an SOS and gone into the water the previous day, evidently after the usual engine failure. Dods located the dinghy in a position about 250 miles south-west of the Scilly Isles, circling overhead and transmitting a position report, which was picked up by Max Mainprize in T/10, who was by then heading out of his patrol area, homeward-bound after completing his task. Mainprize conducted a search in the reported location, finding neither the dinghy nor O/461 before his fuel state dictated a resumption of his homeward course.

By 4.30 p.m., Dods was orbiting around the Whitley crew in the dinghy, sending a signal to base, 'over dinghy, may I land?' He reported the sea as 'calm', so base gave guarded permission for Dods to land at his own discretion. At 5.33 p.m., Dods made his approach to alight, lining the Sunderland up into wind, but across the swell, which meant a landing direction perpendicular to the line of the swell, so that the hull would strike each wavetop in succession. The trouble with open water landings was that the wind and the swell never lined up, presenting flying boat captains trying to alight with Hobson's choice: land along the line of swell, but in a crosswind, or into the wind and accept the hull slamming against the wavetops. Dods entered his final approach, descending gently towards the water with power on, and then easing back the control column to contact the water as slowly as possible for minimal structural impact. Unfortunately, he touched down too soon, while the wing still retained flying speed, for when the bottom of the hull struck the top of the first wave, the hard water contact bounced it back into the air. Dods struggled at the controls, trying to stabilise the aircraft to persist with the landing attempt, but the aircraft was faster than him, hitting the next wave top too and bouncing again. By now, the Sunderland was departing from controlled flight, subject to every pilot's nightmare, pilot-induced oscillations. Dods's control inputs could not get ahead of the aircraft in time to arrest its uncommanded pitching, and the Sunderland bounced again as it struck a third wavetop. Now the aircraft's airspeed finally bled away, stalling the wing.

As the nose pitched steeply down, Dods was left with no height to recover the aircraft to normal flight. The Sunderland flew into the sea, in what was afterwards reported to have been an almost vertical dive. The front section of the hull, from the cockpit forward, was torn away in the violent oblique impact with the water, carrying both pilots away with it. The other crewmen were momentarily submerged in their crash positions aft of the wing spar, but the half-severed wreck 'surged back to the surface' in the seconds after initial impact, shedding 'tons of water' as it heaved itself back up to float for a short time on the surface. In their crash positions on the top deck, the men were shocked and wet, but they were breathing air, granted only seconds in which to regain their wits and to get moving, for the sea at once rushed into the hull 'like a flood'.[39] The wreck floated long enough for the stunned men to get themselves up, keep their heads out of the rising water, and exit through the severed fuselage. Dods was never seen again, considered to have been killed 'instantly'; while the first pilot, Raleigh Gipps, the hero of the squadron's first claimed U-boat sinking a month earlier, bobbed up in the water beside the wreck, in agony from his serious injuries 'inside and out'.

The J-type dinghy in the starboard wing had released itself automatically upon water impact, as it was designed to do, but the other two dinghies were damaged and useless. Each dinghy was designed to take a seven-man bomber crew, albeit in some discomfort, so this one was certainly overcrowded by the time ten men got in. Both pilots were still missing, but FS Wal Mackie, one of the wireless operators, spotted Gipps floating nearby. Mackie launched himself from the dinghy to bring him in, but upon reaching Gipps, found him barely conscious and in great pain; it was all Mackie could do to tread water, supporting the injured pilot and keeping his own head above the waves. He held Gipps up for thirty minutes before the other crewmen managed to manoeuvre the dinghy across the swell to reach them.[40] He was later to be awarded the British Empire Medal for his courageous, single-handed rescue of the injured co-pilot.[41]

With both Mackie and Gipps aboard the dinghy, by 6.30 p.m. the Sunderland crew had managed to paddle across to join the Whitley crew. Both dinghies were lashed together, and both crews prepared for a night at sea. Once O/461 failed to respond to signals from base after 5.33 p.m., No. 19 Group HQ knew that the Sunderland was down, so during the night, a Wellington from 172 Squadron, captained by one of this squadron's most capable pilots, Plt Off. Peter Stembridge, was sent out to locate the dinghy. The Wellington flew straight to the spot, homing on the distress signal transmitted by the newly-introduced T1333 emergency transmitter in the dinghy (operated by rotating a handle), and then appeared blindingly out of the darkness, spotlighting the close-huddled survivors with its powerful submarine-hunting Leigh Light.[42] The shivering men in the dinghies must have been greatly heartened as the Wellington roared by overhead. It then pulled up to orbit the dinghy at a safe height, transmitting position reports to base. There was some light to see by from a waning crescent moon, but as the Wellington circled, sea fog rose and thickened, gradually cutting off visual contact between dinghy and aircraft. The men in the dinghy remember the Wellington staying for only one hour before departing, but

Plt Off. Stembridge reported circling around the dinghy for almost four hours.[43] The Wellington finally departed, signalling base at 4.33 a.m. that it had 'lost contact in fog'. At least it left the men in the dinghies with the assurance that HQ knew their position.

Back at Pembroke Dock, No. 461's ops room staff spent the night closely following the radio traffic and preparing two air sea rescue sorties for arrival over the dinghies soon after dawn the next day. Fg Off. Gordon Singleton's crew was briefed at 12.40 a.m., advised of the positions of the two dinghies, but given unpromising 'Met gen' by the meteorological officer: 'Sea rough, fog down to fifty feet of the water, visibility one hundred yards'.[44] Nonetheless, Singleton took off in E/461 into the darkness at 3.41 a.m., flying into weather that grew worse the further south he flew: by the time dawn was feebly glimmering upon the dull waters of the Bay, Singleton found cloud base hanging down towards the surface mist like a 'dirty grey blanket'. He flew his Sunderland through the narrow band of misty air between cloud and sea, with visibility down to a few hundred yards. Despite these highly unpromising search conditions, three hours after take-off the dinghies appeared in sight 500 yards off the starboard bow. Singleton's navigator, Harry Winstanley, had done a great job in navigating the Sunderland to arrive in the correct patch of sea, while his lookouts had also done fine work in spotting the dinghy in such unpromising visibility. Singleton turned in immediately, before he lost sight of the dinghies behind a patch of passing mist, and made a low pass overhead, 'almost at deck-level'. Down below, his squadron mates were relieved to see a Sunderland suddenly roar out of the fog, low cloud and drizzle, and thunder straight past overhead, dropping both a smoke-float and a marine marker.

With the weather closing in, Singleton was in a hurry to land before the dinghies were swallowed up in the fog and rain; he wanted to get on the water and to rescue them while he could still see them, despite the admonitory precedent set by Dods's own failed attempt to do just that on the afternoon before. Indeed, he was in such a hurry that he went ahead with the landing without either jettisoning the depth-charges or dumping fuel, both of which were standard precautions before a sea landing. With cloud ceiling at 100 feet, there was no height for a normal circuit, so he was obliged to turn tightly around the dinghies, trying to keep them in view while he set up for a landing close by. Although Singleton had judged the sea to be calm from higher up, upon descending closer to the water on final approach, he saw that there was in fact a 'moderate' 8-foot swell rolling by under his keel, coming from an oblique angle. A similar misperception had evidently happened to Dods the previous evening, but Singleton was now committed to his landing. Using the smoke-float to line-up his aircraft into the wind, he accepted the cross-swell, holding the nose up to slow down as much as possible before water contact. As he held off, the inertia of the big flying boat kept it flying, during which the bottom of the hull kept bashing upon the crests of each wave in passing. With its nose still held high, the aircraft was slowing, and as it approached stall speed, Singleton pulled the control wheel back into his lap and put the Sunderland neatly down on the water, right in the trough between two wave crests. It was 7.04 a.m., and Singleton had pulled off a skilled open water landing. By 7.30 a.m., he was taxiing alongside the two dinghies, placing them in the lee of the Sunderland's hull.

From there, E/461 took on board the six Whitley crewmen and the ten survivors from Dods's crew. A bunk was wrenched from the wardroom to make a stretcher for Gipps: he was strapped to it while in the dinghy and then manhandled through the aircraft's entry door. When the improvised 'stretcher' proved too wide to fit within the narrow hatch, the men rotated it onto its side to fit it through, with Gipps held in by the straps. The shocked patient endured this treatment in 'patient silence'.[45] Once the survivors were on-board, Singleton's crewmen saw to their shipwrecked passengers: they got the shivering men out of their wet clothes and into whatever motley assortment of dry flying clothes the men of E/461 could donate at short notice. For example, Winstanley stripped off his trousers, socks, and boots for the survivors' use. Left wearing only his white 'long johns' below the waist, he pulled on one of the old-fashioned one-piece leather flying suits which the aircrews had long since discontinued wearing, but which were kept stored in the aircraft.[46] First aid was also provided to Gipps and to two of the Whitley crewmen who were injured. In the galley, one of the air gunners, Fg Off. George Viner, cooked up a hot meal to fortify the survivors. Viner had already survived a tour on bombers with 460 Squadron, so had already seen a lot—but not this. Besides being his own crew's designated cook, he was a man known throughout the squadron for his culinary efforts in the aircraft galley, for the following July, he was called into the BBC studios to broadcast a talk on 'Cooking in a Sunderland'.

However, with sixteen extra bodies, eight depth-charges, and 1,500 gallons of fuel aboard, the aircraft was now too heavy to attempt a take-off. After landing, Singleton had turned to Winstanley and remarked: 'We've shot ourselves with science. We can't take off. We'd be smashed to matchwood'. The Sunderland's strut-and-wire-braced wing-floats were highly vulnerable to sea impacts, and once a float was damaged, the affected wingtip would drop into the water; if that were to happen, there would then be three crews in dinghies awaiting rescue, not two. While his crewmen saw to their guests, the captain remained at the controls to ride the seas out, using engine power to hold the nose into wind, and using the rudder and ailerons to veer and roll the aircraft to 'keep its floats out of the swell'.[47]

After the landing, the cloud-base began to lift, the wind increased, the mist dispersed, the sunlight grew brighter, and the visibility improved. This boded well for rescue and for getting airborne again but boded poorly if the Luftwaffe came to find them, for the Germans were certainly monitoring the RAF radio traffic. At 9.01 a.m., No. 10's Norm Gerrard arrived overhead in G/10 and saw E/461 on the water, with her port inner still running to hold her head into wind. Soon there were three aircraft orbiting at 200 feet around the Sunderland on the water: Gerrard's G/10, a Sunderland from 228 Squadron, and an ASR Hudson. All four aircraft got in contact via either R/T or visual signalling, in the course of which Singleton advised the orbiting aircraft of his inability to take-off and requested that a destroyer be homed on to the scene to take the survivors off his aircraft. Fg Off. Sherwood's air sea rescue Hudson crew from 279 Squadron successfully contacted a destroyer by wireless and homed it on to the scene.[48]

At 9.48 a.m., Gerrard's crew saw the destroyer appear out of the rain 8 miles away, steaming to the rescue: she was the Free French *La Combattante*, and twenty minutes later, she was hove-to a short distance away from the waterborne Sunderland. The destroyer launched her whaler to go alongside the flying boat, but unused to dealing with floating aircraft, the French sailors rowed directly towards the Sunderland's bows rather than going around the wing and approaching from the beam. In the cockpit, Singleton hastily handed over the controls to his second pilot, FS Pearce Taplin, and climbed up out of the astrodome hatch. From this lofty position atop the aircraft, he screamed at the boat crew in an urgent mixture of French and English, telling them to go around and approach from the side. After that, they did so adroitly in seaman-like fashion, allowing the ship's doctor to go aboard. He calmly and quietly examined the condition of the survivors, starting with Gipps. After that, it took the French seamen two or three trips to take-off all sixteen survivors as well as five 'dispensable' crew members from E/461: Singleton wanted to lighten his aircraft as much as possible to enable a take-off, so he disembarked some of his back-seater crewmen. The Sunderland still had the depth-charges on-board, so Singleton also asked for the ship's armourers to come aboard to defuse them, so that he could jettison them safely into the water beneath his wings. The Frenchmen came aboard, spent some time in the bomb room, and removed the bombs' detonators. On the final whaler trip, the French captain sent over a couple of bottles of Scotch for Singleton's rump seven-man crew; then, at 12.55 p.m., after three hours of shuttling back and forth between ship and Sunderland, the whaleboat was hoisted aboard *La Combattante*, which got away with E/461 under tow, heading for England.

However, in the prevailing seas, the tow was a marginal undertaking, as the Sunderland 'crashed through the seas behind the destroyer, with water pouring across the wings and into the engines'.[49] With all of the Sunderland's engines stopped, Singleton's crew kept the aircraft straight while under tow by trailing a sea anchor rigged up in seamanlike fashion from the galley hatch by the flight engineer, Sgt Harry Hall. Despite this, the waves kept crashing in through the nose turret opening, which had been opened to secure the towline, but the retraction rails had fouled on the rope so that it would not shut. So much sea water crashed into the hull through the bow opening that Viner and one of the wireless operators, Sgt Johnny Lewis, had to slave away at the hand-pump, but despite their energetic efforts, they failed to gain on the flooding. Facing defeat, Hall 'worked like a man possessed' to start the auxiliary motor in the starboard wing root, in order to run the pumps, give Viner and Lewis a breather, and save the aircraft. While the motor was running, the flooding remained at an equilibrium, with the aircraft shipping green seas through its bow hatch, and the pump sending the water straight back out. Despite this stabilisation of the flooding, Singleton was 'profoundly disturbed' at his aircraft getting 'pounded by pile-driver blows' from the oncoming seas. Communicating with the destroyer by signal lamp, he succeeded in getting the towing speed reduced from 10 knots to 5 knots, but even after that, the sea anchor tore away from its mooring, and without its drogue effect, the aircraft swung violently into wind.[50]

With directional control lost, Singleton had to start the starboard outer engine, as without a sea anchor this was the only way he could continue the tow, using the outboard engine's asymmetric thrust to keep the bow pointed on course, counter-balancing the aircraft's powerful tendency to weather-cock into the wind. With an engine running, Hall was now back at his flight engineer's panel at the rear of the flight-deck, monitoring the engine instruments, and was soon reporting the engine's rising cylinder head temperatures—the aircraft was going too slowly to provide the engine with its needed air flow-through for cooling. Singleton anxiously tolerated these temperature readings until Hall suddenly barked, 'Switch off! Danger point!' as the needle climbed into the red. Singleton cut the throttle and pulled the fuel cut-out toggle to stop the engine. At once, the powerless aircraft yawed uncontrollably to starboard, weathercocking into the wind. As it did so, the towline slackened, then tautened suddenly from the destroyer's forward motion. The sudden side force tore away the bollard from the bow compartment of the flying boat, irrevocably severing the tow. It was 5.25 p.m.

Uttering the exclamation, 'That's that', Singleton was left confronting stark choices: either to abandon the aircraft and return home by ship or attempt a take-off. He ordered a visual signal to be flashed to *La Combattante*: 'stand by. We're taking off'. His crew prepared the aircraft for take-off: they winched the inert depth-charges onto the aircraft's bomb racks, wound them out under the wings, and then jettisoned them into the water alongside; they chopped off the base of the snapped-off bollard in the bow, and closed the nose turret; they pumped out all remaining water from the bilges, closed all watertight doors, and went upstairs to assume their crash positions behind the flight-deck. Singleton, Taplin, and Hall started the engines, while the destroyer steamed around them as a 'crash boat' to watch the take-off. By now, the position was 150 nautical miles south-west of Bishop Rock in the Scillies.

At 6.10 p.m., Singleton lined up along the swell and opened the throttle for a crosswind take-off. The six men aboard had to endure a gut-wrenching ride as the Sunderland lurched, slammed, yawed, and bounced its way for 3 miles across the waves: Harry Winstanley recalled that it took three or four times the normal take-off run, and that the crosswind uncontrollably weather-cocked the aircraft so that it yawed into wind and off the line of the swell. Like in Dods's disastrous landing, the weathercocking forced the aircraft to run straight into the waves, smacking its hull hard against each wavetop and bouncing from the top of one swell to another. The aircraft had barely become airborne, staggering along just above the water, when the hull bottom struck a 'huge wave'. This impact 'hurled the Sunderland into the air', so they were at least flying.[51] As the aircraft climbed away, Viner went below, going from compartment to compartment to check for damage. Coming to the wardroom, he found that the door would not open, and had to force it; looking inside, he was shocked to see a gaping 7-foot by 4-foot hole in the floor. Looking through the hole, there was nothing but the bleak, grey surface of the sea racing past below. The bottom hull plating had been torn away during that hard impact with the final wave, and the force of the inrushing water at 100 knots had smashed the entire contents of the room into a pile of debris jammed against the rear bulkhead, leaving only the white porcelain lavatory pedestal hanging in the slipstream. Viner plugged in his headset and said over the intercom, 'Galley to captain. We've been holed. I think you'd better take a look'. Disbelieving, Singleton tried to put him off, but Viner insisted, 'You'd better make it now, Gordon. I'm dinkum!' Singleton came below, took one look inside the wardroom, and conceded, 'That's awkward, George.'[52]

Singleton knew it would be 'suicide' to attempt a water landing with such a large breach in the hull, so decided to land his flying boat on the grass at RAF Angle, using the keel of the flying boat's hull as a sled. Angle was a clifftop airfield inside St Ann's Head, west of Pembroke Dock at the other end of Milford Haven. He signalled base at 6.51 p.m.: 'landing drome, hull gone', and requested that the crash truck and 'blood wagon' (ambulance) be made ready for his arrival. At Pembroke Dock, upon receipt of this signal, the squadron was thrown into uproar, with the 'commanding officer racing for a car'. The news of the impending 'landing' 'startled ambulance men and crash-men half out of their wits', but they got their vehicles ready and raced off along country roads to greet the arriving Sunderland at the nearby airfield. Meanwhile, as the damaged Sunderland winged its way to Milford Haven, Singleton dumped fuel while his crew threw out everything that could be manhandled out of a hatch.[53] They hoped to save the aircraft from structural damage by making touchdown on the grass at minimum possible weight.

Unlike the US Navy's widely-used PBY-5A Catalina flying boat, the Sunderland was not an amphibian, so had no undercarriage for a landing on dry land; but Angle had a wide expanse of unobstructed grass, so was suitable for this unprecedented emergency landing. Arriving on grass was certainly a better option than almost certain death in the violent deceleration and catastrophic airframe disassembly that would follow a water landing with that huge rent in the hull bottom. At 8.40 p.m., Singleton made a couple of circuits of the airfield, then set up for a long, flat, slow approach over the sea cliff running along the airfield boundary. He knew he had an audience, having recognised the CO's car parked at the upwind end of the runway. Singleton held the nose high as he flared above the grass, holding off for as long as possible to make the arrival as gentle as could be. The great hull kissed the grass momentarily before jarring and banging its way across the airfield, while he held the wings level and held the control wheel back into his lap to maximise the deceleration. Meanwhile, the CO was racing alongside in his car at 60 mph.[54] The Sunderland's keel cut a shallow furrow in the soil for 150 yards and then as the speed dropped off, the port wing started dropping.[55] As the wing's weight fell upon it, the port wing-float broke its struts and collapsed; the wing dropped onto the ground, and the aircraft pivoted gently around its port wingtip in a gentle arc.

Despite the stately pace of the arrival, the crew started abandoning ship at once, exiting through the astrodome hatch in haste even before the pilots on the flight-deck had cut the engines. The men got off the aircraft by partly running and partly slipping along the steeply-canted port wing onto the ground, missing the hot engine exhausts as they went by, and at the end stepping neatly off the wingtip onto the grass. The pilots themselves were not far behind the others: they were out and down the wing before the propellers had even stopped turning; these continued to spin perilously close-by as the pilots tottered past only a few feet away. Judging by the haste of the disembarkation, the crewmen were evidently in a great hurry to get clear in case the fuel tanks ignited.[56]

Singleton had certainly pulled off a good landing as an end-point to a highly challenging operational flight, but he was exaggerating when he claimed that he had put E/461 on the ground 'without much further damage to the aircraft'. In fact, that was the last time she either 'flew or floated', at the end of thirty-nine operational flights with No. 461.[57] Meanwhile, *La Combattante* headed for England, docking in Devonport at 6 a.m. the next morning, to put the airmen ashore and to get Gipps to a hospital. He survived, but never flew again, resuming ground duties in the RAAF only after 'a long, long time' in convalescence, suffering from an arm that was permanently crippled.[58] The senior officer who had accompanied Gipps in his famous U-boat attack on 28 April, Air Vice-Marshal Baker, kindly made visits to him in hospital.[59] Thus the man who had been credited with the squadron's first U-boat kill had now finished his tour prematurely before ever attaining his captaincy; he would serve out the war in an administrative role at R.A.F. Pembroke Dock. Singleton could have been awarded a D.F.C. for his unusual piloting feat, but he was not: it may be that Coastal Command did not want to offer any further encouragement to captains tempted to emulate what was now recognised as too dangerous an undertaking: whereas validating the sea landing by awarding a DFC would have had the contrary effect.

The whole affair had considerable parallels with the 461 Squadron incident back in August 1942, when Wg Cdr Halliday had, like Dods, misjudged his ocean landing in sea conditions that were clearly out of safe parameters. In both cases, an attempt to pluck a crew to safety had ended with two dinghies in the water, not one. At least in Dods's case, all but one of his crew survived the attempt, whereas in Halliday's case, all but one of his crew had died. In both cases, however, a fine captain had made a mistake and died for it. Both episodes certainly emphasised the lengths to which Coastal Command crews would go in rescuing downed airmen. After Halliday's disastrous precedent, it is perhaps surprising that Dods had even attempted a similar ocean landing in similarly-marginal conditions. The fact that he did so attests to the enormous moral commitment that aircrew gave to the mission of rescuing their brother airmen from peril on the seas. Singleton's readiness to make yet another sea landing, even after Dods's disaster, further underlines this point.

Nonetheless, after this, the cautionary message about sea landings was now getting through to at least some of the pilots: Phil Davenport, who had flown with both Dods and Gipps, considered the landing attempt 'reckless', and when he himself found a life-raft with four survivors on 24

July, he carefully weighed up the option of alighting to pick them up. It was a tempting option, considering the favourably calm water, but while circling overhead, he deliberately gave himself time to let the 'blood rush' recede from his head before prudently deciding against it. However, this decision was eased by the proximity of a group of Royal Navy warships, which could undertake the rescue instead. Of course, neither Halliday nor Dods had had the luxury of such surface ship back-up. Bill Dods had died on his thirty-ninth operational flight as a captain. Sadly, it was to have been his last trip before finishing his tour: after returning from this mission, he was to have handed over his crew to Raleigh Gipps, who was now deemed ready to take up his captaincy.[60] Now, that was not to be, either.

The Crisis of May 1943

No. 461 had written-off two aircraft in the course of this convoluted rescue operation at the end of May, but these were not the only aircraft losses suffered by the two Australian Sunderland squadrons in this period. On 17 May, the two units had despatched five Sunderlands on Derange patrols, but only four crews returned to base. Sunderland Z/10, flown by the newly-promoted Flt Lt Keith McKenzie, took off at 5.17 a.m. for a day-long patrol, but failed to return, with both aircraft and crew lost without trace.[61] Among the twelve missing men were three particularly unlucky airmen: Plt Off. Vic Corless was a navigator-under-training who had joined the unit on 3 April and was flying his first trip as understudy to the regular navigator, Fg Off. Bob Bowley, DFC; Plt Off. Norm McLeod was a former 10 Squadron wireless mechanic/air gunner, who had retrained as a pilot, been commissioned, rejoined the squadron on 5 March, and was now flying only his third operation as second pilot, and Flt Lt Tom Patrick was the squadron's thirty-three-year-old squadron armament officer, who having become tour-expired and received a posting back to Australia, had taken one last opportunity for a 'jolly', going along on this trip as the crew's 'armourer'.

Z/10 had run into a flight of Ju 88s led by *Hauptman* Hans Morr, a squadron CO with V./KG40, as soon as she entered the patrol area. Morr shot down the Sunderland at 7.20 a.m. with such efficiency that the Sunderland hit the water before the wireless operator could tap out a distress call. Unfortunately for the crew of Z/10, it was a cloudless day over the Bay, so there had been nowhere for a Sunderland to hide; the lack of a radio call suggests that the German pilot achieved complete surprise, presumably by attacking suddenly from out of the sun, or by making an unsighted approach at 'zero feet' over the sea and then pulling up to fire into the Sunderland's belly from below. Despite the violent ambush, McKenzie's gunners evidently took some revenge in the brief and violent encounter, for the Ju 88 flown by *Leutnant* Werner Hensgen was shot down in combat with a Sunderland, with the deaths of all three crewmen.[62] That same evening, the British radio monitoring service picked up a German news broadcast reporting that armed reconnaissance aircraft of the Luftwaffe had shot down a Sunderland that day, and that it had fallen into the sea and exploded. This must have been Z/10, as no other Sunderland from 19 Group was lost that day.[63]

May 1943 had brought not only an escalation in the conflict between aircraft and U-boats in the Bay, but also a spike in aerial combat between Sunderlands and Ju 88s. On 7 May, 461 Squadron's Col Walker escaped from two twin-engined German fighters by climbing into cloud. A week later, on the 14th, the same squadron's Bert Smith had a much closer shave when he ran into six Ju 88s while flying a Derange patrol: he was flying M/461 at 4,000 feet, and was just emerging from a bank of sea fog off the Spanish coast when his lookouts spotted four Ju 88s crossing the Sunderland's nose from right to left, 2,000 yards off; they were getting into position to make an attack from the front. Simultaneously, the rear gunner reported two more Ju 88s, 1,500 yards astern. Smith turned right to evade the attack from the enemy fighters ahead, pulling around to regain the fog. The evasive turn to avoid the Ju 88s ahead brought the two Ju 88s behind into range, and the leading Junkers fired a long burst from the extreme range of 1,000 yards, just before the Sunderland disappeared into the fog. The German pilot was an unusually good shot, for the Sunderland seems to have flown right through the burst of fire, peppered with hits from bow to stern: there were holes shot in the bow turret, pilots' windscreen, port wing, in the centre hull near the astrodome, and in the starboard tailplane and port elevator. The bow turret gunner, Sgt John Barrow, suffered a flesh wound in the right thigh, but no one else was hit. This was lucky, as shells had also struck close to the pilots', navigator's, and wireless operator's crew positions on the flight-deck. It was a random stroke of good fortune that, despite the German pilot's good shooting, no shell hit anything vital, such as men, fuel tanks, or engines. Smith headed back the way he had come, hiding his aircraft in the fog. His gunners had not fired a single round, as the German pilot had fired unexpectedly from far out of .303 range. Once back at Pembroke Dock, M/461 was patched up in time to fly again six days later, on the 20th, flown by the same crew.

On 17 May, the same day as McKenzie was shot down, a No. 461 crew on a Derange patrol also tangled with Ju 88s. That afternoon, John Weatherlake was flying through the patrol area in H/461 when he ran into a formation of six Ju 88s approaching at 500 feet. Three of these climbed into positions all around the Sunderland for co-ordinated attacks, then started coming in one by one: one would come in from either the port or starboard bow, one from the other bow, and then one from head on. Whenever the Sunderland turned to evade one attack, another Ju 88 would be coming in from a different angle. On top of their tactical co-ordination, these German pilots were aggressive, in some instances pushing their attack runs so close that the turret gunners were able to take shots at them from as close as 100 yards. After receiving bursts of return fire, two German aircraft were seen to head away trailing black smoke, to be afterwards claimed by the Sunderland gunners as 'probables', although in fact all seem to have made a safe return to their base after the combat.[64] The Germans were also persistent, for they maintained the engagement for thirty minutes, each making his attack run in turn, reclimbing to regain up-sun positions for the next go, and then coming down again, and so on. The Ju 88s seem to have run out of ammunition by the conclusion of the engagement, for they followed the Sunderland for ten minutes at the end of the fight without attacking, and then sheared off to go home. In the course of all these attacks, the Germans got hits, for H/461 returned to Pembroke Dock extensively damaged, bearing 200 holes. Once again, these were lucky hits from the Sunderland crew's perspective: for example, 20-mm shells had exploded inside the starboard wing without hitting the fuel tanks, or at the base of the dorsal turret without hitting the gunner, or severing control wires to the tail unit without destroying the aircraft's controllability. The resultant damage was so severe that it took three and a half months for 'H' to be repaired by No. 43 Group, returning to the unit only on 3 September.

Dangerous airborne encounters with happy endings, like Weatherlake's, made good news fodder back in Australia, and so were reported assiduously. The Brisbane *Truth* lionised 'the brilliant evasive tactics' in this combat by local boy, John Weatherlake, and itemised the damage to H/461: 'Its wings and fuselage shows cannon shell and machine gun holes, while two turrets have been hit, with damage to their gear; the wireless aerial has been shot away, one prop. has been hit, while the port inner engine is out of action and half the flying instruments have been rendered unserviceable by a burst of fire which struck the windscreen'. Viewing the damaged aircraft back at Pembroke Dock, reporter C. H. Bateson wondered how with so many hits the damage was not more severe, or how the crew had not been hit. The parochial Brisbane newspaper crowed about the number of Weatherlake's fellow Queenslanders in this successful and lucky crew: Plt Off. John Park, the second pilot; Plt Off. John Sullivan, the navigator; FS John Lewis, the wireless operator; and Sgt Norm Wyeth, the nose gunner.[65]

Enemy fighters were certainly not the only hazard faced by the Sunderland crews as they set out on their long Bay patrols in over-loaded aircraft filled with 6 tons of 100-octane petrol. No. 10 Squadron launched three aircraft on Bay patrols in the early pre-dawn darkness of 20 May, and at 5.08 a.m., the Coast Guard stations at Rame Head and Looe on the coast of Cornwall reported a white flash in the sky, followed by an audible explosion, from a position estimated as 4 miles WNW of Eddystone Light. Sunderland U/10, captained by Flt Lt Denis Saunders, neither made nor returned any wireless calls. No. 19 Group HQ got the navy to dispatch a destroyer to investigate, and this vessel discovered a wreckage field in the water, and at 10.45 a.m. signaled the discovery of aircraft floats, said to be similar to those of Sunderland type. No. 10's CO, Wg Cdr Hartnell, took off in a Sunderland to view the reported wreckage. It was only a short trip, as the wreckage was floating in the sea only 14 miles from Plymouth. It was also a melancholy trip, as Hartnell returned to confirm that the floats were indeed those of a Sunderland.[66] After that, a motor pinnace set out from RAF Mount Batten to investigate the floating wreckage close-up. Under the direction of No. 10's Sqn Ldr Marks, it proceeded to the given position, found the wreckage, and recovered two bodies, those of Sgts Ed Dewhurst, an air gunner, and Norm Owen, a wireless mechanic. The other ten crewmen were never found.[67]

After investigation, Hartnell concluded that open flames from the gas stoves in the galley had ignited the aircraft's fuel tanks. He thought that the off-duty crewmen must have started cooking too early, lighting the stoves while the hull was still full of petrol fumes, while the topped-up tanks were still venting fuel from their overflow pipes, and while spilled fuel still lay pooled against the bottom skins of the wings after the refueling. Alternatively, he felt that loose fuel lying pooled against the bottom wing skins might have spilled into the hull while the aircraft banked into a turn, and then been ignited by the lit galley stoves. In either case, the cause would be the same: normally the crews did not light the stove until an hour after take-off, as this gave time for the loose fuel in the wings to vent or evaporate, and for fuel vapour inside the hull to dissipate. If the galley stove was indeed the cause, then it was a tragic and unnecessary loss. The death of this crew came only three days after the shooting down of McKenzie's crew over the Bay, so No. 10 had once again to confront the loss of two crews within days. Despite its tightly-knit society, the squadron would just have to bear up under its losses, for there would be more to come. Despite the losses, the CO thought that 'the chaps are standing up to it well and are quite cheerful', but he himself was left with the salutary task of writing the condolence letters to the men's next of kin.[68]

May 1943 was not only a big month for air combats over the Bay, it was also a big month for U-boat sightings. Frustratingly for the Sunderland crews, however, the U-boats were proving adept at submerging before the Sunderlands could get close enough to bomb. For example, on the 21st, two days after Geoff Rossiter's successful open water rescue, and a fortnight after making his U-boat kill, he contacted yet another submarine while flying a Derange patrol in the western outskirts of the Bay, and despite spotting it at 12 miles range and manoeuvring into cloud to make a covert approach, the submarine had disappeared by the time the Sunderland popped back out of cloud for its attack run. Other crews from No. 10 that found U-boats included those of Gordon Strath, who made abortive sightings on both the 9th and 18th, Norm Gerrard on the 21st, and Keith Sampson on the 23rd; and from No. 461, Chic Clarke made a similarly brief contact on the 15th, and the ill-fated Bill Dods on both the 17th and 24th. During a convoy patrol on the 11th, No. 10's Keith McKenzie came the closest he would ever come to seeing the death of a submarine, six days before his own death. Upon contacting his convoy, McKenzie received a visual signal from the escort commander to investigate a submarine contact, 50 miles away on a bearing of 335 degrees. McKenzie arrived there in time to witness two British warships stopped in the water, with their lifeboats picking up survivors. *U-528* had just been depth-charged by a Halifax from 58 Squadron, then finished off by the sloop, HMS *Fleetwood*.[69] As the Sunderland circled over the scene, McKenzie's crew saw about twenty Germans picked up by the warships' boats. The increasing pace of submarine kills in the Bay during May was such that only four days after this, on the 16th, Ted Farmer's crew similarly obtained a view of the melancholy aftermath of a submarine sinking. He was flying a Derange patrol in the usual place—the south-western extremity of the Bay, 200 miles out to sea from Cape Finisterre in Spain—when he overflew an oil slick, 1 mile long. Farmer circled over the vast pool of 'brown effluent', seeing two dead men floating among the flotsam. This was the death-marker for *U-463*, which had been sunk by another Halifax of 58 Squadron, with the loss of all fifty-seven hands.[70]

Despite these tantalising glimpses of the death and destruction of their enemy, since Smith's and Rossiter's U-boat kills in the first week of May, the intervening month had delivered little to the Australian Sunderland crews but fleeting submarine sightings and elusive U-boat submergences. However, on the last day of the month, No. 10 launched two sorties, each flown by one of its veteran senior pilots, Reg Marks and Max Mainprize. Marks was despatched on what turned out to be a fruitless dinghy search, whereas Mainprize took off after lunch in E/10 on the squadron's final Derange patrol of the month. At 4.50 p.m., he received a message from base instructing him to search for a damaged submarine at a position in the western outskirts of the Bay, nearly 400 miles out to sea from Land's End. By 5.30 p.m., he was searching on a south-easterly course, flying underneath cloud-base at 2,000 feet, when a submarine came into view 5 miles dead ahead. Mainprize at once eased the nose of the Sunderland down for an immediate attack. As he came closer, he saw that two Halifaxes were already orbiting over the submarine, and that the latter was sitting low in the water, trailing a slick of oil, evidently already damaged.

Mainprize circled around to set up for an attack across its bow, to avoid the firing arcs of the AA guns on its rear-facing bandstand. The submarine was still under power, and started turning to avoid the attack, but the Sunderland got there too quickly, thundering across its bow only 50 feet up. Mainprize dropped a salvo of four depth-charges, which straddled the boat perfectly: the closest depth-charges exploded either side of the conning tower, only 20 feet from the hull, and so within killing distance. After the water bursts subsided, the U-boat came to a complete stop. Mainprize turned as quickly as he could for his second attack, this time coming in for an unopposed attack against a sitting target. One of his depth-charges exploded 30 feet short of the hull, opposite the conning tower, while the other three overshot the hull and exploded in a line on the other side. As the Sunderland pulled around into another turn, the submarine's bows were awash, and its stern standing clear of the water. Mainprize's crew could see German crewmen assembling on deck, wearing life preservers. The U-boat was going down.

E/10 had no more depth-charges, so from this point could do little more than observe the sinking. However, other Coastal Command aircraft had received the same position reports, and so were now descending upon the scene with less than pacific intentions. As Mainprize circled around the sinking submarine, Halifax R/58 appeared, and came in for a strafing run, spraying the submarine's upper decks with machine gun fire. Then another Sunderland appeared ('X' from 228 Squadron) and like E/10, it made two separate depth-charge attacks, each time dropping four charges. At the end of this, Mainprize's crew saw the sinking submarine 'disintegrate' with an orange flash, leaving in its place a pool of brown scum, now spreading over a wide area, within which could be seen floating wreckage and bodies. Mainprize composed a message for transmission to base, 'U/ boat is sunk. Crew in water'. With some under-statement, once back at base, he reported himself, 'Satisfied that the U/boat was destroyed'.

Indeed *U-563* was sunk, and all forty-nine of her crew killed.[71] The men had died in their Mae Wests as they tried to abandon ship, some probably machine-gunned off the upper deck by the Halifax, and the unfortunate survivors fatally concussed by the depth-charges from the 228 Squadron

Sunderland. The Luftwaffe's Atlantic Air Command had been following the action through their monitoring of RAF transmissions, and next day sent out a patrol of Ju 88s carrying life rafts for the survivors, but it was all too late.[72] This brutal, disturbing episode was worthy of a scene in Nicholas Monsarrat's *The Cruel Sea*, that searing novelisation of the Battle of the Atlantic. The action certainly encapsulates the implacable and remorseless violence of air-sea warfare, typical of so many other episodes by which overwhelming force was applied to ensure the total destruction of a U-boat—hence Mainprize's pointed report that the crew was in the water, a fact offered as proof of the unambiguous destruction of that boat.

Although Mainprize had made an excellent attack which doomed the boat, *U-563* had been killed by a combined effort from three squadrons. It had begun with Wg Cdr Wilfred Oulton, the ace U-boat killer and CO of No. 58 Squadron, who had already sunk *U-266* on 15 May.[73] He was also (falsely) credited with having previously sunk *U-663* on 5 May.[74] He had first spotted *U-563* running on the surface, and made two successive depth-charge runs upon it, pressing home his attacks through AA fire. After nine depth-charge detonations the submarine appeared to be 'fatally wounded', but it did not sink. Then a second Halifax from 58 Squadron likewise made two attack runs, but its nine depth-charges did not fall accurately.[75] It was then that Mainprize's Sunderland arrived, by which time both Halifaxes were out of depth-charges; while the U-boat was evidently crippled, unable to submerge, but still afloat. The decisive result of Mainprize's subsequent attack we have seen. The late arriving Sunderland X/228 was flown by Fg Off. William French, who saw 'bodies thrown into the air' by his depth-charge explosions, just after thirty to forty men had been visible in the water.

The sinking of *U-563* was correctly lauded as a model attack that had secured the verified destruction of a U-boat, and all those involved became the object of command-wide acclamation. The next day, Air Vice-Marshal Bromet sent a congratulatory message from 19 Group HQ: 'Yesterday's kill after U/boat had been damaged by R/58 was an example of good co-operation and successful homing. Heartiest congratulations to R/58, J/58, E/10 and X/228'. With three U-boat kills recorded to his credit in one month, 58 Squadron's dynamic CO, Wg Cdr Oulton, was awarded both a DFC and a DSO.[76] This official approbation was deserved, for the submarine would not have been sunk without Oulton: he had patiently stalked it while it was running on the surface, made a damaging attack which evidently trapped it on the surface, and thereby pinned it down to be fatally attacked by Mainprize. Also, as a squadron CO, he was self-evidently leading his unit from the front in a highly meritorious manner. French's final attack in X/228 had made certain of the destruction of the

U-boat, but as a by-product, he had killed the submarine crew in the water. For the crews of Coastal Command, the maxim was 'A U-boat damaged isn't a U-boat sunk', and so French had correctly made certain of it.[77] It was all a matter of timing: if X/228 had arrived a minute after the boat sank, he would not have attacked; but he arrived while the submarine still floated, so attacked. No 'benefit of the doubt' could apply in the deadly war between Hitler's U-boat arm and the sea-air forces of the Allies. So long as a submarine floated, there was the chance it would survive to fight again. For Coastal Command crews, the only good U-boat was a sunken U-boat, and 228 Squadron's Bill French had rightly sought to ensure that outcome for *U-563*.

Mainprize and his 10 Squadron crew had certainly made a decisive attack, rupturing the boat's hull and causing the captain to order his crew to abandon ship. This too was a product of timing. Oulton had damaged *U-563* but had expended his depth-charges and so had no remaining means of sinking her. When Mainprize found the U-boat, she was still under power and under control, and could almost certainly have got back to port so long as she was not attacked again. Whereas after Mainprize bombed, the boat was sinking, and her men were abandoning ship. This sinking was the third U-boat kill by the Australian squadrons in one month.

The effective U-boat hunting by Nos 10 and 461 was part of the general upswing in U-boat sinkings during May, during which the squadrons of No. 19 Group sank a total of seven submarines in the Bay of Biscay.[78] This month was the turning point in the Battle of the Atlantic overall, with an unprecedented forty U-boats sunk, after monthly losses of only about fifteen boats from January through to April.[79] It was during May that Admiral Dönitz's command irrevocably lost the ability to win the 'tonnage war' by sinking more Allied ships than the number of U-boats lost. Drawing upon the most comprehensive intelligence data available, the Admiralty's Anti-Submarine Warfare Directorate was able to report that April–May 1943 was 'the critical period during which strength began to ebb away from the German U-boat offensive'.[80]

This realisation of dawning victory in the Atlantic was not merely retrospective historical analysis but was recognised at the time by commanders with access to the full intelligence picture of U-boat buildings, sailings, and sinkings. Air Chief Marshal Charles Portal, commander of the RAF, sent a message to Coastal Command squadrons on the same day as *U-563*'s sinking, in which he expressed his admiration for the devotion to duty and tireless perseverance of the aircrews, congratulating them on the 'welcome reward' for their long months of arduous operations and training: 'Now that you have obtained this remarkable advantage over the

U/boats, I know you will press it home with ever increasing vigour and determination until, in conjunction with the Royal Navy, you have finally broken the enemy's morale'.

German U-boat historian Jürgen Rohwer concluded that from May 1943 onwards, the threat to Allied convoys from Dönitz's U-boat force was 'virtually negligible'.[81] The year of 1943 was the year that Hitler's Germany irrevocably lost the war, with German forces defeated in their campaigns on the Russian Front, in the Mediterranean Theatre, in the air defence of Germany, and in the Atlantic. There would be ongoing sinkings of Allied ships until the end of the war.[82] Nonetheless, the U-boats had lost their status as hunters on the high seas, becoming instead the hunted.[83] The U-boat force's casualty figures for 1939–45 tell the ultimate story: out of 41,000 men who served on U-boats, 26,350 died in action and 4,945 were taken prisoner; including training fatalities, the loss rate was 78 per cent.[84]

As severe as these casualties were, the brutal battle of the Atlantic was also taking its toll on the aircrew of Coastal Command: for example, as we will shortly see, both Australian Sunderland squadrons would need considerable resilience and resolve to see out the rest of 1943 in the face of ongoing heavy losses. In the meantime, in No.461's own estimation, after a year-long adolescence spent in the shadow of its senior sister, it had 'covered itself with glory' by getting the Australians' first U-boat kill of this climactic season. During the squadron's 'most outstanding month', it had demonstrated equal operational proficiency to No.10, and unlike its senior sister had moreover luckily avoided crew losses. It had also trained assiduously to both improve the combat performance of its existing crews, and to train up new crews: during May 1943, the unit had two or three crews out on training sorties every day, in the course of which they fired more than 40,000 rounds of .303 at drogues and targets, and dropped 444 practice bombs to improve the pilots' ability to straddle a U-boat with their first salvo of depth-charges. No. 461's crews had never seen as many Germans as they saw that month, as shown by their also having fired 3000 rounds of .303 at the enemy in the same period.

Junkers Corner

Although Dönitz had ordered the withdrawal of his U-boats from the North Atlantic, his submarines continued to sail from the Biscay ports, albeit assigned to patrol the less well-defended convoy routes in the South Atlantic, Indian Ocean, or Caribbean. Thus, forty-eight boats sailed on war patrols each month over June–July. The aircraft of No. 19 Group continued to exact a toll upon these boats as they made passage for these more far-flung theatres, for in that same two-month period, they sank thirteen of these U-boats as they attempted their transit through the Bay of Biscay.[1] However, despite Coastal Command's overall success, the Sunderland units missed out on their share of the 'trade' during this period, as these attacks on U-boats were dominated by the ASV III-equipped Liberator and Wellington units.[2] Despite the three sunken U-boats chalked up on the Australians' scoreboards during May 1943, the eight weeks that followed were a lean time for Nos 10 and 461, with a mere seven U-boats sighted between the two squadrons in the course of 214 operational sorties.

Although U-boat activity dropped off in June–July 1943, the same could not be said of Luftwaffe activity over the Bay. Indeed, from June to September, there would be twelve air combats between the Australian Sunderlands and the formidable Ju 88 long-range fighters of V./KG40. By the summer of 1943, not only were the Australian crews more proficient at killing U-boats, but by then, the German Ju 88 crews had also become more proficient at killing Sunderlands.

This period of tumultuous air combat was opened on 2 June with an aerial engagement, which was immediately acclaimed by Allied authorities as a symbol of the superior fighting prowess of Coastal Command airmen under fighter attack. That day, the two Australian squadrons despatched a total of five crews on patrols over the waters of the Bay. One of these was Col Walker's crew from 461 Squadron, flying 'N-Nuts' on an afternoon Derange patrol. At 7 p.m., this Sunderland was flying a patrol leg on an easterly course at 2,000 feet when the tail gunner, FS Ray Goode, reported eight Ju 88s, 6 miles to port and higher up, inbound. Walker hoped that the Germans had not yet spotted him, and climbed at once for cloud, but the Germans had indeed seen the portly Sunderland, and moreover the cloud was only 3/10th at 3,000 feet—too sparse to hide in. Walker rang the action stations klaxon, jettisoned the bombload, and headed out to sea at full throttle. The Ju 88s had, moreover, happened upon the scene at an inconvenient time, for fifteen minutes earlier, the Sunderland had developed an engine fault, with the starboard outer showing fluctuating boost and revs; so when the chase began the Sunderland was already sub-par in performance. The navigator, Fg Off. Ken Simpson, took up his fire control station under the astrodome, reporting the Ju 88s' movements as they closed upon the Sunderland and split up into two elements. Soon there were four aircraft queued up on each side, 500 yards out. When action stations sounded aboard the Sunderland, the men who had been on duty at the time in the nine watch positions remained in those positions for the duration of the action, leaving the two off-watch crewmen to man the newly-installed .303-inch Vickers VGO machine guns in the galley hatches, one on each side.

Then the first two fighters rolled in to attack, one from each side, attacking simultaneously to split the Sunderland's defence. The Ju 88 coming in from the port bow fired and hit the Sunderland's port wing and forward hull with an accurate burst of fire: N-Nuts' port outer engine was hit at once and burst into flames. The cockpit too was struck from the same burst of fire: the compass alongside Walker's left knee was struck by an incendiary round, which shattered the glass and ignited the alcohol. This flashed up into an 'extensive fire' with 3-foot-high flames, setting alight Walker's clothing. He stood up to douse the flames with his gloved hands, in time to let the second pilot, Plt Off. Jim Amiss, do the job properly by spraying him 'full on' with the cockpit fire extinguisher.[3] Meanwhile, the first pilot, Plt Off. Bill Dowling, had taken the controls, carrying out the evasive turns called by Ken Simpson from the astrodome. Fortunately, the port outer's Graviner fire extinguisher system worked as advertised, leaving the damaged engine dead, streaming a trail of dense white smoke, with the propeller windmilling in the airflow. Nonetheless, N-Nuts remained hard-to-handle with a dead port outer, now needing the two pilots to heave together at the controls to force the recalcitrant aircraft to obey their will. To make matters worse, the gunfire had severed the controls to the rudder and elevator trim tabs, so the pilots had to hold their control wheels against the aerodynamic forces by brute force alone. The control loads were reduced when, after twenty-five minutes, the dead engine's oil-deprived propeller reduction gear seized and sheared, so that the windmilling propeller spun away into space. That was an improvement, but even then, hard evasive-turns could only be made to the left, as the pilots could only turn the aircraft towards the dead engine.

The pilots sweated and strained at their controls for three-quarters of an hour, during which the 88s made thirty separate attacks. The Germans continued to get hits as they came in one after the other, breaking away after each attack and then moving back out on to the Sunderland's flank to set up for their next firing run. With Simpson calling the attacks over the intercom, Walker's gunners fired back so hotly that they afterwards claimed three of the 88s shot down—reported to have struck the sea or disintegrated after being struck by return fire.

However, as the action went on the Sunderland's return fire slackened: Ray Goode in the tail turret had his head slammed so hard against the turret structure by Walker's violently-yawing evasive turns that he was knocked-out for five minutes. After regaining consciousness, he resumed his firing, but a 20-mm cannon shell then hit the base of his turret and cut the hydraulics; he was reduced to elevating, traversing, and firing his guns manually, which reduced his firing to a scarecrow role only. In the galley, the flight engineer, Sgt Ted Miles, RAF, was hit in the stomach and collapsed at his gun. Jim Amiss, the second pilot, had been ordered aft to check on the tail gunner, and *en route* found Miles lying unconscious in the galley. With the aid of the second flight engineer, Sgt Phil Turner, Amiss got Miles out of the galley and into the adjacent bomb-room, but despite first aid administrations, the wounded man died twenty minutes later. The action remained so hot that while Amiss was standing in the doorway of the bomb-room, talking to Turner, another burst struck the aircraft, with bullets passing between their faces, only 18 inches away.

Further hits at 7.35 p.m. severed the intercom, cutting off the gunners from Simpson's fire control direction. After that, Simpson gave his orders to the pilots to break left by hand signal, looking like an 'orchestra conductor' as he did so, with his signals interpreted by Amiss, who stood behind the pilots and relayed the commands by shouting. Simpson himself had already been wounded, hit by shrapnel, which passed 'right through his calf' and left his leg 'bleeding profusely'. He had been struck by a spray of splinters from a 20-mm shell that had exploded against the radio bulkhead on the flight-deck; these splinters also wounded the first pilot, Bill Dowling, in the palm of his left hand, and the wireless operator, FS Harold Miller, with a slight laceration to his face; while the shell detonation filled the upper deck with smoke. Committed to his vital early warning role at the fire control station, Simpson carried on at first without mentioning his wound, and then suffered Amiss to dress his wound while remaining standing in his position beneath the astrodome.

The midships turret gunner, FS Eric Fuller, RAF, enjoyed the widest firing arc of any gun position on the aircraft, and he kept firing throughout, undeterred by his clear view of the burning engine and of the smoke streaming out of the burning cockpit. Although Fuller was only nineteen years old, the crew prized his status as a permanent RAF airman, and he lived up to this mystique by exhibiting outstanding technical proficiency under fire, maintaining his brisk return gunnery despite 'dozens of hits' striking the hull around his turret. Shouting, 'Come on you bastards, come and get it,' Fuller held his fire until the Ju 88s were within killing range of 250 yards and then 'let them have it'.[4] The number of Ju 88s remaining in the fight fell steadily, from eight, to five, and finally to two, and these finally made off at 7.45 p.m., probably out of ammunition and at the limit of their fuel. One of them, Lt Friedrich Maeder of V./KG40, returned to base to somewhat optimistically claim the Sunderland as shot down.[5]

Walker and his crew returned the compliment, returning home to claim three Ju 88s 'definitely' shot down and two 'probables'. Certainly, the deterrent effect of the gunners' tracer fire had been crucial to the crew's survival, and this must have been predominantly due to Eric Fuller, for his midships turret alone remained operational right through the action and covered the rear quarters from which most attacks came. Walker himself attributed the failure of this large force of Ju 88s to finish off his crippled Sunderland to the gunfire of his gunners; he noted that the German pilots fired from too far out (as much as 1,500 yards) and that they then broke away too early (no closer than 200 yards) more or less as soon as they came within .303-range.

Although N-Nuts departed the scene still flying, she was in a parlous state, with an estimated 400 to 500 holes in the airframe, with one engine gone, the wireless set wrecked, no trimming controls for the rudder and elevators, the port wing-tanks' fuel gauges inoperable, and the hull so twisted by the non-stop violent manoeuvring that none of the watertight doors could be closed or opened afterwards. She still had a three-hour flight ahead of her to get home, flying on only three engines. After forty-five minutes of chaotic manoeuvring, Walker did not know his position, so initially set off for home on a provisional course of 030 degrees. The three surviving engines were hot from continuous full power, but the aircraft would have difficulty maintaining level flight on three engines once power was reduced to bring their temperatures back within limits, so Walker ordered everything removable hacked away and chucked overboard. This included all personal belongings, flying kit, batteries, tool kits, anchor and chain, and all unserviceable equipment. The flight engineer went from bow to stern with the fire axe, chopping away 'all useless gear'.

But first the wounded men had to be attended to, particularly Simpson, who had to navigate them home. Once his wound was dressed and his bleeding staunched, he insisted on standing up again under the astrodome, this time to take a sun-sighting with the bubble sextant. Returning to his chart table, he performed the necessary calculations to provide Walker with a more accurate position and a better course-to-steer: 065 degrees. With the main wireless set wrecked, the wireless operators went aft to open the dinghy pack in the rear fuselage, extracting the T1333 emergency radio set, connecting it to the aircraft's trailing aerial and using that to attempt a call to base on 600 kilohertz. Despite their efforts, none of these signals were received in England, so no one in the ops rooms at Plymouth or Pembroke Dock knew N/461 was still airborne after the initial fighter contact reports. Midway through the action, Walker had ordered a situation report transmitted to base, but the wireless set had been knocked out from a direct hit by a cannon shell mid-transmission. Without a usable wireless transmitter or receiver, no reply came from the aircraft to the continuous calls from base over the following three hours, leaving the listeners back at base with the conviction that N-Nuts had gone the way of so many others, shot down into the sea. Indeed, HQ diverted two patrolling aircraft to the spot to look for survivors in the water.

Simpson's course-to-steer proved good, for the crippled Sunderland made landfall on the extreme western tip of Cornwall. With night falling, Walker resolved to land at once while there was still light, within the closest stretch of sheltered water they could find—Mount's Bay. Although the crew had bunged-up the bullet holes below the waterline with plugs of cloth, Walker knew that with so many rents in her lower hull, his Sunderland could not possibly stay afloat once he put her down on the water. He decided to put her down in a channel close to the beach at Praa Sands, east of Penzance, so that he could run her up onto the shallows before she sank away. The landing worked out just as he had foreseen: as the aircraft touched down on the water, 'Sea spurted into the hull which was perforated like a shower rose so he drove her hard onto the sand'.[6] The flying boat sank so rapidly that by the time the keel grounded on the sand there was almost 5 feet of water inside the hull. It was 10.48 p.m., three hours after the end of the combat.

As the distressed Sunderland 'slewed', 'thumped', 'shuddered and dug in' to her final resting place upon the sands, Walker cut the switches and in the sudden silence yelled, 'all out!' The men started wading through the surf the remaining 300 yards to the beach.[7] A coastguard cutter approached from the sea; it was now so dark that she was already sweeping the inshore waters with her searchlight. Once the first airmen came ashore onto the beach, 'almost straight away' the local people turned up to greet them with 'hot cocoa and cake'. They said, 'You sound like Australians,' and then someone asked, 'What about your aeroplane? Can we do anything to help?' One of the drenched airmen replied, 'No, she's had it, I reckon.' As the subdued group of airmen looked back towards the wreck of their aircraft in the surf, they witnessed the final melancholy scene of their violent flight: the sight of 'Four crewmen wading waist-deep ... carrying Ted Miles ashore'.[8]

Walker was the last to emerge from the surf, and in his burned flying clothes appeared particularly 'filthy and blackened and wet' when he came up to receive his cup of steaming tea. He gave his thanks to the civilians, before they ushered his men off the windswept beach into a nearby house. There the locals restored them to vitality with hot water, soap, dry towels, dry clothes, and hot food, while Walker phoned the officers' mess at Pembroke Dock, asking to speak to the CO. At the time, Wg Cdr Douglas was in the ante-room with 'a few of the boys', 'drinking to the damnation of all Ju-88s'. When Walker told Douglas that it was 'Col' who was speaking on the other end of the phone, the disbelieving CO blurted out, 'Col who?', then, 'Walker! You're dead!'[9]

Left beached within the tidal zone on an open beach, N-Nuts was ground to pieces in the surf, a total loss. She had flown sixteen operational patrols with No. 461 from February 1943 onwards, having previously served as the squadron's crew trainer from November 1942. A replacement Sunderland was taken on strength at Pembroke Dock by 9 June, but coded 'X'.

Walker's entire crew had done an outstanding job in not getting shot down. By rights, they should have been killed, having been caught by a squadron of enemy fighters, exposed to their co-ordinated attacks for forty-five minutes, subjected to forty individual attacks, and hit repeatedly by gunfire. Under these circumstances, to merely survive was good enough, but to top it off, once the crew was returned to Pembroke Dock and debriefed, the three turret gunners were awarded a total of three 'confirmed' kills for the Ju 88s, which they had individually reported to have seen burning and crashing into the sea. However, despite these enthusiastic claims by Walker's adrenalin-charged gunners, all eight of the opposing Ju 88s seem to have returned to base, as there is no record of V./KG40 losses on or around this date, from any cause. It seems that the over-stimulated gunners had mistaken their fleeting glimpses of gun splashes in the sea for crashing fighters—a common enough occurrence in the disorientating chaos of air combat. Nonetheless, the apparent feat of one Sunderland in beating off an attack by eight fighters and shooting down three of them was a made-to-order success story with which to buck up the crews of Coastal Command who were obliged to take their slow-flying patrol planes into the fighter-infested skies of the Bay of Biscay. Indeed, in the preceding three weeks, the Ju 88s had shot down nine Coastal Command patrol aircraft, with the loss of eight of the crews.[10] Every airborne wireless operator and every station wireless room listened in to these stricken aircraft's fighter contact reports, their SOSs, the subsequent unanswered signals from base, and then the radioed instructions to search for dinghies in the reported position of the combats, so the aircrews were well aware of what they were up against, and needed every bit of bucking-up they could get.

News of Walker's air combat feat went viral, passing straight to the top of the RAF command chain and then back down again to all units. Walker and his crew found themselves trumpeted throughout the command as a model of what a well-trained crew could do, even against overwhelming odds. No less a personage than Sir Archibald Sinclair, Britain's Secretary of State for Air, praised the crew's combat as 'outstandingly gallant and successful', and this sentiment was echoed by the commander of the RAF, Air Chief Marshal Charles Portal, who acclaimed it as 'one of the finest instances in this war of the triumph of coolness skill and determination against overwhelming odds'. The Duke of Gloucester came to visit on 4 June, spending most of the day climbing through the aircraft and talking to the men, particularly to Walker's crew. That same day, the CO of RAF Pembroke Dock called a parade in which he elaborated the details of Walker's action to a 'greatly interested' audience of station personnel. On the 7th came a visit by the commander of Coastal Command, Air Marshal Slessor, who heard the story 'first hand' from Walker and his crew and gave an 'interesting and heartening' talk to station personnel.

All this official approbation from high places was given tangible form in the 'immediate' awarding of decorations to four members of the crew: Walker received a Distinguished Service Order (DSO), an award usually given to COs for their leadership of their units in combat; the navigator, Simpson, received the more usual officer's award, the DFC; while the enlisted man's award, the DFM, went to both FS Goode, the tail gunner, and FS Fuller, the midships gunner. As was often customary, the unfortunate Sgt Miles was posthumously commissioned; his bereaved family could now get a larger pension. The squadron conducted his funeral on 7 June, attended by his wife and mother-in-law, 'who expressed their gratitude for the arrangements made'.

Walker's action finally put the spotlight upon No. 461 rather than No. 10: there were now two celebrated Australian Sunderland squadrons in England. With N-Nuts's survival, crash-landing, and three 'confirmed' fighter kills, No. 461 had truly emerged from the senior squadron's shadow. The squadron CO, Wg Cdr Douglas, who had set himself the task of establishing No. 461 'as the Top Flying Boat Squadron in Great Britain', seized upon Walker's feat and the Ju 88 kills as the crowning event he had been waiting for.[11] From now on, high-ranked VIPs would need to detour out of their way to visit Pembroke Dock in Wales, rather than contenting themselves with more conveniently-located Plymouth as formerly.

Flt Lt Walker, DSO, was not only heroised, but he was now too precious a survival icon to be risked on any further operations, so became tour-expired after captaining thirty-two operational patrols with No. 461, having flown the first half of 1942 as a co-pilot in No. 10. As one of the unit's originals, he was the third of No. 461's captains to complete his tour and go off operations. After the famous combat of 2 June, Walker's first pilot, Dowling, was also given a spell from operations: he underwent a month of captaincy training before flying his first mission in command of Walker's old crew on 8 July. The combat was also a watershed for Fg Off. Simpson, DFC, who was likewise taken off operations, but serving on with the squadron as a staff navigation officer, and accordingly promoted to flight lieutenant in August. Of course, the more junior members of the crew simply had to fly on: for example, the second pilot, Plt Off. Amiss, who had only joined the unit in April 1943, commenced training for first pilot duties in July, subsequently going on to captain Sunderland crews on operations into 1945. Walker's non-commissioned back-seaters were given a short reprieve from ops: having been assigned as Dowling's crew, they flew training missions with him for his captaincy qualification, before resuming ops with their newly-qualified captain.

After the blood and thunder of Walker's combat on 2 June, the Australian Sunderlands had only infrequent combat with the Ju 88 fighters over the Bay of Biscay. In the two months following, the Ju 88s of V./KG40 shot down sixteen Coastal Command aircraft, but luckily none from Nos 10 or 461.[12] During that period, the two Australian Sunderland squadrons contacted Ju 88s on only four occasions. On 26 June, Fred Manger was flying N-Nuts's replacement, Sunderland X/461, on an anti-submarine patrol in one of the newly promulgated 'Musketry' search areas, when his lookouts spotted two Ju 88s. Luckily, there was a layer of 10/10th cloud overhanging the patrol area at less than 1,000 feet, so it was a simple matter to pull up into cloud and avoid them. He resumed his patrol, and nearly three hours later, two more Ju 88s came into view; it was again an easy matter to avoid a confrontation by hiding in cloud. Two weeks later, on 8 July, 10 Squadron's Ted Farmer was flying a patrol in more perilous, fine weather; he was cruising at 500 feet when a crewman spotted a Ju 88, 10 miles off, flying low down over the sea at only 200 feet. This time there was no cloud to hide in, so Farmer's crew had to watch it drawing nearer, until it was only a mile away off the port beam. Unaccountably, it then turned away behind the Sunderland and flew off into the distance on a reciprocal course. Given V./KG40's standard patrol tactics of patrolling in fours or eights, it is likely that this single, inoffensive aircraft was a Ju 88 reconnaissance aircraft. If it was a Ju 88 fighter, the pilot had evidently decided it was too dangerous to attack a Sunderland alone.

A week later, on 14 July, 10 Squadron's Plt Off. 'Alan' Williams encountered a more combative Ju 88. Williams was a recently qualified captain who had flown his first patrol in command of a crew in May and was now leading his tenth operation. His gunners spotted the Ju 88 at 6 miles away, upon which Williams pulled up to climb into cloud, but the enemy fighter cut him off. The Ju 88 came in for a firing pass upon the Sunderland's starboard bow, obliging Williams to make an evasive turn and dive to regain some speed. Although the Ju 88 pilot was aggressive, he was not self-sacrificial, at first firing from a safe range of 900 yards before breaking away, at which distance he got no hits. A second attacking run was even less resolute, broken off at 1,000 yards. Meanwhile, Williams had resumed climbing, and he made it into the obscurity of 10/10th cloud before the prudently-flown Ju 88 could attack again. Despite the bracing story of Walker's triumphant victory over eight Ju 88s, it is most evident that no crew was taking any chances with enemy fighters; they knew that their only real security lay in avoidance, not fighting.

It made all the difference in the world not only how much cloud cover there was in the patrol area, but also how many enemy fighters one ran into. On 27 July, both tactical factors bore down heavily upon No. 10's Fg Off. Ron Humble, when he was attacked by four Ju 88s in perilously clear skies. Humble was another newly-qualified captain, having joined the unit in October 1942, flown seven trips as first pilot, commenced captaincy training in May 1943, and captained his first operation on 16 June; this was now his seventh trip in command. By 4.05 p.m., he was three hours into the flight, cruising in E/10 at 2,500 feet within the northern 'Musketry' patrol area, when four Ju 88s appeared, 8 miles away, already distributed into co-ordinated attacking positions off the Sunderland's port and starboard quarters. To make matters worse, it was a dangerously fine day, with 'nil cloud' and 'good visibility'. Humble and his crew had no option but to go to action stations, watch the Ju 88s come closer, and prepare for a fight. The combat that ensued was like Walker's almost two months previously: the Ju 88s made co-ordinated attacks from both sides, they fired well enough to get hits, and their sequence of attacks lasted one hour. To spoil the Germans' shots, Humble pushed and pulled his Sunderland through the standard repertoire of hard evasive manoeuvres: skidding turns underneath each incoming fighter's flight-path, corkscrew dives, and climbing turns. The first pilot, FS Wally Simms, was hit in the heel, but refused first aid as he needed to stay in his seat to watch the incoming Ju 88s, to help call the evasive turns, and assist Humble in heaving, pushing and pulling on the control wheels.

The German gunfire also holed the oil tank behind the starboard outer engine, and without oil, this engine had to be shut down, cutting hydraulic power to the midships turret. Luckily, the last Ju 88 broke off to head home at 5.05 p.m., leaving Humble to set course for the Scillies. Base signalled a diversion to Pembroke Dock, as Mount Batten was 'weatherbound', which meant a longer flight, and that on only three engines. Humble had his wireless operator tap off a reply, advising base that he needed an ambulance, and that his aircraft had hits below the waterline and needed to be slipped (brought up out of the water) straight away. He landed safely at 'PD' at 8.18 p.m. at the end of a twelve-and-a-half-hour flight. A party of airmen from RAF Pembroke Dock fitted beaching dollies to 'E' and pulled her up the slipway on to the hard-standing, so that her hull damage could be inspected and repaired. Meanwhile, FS Simms was taken for treatment at the Station Sick Quarters. It turned out that Humble's Sunderland 'E' had been seriously damaged, for after an inspection two days later by a 10 Squadron maintenance party sent up from Mount Batten, the scope of repairs was deemed too much even for that unit's resources, so she was handed over to No. 43 Maintenance Group at Pembroke Dock at the end of the month, to be repaired by sub-contractors. Once that work was completed, she was flown home from Pembroke Dock on 19 August, resuming operational service on the 20th. Humble and his crew had done very well to withstand an hour-long encounter with four Ju 88s, to get home safely on three engines, and to escape personnel casualties more serious than Simms's wounded heel. Like in Walker's case, the gunners claimed to have hit most of the attackers, with three Ju 88s claimed 'damaged'. However, despite the substantial similarity between the two battles, the crew made no claims for enemy aircraft 'destroyed', so there was no repeat of the crew lionisation seen in Walker's case. Humble's crew was assigned a replacement aircraft, 'K', and after his wound healed, Simms rejoined his crew on operations.

By the end of July, the tempo of air combat over the Bay was hotting up, with the Luftwaffe's Atlantic Air Command responding meaningfully to U-boat Command's calls for air support in the face of the imminent defeat of the U-boat weapon. It was only now, belatedly, that the Luftwaffe made its most convincing attempt to wrest aerial dominance away from Coastal Command in the critical skies over the Bay. During the four months of June–September 1943, the Ju 88s of V./KG40 would shoot down forty-six Coastal Command aircraft.[13] As we shall see, further crews from both Nos 10 and 461 Squadrons would number among these victims. In the meantime, No. 19 Group's offensive against the U-boats' transit routes through the Bay continued, flying patrol lines hundreds of miles from the French coast to put maximum distance between the RAF's vulnerable patrol aircraft and the bases used by the dangerous German twin-engined fighters.

The U-boat 'Trade' Resumes

The Australian squadrons scored no U-boat kills in June, but on the last day of that month, No. 10's Flt Lt Hec Skinner came close: by 9.12 a.m., he had been airborne for almost five hours in T/10 when base signalled him to set course to intercept a submarine reported sailing about 70 miles off Cape Ortegal in Spain. This was within a much fought-over, high-probability area, part of the heavily-trafficked liminal zone for U-boats heading out to sea after taking passage along the northern coast of Spain. The crew of T/10 spotted the submarine two hours later, 4 miles off the port bow, and Skinner turned to make an immediate attack. However, having started at 3,000 feet, he was too close and too high; to lose enough height to make an attack, he banked his aircraft steeply to the left and then to the right, in a series of height-losing S-turns. However, in his impatience to get down close to the water without further ado, he was still at 250 feet when he overflew the U-boat, too high for an effective depth-charge attack.

Circling around for a more careful, second approach, this time Skinner bored in at the correct height and dropped a stick of seven depth-charges across the U-boat's track. The nearest one exploded 50 yards off the boat's port side—too far to damage the hull. The AA fire was severe, and although Skinner's nose gunner fired off three magazines of .303 at the conning tower and saw three men falling under his fire, there were enough gunners firing accurately as the Sunderland went past overhead, hitting the aircraft in the tail turret, port elevator, rear hull, and in both wings. The rear gunner, Sgt John Burnham, got a momentary burst away (a total of fifty rounds from his four guns) before he was severely wounded by a burst of 20-mm, suffering shrapnel wounds to his right leg and both hands, and extensive facial injuries. With a badly wounded man aboard and a severely damaged aircraft, Skinner headed for home at once. However, from the south-western extremity of the Bay of Biscay, it took almost five hours before T/10 was on the water and taxiing for the slipway at Mountbatten. This was too slow for Burnham, who despite being admitted to the Royal Navy Hospital at Plymouth died later that day. On 2 July, the CO led a funeral service at the RAF Mountbatten mortuary, before an interment ceremony at Bath on the following day.[14] The U-boat that Skinner had attacked was *U-518*, which safely made Bordeaux on 3 August.[15]

Despite the losses inflicted by the Ju 88s, the heavy RAF airborne presence over the Bay bore fruit, for it was in this period, the end of July and the beginning of August 1943, that U-boat Command suffered another spate of catastrophic losses, giving Coastal Command a second happy hunting period to rival that of May. The reader will recall that Dönitz had despatched six U-boats to sail for the Atlantic on 27 and 28 July, and that

Dudley Marrows's crew from No. 461 sank *U-461* from this sailing on 30 July, as part of a stunning triple sinking (as we saw in chapter 1). After the loss of both *U-461* and *U-462* in that disastrous battle, Dönitz's U-tanker force had been decimated, with only two Type XIV 'Milch-cow' U-tankers left in service. After 30 July, only three of the six boats despatched on this sailing remained afloat, still sailing west. Aware of the loss on 30 July of the two U-tankers, U-boat Command signalled new orders to these other three boats: they were to sail into the Atlantic and act as improvised tankers by donating their fuel to the boats further out.

One of these boats was *U-106*, and on 1 August, she was found, reported, and attacked by a Wellington of No. 407 (Canadian) Squadron. By then, she was five days out from Lorient, but still within aircraft range because of her slow, mostly submerged, passage through the Bay.[16] This continued exposure to air attack shows the tactical effect of 19 Group's swamping patrols across the Bay's exit points, for without the constant presence of RAF aircraft overhead, *U-106* would have made more surface running, therefore more progress to the west, and hence would already have been beyond the range of patrol aircraft from Britain. In the event, she survived the attack by the Canadian Wellington, but was sufficiently damaged to abort the mission and head back to base for repairs. We will shortly meet *U-106* again in this narrative. Another of the surviving boats, *U-454*, had set out from La Pallice on 29 July, to make an independent passage through the Bay.[17] She too made slow progress, having applied the by-now standard tactical procedure of proceeding mostly submerged, to avoid getting ambushed by radar-equipped Wellingtons. Both these boats were destined for violent collisions with Australian Sunderlands.

Over the first two days of August, the two Australian squadrons between them despatched seven aircraft on patrols into the Bay. On 1 August, No. 10's Flt Lt 'Bob' Fry took off in B/10 for a 'Musketry' anti-submarine patrol to the by-now standard area of conflict in the outer south-west corner of the Bay of Biscay. Fry was a twenty-nine-year-old veteran flying his twenty-eighth mission as captain of a Sunderland. B/10 received a message from base to search for a submarine reported in a position 130 miles north–north-west of Cape Ortegal in Spain, and at 2.20 p.m. was searching the area at 1,700 feet when he saw five warships 6 miles away, evidently engaged on a submarine hunt: these were the sloops of Capt. Johnnie Walker's 2nd Support Group (the same ships met with in Chapter 1). Fry turned towards this activity, and almost at once almost overflew the ships' quarry: a surfaced submarine, only 2 miles off, sailing north-west at 10 knots.

This was *U-454*, which had spent the day so far trying to surface to recharge her batteries, which were heavily drained after cruising all night submerged. However, each time she surfaced, there had come an aircraft alarm almost at once, obliging yet another dive and more battery-draining submerged running. Only twenty minutes before Fry found her, she had had to dive again after only five minutes on the surface because of yet another of these aircraft alerts. According to her CO, *Kapitänleutnant* Burkhard Hackländer, 'The situation was now serious, the batteries were exhausted and the air was foul'.[18] With flat batteries, he now had no choice but to surface again. And so *U-454* popped up again, again surfaced in the Allied patrol area, and this time without enough battery power to submerge. Straight after surfacing, Hackländer's lookouts called yet another aircraft contact, 2 miles off the port beam: it was Fry's Sunderland, B/10. So harried had the U-boat crew been up to this point from the incessant aircraft alarms that they had not detected the five sloops bearing down on him: these were even then only 5 miles away, steaming up the submarine's wake at 18 knots.

Fry was too high and too close to attack immediately, so descended towards the water in a left turn. The U-boat bridge crew saw the Sunderland suddenly drop out of the clouds, cross the boat's bows, and then turn tightly left to dive upon their boat's starboard quarter. Fry was of course unaware that the submarine could not dive, so was in a terrible hurry to attack before it submerged. The resultant geometry of the attack, dictated by angles and distances outside his choosing, placed him on an attack run exposed to the U-boat's full flak-gun broadside. Like Marrows two days earlier, he was now committed, and his survival and that of his crew would depend upon his nose gunner's ability to outshoot the submarine's flak gunners with his 'pop gun' .303. On the other side of the fence, *U-454* had one twin 20-mm on the upper bandstand, and a single 20-mm on the lower bandstand. The Sunderland's nose gunner (probably Sgt John Fryer) sprayed the submarine's conning tower with .303 tracers, but his shooting seems to have been slightly astray, leaving the U-boat's gunners to aim and fire unhindered. As the Sunderland straightened out of its final turn and headed in at minimum altitude, the gunner on the U-boat's twin 20-mm fired in short bursts to find the range, finding it awkward trying to hold his aim while the boat rolled in the swell beneath his feet; but when the Sunderland reached a quarter mile off, he got hits on both of the aircraft's starboard engines. The 20-mm shell impacts ruptured the starboard main fuel tank as well, and with fuel flooding into the cockpit and the starboard inner engine 'shattered', the Sunderland's pilot had his work cut out to keep the aircraft flying straight and level, tracking towards the U-boat for bomb release. *U-454*'s captain saw 'numerous bursts of fire' hitting the Sunderland's hull, but it flew steadily on nonetheless, boring in for the kill. From *U-454*'s conning tower, Hackländer saw the flying boat pass overhead at 50 feet, releasing a stick of six depth-charges which fell in a perfect straddle, three each side of the submarine.

The Sunderland's depth-charges were 'all aimed with extreme accuracy': three exploded in the water just past the hull, and the other three hit the U-boat squarely. These three bombs struck the upper deck in a line running from just forward of the conning tower to the extreme bow, then rolled off the deck into the water. Exactly as they were fused to do, they then exploded at a depth of 25 feet, right underneath the forward hull. These detonations catastrophically ruptured *U-454*'s hull: she 'broke in two' and was gone in 'barely 30 seconds'. As the Sunderland flew past, the tail gunner, FS Don Conacher, 'saw the target disappear momentarily in a monstrous plume of water and spray and then watched the U-boat rapidly sink'. This U-boat's demise came in a very similar fashion to that of *U-461*: only one man made it out of the hull alive, and he reported that the depth-charges wreaked such violent destruction in the control room that 'most of the instruments and apparatus had been torn from their supports', followed by 'a massive inrush of water from above'. Only thirteen men survived to find themselves swimming in the water, and like in *U-461*'s case, the survivors with only a single exception were limited to the small parties of watch-keepers on the bridge (including the CO and first lieutenant), the gunners on the bandstands, and the flak-gun ammunition parties. Most of these men simply found themselves in the water as their boat sank away beneath them. The other thirty-four men, trapped down below, went down with her.[19]

Fry's flak-hit Sunderland headed away, flying to the south with wings level, aiming towards the approaching sloops about 5 miles away. The flak hits in the hull had evidently knocked out the intercom, as no one heard anything more from the pilots on the flight-deck. With two engines hit, the aircraft had no hope of flying the 400 miles to St Mary's in the Scillies: a Sunderland struggled to maintain height even with only one engine out, so this one would need to force-land on the ocean, and soon. After flying straight for 6 miles, the Sunderland approached the Royal Navy taskforce, then turned 180 degrees left, setting up to force-land on the sea near the ships. With frontal conditions passing over the Bay, the weather was described as 'bumpy' and 'turbulent', and the height of the swell was estimated as 15–20 feet, too high for a safe Sunderland sea landing. HMS *Wren* was nearby as the Sunderland made its final approach, and aboard the sloop was Flt Lt John Jewell, No. 10 Squadron's navigation officer, who was on a two-week professional exchange with the Royal Navy. He saw the 'obviously crippled' Sunderland line up on a northerly course to land along the swell, a task made difficult by the stiff crosswind from the west.[20]

Although the pilot of B/10 had set himself up for the best chance of a successful forced landing, in fact the sea conditions were far outside the safe parameters for Sunderland aircraft. The aircraft made a stable approach, but upon touchdown bounced twice upon the tops of the waves, and at the top of the final bounce stalled and dropped the starboard wing with such force that the wing was torn off in the impact—not unlike the earlier catastrophic arrivals of Neville Halliday and Bill Dods. The pilot had likely tried to add some power after the second bounce to arrest the rate of descent, but with two engines out on the starboard side, he could not hold the swing, and the aircraft had rolled and yawed uncontrollably, cartwheeling into the next wave. Aboard HMS *Wren*, John Jewell saw the Sunderland 'plunge straight into a 15 foot swell'. This third and final touchdown was violent and final, snapping off a wing, severing the forward hull and sinking rapidly.

Because the intercom was knocked out, the four gunners in their positions in the fuselage had evidently received no warning from the pilots about the imminent landing, as shown by the fact that the tail and dorsal turrets were still manned when the landing was made, with their turrets trained fully to the left: if the crew had been advised of the landing, these gunners would certainly have vacated their turrets at once and taken up crash positions behind the wing spar. It seems both turret gunners had belatedly perceived that the aircraft was about to make a forced landing, for they had rotated their turrets to the beam to enable quick escapes through their turrets' rear doors if things came unstuck in the landing. Down on the bottom deck, the galley gunners were not enclosed by any turret structure, and so were free to climb up the ladder to the upper deck as soon as they recognised that the aircraft was turning in for a landing. The fact of their survival indicates that they made it in time, for the hull was split open so violently in the crash that the bottom deck must have been destroyed in the impact and violently immersed.

With the desperation of survival, all six men in the rear fuselage managed to struggle out of their positions and get clear of the rapidly sinking wreckage; none of them were afterwards able to give any coherent account of events prior to getting free of the wreck and finding themselves able to swim in the water.[21] The survival of both turret gunners is remarkable, for both the tail gunner, Don Conacher, and the dorsal gunner, FS Ron Welfare, suffered broken right ankles and lacerations to the right side of their bodies as they were flung violently forward against their turret fixtures in the final water impact.

None of the crewmen on the flight-deck survived: all three pilots, the trainee navigator, and the flight engineer; as well as the nose gunner. That area had taken the full brunt of the nose-first hull impact, and the shattered forward fuselage had buried itself deeply in the water. The survivors were the navigator, Fg Off. John Portus, four gunners, and the second flight engineer. All six crew members who failed to survive the crash were on the flight-deck or forward of it, while all those who survived were further aft in the fuselage. The nose gunner may well have been hit by gunfire in his turret, given the all the flak hits that the Germans observed on the hull, and either died from his wounds or failed to get out of his turret before the crash. Certainly, if he was still in his turret upon water impact, he had no chance. Thus it was seating position at the moment of the crash that determined the survival of any one crew member: those in the torn-off and submerged front hull died; those in the still-floating centre and rear fuselage survived.

It was believed that Fry and the other pilots had been hit by the burst of 20-mm that crippled the aircraft, and this might have been so.[22] However, someone had certainly been flying the aircraft, for it was clearly under control, and being flown purposefully for a controlled forced-landing. Furthermore, during the bomb run, at least one of the pilots had very capably counteracted the involuntary roll and yaw effect of the knocked-out starboard inner engine, had precisely held the optimum attack height of 50 feet, and had then made the most accurate depth-charge attack ever recorded in this book. With this seamless performance, there can be little doubt that either Fry or his first pilot, Fg Off. 'Bob' Budd, or both, remained alive and functional on the flight-deck. After the gunfire ruptured the wing fuel tank, however, it is possible that petrol fumes were filling the aircraft's upper deck and making the flight-deck unbearable, which may then have hastened the landing attempt. Fry's crash was another instance of the unhappy Sunderland open-water-landing syndrome, exacerbated by the barely-controllable aircraft, with two dead engines on one side. Fry and the others thus died straight after their greatest triumph, but that was the way of things in operational flying.

Not one of the three aircraft dinghies deployed in the violent crash, leaving the six survivors swimming in the water, held up only by their Mae Wests. Luckily, the torn-off starboard wing, with its wing-float still attached, continued to float nearby, so five of them swam over and climbed onto the stump of the wing, using it as an improvised survival raft. The man who did not do so was the tail gunner, Don Conacher, who had suffered such a painful broken ankle that he could not swim. Fortunately, HMS *Wren* was racing 'to the spot', and was soon alongside Conacher. The sea proved to be too rough for the *Wren* to launch the ship's boats, even after pumping a pool of oil over the side to calm the sea, so the sailors threw Conacher a lifebuoy and then hauled him painfully up the side of the ship onto the deck. After that, the sloop manoeuvred over to the floating wing stump, and let the five other men jump into the sea, swim to the ship's side, and climb up the scrambling net hung over the side. However, the navigator, John Portus, was so exhausted that he could not make it from the wing stump to the ship, and so some sailors dived in to shepherd him across to the ship and then manhandle him up the side and aboard. All six men were rescued within thirty minutes of the crash.

Had it not been for the serendipitous proximity of the Royal Navy task force, there would have been little chance of anyone surviving.

Back at RAF Mount Batten, 10 Squadron's ops room received the signal from the ships that B/10 had crashed, and then the signal that there were only six survivors, unnamed. The squadron CO, Wg Cdr Hartnell, confided in his diary that 'They are the best crew in the squadron by far and Bob Fry and Bob Budd in particular will be sadly missed if they are gone.'[23] Fry would also be missed by his wife, waiting for him back in Glenelg, South Australia. Budd was a 'brilliant pianist' from the Sydney Conservatorium, who was known for arriving back from a twelve-hour trip, getting debriefed, then going to the piano and playing 'solidly for two hours'.[24] Hartnell had to wait until the ship docked at Devonport on the morning of 6 August before finding out who was dead. Of course, it was even worse for the next of kin, for the families of all twelve crewmen had in the meantime been notified by telegram that their loved one was missing. Hartnell met the ship, thanked the captain, and drove the men back to Mount Batten, dressed in their motley assortment of naval uniform items from the ship's stores. Afterwards, the survivors 'spoke glowingly' about the hospitality the Navy had provided. With their fractured ankles, Conacher and Welfare were admitted to the Royal Navy Hospital at Plymouth, while even the uninjured men were still suffering from shock, with all four admitted to the station sick bay at Mount Batten. While the survivors were being cared for, another set of telegrams were prepared for the next of kin: six families would be relieved of their anxiety, but another six would learn that what they had feared had come true.

As well as the survivors of Fry's crew, the *Wren* also disembarked a party of U-boat survivors at Devonport, who were similarly clad, but unlike the airmen, they were led off the ship 'Indian file', blind-folded. Hackländer was reunited in captivity with his officer colleagues, Stiebler and Vowe, and the rest of the survivors from *U-461* and *U-462*, spending the next four and a half years together in POW camps. During the interrogation process, the British intelligence officers found Hackländer to be 'a pleasant type of non-political German naval officer', whereas by contrast, his second lieutenant, *Leutnant* Gerhard Braun, was judged to be 'a fanatical National Socialist'. The intelligence officers were amused by the ironically contradictory political opinions of these officers: whereas the mild, 'non-political' Hackländer continued to believe Hitler to be a 'military genius', despite the decisive and disastrous turn of the war against Germany on all fronts in 1943, the diehard Nazi, Braun, was 'convinced Germany will lose the war'.[25]

With *U-454* sunk, the reader will recall that *U-106* was still underway, making her passage into the Atlantic, and that on the next morning, 2 August, she was attacked and damaged by a Wellington of 407 (Canadian) Squadron. Under the command of *Oberleutnant* Wolfdietrich Damerow, her crew patched her up sufficiently to allow her to submerge again, but she sent a distress signal to U-boat Command advising that she was aborting her mission and returning to port for repairs. She was then advised that three destroyers had been despatched to escort her home and was given a mid-ocean rendezvous point north-west of the Spanish port of El Ferrol. She reached the rendezvous late that afternoon, but the destroyers were not there. However, the submarine's hydrophones picked up the sound of destroyer propellers, heading away to the north. Fearful of missing the rendezvous and losing the flak protection of the friendly warships, Damerow surfaced his submarine and headed north to cut them off at best speed.[26]

U-106 did not find the German destroyers, but a Sunderland crew from 461 Squadron did: Flt Lt Chic Clarke had taken off from Pembroke Dock in aircraft 'M' at lunchtime, proceeded to the usual south-west corner of the Bay to commence his Musketry patrol, and at 4.44 p.m. spotted the three destroyers 5 miles off. He shadowed them outside the range of their 20-mm flak, but the German ships engaged him with their 4.1-inch guns whenever he got too near. Drawn by M/461's sighting report, another Sunderland appeared: this was N/228, also based at Pembroke Dock, and flown by Fg Off. R. D. Hanbury. Together, these two Sunderlands saw the German destroyers turn around and head back to France.[27]

The German warships might have given up their search for *U-106*, but the Sunderlands kept looking and found her as well: Hanbury spotted her first, attempted a prompt attack, but sheared off when he saw the wall of flak put up by her 20-mm battery. By 8.05 p.m., Clarke's M/461 had joined N/228 in orbiting around the U-boat from 3 miles away. After a few minutes of this, the two Sunderlands rolled in for co-ordinated, simultaneous attacks: Hanbury dived upon the submarine's starboard bow, while Clarke dived upon its port bow. This split the boat's flak: Hanbury's Sunderland was taken under fire from the quad 20-mm, while Clarke's was engaged by the single 20-mm and the 7.92-mm machine guns on the conning tower. Clarke levelled out just above the sea, at 50 feet, with his nose turret gunner, FS John Royal, firing bursts of .303 at the U-boat's bandstands. Royal got hits: on the submarine's conning tower, Damerow saw all four men on his quad 20-mm cut down by the fire from the Sunderland, while the pilots on Clarke's flight-deck saw the bodies of German crewmen falling off the conning tower into the water. As we have seen with the earlier attacks by Marrows and Fry, obtaining fire superiority over a U-boat's flak gunners was essential to an attacking aircraft's survival, and Royal had shot as accurately as had 'Bubbles' Pearce and 'Pierre' Bamber three days previously.

Both Sunderlands roared across the U-boat within seconds of each other, with Hanbury's salvo of depth-charges going into the water 50 yards astern of the submarine, close enough to cause 'severe concussion' within the boat's hull. Then Clarke's Sunderland went across the U-boat's bows at 50 feet, dropping seven depth-charges. These fell obliquely across the submarine's hull in a perfect straddle, centred on the conning tower. From the U-boat's perspective, these detonations came 'almost simultaneously' with the earlier blasts but were much closer: they knocked out the starboard diesel engine, with an electrical fire in the port engine-room switchboard as well. Although the boat was still under power from her port diesel, her pressure hull had been breached, so she was unable to submerge; her compartments were filling with smoke from the electrical fire in the engine room, and she was starting to flood, listing to port from a 'bad leak'.[28]

With the U-boat left wallowing in this parlous state, both Sunderlands came back in to get rid of their last depth-charges. Five minutes after their earlier attack, Hanbury came in with the sun right behind him to blind the flak gunners, followed by Clarke coming in from another direction. The interval was long enough for new gunners to come up from below to man the submarine's quad 20-mm, but these men were not trained gunners and so shot ineffectively: once again, the Sunderlands' .303-inch fire struck the bandstands, knocking the single 20-mm 'out of action', and again the resultant fire superiority allowed the Sunderland pilots to bomb accurately. Each aircraft had only a single remaining depth-charge to drop, but both fell 'very close'. On *U-106*'s conning tower, Damerow heard the resultant damage reports: the port diesel too was now knocked out, as well as both electrical motors. The boat was now dead in the water, her hull spaces filling with chlorine gas from burst batteries, and with uncontrolled flooding aft. Up above, the crews of the circling Sunderlands saw the U-boat settling by the stern in a great welling pool of diesel oil, streaming dark smoke from her starboard side. When Damerow's senior engineer announced that the boat could no longer be kept afloat, the captain ordered 'Abandon Ship!' The crew grabbed their dinghy packs, hurried up on to the upper deck, inflated their dinghies, and took to the water. Damerow remained on board the still-floating boat with five men to guard the men in the water with the AA gun.[29]

By now, Clarke's aircraft had been airborne for nearly eight hours, so upon reaching minimum fuel he had to depart the scene and head home. He therefore missed observing the final destruction of *U-106*. With the submarine still floating, and with all his depth-charges expended, Hanbury made a series of strafing attacks on the sinking boat and its distressed survivors, shooting up 'a number of rafts'. As we have seen before, in the brutal logic of the Battle of the Atlantic, so long as the U-boat itself floated, the attack had to continue, for the crew could potentially reboard the still-floating boat and get her underway again. Finally, when the gunners on the boat ran out of ammunition, Damerow ordered them off into the water, and then jumped in himself. Soon after, the men in the water saw and heard a 'heavy explosion' aboard the U-boat, after which she sank rapidly by the stern, farewelled by 'the cheers of the swimming crew'. From overhead, at 8.40 p.m., Hanbury's crew saw the boat suddenly explode, leaving the sea 'littered with debris and four dinghies full of survivors'. Hanbury's Sunderland then made low passes over the survivors, dropping two smoke floats to help rescuers locate their position, before following Clarke back to Pembroke Dock.[30] By now, U-106's distress calls had prompted the three destroyers to turn about once more, and these reached the survivors just before nightfall, rescuing thirty-five men. Another twenty-five had died on the boat and in the water.[31]

Back at Pembroke Dock, the crews were buoyed by another congratulatory message from Air Vice-Marshal Bromet at Plymouth: 'Today's operations have been a smashing success. Co-operation between all units has been beyond reproach. Well done and keep it up. They can't keep this pace up for long'. Clarke had shared this latest kill with Hanbury's crew from No. 228 Squadron, while U-106's presence on the surface was the direct result of the 407 Squadron Wellington's attack earlier in the day. Nonetheless, this could be chalked up on No. 461's scoreboard as a definite kill. Clarke's attack had moreover been the most accurate of all, crippling the U-boat and leaving her sinking. This kill meant that the two Australian squadrons had killed three U-boats in only four days—an unprecedented achievement for them. For the Germans, it was much worse than that: in the six days commencing 28 July, they had lost nine boats trying to make passage through the Bay, all but one of them killed by the aircraft of No. 19 Group.

The weight of these losses was 'catastrophic' for Grand Admiral Dönitz's U-boat Command. These sinkings of boats attempting to transit through the Bay at the turn of the month from July to August 1943 were so extreme as to suggest it was almost suicidal to continue the attempt: indeed, only a single boat from the end-of-July sailings had survived. Accordingly, Dönitz recalled the four boats that had subsequently set sail on 1 August and halted further sailings from the Biscay ports. Hitler's Grand Admiral and his staff officers at U-boat HQ were staring stark defeat in the face—defeat at the hands of Allied anti-submarine forces that had grown so numerous, so hyper-active, and so proficient as to reduce his hitherto mighty submarine weapon to the status of mobile targets, and his submariners from conquering heroes to the pitiable victims of overwhelming force. For Dönitz and his staff officers, it was back to the drawing board. They used the ensuing hiatus in U-boat operations to replan their strategy and reconfigure their boats upon some viable basis for a resumption of the campaign later in the Autumn.[32] They would try, but they would not succeed. Germany had irrevocably lost the 'Battle of the Atlantic'.

Bearing the Cost of Victory

Despite the triumph of these U-boat sinkings at the beginning of August, they proved to be the last anti-submarine successes by the Australian Sunderlands in 1943. For the balance of the year, the Australian crews would have to content themselves with practise attack exercises against 'tame' British submarines which conveniently surfaced and submerged like clockwork mice within the exercise area in the English Channel. The year would thus end as August had ended, with a total of six U-boats sunk by Nos 10 and 461; honours were even, with three to the credit of each squadron. None of the crews knew it at the time, but the rest of 1943 would be chiefly characterised by combats with German fighters, rather than with U-boats. The Luftwaffe would exact a belated revenge for the Australians' leading role in the destruction of U-boats in the Bay.

On 3 August, the day after Clarke's U-boat sinking, Alan Williams's 10 Squadron crew ran into another flight of Ju 88s, in an encounter very reminiscent of Col Walker's famous action of two months before. After escaping a previous fighter attack on 14 July, this time Williams ran into seven Ju 88s while flying a Musketry patrol in J/10. Unfortunately, it was a beautiful day with visibility of up to 25 miles, only scattered cumulus clouds, and a thin layer of cirrus cloud at 3,500 feet. Recognising the heightened danger of flying in these conditions, all his gunners were 'keyed up' as their Sunderland traversed the wide blue sky.[1] At 6.16 p.m., J/10 was cruising at 3,000 feet when the sharp-eyed first pilot, Fg Off. Ray Behrndt, searching below the horizon through his binoculars, called three 'bogeys' 8 miles off. Williams climbed for a cumulus cloud big enough to provide cover, and after hiding in cloud for nine minutes, he resumed the patrol, flying off on the designated search leg to the south, crossing the wide expanse of blue sky. Soon after, at 6.37 p.m., Behrndt spotted three bogeys at 12 miles. Williams reversed course and made for the same isolated cumulus cloud to the north he had left only minutes before, but the Ju 88s came after them: the tail gunner, Sgt Angus McVinish, and the midships gunner, Sgt Bart Simon, saw the pursuing Ju 88s leaving trails of black smoke from their engines. Like the Sunderland, they were running their engines at full throttle, burning their fuel in rich mixture to get some speed.

Soon the fighters caught up and deployed into the standard attacking positions, with aircraft queuing up off each beam, preparatory to starting their firing runs. To make matters worse, McVinish and Simon then spotted a second flight of three Ju 88s, moving up from behind to join the attack. But the battle opened with a head-on pass by a hitherto-unseen Ju 88, which suddenly appeared from behind a cloud up ahead. It may be that Williams's gunners and lookouts had fixated too much upon the six enemy fighters previously spotted, for it was while they were watching these that the seventh one suddenly arrived. Ray Behrndt spotted it at the last moment and called out a warning. Seeing this Ju 88 looming up in front, Williams used the flight controls to line up his gunsight on the incoming 88 and fire back with his four front guns: Sunderland J/10 was the very first Sunderland to fly an operation retrofitted with the newly-introduced anti-submarine armament of four fixed .303-inch Brownings in the nose, aimed by the pilot, fighter pilot-style. However, Williams immediately regretted using his aircraft in this fashion, for it had left the Sunderland flying straight for critical seconds, simplifying the German pilot's gunnery problem. The venturesome German fighter pulled up only 100 yards in front and passed closely over the top of the Sunderland, too quickly to be hit. In the midships turret, Sgt Simon saw the Ju 88 go past only 200 feet above and sent his tracers after it. The nose turret had also returned fire momentarily as this first Ju 88 came in, but had then fallen silent: the gunner, FS 'Alan' Bird, had been struck and killed by the German pilot's accurate gunfire.

While the head-on attack distracted Williams, the first of the flanking Ju 88s had rolled into their attack runs, one after the other, coming in to fire from alternative sides at the momentarily non-manoeuvring Sunderland. The first of these fired as accurately as the very first attacker, for a 20-mm cannon shell exploded in the starboard wing root, scattering shrapnel into the flight-deck. The crew's fighter controller in the astrodome, Fg Off. Reg Gross, who had been watching the incoming 88s and calling the evasive turns for the captain, fell to the floor, struck in the side by splinters; while the wireless operator, FS Jim Guy, was struck in the face by shell fragments. This same shell-hit also cut the hydraulic lines to both the nose and midships turrets, as well as cutting the intercom. The wounded Gross took position again in the fighter lookout position underneath the astrodome, but without intercom he was reduced to passing manoeuvring instructions to the pilot 'by hand', which given the resultant time lag, was hardly likely to work as well as real-time verbal instructions in the pilot's earphones, despite the assistance of the second pilot, Fg Off. Alan Murray, as an intermediary. With significant damage already inflicted upon his aircraft in the first two firing passes, Williams jettisoned the depth-charges and settled down to a torrid fight for survival.

For the next hour, the seven Ju 88s came in one after the other in 'continual' attacks, repositioning after each firing run before making a new run from a different direction. Williams was reduced to manoeuvring almost blindly, able to respond to not much more than what he and Ray Behrndt could see out of the cockpit windows. Despite the handicapped vision, he put the aircraft through an interminable succession of full-throttle climbing and diving turns, as well as 'hedgehops'—a sharp pull up to cause the attacker to overshoot, followed by a bunt to push the nose down and regain flying speed for the next manoeuvre. This evidently worked well enough, for after their first fusillades the Germans never again succeeded in hitting anything vital, although the starboard main fuel tank was holed. With great dedication to duty, the first fitter, Sgt Bill Moser, crawled out into the wing cavity to bung the leak. The starboard galley gunner, Sgt 'Tony' Owen (the first flight engineer), was hit in the legs during one of these attacks but stayed at his gun until relieved by Moser. Crucially, all four engines continued to deliver full power, enabling the Sunderland to corkscrew in the general direction of the much sought-after cumulus cloud without losing height.

With considerable understatement, Williams afterwards reported that he had tried to make cloud, but that it was very difficult to do so because of the continuous turns he was making. Remarkably, despite that he succeeded in finally reaching a patch of cirrus at 3,500 feet, but it was too thin to obscure the Sunderland from the fighters, so he maintained his corkscrewing progress towards the larger cumulus cloud, his original goal. Even more remarkably, Williams survived the attentions of the fighters to cross the intervening expanse of blue sky and to finally enter that friendly cloud. It proved none too large, requiring continuous circling within for the Sunderland to remain hidden. Williams emerged occasionally to see if the coast was clear, each time spotting four Ju 88s lurking on the fringes of the cloud like a pack of killer whales circling around a seal on the ice. The Germans resorted to firing blindly into the cloud: the Sunderland's midships turret gunner, Bart Simon, saw the flashes of time-fused 20-mm shells exploding eerily within the blank grey interior of the cloud. After circling inside for fifty minutes, the Sunderland finally emerged to find that the 88s had given up: there was a flight of five of them visible in the distance, heading away towards Brest. When the Germans got home, they accurately and modestly made a claim for one Sunderland damaged in combat.[2] Williams meanwhile set course for Mount Batten, signalling base that he needed an ambulance and a doctor upon arrival. To get home as directly as possible, as soon as his wounds were dressed, Reg Gross resumed his place at the navigator's position, using a sextant to fix the aircraft's position and a drift recorder to find the wind.[3]

Alan Bird's funeral was held on 5 August: first there was a short memorial service at Mount Batten, attended by officers and other ranks from the unit, and then the coffin was taken by road to Millbay Railway Station in Plymouth, for onwards carriage to Bath. There the burial service proper took place at Haycombe Cemetery, with the squadron radio officer, Plt Off. Noel Medlin, in attendance as the head of Bird's section. Meanwhile, up on her beaching wheels on the hard-standing in front of the hangars, No. 10's maintenance flight ascertained that Sunderland J/10 was seriously damaged, with numerous holes through her hull, wings and main spar. The aircraft was handed over to the manufacturer, Short Bros, for repairs at their RAF Mount Batten work site. She had only been with the unit since May 1943, and it was not until November that she returned to the unit repaired from the contractor.

The death of Alan Bird and the wounding of the other crewmen, on top of the successful defence of the aircraft against sustained attack from seven enemy fighters, triggered the awards process, in a manner not dissimilar to that experienced by Walker and his crew previously. As early as 11 August, scarcely more than a week after the event, the squadron received notice of the 'immediate' awarding of DFCs to Williams and Gross, and DFMs to Owen and Moser. As was customary, the crew was put on light duties afterwards: Williams did not fly again until 20 August, when he took a skeleton crew to Pembroke Dock to fly Sunderland 'E' back to Mount Batten; this was Ron Humble's aircraft, now repaired after the damage she suffered in the fight on 27 July. On 22 August, he was assigned a similar duty, ferrying one of the unit's new aircraft back to Mount Batten from Wig Bay. On the 27th, he was promoted to flight lieutenant, before resuming operational flying on 1 September, assigned to the same brand-new aircraft, 'P', which he had ferried in from Wig Bay only days previously.

Less than a week after Williams's big combat, on 8 August, 10 Squadron's Norm Gerrard was patrolling within his assigned Musketry patrol area when he was overtaken by a flight of Ju 88s, on another perilously-fine day of wide-open skies. At 12.58 a.m., he had only been on station in the patrol area for fifteen minutes, cruising in F/10 just above a layer of scattered cloud at 2,500 feet, when his gunners reported six Ju 88s at 2,000 yards, approaching from behind. These fighters followed their standard tactical drill, getting into position out on the Sunderland's flanks and then starting in from either side, attacking in ones and twos. Luckily, these German pilots displayed more caution than some had done recently, firing from long range and then breaking away at 600 yards. They made only a single firing pass each, then regathered and headed home, having got two hits on the Sunderland, one in the top of its port wing and one on the port wing-float. Gerrard's gunners fired back, but the combat had been so indecisive that Gerrard simply resumed his U-boat search afterwards. By August 1943, Gerrard had become one of the squadron's most experienced captains: this was his thirty-first operational trip. He was lucky to have run into a group of German pilots as relatively inoffensive as these had been.

The gunfire damage to 'F' was only superficial, for she was serviceable again in time to take-off on Gerrard's next patrol, only three days later, on the 11th. It was another anti-submarine patrol in one of the Musketry search areas. The same unit's Hec Skinner was flying W/10 on a patrol in the same area that afternoon, and at 2.10 p.m., he passed another Sunderland, presumed to be Gerrard's aircraft, flying at 2,000 feet on a reciprocal course. That was the last contact anyone ever had with Gerrard and F/10, which did not return to base and sent no signal. None of Gerrard's crew was ever seen again.[4] Skinner's crew had also come into contact with the source of F/10's demise, having earlier spotted three Ju 88s flying on a northerly course through the patrol area, low down just above the water. He had avoided them by climbing into cloud and then watching them go past below. Ju 88 pilots from V./KG40 made a claim that day for a Sunderland shot down.[5] Particularly unlucky was the twelfth man aboard, Plt Off. Roy 'Happy' Adams, the squadron gunnery officer, who had picked the wrong day to accompany his gunners on an operational flight. Wg Cdr Hartnell had the melancholy duty of writing another twelve condolence letters: to Adams's mother, Alice Adams in Caulfield, Victoria, he gave special tribute to 'Happy' for being 'the most efficient gunnery officer I have had the pleasure to work with'. He was one of the squadron originals, having been an air gunner since 1939, and only commissioned from NCO rank five months before he was lost, promoted specially to take up the role as officer in command of the squadron's gunnery section.[6]

After deftly avoiding the marauding Ju 88s on the 11th, Hec Skinner too was fated to fall victim to the voracious appetite of these airborne predators. He flew his next operation one week later, on the 18th, flying T/10. He took off from Mount Batten at 10.26 a.m., for an anti-submarine patrol in a Musketry search area. At 6.50 p.m., the RAF's No. 4 RDF Station at St Eval received a message from 'T' that she was under attack by enemy aircraft, followed shortly after by an SOS. The details of the signal were hard to read because of interference, but the transmission was fixed as emanating from a bearing of 222 degrees.[7] The message ended with '2020', which was presumably the crew's ETA back at base: they were evidently struggling home in a damaged aircraft, just as a succession of crews had successfully done before them. They never made it, however, and nothing was ever seen again of the twelve-man crew. Everyone assumed that T/10 too had tangled with Ju 88s, and such was indeed the case, for *Hauptmann* Horst Grahl from V./KG40 made a claim for a Sunderland shot down that day.[8]

This latest shoot-down left 10 Squadron's CO with another melancholy round of condolence letters to write, but his letter to Hec Skinner's father, Mr W. H. Skinner of Tramere, South Australia, included such personal touches as to suggest that Wg Cdr Hartnell had known his son well: the CO wrote that Skinner had been 'such good company in the mess that it is hard to write and tell you just how much we thought of him'. Just before the fatal flight, Skinner had divulged to the CO that he was engaged, intending to get married in September. Hartnell now assured Skinner's father that the fiancée was 'a very nice lass', and that she 'has been rather upset but very brave' after hearing the bad news; Hartnell reported that he had taken the liberty of giving her a 'small brooch' from Skinner's belongings as a keepsake of the relationship. As was so often the case, the victims included men who had so narrowly escaped death in a previous action: one of Skinner's wireless operators was Sgt Ron Gibbs, while one of his air gunners was FS Hugh Burbidge, both of whom had previously been wounded by shrapnel from a U-boat's AA fire during an attack on 18 April, as part of Ted Farmer's crew. Burbidge too had become engaged to a girl in England, leaving another bereaved fiancée, while three of the other men left bereaved wives.[9]

Wg Cdr Hartnell had been shocked by Gerrard's loss only a week before, and now Skinner too had failed to return; Hartnell was left to ruminate: '...again we've lost an excellent captain and crew'.[10] Indeed, the losses put the squadron into tactical crisis: Hartwell at once convened meetings to discuss ways of countering the fighter threat. Real solutions would be hard to find, but these losses left No. 10 in such urgent need of aircrew replacements that on 13 August, Hartnell despatched Flt Lts Jewell and Rossiter to visit the personnel pool at Brighton. These trusted squadron officers evidently had a mission from Hartnell to 'cherry pick' airmen from the RAAF aircrew pool there, as had long been No. 10's prerogative because of its privileged status as the RAAF's flagship unit in Britain. After this visitation, batches of aircrew started arriving from Brighton: four new navigators on the 25th, four new pilots on the 27th, and eight wireless operator/air gunners on the 29th. Replacement aircraft too were needed, and on the 22nd, Alan Williams and Keith Sampson were flown off to RAF Wig Bay to fetch two new Sunderlands back to Mount Batten.

'The show must go on', but such a spate of cruel losses inevitably shook the unit. Ivan Southall, one of the later 461 Squadron pilots, expressed the feeling aptly:

> Upon some squadrons luck may smile, upon others luck may frown severely. Luck, good or bad, is constitutional. A squadron may fly for months without losing a man, then the balance may suddenly topple. In a week the familiar faces have gone and the mess tables are half-empty and the humour has gone out of life for a while. At the beginning one prays for luck.[11]

Command Responses to the Crew Losses

To make up the losses, new crews needed to be formed, new captains graduated in a hurry, and new aircraft assigned; newly-obtained airmen commenced the in-squadron training program, to get them up to operational standard as soon as possible. By now, in-unit training was so professionalised that No. 10's new pilots were rotated through a three-week-long Sunderland pilot's course. Similarly, on No. 461, the new crews under training were rotated through a curriculum, which included night flying, air-to-air and air-to-ground firing, low-level bombing, and practising defensive manoeuvres against simulated fighter attack. Operations were only part of a Sunderland squadron's flying duties: the other ceaseless commitment was crew training.

It was not only 10 Squadron's CO who was alarmed at the upswing in losses: Coastal Command HQ responded to the rising losses to the Ju 88s by trialling a range of initiatives. Firstly, in recognition of the Sunderland's inadequate armament, the aircraft were up-gunned to give them a better chance of fighting back. This involved modifications to add beam guns, one per side in the galley; to upgrade the front turret armament to twin belt-fed .303-inch Brownings, rather than the single magazine-fed Vickers gun employed hitherto; and finally, the installation of a wholly-new, fixed forward-firing armament of four .303 Brownings, aimed by the pilot. As we have seen, the galley guns had recently appeared in the Sunderland fleet within both Nos 10 and 461. This was a comparatively simple modification, with a single Vickers K-gun mounted each side of the galley, firing out of the open hatches to port and starboard. No. 10's Flt Lt Phillip Witchell and FS Ernie Blundell produced the galley gun engineering drawings that would be duly adopted and applied to Coastal Command's entire Sunderland fleet.[12] On the other hand, it was No. 461 that had pioneered the concept and fitted the first such gun mountings, designed by FS Len Burn.[13] The junior squadron also had them in action first, taking them on operations as early as the beginning of June; whereas at No. 10, Witchell did not finalise his design until 6 August. It was quick work after that, however, with work starting that night, progressing so expeditiously that No. 10's engineers had retro-fitted the new galley guns to all squadron aircraft by the 21st. In truth, the galley gun installation had a poor arc of fire because of the requirement for a mechanical 'cut-out' device to stop the excited gunner shooting off his own aircraft's propellers and wing float.

Besides pioneering the new galley-gun installation, No. 461's maintenance flight also undertook the engineering work to accommodate a two-gun F.N.5 turret in the nose of the Sunderland, in order to beef up the aircraft's forward-firing armament, both against U-boats and fighters. By August 1943, this project was on the cusp of command-wide adoption, thanks to the organisational support and political advocacy provided by No. 461's CO, Wg Cdr Douglas, and to the design work and prototyping undertaken by FS James Lavery, one of the squadron's armament fitters. However, the first trial installation on an operational aircraft was not made until September 1943, when S/461 got the treatment.

The third armament upgrade was the four-gun battery in the nose. This modification was proposed by Grp Capt. Jim Alexander, former 10 Squadron CO and now station commander of RAF Mount Batten, in collaboration with No. 10's gunnery officer, Flt Lt Bob Asker, the engineering officer, Flt Lt Witchell, and his right-hand man, FS 'Ossie' Ferguson. By 6 August, No. 10 was trialling a prototype installation of four fixed forward-firing .303-inch Browning machine guns in the Sunderland's nose, two on either side, and had two aircraft so fitted. After that, the squadron's Cpl Geoff Swinson, a professional draughtsman before the war, provided Short Bros with the necessary technical drawings, allowing for the bow guns to be fitted across Coastal Command's Sunderland fleet.[14]

The technical staff on both Australian squadrons had thus been instrumental in conceiving, trialling, and fitting all three of these armament modifications, which would in time be applied to Coastal Command's entire fleet of Sunderland aircraft. To get the technical details finalised and obtain command approval, a series of armament conferences took place through August–September–October. However, it was not until October 1943 that approval was finally given for this three-part armament upgrade to be retrofitted to all Coastal Command Sunderlands.[15]

The fourteen-gun Sunderland that emerged from this process was thus a feature of 1944 operations, too late for the critical battles of 1943. Indeed, most of the air battles of 1943 were fought with either 'stock' seven-gun Sunderlands, or only slightly upgraded eight or nine-gun aircraft. Nonetheless, thanks to feats such as Colin Walker's famous combat on 2 June, the type was acquiring a propagandised reputation as a 'flying porcupine'.[16] The implied claim that the aircraft was near impossible to attack made a certain amount of sense to an unschooled and optimistic public, but the reality was that the modifications arrived too late, and even then failed to fundamentally alter the aircraft's essential vulnerability: even a fourteen-gun Sunderland remained a prey species to an entire squadron of predatory German fighters working together.

A further command-wide initiative to arrest the losses was the provision of Allied long-range fighter patrols over the Bay, and thus squadrons of Beaufighters and Mosquitoes were deployed to hunt the hunters by patrolling across the Ju 88s' hunting grounds. Regular combats ensued, inflicting rising losses upon V./KG40: the unit suffered a total wastage of thirty-six Ju 88s to enemy action from January to August 1943, of which the RAF long-range fighters shot down twenty-six, causing the loss of twenty-four of the Germans' three-man crews.[17] This represented a significant rise in the German unit's operational attrition.[18] The visible presence of patrolling Allied fighters in the Bay also gave a fillip to Allied aircrew morale, for the Beaufighters and Mosquitoes were frequently spotted while on patrol, and almost as frequently mistaken by nervous Sunderland lookouts for Ju 88s. It was a great relief for the crews of the vulnerable patrol aircraft to know that it was no longer a one-sided fight over the Bay. For example, during a patrol on 7 September, Phil Davenport's crew reported a swarm of Ju 88s; Davenport was about to jettison depth-charges and dive for the sea when one of his gunners realised that some of the aircraft were friendly, shouting over the intercom, 'They're being attacked! It's a Mosquito! They're being attacked by Mozzies!'[19] The relief was palpable. A third counter-measure against the Ju 88 threat was bombing raids upon V./KG40's bases; by this means, ten of V./KG40's Ju 88s were destroyed in a raid on Lorient on 23 September.[20] This direct, aggressive air action against the Ju 88s, both in their hunting grounds and in their lair, must have degraded the air threat over the Bay.

Another RAF measure taken in response to the rising losses was to reroute Coastal Command air traffic. On 13 August, No. 19 Group HQ instructed all crews transiting to and from the Bay to pass through a datum point at 5 degrees north and 8 degrees 30 minutes west; this was a point in the ocean about 220 miles west of Land's End, and about the same distance from the closest German Ju 88 base at Brest. The intent was that by flying this exaggerated dogleg out to sea on both inbound and outbound flights, Coastal Command's air transit corridor between England and the Bay would be helpfully displaced away from the enemy fighter base. Paul Bird from 461 Squadron recalled that in 1942, the air corridor dogleg off the German-occupied coast had been located at 6 degrees west, and that the congregation of Ju 88s patrols across that point had given rise to the Sunderland crews' naming the datum point, 'Junkers corner'. He recalled that when the datum point was moved even further offshore to 10 degrees west, this merely shifted the location of Junkers corner—the Ju 88s followed them there.[21] However, displacement of the air corridor was not in vain, as the fighters' resultant longer transit flights necessarily reduced their time on patrol in the target-rich operational area. In a campaign of marginal arithmetical gains, every bit helped. Another tactical deviation was instituted on 13 October, when HQ instructed crews to adopt further evasive routing *en route* to the patrol area: departing from the standard datum point of Bishop Rock in the Scillies, aircraft were to deviate to the west, on a course of about 220 degrees, before heading south to reach their patrol areas, and to fly the reciprocal when heading home. While the long-range Ju 88s could make the resultant extra distance, this rerouting too must necessarily have had the effect of reducing the German fighters' patrol duration within the air corridor.

An additional measure was to suppress the electronic emissions of Coastal Command aircraft on patrol within the Bay. During 1943, the Luftwaffe developed the capability of tracking the movements of RAF Bomber Command aircraft through the night skies over Germany by monitoring the bombers' IFF transponder emissions. The IFF 'black boxes' in RAF aircraft functioned by emitting an electronic 'squawk' in response to friendly radar signals, in order to indicate their friendly identity to RAF air defence radar operators. It was a comparatively simple technical task for designated German signal units to 'challenge' overflying British aircraft with a radio signal of their own on the correct frequency; this triggered the IFF sets to automatically send their response 'squawk', enabling the Luftwaffe fighter control organisation to plot these transmissions and hence track the bombers' movements through their airspace. By this means, German fighter controllers could follow the movements of individual bombers accurately enough to achieve ground-controlled interceptions without the use of radar. It was not until the end of 1943 that the RAF realised this, when their monitoring of German radio traffic during British raids concluded that on three particular nights, about one-quarter of bomber losses had resulted from the Germans' tracking of their IFF transmissions. As a result of this unsettling realisation, Bomber Command ordered its crews to switch off their IFF sets while over enemy territory, and this became the tactical norm in 1944.[22] By the autumn of 1943, Coastal Command was coming to a similar realisation: on 20 October, the Sunderland squadrons received a signal from 19 Group HQ, instructing the crews to switch off IFF unless within 150 miles of friendly territory or operating in the vicinity of friendly warships. In such cases, the IFF was needed to identify the aircraft to friendly units and thus avoid friendly fire incidents, which was precisely the purpose of IFF in the first place.

All these measures were soundly conceived, so must have had some cumulative effect in reducing losses to the Ju 88s. However, V./KG40 was an unusually large air group, with about forty-five Ju 88s constantly on hand, and kept up to strength by a regular flow of replacement aircraft and crews.[23] So it was not until the final quarter of the year that the German fighter unit became significantly degraded, as shown by sharply-declining air combat results over October–December.[24] In the meantime, the severe threat persisted, as shown by the Ju 88s' success in shooting down six Australian Sunderlands in the two months of August–September 1943.

The Air Combats Continue

It might look as if No. 10 was monopolising all the malevolent attention from the German fighters, but the crews of No. 461 would not be left out for long. On 13 August, it was No. 461's turn: the newly-promoted Fg Off. Dowling (Col Walker's former co-pilot) departed Pembroke Dock at 7 a.m., to fly a Musketry anti-submarine patrol in M/461. Almost eight hours into the flight, 'M' transmitted a message that she was under attack from six Ju 88s. After that, silence. Neither aircraft nor crew ever returned. In the meantime, *Leutnant* Artur Schroeder from V./KG40 returned to base to claim a Sunderland shot down.[25] Out of the eleven lost men in this crew, eight (including Dowling) had flown with Walker in his famous combat on 2 June. On that occasion, they had survived an attack by eight Ju 88s, but this time, they were not so lucky. Sadly, the dead included three of the four airmen who had been decorated for that earlier combat, namely the navigator, Simpson, and the gunners, Fuller and Goode. Another sad loss was the first pilot, Fg Off. David Galt, DFC: like Les Baveystock who had joined the squadron earlier, Galt had won his 'gong' flying ops with Bomber Command, in his case completing a tour of operations with the Australian No. 460 Squadron. Having cheated death flying with Bomber Command, he had now died after volunteering to fly a second tour of operations with the 'far-safer' Coastal Command. Death was random and capricious over the Bay of Biscay. The next day, Gordon Singleton flew a search in the deduced area of the loss, looking for dinghies or survivors, but despite extending his Sunderland's time in the air to thirteen hours, had no joy.

Two days later, it was No. 461's turn again. Phil Davenport, whom we have met previously flying as first pilot to Fred Manger, had, like Dowling, recently qualified as captain and been promoted to flight lieutenant and was now flying his sixth operation in command, at the head of Manger's old crew. Manger himself had finished his tour in July, having captained forty-six operational flights with No. 461. At 6 p.m. on 15 August, Davenport was flying Manger's former aircraft, X/461, through an ominously fine sky. He had completed his anti-submarine patrol off the Spanish coast and was heading home, approaching the notorious Junkers corner out to sea from the Brest Peninsula. After the recent spike in losses, Davenport had become keenly aware of the vulnerability of the Sunderland to fighter attack, to the extent that he had been suffering disturbed sleep, given over to 'sleepless pondering' during the night about how to combat an attack by a coordinated flight of Ju 88s. From his very first operation in command, he was so anxious about aircraft contacts while on patrol that he made a practice of avoiding even friendly aircraft, just to be sure.[26] Davenport was certainly not the only Sunderland pilot intimidated by the risks they faced: Russ Baird afterwards admitted to being 'dead scared all the time'.[27]

As Sunderland X/461 droned on towards the north through the anxiety-provoking blue sky, the pilots were encouraged to see that there were some heavy clouds up ahead. The wireless operator, FS Paul Bird, received a fighter contact report from another aircraft, and from the strength of the signal knew it was fairly close. This meant there were enemy fighters in the area. He handed the contact report on to the navigator, Flt Lt 'Wonk' Kennedy, whose plotting table was just across the corridor from Bird's wireless station. However, the navigator was at the moment caught up in the middle of executing the complex procedure of measuring the aircraft's drift, in order to find the wind, 'fix' the aircraft's deduced position, and recalculate the heading-to-steer for the pilots. At the same time, the crew was distracted by a change of watch, with the men rotating between lookout positions. Paul Bird was scheduled to relieve FS Ross Woolhouse in the midships turret, as per the scheduled crew roster, but Kennedy asked him to go aft and drop a smoke flat instead. Bird did so, leaving Woolhouse in the turret for now. Bird ejected the flame float through the flare chute in the rear fuselage, and the tail gunner, Sgt Alan Craig, busied himself reporting the float's drift angles to Kennedy over the intercom, so that the navigator could calculate the wind velocity.[28] All this activity occupied the crew, evidently degrading their lookout.[29] Suddenly the involved process of obtaining the drift readings was interrupted by a shout over the intercom from Sgt Ron Fowles, standing watch in the nose turret: 'Enemy aircraft coming in hard from the starboard bow!'

Kennedy abandoned his drift calculations, stood up beneath the astrodome, and spotted a flight of Ju 88s emerging from behind that bank of cloud up ahead; now he amplified the sighting with, 'Phil, go for cloud; they're 88s!' Davenport starting corkscrewing towards the cloud, while the crew went to action stations: Woolhouse stayed in the midships turret, while Bird took position at the galley guns; he had only enough time to mount his Vickers gun in its firing position in the galley hatch before the Sunderland fell away into a 'screaming dive' to dodge the fighters. As Bird recalled, on looking out the galley window, 'all I could see were Ju-88s', but he could not draw a bead on any of them for fear of shooting through his own aircraft's wing. Then he heard 'an awful commotion; you could hear the shells hitting the aircraft'. Sunderland 'X' had been ambushed; as Bird admitted, 'They jumped us from round a big bank of cloud'.[30]

None of the gunners fired a shot before the incoming fire struck the Sunderland. In the cockpit, a cannon shell flew straight past Davenport's head to explode in the wing root just behind him, striking the wireless operator, WO Ian 'Jonah' Jones, with flying shrapnel. Although in considerable pain and distress, Jones stayed at his set and tapped out a fighter contact report to base. At the controls, Davenport was now facing his greatest fear: in an almost catatonic state, he went through the drill of flying the Sunderland through the practised sequence of skidding corkscrew turns:

For me those first moments were filled with an intense and unique fear. I felt remote, comfortably seated, slightly amused, looking down on myself, a lesser individual, desperately heaving on the controls; an automaton functioning faster than thinking and performing to programs modified by practise and by sleep lost pondering about such an attack.

His disturbed nocturnal cogitation on tactics seems to have put things on the right track, for after the initial fusillade struck home, he made the Sunderland a more elusive target, zigzagging towards the cloud with all four engines going strong, helped by Kennedy in the fire controller station, who kept his head turning in the astrodome, calling the evasive turns. The initial hits had, however, inflicted 'critical damage', with most flight instruments in the cockpit knocked-out, and the hydraulic lines to all gun turrets severed. With no hydraulic power the turrets were nearly immobilised for practical air-to-air gunnery purposes, reducing them to the scarecrow role of firing admonitory tracers through the intervening void in the general direction of the incoming fighter. The aircraft's fully-functioning armament was reduced to the two largely-ineffectual galley guns.[31]

Kennedy, looking aft from the astrodome, saw that the midships turret had been hit, and over the intercom, said, 'Looks like Birdie's got it'— thinking that Paul Bird was in that position as per the crew roster. Once Bird himself replied over the intercom from the galley, alive and well, Kennedy told him to go to the turret and help the gunner. Bird climbed the ladder to the upper deck, but arriving at the shattered turret, he found Woolhouse 'very dead', having 'taken a cannon shell through the side of the head'. Helped by his fellow wireless operator, FS Gordon Smith-Gander, RAF, Bird tried to extract the dead gunner, but could not rotate the jammed turret to gain access to the body. Afterwards, when they returned to the flight-deck to report to Davenport, the pilot was 'horrified by the blood on their clothes, and most of all, on Smithy's face'. Kennedy now asked Bird to relieve the wounded Jones at the wireless, so Bird helped Jones below to the galley, gave him a shot of morphine, and then returned to the flight-deck to take position at the wireless. Once he sat down behind the set, he was shocked to see a cannon hole in the fuselage skin beside him, 'big enough to drive a truck through'.

By that time, the aircraft had gained the cloud cover. Bird was sure that this was 'the only thing that saved us'. Meanwhile, he worked the set, 'as busy as a one-armed fiddler' to get an amplifying report away to base advising of the combat, the casualties, and the damage.[32] Without flight instruments, when the Sunderland reached cloud, Davenport had to resort to an imprecise blind-flying reference to keep the aircraft wings-level: 'When the cloud thinned, a glimmer of the sun was not where it should have been but it was high enough to show that we were almost right side up'. Having obtained his bearings about which way was up, he made a series of turns to stay within the cloud, keeping that up for thirty minutes before venturing outside again. Because of the damage to the cockpit systems, and the damage to the starboard inner engine, which was now overheating, Davenport had trouble adjusting the throttle settings to obtain an even power setting from all engines.

In the tail turret, Alan Craig had during the combat been 'slung about like a stone in a sling shot' by Davenport's violent manoeuvring, and a shell had moreover exploded right underneath his turret during one of the Ju 88s' fusillades. The turret's protective armour plating had saved him from injury, but the detonation had left him 'in shock and disorientated', and perhaps concussed as well from having his head banged against the turret structure by the violent yawing of the Sunderland's tail. Now Craig came on to the intercom asking to be relieved, but with two men incapacitated, and with casualties and damage still to attend to, Davenport had to ask him to stay in his turret for a bit longer, as he remained anxious about Brest-based Me 109s coming out to intercept them. Bird changed the wireless frequency to a direction-finding station and started making transmissions so that RAF ground stations could get a fix on the crippled Sunderland's position, in case she had to ditch. Sgt Jack Edge remembered that 'there wasn't much talking' among the sombre and sobered crewmen. Davenport recalled that it was 'sadly and gingerly' that he flew the damaged Sunderland the 300 miles to the Scillies. With fuel leaking from damaged tanks and with too much fuel already consumed in full-throttle manoeuvring, Davenport judged that the aircraft did not have the fuel margin to fly the extra 140 miles to Pembroke Dock, so decided to land in the Scillies, at St Mary's.

After thirteen hours in the air, Davenport made a 'masterly' landing at St Mary's, despite the two inner engines cutting out when he throttled back to flare. As soon as the aircraft touched down, he cut all engines. As the way came off the aircraft, it gently weathercocked into the wind and wallowed in the swell. In the sudden silence, the crew listened as 'Wavelets slapped gently and soothingly against the hull'. They waited for a pinnace to come out to tow them into harbour, but when the motor boat came alongside, the coxswain was so shocked to see the gory mess within the midships turret that during the last moments of his run-in, he lost concentration and bumped his boat into the Sunderland's hull. Standing on top of the wing, the watching Davenport was so uptight by now from the extremities of his experience that he yelled 'unjust abuse' at the man in protest at his clumsy boat-handling. Jones spent a month in the maternity ward of St Mary's hospital, becoming their 'star patient'. The body of Woodhouse was cut free of the turret and taken ashore.

The German pilots had meanwhile returned to base to claim one Sunderland shot down.[33] Davenport himself thought that his damaged aircraft, X/461, was written-off, but in fact she was returned to the squadron repaired, and in November 1943 resumed operational flying, assigned to a newly qualified captain, Fg Off. Dick Lucas. The remaining crewmen were flown out next day by No. 461's training officer, Sqn Ldr Harry Cooke, who arrived at St Mary's in the squadron 'hack', Sunderland 'D'. Davenport's strung-out crew stood in need of an uneventful flight, but it was not to be, for Cooke struck a rock on take-off and tore a gash in the bottom of the aircraft's hull. Once airborne the crew plugged the hole, but upon touch-down at Pembroke Dock, the plugging material 'popped out' from the pressure of the water, and the affected compartment, the bomb room, started flooding. The crew had of course closed the watertight doors—a standard part of the pre-alighting drill—so the flooding was confined to that single compartment of the hull. Nonetheless, Cooke taxied as expeditiously as he could towards the slipway, intent on getting 'D' pulled up on to the ramp before she sank. The fire tender came alongside to pump out the flooded compartment, but the pump failed, prompting FS Howells to order his men into the flying boat to save her by bailing her out. However, Arthur Barraclough had just completed a course at Short Bros, where he had learnt that a Sunderland had sufficient buoyancy that it would not sink even if three hull compartments were flooded. The well-informed Barraclough therefore told Howells, 'Not to panic, Flight', explaining that the aircraft was in no danger of sinking as she had only one compartment flooded. Perhaps sarcastically, Howells announced to his toiling party of bailers, 'Right lads, stop bailing, Brain-Box Barraclough says she won't sink.' And she did not: the men of the Marine Section had enough time to get the aircraft's beaching gear fitted; and the holed flying boat was towed up the slipway, with water streaming from the gash in her hull. As D/461 was the oldest aircraft in the squadron, an obsolescent Mk I model, and already relegated to second-line duties, squadron personnel considered that she would be written-off and scrapped for spare parts.[34] In fact, she was repaired at Wig Bay for reallocation to No. 228 Squadron.[35]

On the 18th, Tom Egerton flew out to the Scillies to bring Woolhouse's body back to Pembroke Dock, and on the 19th, Woolhouse was given a soldier's funeral at Llanion Barracks, attended by a large number of his squadron comrades, with squadron personnel serving as the pall-bearers and firing party, and with Davenport leading his men in a slow-march to their comrade's graveside.[36]

The survivors of Davenport's crew had come through the most dangerous period in the war for the two Australian squadrons, with a total of three crews lost in eight days—and they had nearly been lost as well. This crew was very lucky to have survived, for they had been ambushed so effectively by a flight of well-drilled Ju 88s that not one gunner other than the nose gunner had got off a single aimed burst; the Junkers' first volley had disabled all three turrets, leaving the Sunderland more or less defenceless above and behind. Given that a Sunderland's defence relied upon both return fire from her defensive armament and upon radical manoeuvring by her pilot, Davenport had done exceedingly well to dodge most of the subsequent attacks without the support of accurately aimed return fire from his gunners. He had believed that it was standard practice for Ju 88 pilots first to aim at and silence the gun turrets, and then to methodically despatch the undefended victim with impunity.[37] If this were true, then he had faced the worst possible scenario, and yet he had survived. In reality, once the Sunderland starting manoeuvring—mostly skidding turns into and under each attack—it was all any German pilot could do to get a shot anywhere on the flying boat's airframe, rather than on any particular spot. In combat against a manoeuvring Sunderland, hits from fighter gunfire were thus distributed randomly across the airframe. Moreover, the Sunderland was so big that it contained many large voids in its interior, spaces within which a 20-mm cannon shell might explode but cause little critical damage. The fact that X/461 lived to fight another day was therefore attributable to two things: Davenport's effective evasive manoeuvring, and the proximity of cloud which enabled him to end the engagement before an arriving shot finally hit something vital.

As we have seen, it was three days after Davenport's engagement, on 18 August, that Hec Skinner's crew from No. 10 was shot down by the Ju 88s. As if to underline the severity of the ongoing threat, over the following seven days, four crews from 10 Squadron encountered enemy aircraft while out on patrol. On 21 August, Fg Off. Fred Lees, on his debut patrol as captain, twice escaped a shadowing Ju 88 by climbing straightaway into cloud. Two days later, on the 23rd, Fg Off. Dick Gray encountered a much more formidable enemy, a gaggle of fifteen bogeys. Fortunately for him, his lookouts spotted the enemy formation 20 miles away, and there was a patch of 10/10th cloud above, so it was a simple matter to climb at once into cloud and continue with his patrol, flying blind inside the cloud and using radar to search for U-boat trade. An hour later, his wireless operator monitored an SOS call from another aircraft, which reported itself under attack from fourteen Ju 88s. This was probably a USAAF B-24 Liberator from the 479th Anti-Submarine Group, which luckily survived the encounter.[38]

Two days later, on the 25th, two crews from No. 10 eluded interception by German fighters thanks to just-in-time radioed warnings received from base. Coastal Command was exploiting a new capability in electronic surveillance, thanks to the recent deployment of task-groups of Royal Navy warships in the western Bay. Either using direction finding to plot the radio transmissions from German aircraft or taking advantage of the air search radars of the ships, the movements of the Ju 88 marauders could now be tracked reasonably effectively across the patrol area. As a result, while flying his 'Percussion' search pattern on the 25th, Plt Off. Keith Sampson received repeated warnings from base about enemy aircraft in his vicinity. In each case, he took avoiding action by altering his course, and then resumed his search afterwards. Similarly, Fg Off. Ron Humble was repeatedly warned of enemy aircraft flying on an interception course towards him, including a very specific warning of four Ju 88s inbound towards his Sunderland. Humble found two separate cloud layers to choose from, evading the enemy by gaining cloud cover and then making course alterations within the cloud.

Of course, these relatively easy escapes did not represent a fundamental change in the tactical conditions over the Bay, for five days later another Sunderland failed to return. On 30 August, four Australian Sunderland crews took-off on Percussion anti-submarine patrols. This was a typical day's output, for throughout August, the two Australian squadrons had each sent out two crews on patrol daily. During these patrols, there was plenty of German fighter activity evident, for like on the 25th, the crews received repeated radio warnings of incoming enemy aircraft, using these to manoeuvre to avoid the fighters. It may be coincidental, but the three captains who that day evaded successfully and returned with their crews alive were experienced men: No. 10's Ted Farmer and Dick Gray, captaining their thirty-third and eighteenth operation respectively, and No. 461's Chic Clarke, captaining his twenty-fourth mission. By contrast, No.

461's Fg Off. Cedric Croft was a new-graduate captain on only his sixth operation. At 9.53 a.m., almost seven hours into the flight, his wireless operator signalled that their aircraft, Z/461, was under attack from three enemy aircraft. At 10.20 a.m. came relief in the form of a message that they were safe, but at 11.05 a.m., the aircraft again signalled that it was under attack from three enemy planes. A Liberator reported seeing a Sunderland crash into the sea.[39] Meanwhile, three Ju 88 pilots from V./KG40 returned to base to claim shared credit for one Sunderland shot down, in a position 75 miles northwest of Cape Ortegal.[40] All eleven men aboard were lost.[41]

Despite the assistance provided to the crews on patrol by the radioed fighter warnings, August 1943 was the costliest month of all for the Australian Sunderland squadrons, with five aircraft shot down, forty-nine crewmen killed, and five wounded.[42] However, for the fighter crews of V./KG40, the best hunting season of the war was now behind them: after shooting down nineteen Coastal Command aircraft in August, in exchange for the loss of only four Ju 88s in combat, these results deteriorated in September, to ten kills for six losses. The tipping point in the battle for air superiority over the Bay had passed, and after that, the balance shifted in the RAF's favour: over October–December 1943, the Ju 88s' balance sheet was a mere nine kills to set against thirteen losses.[43] For our two Australian squadrons, after their four air-to-air losses in the crisis month of August, the trend of their combats afterwards followed a similar diminution, with two Australian Sunderlands shot down in September, and another two in November. By persisting with their patrols even in the face of a frightful level of airborne challenge within their patrol areas, and by shrugging off their losses by replacing aircraft and training new crews, the battered units of Coastal Command's No. 19 Group had cemented their May 1943 victory over the U-boat. Through August, they emerged from a bloody trial exhibiting a degree of air superiority over the Bay that was commensurate with their air-sea superiority over the U-boat, as measured by Coastal Command's ability to maintain the program of anti-submarine patrols despite losing so many aircraft to fighters.

It was perhaps in an endeavour to provide some relief from the stress and fear of operations that No. 461 held a 'very successful' dance in the officers' mess on the evening of 6 August, attended by the Pembroke Dock station commander, Grp Capt. A. M. Carey, RAF. The enlisted men had their chance to let their hair down the following night, with a dance in the airmen's mess, and without the presence of high-ranking officers, the other ranks enjoyed 'a very enjoyable informal affair', spiced up by the presence of 'a good number' of ladies who came as guests of the airmen—not only WAAF's, but civilian women as well. The success of No. 461's enlisted men in getting so many non-WAAF women to their dance changed the rules hitherto applying at Pembroke Dock: when a similar event was held on the 13th, this time run by the RAF station, the welcome announcement was made that the men were now permitted to bring civilian women, and the resultant event proved 'very successful', setting a precedent for regular repetition. As usual, No. 10 did not lag behind on the leisure and entertainment front, similarly hosting successful dances, and these were enlivened by the formation of a squadron dance band of such unusually high quality that it was boasted of in the unit war diary.

Battered but undeterred by the losses of August, Coastal Command's operational tempo was maintained in September, with each of the Australian squadrons flying two or three patrols daily. Both these squadrons sustained an aircraft strength of eleven Sunderlands, both fulfilled their monthly quota of operational hours, and both successfully fielded replacement crews for those lost: for example, No. 461 debuted three new captains on operations over August–September, while No. 10 fielded five debutants. Matching the personnel replacements, the RAF topped up the squadrons with replacement aircraft over the same period: in August, each squadron received three replacement Sunderlands. It was in this manner that Coastal Command showed itself organisationally resilient in the face of the recent losses inflicted upon it over the Bay.

Nonetheless, the fighter threat had not gone away. During September, crews continued to receive sharp reminders of the presence of lurking formations of German fighters: for example, on the 5th, both the 461 Squadron crews airborne received repeated messages from base warning of incoming enemy aircraft. On 16 September, four Australian Sunderland crews were despatched on Bay patrols in reasonably favourable weather conditions, namely with enough cloud to give a good chance of avoiding fighters. By the afternoon, frontal conditions were moving across the Bay, with bad weather to the north and east, but clearing to the south and west of the operational area. As a result, all three of the crews despatched by No. 10 found difficult flying weather in their patrol area, with heavy cloud, rain, and turbulent, gusty winds. These crews returned home to complain of the lousy weather, but it had at least hidden them from the fighters.

By contrast, Flt Lt Dudley Marrows was despatched on an afternoon 'Percussion' patrol further south, near the Spanish coast, and once he flew beyond the weather front's line of unsettled air, he found forbiddingly fine weather in his allocated patrol area; as he recalled, the day was 'beautiful, sunny and warm'. This was, of course, the same Marrows who had sunk *U-461* on 30 July; he was flying with the core of his old crew, but had a new aircraft, E/461. This was to be Marrows's last trip before completing his tour and heading home to Australia. As his Sunderland droned along its patrol line, the crew's discomfiture at the fine weather can only have been increased by the succession of wireless warnings they received from base of enemy aircraft nearby. At 3.37 p.m., E/461 was cruising west at 4,000 feet when Fg Off. Pete Jensen, the tail gunner, reported five bogeys 'dead astern', 17 miles away. Marrows at once made for the nearest cloud visible to the west, but this was 30 miles off, an excruciating twelve minutes away at full throttle. His wireless operator meanwhile transmitted a fighter contact report to base, to provide a positional fix in case they went into the water.

The five bogeys turned out to be six of the dreaded Ju 88s, and as these drew nearer, they shook themselves out into their usual attack drill, with four aircraft overhauling the Sunderland off its starboard beam, and the other two to port. Marrows jettisoned the depth-charges, and his new navigator, Plt Off. George Done, took up his fire controller station beneath the astrodome, ready to call the breaks for his pilots. As the first Junkers rolled in to attack from the Sunderland's starboard bow, Done announced over the intercom, 'Get ready to turn to starboard— Go!' At once Marrows rolled into a tight, diving turn. He had fitted his new aircraft with his favoured armament upgrades, namely a .303-inch Vickers K-gun in the first pilot's cockpit window, and an American .3-inch Browning in the nose bombing window. The first pilot, Plt Off. Jimmy Leigh, used the Vickers to fire a spray of tracer at the incoming Junkers. Between that and Marrows's turn, this ruined its attack, but this Junkers was quickly followed by the first one in the queue from port. As usual, the Germans sought to catch the evading Sunderland in a deadly scissors, where only one of the incoming fighters could be evaded, giving the other one a feasible shot from the Sunderland's beam. Once the attacks started coming in, there was no time for sophisticated manoeuvring: Done just kept calling each attack, and Marrows kept rolling into turns to make the German pilots' gunnery as difficult as possible. In a repeated sequence, one Ju 88 came in from the port bow, followed by its colleague from the starboard quarter. These tactics were both well-practised and well-proven. The Sunderland's galley-gunners fired at any Junkers that came in from that side as the big flying boat banked into its turns, but the German pilots attacked as much as possible from above, where they were out of the galley guns' firing arc because of the huge plank of Sunderland wing that interposed itself between gun and target. The galley gunners were also injured mid-action when the tea urn on the galley stove was upset during the violent manoeuvring: Bob Webster was struck in the face by the flying kettle, suffering a 'nasty cut on the bridge of his nose', while 'Bunny' Sidney was scalded when the boiling water was flung all over him. Sidney was a 'larger than life' air gunner and a notorious home-brewer who had had the temerity to use his barrack block's only bath as his brewer's 'fermentation vessel'. It seems Sidney's predilection for producing a 'brew' had now rebounded painfully upon him.

Marrows's manoeuvring had undoubtedly prevented the Sunderland from being shot down in the first combined assault, but the action went for nearly an hour, far too long to escape hits. In the tail turret, Pete Jensen heard enough impacts in the airframe to think that the aircraft was copping hits in every firing pass. From the cockpit, Marrows could also hear the cannon shells hitting the hull, and the damage mounted up: Jensen reported from the tail that he had lost hydraulic power, thereby neutering the aircraft's only four-gun mounting; one of the guns in 'Bubbles' Pearce's midships turret was struck and knocked-out of operation; the wireless set was hit and rendered useless; the bow turret was knocked out; the bow gunner, 'Pierre' Bamber, was hit; the port inner engine was knocked out; and then the port outer was hit too. The complete loss of power on one side made the aircraft increasingly difficult to manoeuvre, and Marrows could no longer maintain height in his turns. With the aircraft now losing height through each manoeuvre, and no longer able to climb for the cloud on only two engines, Marrows stole glances at the sea surface below, knowing that he would be obliged to land upon it soon. The sea was moderately rough, so in between wrestling his crippled aircraft through evasive turns he noted that he would need to alight crosswind, along the swell. Then one of the Ju 88s got a hit on the starboard outer engine.

With only a single engine left to deliver full power, Marrows ordered his crew to ditching stations. E/461's seven gunners, with their combined total of eleven machine guns, had fired 3,500 rounds at their six assailants, aiming well enough to extend the action to almost one hour, but the game was now up. Jensen abandoned the tail turret and went forward to his ditching station, finding a 'shambles' inside the aircraft, with the hull shot full of holes like a colander; 'oil everywhere from busted hydraulic lines … a lot of fixtures and stowed equipment had broken loose and was … being tossed around'. In the nose, the men found that Bamber and his American Browning gun had been almost blown 'back into the wardroom' by the cannon shell that had struck his gun position beneath the nose turret. With a severe wound to his leg, Bamber was dragged out of the nose compartment, and painfully pushed and pulled up the ladder to the upper deck ditching station.

Some 10 miles away, Marrows's colleague, Flt Lt Russ Baird, was patrolling in W/461. At 4.05 p.m., he reported a Sunderland off to starboard, down to 500 feet, under attack by two enemy aircraft. After that, he saw the Sunderland descend to land, leaving a large, white streak on the surface of the sea. Baird was already heading home at the limit of his aircraft's endurance, so could not hang around to watch, or to orbit the dinghy afterwards. With fighters around, he prudently transmitted this report, climbed into cloud, and headed for base.

Marrows executed a fine landing, except that the port wing float collapsed, the stays having been shot away. As the unsupported wing dropped into the water, the crew carried out their ditching drill, evacuating through the astrodome escape hatch, collecting together on the top of the wing, and inflating two dinghies. The Germans made a final gunnery run to strafe the downed but still-floating Sunderland, just as Marrows emerged from the hatch, the last man out. He saw a line of bullet holes run across the starboard wing, but his crew's luck held; no one was hit. The German pilots chivalrously left it at that, took a photo of the wallowing, lopsided Sunderland, and departed to scrupulously claim one Sunderland probably destroyed (because they had not seen it sink).[44] As the Junkers departed, Marrows took stock of his men's wounds and injuries, and noted that the men had collected only two of the aircraft's three dinghies. He went back into the hull to retrieve the missing dinghy from its stowage in the rear fuselage, also grabbing a few items that would assist their survival—signal pistol, signal cartridges, bread, and smoke floats. While down below, he saw water squirting through the many bullet holes in the bottom of the hull, so he knew that the aircraft would definitely sink. Anxious that the aircraft might capsize on to its sunken wing while he was still inside, Marrows saved time by throwing the dinghy pack out through the rear entry hatch. While his men packed the survival equipment into the other two dinghies on the top of the wing, they saw this dinghy pack floating away from the aircraft. Jimmy Leigh volunteered to dive in after it. He swam after it, reached it, inflated it, boarded it, and started paddling.

Once the two dinghies on top of the wing were packed, the men launched them and boarded them. These were the larger, six-man, H-type dinghies, while Leigh's dinghy was one of the smaller types. No sooner had the men settled into their allocated dinghies than one of the H-type dinghies burst, due to a shrapnel graze sustained in the action. The sudden deflation dumped the occupants and their carefully-packed survival gear into the water. By the time they had swum across to the second H-type and loaded it with whatever gear they had managed to salvage, this remaining six-man dinghy was grossly overloaded. To make matters worse, the signal pistol had been lost in the dinghy sinking, and the carrier pigeons drowned. Jimmy Leigh was meanwhile still paddling his small dinghy across the sea towards this scene of alarm and water-logged confusion. The ten bedraggled men crammed into the sole remaining H-type now saw Leigh's dinghy suddenly burst as he paddled intently towards them. Leigh swam the remaining distance, grabbed on to the side of the dinghy, and asked whether there was room aboard for him too. There was, but the eleven-man crew had to be packed into the dinghy in two tiers, with the inner tier sitting on the floor, and the outer tier sitting on top of the inflated flotation ring, with their backs supported by the splash ring. They propped up Bamber's 'shattered leg' as best they could, on top of the flotation chamber. Marrows afterwards singled out Bamber for his cheerfulness despite the extremity and pain.

The men started discussing whether they should eat the drowned pigeons, but by now they were becoming sea sick, which made the thought doubly repulsive, so the dead birds were 'jettisoned' along with the now-useless signal pistol cartridges. By contrast, the sole smoke float was 'virtually nursed', although the dinghy also had a stock of signal rockets as part of its standard inventory—all considered vital to survival. Nightfall came quickly, leaving the seasick men to endure a night noisy from the waves slapping against the sides of the dinghy and breaking against it, as well as wet, from the resultant flooding and bailing. More positively, the 'eerie' night carried the sound of aircraft engine noise. The men comforted themselves with the thought that the aircraft they could hear was 'ours', and that it was searching for them. They fired a signal rocket as the engine noise approached and were almost at once spotlighted by a 'bloody great light'—a Catalina flying boat's submarine-hunting Leigh Light. Their position was fixed, they would be rescued.

The Catalina was from 210 Squadron, the unit which had swapped places with No. 461 back in April, moving into the unpopular Hamworthy; it was captained by Plt Off. John Cruickshank, a pilot who would become famous the following year by winning the Victoria Cross through pressing on with an attack to sink *U-361*, despite suffering seventy-two shrapnel wounds from the boat's return fire.[45] After locating the Australians' dinghy at 3 a.m., Cruickshank's Catalina orbited the dinghy until the limit of its endurance, handing over to a Liberator from 53 Squadron at 8.45 a.m. Things were certainly looking up in the light of day, when Marrows's men were greatly excited to spot ships' smoke on the horizon. Now they lit the smoke float and threw it overboard. The Liberator flew straight overhead, evidently homing the ships upon the dinghy, and soon after five warships loomed over the horizon, heading towards them. This was once more Capt. Johnnie Walker's support group, the same group which had cooperated with Marrows's U/461 in the sinking of the three U-boats on 30 July. Steaming towards the dinghy, Walker's ships had earlier located the wreck of Marrows's Sunderland, still floating but awash, sinking it with gunfire.

Walker brought his own ship, HMS *Woodpecker*, alongside and launched one of the ship's boats. This came alongside the dinghy to get the wounded Bamber and Webster on board the sloop and into the sick bay as quickly and painlessly as possible. The latter protested at his special treatment as he was hauled aboard the boat, leaving the others to clamber up the side of the warship via a scrambling net.[46] With the survivors aboard, the task group sailed for its home port of Liverpool. Walker himself was bound to be very interested when he discovered that the Sunderland crew was the same crew that had sunk *U-461* on 30 July, and so he presented Marrows and his men with some souvenirs of that battle: the life preserver and escape apparatus used by *U-461*'s commander. This was later lodged with the RAAF Overseas HQ, displayed as a war trophy at its Kodak House premises. Walker gave a further sign of his recognition and esteem, delivering the airmen directly to Pembroke Dock rather than suffering the delay and inconvenience of returning via Liverpool; he transferred them to HMS *Starling*, and she called into Milford Haven on 20 September.

On that day, No. 461's CO, Wg Cdr Douglas, came out on to the harbour in a pinnace to see them arrive, overjoyed at their survival. Once ashore, the airmen were debriefed, given a hot meal, a hot bath, and their own beds. Having heard their story, Douglas championed the combat airmanship of Marrows and his men, reporting that they had fought an action as great as had Colin Walker and his crew in N-Nuts on 2 June. His viewpoint was endorsed by the higher commanders, for Marrows received a DSO to go with the DFC earned in his 30 July action against *U-461*, while two of his air gunners, Sgts Bamber and Pearce, got the DFM.[47] These men were deserving recipients, being the very same two whose highly effective gunnery had suppressed *U-461*'s flak guns on 30 July, enabling Marrows to make his successful bomb drop, and enabling the rest of the crew to get home alive. Marrows had got home from his last trip, and thus survived his tour: he would be one of a lucky party of tour-expired Australian Sunderland airmen who ferried back to Australia the home-based RAAF's first Sunderlands in February 1944, thereby belatedly fulfilling the intent of the original 10 Squadron Sunderland ferry plan of 1939. The six aircraft formed No. 40 (Transport) Squadron, spending the rest of the war running personnel and freight up and down the east coast of Australia between Sydney and Port Moresby.[48]

Despite the lucky survival of Marrows and his crew on 16 September 1943, that was not the last violent encounter between the Australian Sunderlands and the Ju 88s of V./KG40, and not all such incidents would turn out so well. The day after Marrows's men docked in Milford Haven, the 21st, three Australian Sunderlands departed on Percussion anti-submarine patrols in the Bay. One of No. 10's newly qualified captains, Fg Off. Glenn Jennison, was flying his fourth patrol as captain, in E/10. At thirty-two years old, he was known on the squadron as 'Pop'. His younger but more experienced colleague, Flt Lt Williams (he was thirty), was flying P/10 on a concurrent patrol in the same area, almost 400 miles out to sea from Brest, and in mid-afternoon made radar contact with an aircraft,

10 miles off the beam. This was thought to be Jennison's aircraft, and ten minutes later, Williams's wireless operator picked up an incomplete message from E/10, the decipherable part including a report of fighter attack by six Ju 88s. Ominously, the signal then 'faded out with a high frequency note'. Twenty minutes later, Williams's crew spotted five bogeys 8 miles away, giving him enough time to turn away to the west and climb into cloud. A Sunderland was afterwards claimed shot down by Ju 88 pilots from V./KG40 after their return to base.[49]

All eleven men aboard 'Pop' Jennison's E/10 were lost. Mr Alfred Buckland from Croydon in NSW, the father of Fg Off. Neil Buckland, the first pilot, received the usual promptly-despatched casualty notification from the Air Board, as well as advice that the Germans had made a short-wave radio broadcast on the night of 21 September, announcing that they had shot down a 'big British flying boat'. Wg Cdr Hartnell sent the grieving father a rather formulaic CO's condolence letter:

Your son had been doing sterling work in the Squadron and was held in high esteem by all with whom he came in contact. I had flown with him on a number of occasions and knew just how reliable he was, either in the air or in the mess. His loss has been sorely felt by all of us.

Despite Hartnell's attempt to set a tone of empathy, Mr Buckland was neither mollified nor convinced: within months of his son's disappearance, he had grown so distrustful of the air force authorities that by April 1944 he was asking pointedly for assurances that in the event of a distress signal, such as that received from his son's aircraft, 'would any effort be made to save this crew, and what was done in this instance?' Mr Buckland received the usual soothingly-intended reassurances, followed a month later by the official notification of his son's presumed death.[50] Most families received the distressing news of their bereavements with the stoicism customary in those times, but there were many angry exceptions.

The week following the loss of Jennison's crew, the Australian Sunderlands continued to encounter Ju 88s, but were lucky enough to succeed in avoiding them. On 23 September, No. 10's Flt Lt Merv Jones was out on a dinghy search, flying W/10 low down over the sea at only 300 feet, when his rear gunner reported three bogeys, probably Ju 88s, crossing the Sunderland's tail, 7 miles away. The day was dangerously fine, but hazy, but the low-flying Sunderland seems to have been swallowed up in the haze layer over the sea, escaping detection. On the same day, the same squadron's Flt Lt Fred Lees similarly spotted three bogeys going past 9 miles away, but it was gathering dusk, allowing him to hold course and disappear into the obscurity of night. On the 27th, while *en route* to base after a patrol, nearing the Scillies,

No. 10's Flt Lt Williams saw a flight of four bogeys 10 miles astern, but again they seemed to have failed to see the Sunderland, for they turned 180 degrees and flew away. These easy escapes were similar to that of Fg Off. Rodger Newton on the 18th, when his No. 461 Squadron crew saw four Ju 88s circling in the patrol area, but he was able to take shelter at once in cloud. The Sunderlands' on-board radar also proved useful on occasion in delivering early warning of fighters: in the early hours of 13 October, 10 Squadron's Dick Gray was on patrol in H/10 in the far south-western corner of the Bay, more than 400 miles off the enemy coast, when his radar operator reported four bogeys inbound. Gray's crew might have thought themselves safe from visual observation in the predawn darkness, but the fighters came unsettlingly close, passing by only a mile away.

For the Australian Sunderland squadrons, 1943 was an unprecedentedly bloody year due to the predatory presence of V./KG40's Ju 88 fighters over the Bay. Fortunately, the same level of carnage would not be repeated in 1944, as the battle swung decisively against the sea-air forces of the Germans around the western perimeter of Nazi-occupied Europe: in that year, only two Australian Sunderlands would be shot down by German fighters. In the crisis year of 1943, however, ten Australian Sunderlands were shot down by the Ju 88s (five from each squadron), with the deaths of eight crews: five crews from No. 10 and three crews from No. 461. These were dismaying losses, but the Australians were certainly not alone in their victimisation by V./KG40: the RAF's No. 58 (Halifax) Squadron lost six crews to the Ju 88s in the same period, No. 224 (Liberator) Squadron lost four crews to the same cause, 10 OTU similarly lost four Whitley crews while engaged on Bay patrols in the first half of the year, while No. 228 Squadron, joining the fight in April, lost three Sunderland crews while engaged in the same patrol duties as the Australians. Despite only commencing operations in July, the Americans too paid their tithe in lives, losing four Liberator crews to the Ju 88s. The suffering was thus spread more or less evenly amongst the squadrons that flew Bay patrols in daylight. It must be said, however, that 19 Group's three Sunderland squadrons could claim the place of greatest honour in Coastal Command's confrontation with the Ju 88s, losing a total of fifteen aircraft shot down in 1943. By contrast, the four Allied Liberator units, patrolling even further out to sea, lost eleven aircraft in total to the Ju 88s.[51]

Hazardous In-Flight Technical Failures

As the year wound on towards the winter of 1943–44, the weather worsened, the cloud cover thickened, and the Ju 88 threat receded. But as we have seen, Sunderland crews faced life-threatening hazards not only from enemy fighters, nor just from the flak gunners on U-boats, but also from the casual, capricious vindictiveness of the element they flew in, and from the wear and tear of their aircraft's mechanical components. The high tempo of flying operations in the sustained 1943 Bay offensive, and the remorseless requirement for each squadron to provide its allocated quota of operational sorties, was attended during this period by increasing mechanical unreliability. Even as early as June–July, there came a sequence of technical mission aborts. On 6 June, both of No. 10's missions were aborted: for example, Hec Skinner aborted his Derange patrol in T/10 when his port outer engine started emitting oil and blowing smoke. The same squadron's Ted Farmer experienced two aborts caused by a malfunctioning port inner engine in G/10; the first was on 19 June, but the problem was evidently not fixed, for it recurred on a patrol on the 25th. Each engine-related abort necessitated the jettisoning of the full load of eight depth-charges, and often the dumping of fuel as well, in order to permit the aircraft to safely maintain height on three engines and to keep within its maximum safe landing weight: in Farmer's case, he dumped 1,000 gallons.

No. 461 too had its share of technical aborts. For example, on 6 July, John Weatherlake experienced an engine fire in A/461's starboard inner just after take-off; fortunately, the Graviner fire extinguisher in the engine bay worked, allowing him to turn around and land at once. Russ Baird was next, forced to abort a U-boat search on 9 July, when S/461's port outer developed a serious oil leak. The squadron's four operational aborts in July were far more than normal incidence, but there was no common thread. An internal investigation by the squadron's maintenance flight revealed causes sufficiently diverse as to confound any single theory of causation: a blown piston ring, unserviceable spark plugs, and incorrect cockpit drill (leaving the engine cooling gills closed while taxiing on the water, and hence overheating the engines).

The Sunderland was a large aircraft with complex systems, so not all aborts were attributable to the engines. For example, on 22 September, Plt Off. Ross Watts suffered a string of failures in F/461, despite the aircraft being only newly-delivered: first there was a failure in the front turret's hydraulics, because a generator had become unserviceable due to overcharging; and then the H/T switch on the radar receiver 'went u/s'. Without a front turret and without radar, Watts aborted. Similarly, when on 6 June J/10's intercom failed and could not be restored to function, Bob Fry had similarly turned for home: without an intercom, the pilots, lookouts, and gunners could not communicate, so the aircraft would be virtually defenceless.

Engine failures remained the most common type of failure, nonetheless, and they were alarming in direct proportion to the aircraft's distance from base and the number of engines that failed. Both factors came together on 28 July, when Gordon Strath suffered an engine failure in T/10 in the worst possible location: in the southernmost reaches of the Bay of Biscay, only 10 miles from the Spanish coast, and with a five-hour flight to get home. At 1.52 p.m., the oil pressure on the starboard inner engine dropped to almost zero, necessitating an engine shutdown. Because the crippled aircraft needed to traverse 'Junkers Corner' *en route* to home, and because Strath knew that the Germans monitored RAF transmissions, he did not yet advise base of the emergency, but maintained radio silence and headed north, flying as stealthily as he could from cloud to cloud. Then the port outer too started to ail, with oil pressure dropping to between 10 and 25 pounds per square inch (psi). Despite reducing power to nurse the engine along, within ten minutes, the oil pressure dropped to only 5 psi, so he shut down this engine as well. Now presented with a severe emergency, Strath now started signalling to base, giving his position as the aircraft passed abeam the Brest Peninsula. He also ordered the crew to execute the usual lightening routine of jettisoning every item that was not 'nailed down' inside the hull, as well as dumping as much fuel as he dared without running the risk of running out of fuel before reaching the nearest friendly territory, the Scillies.

Alan Williams from the same squadron was on patrol at the same time in J/10, and base tried to arrange for him to undertake a mid-air interception of the crippled Sunderland, ordering Strath to transmit on the homing frequency, and for Williams to home on its signal by radio, and then to pick up the other Sunderland on radar. Evidently someone had given a wrong position, for Williams failed to find the other aircraft. With only two engines, Strath knew there was now no hope of staying in the air long enough to get to Mount Batten, but fortunately the dead engines were not on the same side, allowing both the remaining engines to be run at high power without imposing impossible control problems. Fortunately, the starboard outer and port inner kept going, allowing Strath to send a relieved message to base cancelling his SOS, and then to make a normal landing at St Mary's, ending a very stressful flight for his anxious crew. On the following day, the 29th, Sqn Ldr Marks flew out to the Scillies with a maintenance party, and then took home most of Strath's crew; on 7 August, the lightened aircraft was patched up sufficiently for Flt Lt Terry Brown to fly her home on three engines.

Strath had been both lucky and skilful to get his aircraft and crew home safely after a double engine failure, but the engine troubles continued. By the end of August, 10 Squadron was blaming the 'deplorable standard' of the reconditioned engines being received by the squadron: one aircraft had gone through seven engines in only forty flight hours. On 4 September, official recognition of the problem was shown by the arrival at Mount Batten to discuss the problem of a delegation of staff officers from higher up the chain of command, led by Air Commodore W. C. Ware Browne from Coastal Command HQ, and Wg Cdr R. Milroy-Hayes from 19 Group HQ.

Of course, flying twelve-hour missions more than 500 miles out to sea with unreliable engines had inevitably to exact a toll upon the Sunderland crews. On 2 October, Fred Lees's crew in M/10 were on a Percussion patrol in the outer reaches of the Bay. Lees was on only his seventh trip in command, having joined the squadron as a green second pilot in September 1942. Upon qualifying for captaincy, he had been assigned the newly-arrived aircraft 'M'. However, this aircraft was a second-hand aircraft, having previously flown with No. 119 Squadron before that squadron's disbandment at Pembroke Dock in April, and she proved to be a 'hangar queen': Lees was able to fly her on only a single mission before she was taken offline for six weeks. While awaiting the return of his own aircraft to the flight-line, Lees and his crew operated by borrowing a succession of other crews' aircraft. 'M' was thus flying on only her second patrol with No. 10 when Lees took off in her on the night of 2 October, no doubt hoping that the 'gremlins' in his aircraft had been ironed out.

However, at 7.25 a.m. that day, base received a signal from M/10, advising that the aircraft was experiencing engine trouble, had aborted the mission and was returning to base from a point about 200 miles south-west of the Scillies, with an ETA at Mount Batten of 10.20 a.m. At 7.55 a.m., base transmitted a signal instructing 'M' to change radio frequency to 333 kilohertz, and this signal was acknowledged. However, nothing further was heard of the aircraft. Air and sea searches were made across the deduced track of the crippled Sunderland, with no joy. RAF Fighter Command's No. 10 Group, tasked with the air defence of England's south-west approaches, advised 19 Group HQ of an unidentified radar contact 20 miles south of the Scillies at 9.49 a.m., suggesting that this was the ditching position of the missing Sunderland.[52] That afternoon, Wg Cdr Hartnell despatched Gordon Strath in K/10 to conduct a creeping line ahead search along M's inbound track, but Strath's crew saw nothing. As we have seen, Strath himself had experienced a similar in-flight emergency back in July, but despite a double engine-failure had found better luck than Lees and survived. By the 4th, Hartnell confided to his diary: 'No news of Freddie, so we can't hold out much hope now'.[53] None of the eleven men flying in M/10 were ever seen again.

A month later, 10 Squadron had another engine incident, when Flt Lt Alan Williams's P-Peter suffered a catastrophic double engine loss. At 9.10 a.m., while the aircraft was cruising at 2,400 feet, heading home from the Percussion Patrol area, 'smoke' suddenly started streaming from the starboard inner. In fact, it was oil, and before the pilots had time to respond—'within seconds'—the propeller suddenly sheared off and spun away. On the Bristol Pegasus engine, the propeller rotated to the right, and so this propeller flew right into the spinning propeller of the adjoining starboard outer, carrying that away too. With both propellers almost instantaneously sheared, the aircraft yawed and rolled violently to the right, under the sudden asymmetrical power of the port engines. Williams and his co-pilot cut the switches to both dead engines, pulled back the throttles on the live engines, rolled back to wings level, cranked on full opposite rudder and aileron trim, and reapplied power to regain level flight in the new condition. As we have seen, it was often touch-and-go whether a Sunderland would maintain height on three engines, let alone only two, and despite immediately jettisoning the depth-charges and 1,000 gallons of fuel, the aircraft was still rapidly losing height as Williams tried to hold her on a course to make the Scillies. Two minutes after the propeller failures, and having already lost 1,000 feet of height, he ordered the crew to throw out everything that was not nailed down, and at 9.22 a.m. managed to get a signal away to base advising of the emergency and that he might be force-landing on the sea imminently. It was lucky that he had been cruising at 2,400 feet when it happened, and so had a little height to lose, and was also lucky that he was only half an hour out from the Scillies. If the same emergency had occurred while the aircraft was cruising at under 1,000 feet, they would have been in the water even before the wireless message could be transmitted. As it was, it took a while for the crew to throw out enough guns, ammunition, and pyrotechnics to lighten the aircraft, and at 9.32 a.m., Williams had an SOS transmitted, giving his position as 40 miles west of the Scillies.

Unfortunately, one of his crewmen, LAC Keith Burleigh, suffered a serious accident while throwing one of the machine guns overboard: in his haste to do so (it was his first operational flight), he had incorrectly unloaded the gun before hurling it over the side, and it fired as it went out of the hatch. A bullet struck his left leg, severing the heavy tendon behind his knee. Despite this unfortunate accident, the men's efforts appear to have succeeded in lightening the aircraft sufficiently for it to sustain level flight on two engines, for Williams was finally able to hold it in level flight at the nail-biting altitude of 300 feet. By this means, P-Peter reached the Scillies, allowing Williams to put her safely on the water there at 9.48 a.m. He cancelled the SOS in a message to base transmitted from the water.

Burleigh was taken ashore for treatment, later evacuated to Truro Hospital in Cornwall, but although his leg was amputated, he died on 15 December from a second haemorrhage. A twenty-two-year-old native of Maryborough, Queensland, he was buried on 21 December in Haycombe

Cemetery at Bath. The funeral was officiated by Sqn Ldr Raymond Russell, the Presbyterian padre from RAAF HQ in London, and attended by Alan Williams and two other crew members.[54]

Four men in this crew had already narrowly escaped destruction in the air combat with seven Ju 88s on 3 August, in the combat for which Williams had been awarded his DFC, and they had now for a second time lived to fly and fight again. Williams too was lucky and would go on to complete his tour in 1944. P-Peter was towed back to Mount Batten by an ASR launch, arriving there on 21 November, and receiving such a rapid double-engine change that she flew again for her next operation on 3 December.

Despite the anxious insecurity of such engine unreliability, from the start of October, the Sunderland squadrons were deployed mostly on to night-time 'Percussion Love' patrols, the purpose of which was to flood the Bay with radar transmissions to keep transiting U-boats submerged at night, which increased the chances of their running on the surface in the daytime, where they would be found and sunk more easily. These nocturnal operations greatly reduced the threat posed by enemy fighters: only two fighters were sighted by 461 Squadron crews in the entire month. However, these patrols were regarded by the crews as an unrewarding and unglamorous task, as there was little hope of the Sunderlands making realistic attacks at night: No. 461 made not a single U-boat sighting in that same month. This left the serious sub-hunting to the Liberator, Halifax, and Wellington squadrons, which were equipped with the newer and more capable ASV III radar. Even so, with the downturn in U-boat operations since their defeat in May–August, pickings were slim even for them, with only five U-boats sunk by No. 19 Group aircraft in the Biscay operational area over the four months from September to December.[55]

The Australian Sunderlands' sequence of U-boat kills during the summer, as well as their well-publicised air combats against the Ju 88s through the autumn, had put both units on the media map, such that both became fixtures for visiting journalists and VIPs. At Mount Batten, the RAAF's Air Vice-Marshal Wrigley visited No. 10 on 11 October, followed by Air Marshal Williams on the 20th. At Pembroke Dock, Fg Off. Collins of the British Film Unit arrived to visit No. 461 on the 15th, during his two-day stay taking footage for newsreels, also spending 'two very enjoyable evenings' with squadron officers in the officers' mess.

No. 461 was certainly pleased with itself, having in effect claimed the status of an elite unit, worthy of being placed alongside No. 10 towards the top of Coastal Command's pecking order. The unit diarist boasted not only of being one of only two squadrons in 19 Group that achieved their planned flying program in October, but even of exceeding its quota by four sorties. The unit had received special mention in the RAF-wide training magazine *Tee Emm*, for its recent sequence of air combats against Ju 88s, and in the command-wide training magazine *Coastal Command Review*, for its U-boat kills. Had the unit's founding CO, Neville Halliday, lived to see it, he would have been proud to see the fruit of all that hard work during the squadron's early months. No. 461 crews had gained so much in efficiency that out of thirty Coastal Command squadrons whose crews were rotated through the armament camp at Pembroke Dock, the Australian unit finished that month in first place on the bombing table, and in second place for gunnery.

Alongside its operational commitments, the squadron maintained the momentum of its training program, as shown by the seventy training flights conducted in October and the six new captains qualified over September–October. To help maintain the through-put of trainee captains, four new pilots joined the unit earmarked for fast-tracked captaincy qualification, having already either graduated from the Sunderland conversion course at 4 OTU, or having obtained instrument-flying gradings at No. 20 Advanced Flying Unit. Another seven pilots joined the unit less well-qualified, posted straight from the personnel depot at Brighton, and thus earmarked for on-the-job apprenticeships in co-pilot roles. On the technical side, the squadron's maintenance flight had completed the first installation of the new four-gun, forward-firing armament; was retrofitting to squadron aircraft a new, squadron-designed mounting for a machine gun fitted in the co-pilot's windscreen; and was expecting delivery of the first batch of two-gun nose turrets.

Despite all these milestones of technical progress, the war seemed to have passed the unit by during October 1943. But November would bring some sharp re-acquaintance with the enemy. On 9 November, Fg Off. Johnny Dobson's crew in S/461 ran into four Ju 88s. Dobson had joined the unit in April, been trained up as a captain, and was now flying his third operation in command. His Sunderland was on a Percussion anti-submarine patrol, cruising at the very low height of 200 feet to remain as inconspicuous as possible to both airborne and shipboard observers. However, the midships gunner reported four Ju 88s approaching from the beam, more than a thousand feet higher. Dobson climbed at once to get some manoeuvring height, while jettisoning both the bombload and the parachute flares to gain a little manoeuvrability. The 88s followed standard tactics, splitting up into one pair on both the Sunderland's port and starboard beams, then started coming in one after another, from either direction in a continuous sequence. Dobson too employed by-now standard tactics, evading by turning into each attack, diving underneath each incoming attacker, and opening up as many of his gunners' firing arcs as possible by heeling the aircraft over in a bank.

Over the course of a half-hour-long engagement, the gunners fired 1,170 rounds, the bulk of them (800 rounds) from the tail gunner in his four-gun turret. All this firing seems to have helped to keep the German pilots' heads down, for these Ju 88s fired from relatively long range and then broke off before pressing the attack into decisive range—turning away at ranges from 700 to 1,200 yards. The Sunderland took twelve hits, but nothing vital was damaged, all crewmen emerged unscathed, and Dobson was able to make a normal landing back at Pembroke Dock. S/461 was repaired in time to fly her next mission on 19 November, but this next flight must have done little to allay the crew's keen awareness of the German air threat, for this time the Sunderland was shadowed for fifteen minutes from 3 miles away by a twin-engined enemy aircraft.

Only two days before that, on 17 November, a 10 Squadron crew had failed to return after running into fighters. Fg Off. Ray Behrndt had graduated from first pilot to captain in September, now flying his eleventh operation in command. He took off in T/10 at 11.01 a.m., on a Percussion anti-submarine patrol, and at 2.30 p.m. sent the message 'O-A'—the coded emergency message indicating that the aircraft was under fighter attack. Next day, the squadron received advice from HQ that Behrndt had been promoted to flight lieutenant, but it would not do him much good now, for nothing more was heard from 'T', and all eleven men aboard the aircraft were lost.[56] Two Ju 88 crews, piloted by *Unteroffizier* Fritz Haenel and *Leutnant* Ulrich Hanshen, returned to base to report a Sunderland shot down at 2.30 p.m.[57] Keith Sampson, on patrol in a nearby search area, was ordered to divert to T/10's estimated position to search for survivors, but Berhrndt's last transmission had been corrupted, so the wireless receiver at RAF St Eval was only able to make an educated guess of the aircraft's reported position—47 degrees north and 10 degrees west. With inexactitude like that, it was unsurprising that Sampson found nothing, and nor did Ron Humble when he was sent out to search for the dinghy next day, while conducting a Percussion patrol.

After the relative quiescence of October, the loss of Behrndt and his crew signalled an evident upswing in German fighter activity within the Bay. On 19 November, Keith Sampson was seven hours into his Percussion patrol in R/10 when four Ju 88s were seen approaching. Fortunately, his gunners saw them early, while they were still 11 miles away, giving Sampson time to climb into cloud. The same day, Don Sinclair's crew from No. 461 was five hours into a Percussion patrol when they received an 'O-A' signal from Sunderland 'W' of 228 Squadron. Sinclair diverted to the indicated position to look for survivors but found nothing and resumed his patrol track an hour and a half later.

The perception of increased fighter hazard was confirmed on 29

November, when Fg Off. Don Howe's P/461 failed to return from a patrol. He was one of the newly qualified captains, having joined No. 461 in January 1943, flown nine operations in co-pilot roles, commenced training for captaincy by June, and flown his first operation as captain during October. He was on his thirteenth operation in command on 29 November, when four hours after take-off on a Percussion patrol his aircraft transmitted one of the dreaded 'O-A' messages, giving a position deep within the Bay. Nothing more was heard from the aircraft, but a German radio message was intercepted reporting an RAF aircraft shot down in flames. When squadron aircraft failed to discover any sign of survivors in dinghy searches the next day, the squadron concluded that there was 'no hope' for Howe's crew. Thirteen men were gone.[58] Four Ju 88 pilots had returned to base on the 29th to file a joint claim for one Sunderland shot down at 2.10 p.m.[59]

Fg Off. Jaques Dupont, Howe's co-pilot, was a particularly unlucky man, having joined the squadron only the previous month, already wearing the prestigious ribbon of a DFM, earnt on another squadron, as Les Baveystock had done before him. Dupont's DFM was so recently awarded that it was only after arriving on the squadron that he had been summoned to Buckingham Palace for the investiture to receive his medal. This was an NCO's award, the sergeants' equivalent of the officers' DFC, so he had won his gong as a sergeant pilot but was now being invested with it as an officer. The fact that he had jumped two ranks straight to flying officer shows that he had been earmarked for advancement. However, he and his promising service career had now been cut off after only a month on the squadron. Dupont left behind an Austin 7 saloon to be sold off to his squadron mates for his estate, while Howe left a 7-hp Fiat to be disposed of in similar manner. It fell to No. 10's acting CO, Sqn Ldr Cooke, to write the condolence letters to the next of kin. A native of Toorak, Dupont had been well-connected within the air force, for his brother was Grp Capt. Richard Dupont, RAF, who was at the time of Jaques's death *en route* from England to Australia. Cooke wrote to Dupont's mother, Mrs Lucy Dupont: 'Your son was one of the most popular men on the Squadron, efficient in his duties and always keen to meet the enemy. He has already distinguished himself in action'. With no trace ever found of the men in Howe's crew, Mrs Dupont remained unconvinced that her son was dead, in June 1944 still writing to the Air Board that 'I have not given up hope'.[60]

The very day after Howe's loss, Flt Lt C. C. 'Ted' Clark's crew from No. 10 ran into six Ju 88s. Clark had joined the squadron as a new sergeant pilot back in October 1942, begun operations as a second pilot in November that year, become apprenticed as first pilot to Max Mainprize in February 1943, commissioned in June in preparation for attaining his captaincy, and flew his first operation in command that August. The RAAF's policy that its Sunderland captains be of officer rank had meant rapid promotion for up-and-coming sergeant pilots like Clark: to make up for lost seniority, he was promoted to flying officer rank in October, after only two months as a pilot officer, and then to flight lieutenant the very next month. Promotion through the ranks was a rough index of operational experience, for by the time Clark put up the second ring on his sleeve on 18 November, he had flown twenty operations in command, his newly-acquired flight lieutenant rank marking him as a senior captain within the unit, half way through his tour.

On 30 November, Clark was flying his twenty-seventh operation, having taken off at 5.10 a.m. on a Percussion anti-submarine patrol. By 2.10 p.m., he and his crew were nearing the end of the patrol, cruising at 2,000 feet, anticipating setting course for home. The first pilot, Fg Off. Stan Chilcott, was on the radar set and reported six radar contacts at 55 miles range. It would have been a remarkable radar performance to detect airborne aircraft at that range, but only a minute later, the two pilots at the controls, Clark and Plt Off. Phil Oakley, looked out of the windscreen to see six twin-engined aircraft only 5 miles away, off the starboard bow. Chilcott, evidently somewhat inexperienced on the radar, had misinterpreted the scope's range scale. Oakley, the second pilot, had been taking a turn at the controls when he made the sighting, so as Clark rang the action stations alarm, all three pilots changed position to get ready for the coming combat: Clark took over the left-hand captain's seat from Oakley, Chilcott slipped into the co-pilot's seat, while Oakley was rendered supernumerary, left to stand behind the captain's seat, obliged to watch proceedings and await developments. The navigator, Fg Off. Col Stanfield, left his plotting table to take up his fire control position in the astrodome. The nearest cloud was 20 miles away, but Clark headed for it, demanding maximum continuous power from his engines, ordering the depth-charges jettisoned and directing the wireless operator to send the 'O-A' signal to base, warning of fighter attack and giving the position in case they were shot down.

As the Sunderland laboriously headed towards the devoutly-desired cloud in the distance, the Ju 88s executed the standard tactics, splitting up into two groups, each of which positioned themselves off either the Sunderland's port or starboard bow. Then they took their usual turns, peeling off for their attack runs from each side in succession. Clark was just as methodical, turning into each attack before rolling out and resuming his halting progress towards the cloud. The Sunderland's gunners succeeded in putting enough tracer bursts across the noses of the incoming 88s to deflect them from their attacks before they got too close: mostly the

German pilots broke away at an indecisive 1,000 yards range. However, a couple of them were more aggressive than that, and so some attacks were pressed in to the potentially decisive range of only 200 yards. Several hits reverberated through the Sunderland airframe, with the interior filled with a 'heavy cordite smell' from the Sunderland's own machine guns. Oakley was looking out through the windscreen past the pilots' heads when there was suddenly 'a bang and a blinding flash' in front of the instrument panel: there were now bullet holes through the now-cracked windscreen, most of the instrument glasses were broken, the throttle control quadrant was displaced, and alcohol spilling from the shattered P4 compass had ignited in a pool of fire on the cockpit floor. Oakley watched as Chilcott bent down out of his seat, trying to the blow the fire out. The 20-mm shell had exploded forward of Clark's left rudder pedal and the shell splinters had also pierced his flying boot and penetrated his foot. He needed that foot to press on the rudder pedal, however, so stayed on the controls.

As the combat progressed and the Sunderland edged towards the cloud, the Ju 88s found themselves further and further aft as they broke away after each attacking run. Their later attacks therefore were increasingly made from the Sunderland's rear quarters, rather than its bow or beam. This placed them within the firing arc of the four-gun tail turret, manned with some aplomb by FS Frank Callander, who shot so well that he reported two of the Ju 88s leaving the combat with engines afire. He had been struck in both legs in the first attack, but he stuck to his post and concentrated on his gunnery. The Sunderland's return fire made a significant contribution to the aircraft's survival, for Clark reached the cloud after an agonising twenty minutes of facing off against successive firing passes from the 88s. Callander's determined resistance under duress was to be rewarded by the award of a well-deserved DFM.[61]

Once safely ensconced within the cloud's misty embrace, Clark requested a damage report and head count. This established that one of the galley gunners, Sgt Lennie Lang, had also been hit in the leg. Oakley went aft to check on the wounded, finding Lang bleeding from a thigh wound. He went aft to help Callander out of his turret, finding the fuselage 'an absolute shambles', with the IFF transmitter literally blown out of the hull by an explosive shell hit, leaving a 'gaping hole' in the fuselage skin where it had been. Oakley reached the tail turret, centralised the turret so that he could open the turret doors, and helped Callander out. He found that the doughty tail gunner had 'several bullet wounds in each knee'. Together, they managed to get forward to the galley, where Callander collapsed on one of the bunks; Lang was in the other. There were three wounded crewmen aboard, but luckily none of their wounds were life-threatening. A preliminary damage assessment showed that the aircraft had been hit by three 20-mm cannon shells and many 7.92-mm bullets: one of the dangerous 20-mm shells had exploded behind the pilots' instrument panel, one had demolished the IFF set, and the third was later discovered to have 'penetrated the port main fuel tank but luckily had not exploded!'[62]

Despite the lucky survival of both aircraft and crew, the cockpit cannon hit had broken the throttle quadrant, so Clark was left with his engines running at maximum continuous power. He had no way of throttling back but was at least able to change from RICH mixture to WEAK. This saved more than 100 gallons per hour, but at 2,250 rpm, even in weak mixture the four engines were together gobbling up 153 gallons per hour, with home still five hours away. Normally, on the way home in a lightened aircraft, it was possible to reduce the fuel burn to below 100 gallons an hour, so over a five-hour stretch, the uncontrolled extra fuel consumption was equivalent to two and a half hours' normal use. The damaged aircraft's fuel consumption was thus extreme, but it was standard practice to return to base with a couple of hours of reserve fuel still aboard as a contingency against just such a situation as this, so they might just make it. Despite this safety reserve, Clark nonetheless had no good reason to be sure that the aircraft's fuel would last long enough to make landfall, so with two seriously wounded gunners and out-of-control fuel consumption, he did not want to waste time, fuel, and distance in circling inside the cloud: as soon as Oakley went back on to the radar set and reported that the 88s were retiring, Clark broke cloud and headed for home. The turrets were re-manned by fresh crewmen, the guns tested in case of any further fighter encounters, and radio silence maintained until the aircraft had removed itself from the Ju 88s' hunting grounds.

Only at 4.30 p.m., when about one hour and fifteen minutes from base, did Clark finally break radio silence, sending a signal advising base of the damage and casualties, and warning that his aircraft was approaching English airspace but without IFF. He was concerned to prevent a friendly fire incident should the unidentified radar contact be misidentified as enemy. Clark also requested an ambulance for his wounded, and the beaching gear to be readied, to get his colander-hulled aircraft up the slipway straight after landing. The flight engineers, Sgts John Cox and Ian Speirs, took turns checking the fuel gauges religiously, calculating and recalculating the total fuel remaining: there was only 125 gallons left when they passed the Scillies. It might have been prudent to land there, and indeed Clark initially preferred to do so, but the weather remained good and he wanted to get the wounded to hospital at Plymouth, so after a council of war on the flight-deck, he decided to press on and try to make Mount Batten. However, when abeam Lizard Point in Cornwall, there was only 50 gallons left, so everyone realised it would be 'touch and go' whether they could reach base. Sure enough, 8 miles past Rame Head, with the fuel gauges reading zero, all four engines cut at once: Clark now had command of a 45,000-pound glider. He took over control from Chilcott and pushed the nose down to gain and maintain a safe gliding speed. Chilcott grabbed the flare pistol and started firing red signal cartridges out the cockpit window as fast as he could reload. The rest of the crew took ditching positions aft of the flight-deck, including the wounded Callander and Lang, who with help made it up the ladder in time, before the aircraft touched down on the water.

Fortunately, the sea conditions were moderately good, with a 'low four feet swell', and Clark made a skilful glide approach, pulling the control yoke back to achieve a 'smooth "dead stick" alighting', running along the line of the swell. It was 5.45 p.m., and the aircraft had safely alighted on the sea just outside Plymouth Harbour with only petrol fumes in its fuel tanks. As soon as the aircraft stopped, rolling and pitching in the swell, the engineers opened the escape hatch, and Callander and Lang were helped out of the hull and on to the wing. The rest of the crew set to the task of pumping and bailing out the water that was flowing into the hull 'through the countless holes in the fuselage'. The aircraft's salvation came in the form of a small trawler, the crew of which offered a tow, which was gratefully accepted. The trawler men threw a line, which was duly secured to the bollard in the Sunderland's bow compartment, allowing her to be towed through the breakwater. Despite the crew's efforts, the flooding was gaining on their pumping and bailing, so to prevent her sinking in deep water, the holed aircraft was beached at Mount Batten. At the rate at which she was settling in the water, there had been no time to fit the beaching gear and get her up the slipway. Despite the temporary inundation of the hull at high tide, at low tide, the men from maintenance flight bunged the holes in her hull below the waterline, allowing her to be refloated the next tide and brought up the slipway with dignity. L/10 was repaired on the squadron and was flying again in time to be damaged in a taxiing accident after landing from a flight on 30 January 1944. After repairs, she flew on with No. 10 right through 1944. After debriefing, Phil Oakley went into town with the navigator, Colin Stanfield, and their friend, Fg Off. Maurie Ryan (a pilot), to celebrate their 'escape'. Despite the supposed secrecy of operational matters, upon entering their favourite pub, The Ship Inn, they were greeted warmly by the publican, who made it clear that he knew what had happened to them, serving them drinks 'on the house' all night. Callander's DFM was announced on 10 December.[63]

10

Evaluation and Reflection

Howe's was the final Australian Sunderland loss in 1943, thankfully bringing to an end the run of heavy casualties occasioned by the predatory activities of V./KG40. The Ju 88s had done their job well, destroying ten of the Australian Sunderlands in the seven months from May to November. Two of these crews (Walker's and Marrows's) survived the loss of their aircraft, both from No. 461, so eight full crews had been killed by the enemy fighters. Three more crews had been lost to operational accidents during 1943. In addition, Bill Dods was killed in an operational crash on 28 May, Bob Fry and five of his men were killed after being shot down by flak on 1 August, and four other men had been killed as part of crews that otherwise returned alive. In total, therefore, the equivalent of twelve crews had been lost in the course of this most costly year of operations, eight from No. 10 and four from No. 461. The scale of these losses can readily be seen in proportion to the number of operational crews on each squadron's strength—up to twelve.

No. 10's CO, Wg Cdr Hartnell, also moved on, in accordance with the RAAF's policy of furthering the careers of its pre-war officers: in December, he left the squadron to take up a staff post at RAAF HQ in London. Hartnell had flown ten operations in his eight months' incumbency, which was a creditable level of operational involvement for a CO. However, his tour of duty was short compared to that of squadron stalwarts like Reg Marks and Terry Brown. Marks had flown through 1941 as a co-pilot, flew thirty-two operations as captain in 1942, then at the end of that year was appointed to an executive role as squadron flight commander. In that role he had flown another twelve operations before finally ending his tour in September 1943, having amassed 1,346 Sunderland hours in an almost three-year-long tour. Similarly, Brown was more-or-less tour-expired in April 1943, by which time he had captained the impressive total of sixty-three operations, on top of a year's worth of operations before that in co-pilot roles, for like Marks, he had begun his apprenticeship as first pilot in early 1941. Brown was made training officer as a fitting way of closing off his operational tour, but still managed to fly two more ops, before definitively ending his tour by being appointed to the role of squadron flight commander in September 1943.

Tours in Coastal Command could be remarkably long, especially for officers destined to put up their third stripe, earmarked to ascend the ladder of the squadrons' executive roles: good examples are No. 10's Ron Gillies and Tom Egerton. Gillies had joined the squadron back in March 1941, completed his operational flying in January 1943, served throughout 1943 instructing the new pilots as squadron training officer, and accruing more than 1,100 Sunderland hours by the time he took over as the squadron CO in December 1943. As we have seen, Egerton had flown through 1941–42 with No. 10, captaining fifty-two operations, then ended his operational tour to become No. 10's squadron training officer at the end of 1942, before getting posted to No. 461 in the New Year to take over the same role. However, for officers not earmarked for the executive officer pathway, as these men had been, tours were a little shorter. Two examples are Flt Lts John Weatherlake and Chic Clarke, who completed their tours with 461 Squadron in October 1943: Weatherlake had flown fifty-four operations since early 1942, forty of them as captain; while, since October 1942, Clarke had flown fifty ops, twenty-nine of them as captain.

Although thirteen of No. 10's captains completed their tours during 1943, another eight had their tours prematurely terminated that year by death.[1,2] This provides a reasonable snapshot of survival statistics for 10 Squadron aircrew during that most dangerous and decisive year of the war. Another way of obtaining an impression of the squadron's casualty rate is to take a roll-call of squadron captains at the beginning of May 1943, before the coming spike in casualties during 19 Group's decisive Bay offensive. At that month's beginning, No. 10 had on its ops board the names of twelve captains: Brown, Farmer, Fry, Gerrard, Griffiths, Mainprize, Marks, McKenzie, Rossiter, Saunders, Skinner, and Strath. Of these, five were killed before the year was out, while another five completed their tours within the same period. As we have seen, April–November 1943 was by far the most dangerous phase of the war for our Sunderland squadrons, so these odds cannot be taken as representative of the whole, multi-year campaign. The longer-term average casualty rate can be seen in another statistical sample: out of forty-four captains who flew with No. 10 during the whole period covered by this book (March 1942 to December 1943), twelve were killed, a fatality rate of 27 per cent.

The figures for No. 461 provide a similar picture of the hazards of flying Sunderland operations during 1943. At the start of May that year, the junior squadron had ten captains available for operations: Baird, Clarke, Cooke, Dods, Manger, Marrows, Singleton, Smith, Walker, and Weatherlake. Within months, four of these would be dead, with another seven completing their tours in the same timeframe. As in No. 10's case, these relative proportions are not representative of the whole extended period of the 1942–43 campaign: from the commencement of No. 461's operations in July 1942 to the end of 1943, the squadron employed a total of twenty-nine captains, of whom six were killed; this provides a metric of aircrew fatality rates within the squadron during that period— about 20 per cent. No. 461's casualty rate was thus a little lower than No. 10's, despite No. 461 having attracted its fair share of attention from hostile aircraft, and despite the similarity in the two units' sortie outputs in the costly period of May–November 1943, during which 383 patrols were flown by No. 10, compared to 351 from No. 461. It follows that on average, the aircrew of the Australian Sunderland Squadrons in this period had stood about a 75 per cent chance of completing their tours alive.

Both units showed similar organisational resilience in replacing their heavy crew losses from May 1943 onwards. As the unit suffering the greatest losses, No. 10 was particularly impressive, for in the six-month period from May, the unit qualified twelve new captains and added them to its operational program. In order of starting, these were Dick Gray, Keith Sampson, Alan Williams, Ron Humble, Merv Jones, Ted Clark, Fred Lees, Ray Behrndt, Glenn Jennison, John McCulloch, Bede Lean, and Phil Edwards. In the context of obtaining an impression of No. 10's casualty rate over this period, it is salutary to observe that of the twelve newly-qualified captains named above, three were dead by the end of November.[3] To emphasise the scale of the in-squadron training effort needed to replace its losses, it is worth pointing out that beside replacing the eight lost captains, the squadron had also to replace all the other lost men in the lost crews, at least ninety air-crewmen in total. The extent of the squadron's organisational resilience is shown in the fact that No. 10 finished November 1943 still with eleven crews on its flight roster, after having lost eight crews inside half a year.

No. 461 presents a similarly robust picture, adding thirteen captains to its crew line-up over the July–November 1943 period: in order of appearance, these were Phil Davenport, Bill Dowling, Jack Nicholls, Cedric Croft, Rodger Newton, Pearce Taplin, Ross Watts, Jim Dawson, Don Howe, Jimmy Leigh, Dick Lucas, Johnny Dobson, and Don Sinclair. Once again, of the new captains named above, three were killed by the end of November.[4] By virtue of the training effort these numbers represent, the squadron ended November 1943 with ten captains and ten crews on its ops board, the same as it had started with at the beginning of May (the apparent arithmetical discrepancy is explained by the fact that nine captains had become tour-expired during that period).[5]

The first and only year of the Sunderland squadrons' war when the crew loss rate rose to something comparable to that pertaining within Bomber Command was in 1943. The men who came through this phase of the squadrons' war had undertaken risky service indeed, but with the consolation of concrete evidence of their operations' effect: six sunken U-boats. Thus, in broad terms, the Australians had exchanged two Sunderlands for every U-boat. A total of 253 German sailors had lost their lives in the course of these sinkings.[6] When laid alongside the 101 airmen lost in action by the two Australian squadrons this also produces a ghoulish exchange rate of about 2.5 German sailors for every airman. Within Coastal Command as a whole, a total of 169 enemy submarines were destroyed for the loss of 741 aircraft, giving a ratio of more than four aircraft for every enemy submarine. To put Nos 10 and 461's 101 dead into context, Coastal Command lost 8,874 men killed during the war, 6,022 of them while flying operations.[7]

The campaign was not decided by such callous arithmetic alone. The fundamental fact was that the patrol aircraft of No. 19 Group had plied their trade over the Bay of Biscay's submarine transit zones without let-up, in spite of the casualties. They could sustain this because of the deep resourcing, which enabled the RAF to replace the lost men and provide replacement aircraft, thereby 'topping up' depleted units to sustain the sortie rates necessary to continue to 'swamp' the Bay with aircraft patrols and radar emissions. The losses exacted by the Ju 88s of V./KG40 had been dismaying, but as we have seen they had not broken the resilience of the squadrons as war-fighting organisations, or even significantly degraded the proficiency of the airmen who carried on with the job after the losses. By now, Coastal Command's program of conversion training, on-the-job training, specialist courses, and ongoing operational tuition was so effective that new crews were ascending the proficiency ladder more quickly than existing crews could be eliminated by the marauding 88s. By 1943, Coastal Command had not only attained the scale of forces necessary to fight a big campaign, but the organisational depth to allow it to shrug off losses and remain effective.

By contrast, U-boat Command did not recover from the losses it suffered. The tithe exacted by Coastal Command and its co-operating naval forces in the peak mid-year hunting season of 1943 rendered the Bay transit so questionable a proposition for Dönitz's U-boats as to impel him in turn to suspend the campaign, to scale back his sailings, and then to resume the campaign within truncated bounds. In short, Allied anti-submarine action had restricted the freedom of operation of the U-boats, in effect imposing limits on where they could sail, when they could sail, in what numbers, and especially when and where they could surface. The consequence was to diminish the rate of sailing, to lengthen transit times across the Bay, and to restrict the number of U-boats reaching their patrol areas. Besides the U-boats actually sunk by Nos 10 and 461, the Sunderland operations had also reduced the number of enemy submarines actually on patrol in the Atlantic. This was an unmeasurable, intangible secondary effect, but was substantive nonetheless, and needs to be placed alongside the six tangible sinkings in any evaluation of the squadrons' operational impact. In summary, whereas the Luftwaffe counter-action had quite failed to diminish the patrol density of Coastal Command aircraft over the Bay, No. 19 Group had indeed diminished the patrol activity of the U-boats.

Unusually for a home-based RAF command, Coastal Command was able to pursue concrete, measurable, and achievable objectives: to find U-boats, sink U-boats, damage U-boats, prevent U-boat transits into the open ocean, shorten the duration of U-boat patrols, and to diminish the U-boat force, both in its numerical strength and its operational freedom of action. Once the command was re-equipped with aircraft, weapons, and sensors fit for the task from the end of 1942, once its operational research staff started 'crunching the numbers' to analyse results, discover patterns, and refocus operations upon high-yield areas, and once crews were trained and indoctrinated in the application of the most effective tactics and methods, then Coastal Command had articulated a meaningful relationship between means and ends. The men of Coastal Command therefore were able to fight a campaign in pursuit of realisable, practical objectives, with tools and methods fit for the task.

Another point of advantage for Coastal Command was in crew experience, as splendidly exemplified by the men of Nos 10 and 461 Squadrons. This was related to loss rates, which were low enough for many men to survive long enough to acquire considerable experience and to finish their tours, by contrast, for example, with Bomber Command. There can be no doubt that the long-range maritime-patrol crews of Coastal Command were numbered among the most proficient airmen of World War II, attaining levels of professionalism that would be matched only by the regular, long-service airmen of the Cold War era and beyond. This was certainly true of both Nos 10 and 461 Squadrons, both of which secured well-deserved reputations for being among the most redoubtable airmen within the Allied air forces.

APPENDIX I

U-boat Kills

Date	Submarine sunk	10 Sqn aircraft	461 Sqn aircr
10 Sept. 41	Alessandro Malaspina	U/10	
02 May 43	U-465		M/461
07 May 43	U-663	W/10	
31 May 43	U-563	E/10	
30 July 43	U-461		U/461
01 Aug. 43	U-454	B/10	
02 Aug. 43	U-106		M/461
08 Jan. 44	U-426	U/10	
28 Jan. 44	U-571		D/461
08 July 44	U-243	H/10	
11 Aug. 44	U-385		P/461
12 Aug. 44	U-270		A/461
Total submarine kills in 1943		3	3
Grand total submarine kills in the Second World War		6	6

in	Enemy casualties	Details
Wearne	all 60 killed	
Smith	all 48 killed	
Rossiter	all 49 killed	
Mainprize	all 53 killed	Kill shared with Halifax R/58 & Sunderland X/228
Marrows	54 killed, 15 rescued by Royal Navy	
Fry	34 killed, 13 rescued by Royal Navy	Sunderland shot down by U-454's AA
Clarke	25 killed, 36 rescued by German navy	Kill shared with Sunderland N/228
F. Roberts	all 50 killed	
Lucas	all 52 killed	
F. Tilley	11 killed, 39 rescued by Canadian navy	
f. Southall	1 killed, 42 rescued by Royal Navy	Kill shared with HMS Starling
F. Little	10 killed, 71 rescued by Royal Navy	

APPENDIX II

Sunderland Losses (1942–43)

Date	Callsign - 10	Callsign - 461	Serial	Captain
21 June 42	Y/10		W3999	Flt Lt Judell
30 July 42	X/10		W3994	Flt Lt Martin
08 Aug. 42	A/10		W4019	Flt Lt Yeoman
12 Aug. 42		B/461	T9090	Wg Cdr Hallic
01 Sept. 42		F/461	T9113	Plt Off. Hosba
12 Nov. 42	D/10		W6054	Fg Off. Thorpe
21 Jan. 43		A/461	T9085	Flt Lt Buls
21 Mar. 43		C/461	T9111	Flt Lt Manger
17 May 43	Z/10		W4004	Flt Lt McKenzi
20 May 43	U/10		W3986	Flt Lt Saunder
28 May 43		O/461	JM675	Flt Lt Dods
29 May 43		E/461	T9114	Fg Off. Singlet
02 June 43		N/461	EJ134	Flt Lt Walker
01 Aug. 43	B/10		W4020	Flt Lt Fry
11 Aug. 43	F/10		DP177	Flt Lt Gerrard
13 Aug. 43		M/461	DV968	Fg Off. Dowlin
18 Aug. 43	T/10		W3985	Flt Lt Skinner
30 Aug. 43		Z/461	JM707	Fg Off. Croft
16 Sept. 43		E/461	EK578	Flt Lt Marrow
21 Sept. 43	E/10		DV969	Fg Off. Jenniso
02 Oct. 43	M/10		DP179	Fg Off. Lees
17 Nov. 43	T/10		DV993	Flt Lt Behrndt
29 Nov. 43		P/461	JM676	Flt Lt Howe

ties - combat	Fatalities - non combat	Details
11		Shot down by Arado 196
12		Probably shot down by Arado 196s
	12	Unexplained loss after SOS
	10	Crashed while attempting sea landing
11		Shot down by Junkers 88s
	5 passengers	Crash landing in fog at night
	11	Crashed after technical failure in bad weather at night
	0	Take-off crash at night after engine failure
12		Shot down by Junkers 88s
	12	Airborne fuel explosion
	1	Crashed while attempting sea landing, Dods killed
	0	Damaged taking off from the sea, crash-landed Angle airfield
1		Damaged by Junkers 88s, crash-landing in sea
6		Shot down by flak from U-454
12		Shot down by Junkers 88s
11		Shot down by Junkers 88s
12		Shot down by Junkers 88s
11		Shot down by Junkers 88s
0		Shot down by Junkers 88s
11		Shot down by Junkers 88s
	11	Lost at sea after engine failure
11		Shot down by Junkers 88s
13		Shot down by Junkers 88s

APPENDIX III

Sunderland Aircraft in Use

10 Squadron

Callsign	Serial	Mark No.	On unit	Off unit
A/10	W4019	Mk III	Feb. 42	09 Aug. 42
B/10	W4020	Mk III	Mar. 42	01 Aug. 43
C/10	T9110	Mk I	June 42	Aug. 44
D/10	W6054	Mk II	Aug. 42	Nov. 42
E/10	DV969	Mk III	Sept. 42	Sept. 43
F/10	DP177	Mk III	Nov. 42	Aug. 43
G/10	W4024	Mk III	Apr. 43	May 44
H/10	W4030	Mk III	Apr. 43	Nov. 44
J/10	DD852	Mk III	May 43	Sept. 44
K/10	JM684	Mk III	May 43	June 45
L/10	DD865	Mk III	Aug. 43	Jan. 45
M/10	DP179	Mk III	Aug. 43	02 Oct. 43
P/10	EK573	Mk III	Aug. 43	May 45
Q/10	EK574	Mk III	Aug. 43	June 44
R/10	W3983	Mk II	June 42	Feb. 44
S/10	W3984	Mk II	Aug. 41	Dec. 43
T/10	W3985	Mk II	Aug. 41	18 Aug. 43
T/10	DV993	Mk III	Oct. 43	17 Nov. 43
U/10	W3986	Mk II	Aug. 41	20 May 43
U/10	EK586	Mk III	Oct. 43	Dec. 44
W/10	W3993	Mk II	Nov. 41	Dec. 43
X/10	W3994	Mk II	Oct. 41	30 July 42
Y/10	W3999	Mk III	Jan. 42	21 June 42
Z/10	W4004	Mk III	Feb. 42	17 May 43

‹s
‹ to return, possibly shot down, Yeoman crew lost
down by U-boat, 6 men lost (Fry crew)
‹ged in landing accident 5 Jan. 44, to Short Bros, scrapped
‹oyed in landing accident 13 Nov. 42 (Thorpe crew), 5 passengers killed
down, Jennison crew lost
down, Gerrard crew lost
Group as instructional airframe
‹ged in take-off accident 16 Sept. 44, to No. 43 Group, scrapped
‹k by ship while at moorings, written-off
‹F Wig Bay, struck off charge July 45
‹ottish Aviation, struck off charge
‹ental loss, Lees crew lost
‹. 4 (C)OTU
‹n take-off accident 1 June 44
‹ne instructional airframe
‹ort and Harland, scrapped
down, Skinner crew lost
down, Behrndt crew lost
‹ental loss, Saunders crew lost
‹ottish Aviation, struck off charge Dec. 45
‹ged in taxiing accident 7 Oct. 43, to Short and Harland, scrapped
down, Martin crew lost
down, Judell crew lost
down, McKenzie crew lost

461 Squadron

Callsign	Serial	Mark No.	On unit	Off unit
A/461	T9085	Mk I	April 42	21 Jan. 43
A/461	DV961	Mk II	July 42	March 44
B/461	T9090	Mk I	April 42	12 Aug. 42
B/461	DD866	Mk III	Aug. 43	Aug. 44
C/461	T9111	Mk I	May 42	21 March 43
C/461	EK575	Mk III	Aug. 43	March 44
D/461	T9109	Mk I	April 42	Sept. 43
D/461	EK577	Mk III	Aug. 43	April 44
E/461	T9114	Mk I	July 42	29 May 43
E/461	EK578	Mk III	Aug. 43	16 Sept. 43
F/461	T9113	Mk I	June 42	01 Sept. 43
F/461	DV989	Mk III	Sept. 43	Oct. 44
G/461	JM678	Mk III	Sept. 43	Feb. 44
H/461	DV960	Mk II	July 42	Aug. 44
I/461	see A/461–DV961 was recoded from 'I' to 'A' after loss of T9085			
J/461	EJ138	Mk III	Nov. 43	Aug. 44
K/461	T9115	Mk I	July 42	April 43
L/461	W6050	Mk II	Aug. 42	Jan. 44
M/461	DV968	Mk II	Sept. 42	13 Aug. 43
N/461	EJ134	Mk III	Dec. 42	02 June 43
O/461	JM675	Mk III	March 43	28 May 43
P/461	JM676	Mk III	April 43	29 Nov. 43
R/461	DV962	Mk II	April 43	June 43
S/461	EJ142	Mk III	April 43	May 44
T/461	EJ133	Mk III	April 43	Dec. 44
U/461	W6077	Mk III	May 43	Aug. 43
W/461	JM683	Mk III	June 43	April 44
X/461	JM685	Mk III	June 43	Nov. 43
Y/461	JM686	Mk III	June 43	April 44
Z/461	JM707	Mk III	June 43	30 Aug. 43

s
ntal operational loss, Buls's crew lost
4 (C)OTU as an instructional airframe
ntal operational loss, Halliday's crew lost
302 Ferry Training Unit
ff accident (Manger's crew), destroyed
228 Squadron
ff accident 16 Aug. 43, to RAF Wig Bay
4 (C)OTU
landed RAF Angle (Singleton's crew), written-off
own (Marrows's crew)
own, Hosband's crew lost
131 OTU
228 Squadron
131 OTU
330 Squadron
rt and Harland, Belfast
ed in gale 24 Jan. 44, written-off
own, Dowling's crew lost
landed from combat damage (Walker's crew), destroyed
landing (Dods's crew), destroyed
own, Howe's crew lost
ed 7 June 43 in hangar by accidental fire, written-off as beyond economical repair
4 (C)OTU
yed in landing accident
rt Bros for repairs after flak damage 30 July 43
4 (C)OTU
228 Sqn
4 (C)OTU
own, Croft's crew lost

Endnotes

10 and 461 Squadron ORBs in NAA: Series A9186, Items 25 and 148.
Casualty files in NAA: Series A705.

Chapter 1

1 Blair, C., *Hitler's U-boat War: The Hunted, 1942–1945* (London: Cassell & Co., 1998), pp. 695, 353, 339, 361.
2 *Ibid.*, p. 274.
3 Mallmann Showell, J. P., *Dönitz, U-boats, Convoys: The British Version of His Memoirs from the Admiralty's Secret Anti-Submarine Reports* (London: Frontline Books, 2013), p. 71.
4 Blair, *op. cit.* pp. 307-308, 311.
5 Mallmann Showell, *op. cit.*, p. 176.
6 Blair, *op. cit.*, pp. 381, 382, 404, 419.
7 Blair, *op. cit.*, pp. 391-393.
8 White, J., *The Milk Cows: U-boat Tankers At War 1941-1945* (Barnsley: Pen & Sword, 2009) p. 124.
9 *Ibid.*, pp. 131-132, 134-135.
10 *Ibid.*, pp. 125, 127.
11 *Ibid.*, pp. 132-136.
12 Mallmann Showell, *op. cit.*, pp. 135, 141.
13 White, *op. cit.*, p. 136.
14 Bowman, M. W., *Deep Sea Hunters: RAF Coastal Command and the War against the U-boats and the German Navy 1939–1945* (Barnsley: Pen & Sword, 2014), pp. 111, 170.
15 'U.454. Interrogation of Survivors. September 1943', www.uboatarchive.net, accessed 21.10.2017.
16 Mallmann Showell, *op. cit.*, p. 179.
17 Bowman, *op. cit.*, p. 170.
18 White, *op. cit.*, p. 137.
19 Blair, *op. cit.*, p. 316.
20 'U.461. Interrogation of survivors', www.uboatarchive.net, accessed 21.10.2017.
21 White, *op. cit.*, p. 138.

22 'U.462. Interrogation of survivors', www.uboatarchive.net, accessed 21.10.2017.

23 Terraine, J., *Business in Great Waters: The U-boat Wars 1916–1945* (London: Mandarin, 1989), p. 421.

24 Wynn, K., *U-boat Operations of the Second World War, Vol. 1: Career Histories, U1-U510* (London: Chatham Publishing, 1997), p. 307.

25 White, *op. cit.*, p. 137.

26 Wynn, *op. cit.*, Vol. 1, p. 308.

27 Southall, I., *They Shall Not Pass Unseen* (Sydney: Angus & Robertson, 1956), p. 106.

28 Blair, *op. cit.*, pp. 322-323.

29 White, *op. cit.*, p. 139.

30 Franks, N. L. R., *Conflict Over the Bay: Momentous Battles Fought by RAF and American Aircraft Against the U-Boats, Bay of Biscay May–August 1943* (London: Grub Street, 1999), p. 135.

31 Southall, *op. cit.*, p. 107.

32 Peter Jensen, in Franks, *Conflict Over the Bay*, p. 137.

33 Dudley Marrows, in Franks, *Conflict Over the Bay*, p. 136.

34 Southall, *op. cit.*, p. 107.

35 Marrows, in Franks, *Conflict Over the Bay*, p. 136.

36 Paddy Watson, in Franks, *Conflict Over the Bay*, p. 137.

37 Watson, in Franks, *Conflict Over the Bay*, p. 138.

38 Jensen, in Franks, *Conflict Over the Bay*, pp. 137-138.

39 Marrows, in Franks, *Conflict Over the Bay*, p. 138.

40 White, *op. cit.*, p. 138.

41 Jensen, in Franks, *Conflict Over the Bay*, pp. 137-138.

42 Marrows, in Franks, *Conflict Over the Bay*, pp. 139.

43 Southall, *op. cit.*, p. 110.

44 Jensen, in Franks, *Conflict Over the Bay*, p. 138.

45 Marrows, in Franks, *Conflict Over the Bay*, p. 139.

46 White, *op. cit.*, p. 140.

47 Southall, *op. cit.*, pp. 111-112.

48 Franks, *op. cit.*, p. 139.

49 White, *op. cit.*, p. 141.

50 Ashworth, N., *The Anzac Squadron: A History of No 461 Squadron Royal Australian Air Force 1942–1945* (Perth: Hesperion Press, 1994), p. 109.

51 Marrows, in Franks, *Conflict Over the Bay*, p. 140.

52 'U.461. Interrogation of survivors', www.uboatarchive.net, accessed 21.10.2017.

53 Franks, *op. cit.*, p. 141.

54 'U.462. Interrogation of Survivors', www.uboatarchive.net, accessed 21.10.2017.

55 Franks, *op. cit.*, p. 143.

56 White, *op. cit.*, p. 141.

57 'U.461. Interrogation of Survivors', www.uboatarchive.net, accessed 21.10.2017.

58 Blair, *op. cit.*, p. 392.

59 Wynn, *op. cit.*, Vol.1, pp. 322-323.

60 Blair, *op. cit.*, p. 392.

61 Ashworth, *op. cit.*, p. 111.

62 Southall, *op. cit.*, pp. 114-117.

63 Franks, *op. cit.*, pp.143, 145.

64 Ashworth, *op. cit.*, p.112.
65 Hendrie, A., *Short Sunderland in World War II* (Shrewsbury: Airlife Publishing, 1994), p. 160.
66 461 Squadron ORB, NAA: A9186, 148.
67 Ashworth, *op. cit.*, p. 112.
68 Blair, *op. cit.*, pp. 274, 381.

Chapter 2

1 'Percy Howard Smith RAAF UK Service Diaries', via Peter Dunn, p. 3.
2 Smith, R. K., *'The Superiority Of The American Transoceanic Airliner 1932–1939: Sikorsky S-42 Vs. Short S.23, A Tale Of The Tares Of Two Airplanes'*, *American Aviation Historical Society Journal*, Vol. 29 No. 2 (Summer 1984), pp. 82-94.
3 Bowyer, C., *Sunderland at War* (Shepperton, Surrey: Ian Allan, 1989, *Sunderland At War*), p. 30.
4 Smith, *op. cit.*, pp. 82-94.
5 Bowyer, *op. cit.*, p. 48.
6 Ashworth, N., *The Anzac Squadron: A History of No 461 Squadron Royal Australian Air Force 1942–1945* (Perth: Hesperion Press, 1994), p. 64.
7 *Ibid.*, pp. 73-74.
8 Gallagher, E. B., and Timmermans, T., *PS: Love Me? The War Memoirs of Flight Sergeant Ed Gallagher* (Victoria, British Columbia: Tricia Timmermans, 2013).
9 Jefford, C. G., *Observers and Navigators and Other Non-Pilot Aircrew in the RFC, RNAS and RAF* (London: Grub Street, 2014, p. vii.
10 Dudley-Gordon, T., *Coastal Command at War* (London: Jarrolds, 1942), p. 127.
11 Ashworth, *op. cit.*, p. 64.
12 Nelson, H., *Chased By The Sun: Courageous Australians in Bomber Command in World War II* (Sydney: ABC Books, 2002), p. 31.
13 Herington, J., *Air War Against Germany and Italy 1939–1945* (Canberra: Australian War Memorial, 1954), pp. 532, 537.
14 Ashworth, *op. cit.*, p. 76.

Chapter 3

1 Coulthard-Clark, C. D., *The Third Brother: The Royal Australian Air Force 1921–39* (Sydney: Allen & Unwin, 1991, pp. 441-464.
2 Clark, C., 'R.A.A.F. Support For An Australian Maritime Strategy Before World War II', Air Power Development Centre, Seminar paper 26.4.2012, airpower.airforce.gov.au, accessed 16.1.2019.
3 Stephens, A., *Power Plus Attitude: Ideas, Strategy and Doctrine in the Royal Australian Air Force 1921–1991* (Canberra: Australian Government Printing Service, 1992), p. 44.
4 Wilson, D. J., *The Eagle and the Albatross: Australian Aerial Maritime Operations 1921–1971* (PhD Thesis, University of New South Wales, 2003), pp. 53-54.
5 Cooper, A., *Kokoda Air Strikes* (Sydney: NewSouth Publishing, 2014), pp. 1-89.
6 Ewer, P., *Wounded Eagle: The Bombing of Darwin and Australia's Air Defence Scandal* (Sydney: New Holland Publishers, 2009), pp. 112-114, 140-143.

7   Baff, K. C., *Maritime is Number Ten: A History of 10 Squadron RAAF, The Sunderland Era* (Adelaide: K.C. Baff, 1983), pp. 1-40.
8   Wilson, S., *Anson, Hudson & Sunderland in Australian Service* (Canberra: Aerospace Publications, 1992), p. 159.
9   Gillison, D., *Royal Australian Air Force 1939–1942* (Canberra: Australian War Memorial, 1962, p. 63.
10 Hewitt, J. E., *Adversity in Success* (Melbourne: Langate Publishing, 1980, p. 1.
11 Baff, *op. cit.,* pp. 20-21.
12 Gillison, *op. cit.,* pp. 58-60, 63-65.
13 Stephens, A., *The Royal Australian Air Force* (Melbourne: Oxford University Press, 2001), p. 61.
14 Jones, G., *From Private to Air Marshal: The Autobiography of Air Marshal Sir George Jones* (Melbourne: Greenhouse Publications, 1988), pp. 68-69.
15 Stephens, *op. cit.,* p. 62.
16 McCarthy, J., *A Last Call of Empire: Australian Aircrew, Britain and the Empire Air Training Scheme* (Canberra: Australian War Memorial, 1988), p. 65.
17 Kingsland, R., *Into the Midst of Things: The Autobiography of Sir Richard Kingsland* (Canberra: Air Power Development Centre, 2010), p. 51.
18 Baff, *op. cit.,* pp. 3, 456.
19 Percy Howard Smith Diaries, via Peter Dunn, p. 6.
20 Baff, *op. cit.,* pp. 22-23.
21 Herington, J., *Air War Against Germany and Italy 1939–1945* (Canberra: Australian War Memorial, 1954, p. 534.
22 Hewitt, *op. cit.,* pp. 5-6.
23 Gillison, *op. cit.,* p. 475.
24 Baff, *op. cit.,* pp. 28, 32.
25 Kingsland, *op. cit.,* p. 51.
26 Baveystock, L., *Wavetops at My Wingtips: Flying with RAF Bomber and Coastal Commands in World War II* (Shrewsbury: Airlife, 2001), p. 152.
27 Hendrie, A., *The Cinderella Service: RAF Coastal Command 1939–1945* (Barnsley: Pen & Sword, 2006, pp. 201, 203, 205-206.
28 Storr, *RAAF Fatalities in Second World War in Number 10 Squadron* (Canberra: Alan Storr, 2006).
29 Southall, I., *They Shall Not Pass Unseen* (Sydney: Angus & Robertson, 1956), p. 1.
30 Blair, C., *Hitler's U-boat War: The Hunters, 1939–1942* (New York: Random House, 1996), p. 170.
31 Australian War Memorial Image 128165.
32 '"Submerged" History Brought to the Surface!', www.3squadron.org.au, accessed 7.5.2018.
33 Wynn, K., *U-boat Operations of the Second World War, Vol. 1: Career Histories, U1-U510* (London: Chatham Publishing, 1997), pp. 58-59.
34 'R.Smg. Alessandro Malaspina', www.regiamarina.net, accessed 7.5.2018.
35 Baff, *op. cit.,* p. 200.
36 Herington, *op. cit.,* pp. 262-263.
37 Herington, *op. cit.,* pp. 262, 272, 149.
38 Roskill, S. W., *The War at Sea 1939–1945, Vol. II: The Period of Balance* (London: HMSO, 1956), p. 81.
39 Herington, *op. cit.,* pp. 269-270, 274.
40 Terraine, J., *Business in Great Waters: The U-boat Wars 1916–1945* (London: Mandarin, 1989), p. 428.

41 Blair, *op. cit.*, p. 695.
42 Padfield, P., *War Beneath the Sea: Submarine Conflict 1939–1945* (London: Pimlico, 1995), p. 221.
43 Herington, *op. cit.*, p. 274.
44 Roskill, *op. cit.*, Vol. II, p. 83.
45 Herington, *op. cit.*, p. 283.
46 Ashworth, N., *The Anzac Squadron: A History of No 461 Squadron Royal Australian Air Force 1942–1945* (Perth: Hesperion Press, 1994), p. 20.
47 *Ibid.*, pp. 16-17.
48 Herington, *op. cit.*, p. 149.
49 Cooper, A., *R.A.A.F. Bombers Over Germany 1941–42* (Sydney: Rosenberg, 2016), pp. 25, 28, 31, 34, 45-46, 55.
50 Ashworth, *op. cit.*, p. 16.
51 'R.A.F. Hamworthy', http://pastscape.org.uk, accessed 17.5.2017.
52 'Poole Flying Boats Celebration', http://www.pooleflyingboats.com/map.html, accessed 17.5.17.
53 Ashworth, *op. cit.*, pp. 17, 18.
54 Southall, *op. cit.*, pp. 2, 3.
55 Ashworth, *op. cit.*, p. 22.
56 Russell Baird Interview Transcript, dated 25.11.2003, Archive No. 1143, australiansatwarfilmarchive.unsw.edu.au, accessed 15.2.2019.
57 Southall, *op. cit.*, p. 4.
58 Gallagher, *op. cit.*, p. 267.
59 Gallagher, *op. cit.*, pp. 242, 264, 265, 267.
60 Gillies, in Ashworth, *Anzac Squadron*, p. 20.
61 Ashworth, *op. cit.*, pp. 17-18.
62 Ashworth, *op. cit.*, pp. 24, 32.
63 Southall, *op. cit.*, p. 6.
64 Baveystock, L., *Wavetops at My Wingtips: Flying with RAF Bomber and Coastal Commands in World War II* (Shrewsbury: Airlife, 2001), p. 142.
65 Gallagher, *op. cit.*, p. 265.
66 Southall, *op. cit.*, p. 6.
67 Ashworth, *op. cit.*, pp. 22-23.
68 Southall, *op. cit.*, p. 6.
69 Williams, R., *These Are Facts: The Autobiography of Air Marshal Sir Richard Williams* (Canberra: Australian War Memorial, 1977), p. 267.
70 Ashworth, N., *How Not to Run an Air Force! The Higher Command of the Royal Australian Air Force During the Second World War, Vol. 1* (Canberra: Air Power Studies Centre, 2000), pp. 276-277.
71 Williams, *op. cit.*, p. 268, 271, 279.
72 Coulthard-Clark, C. D., *McNamara V.C.* (Canberra: Air Power Studies Centre, 1997), p. 93.
73 Williams, *op. cit.*, pp. 301-302.

Chapter 4

1 Davenport, P., *Hurrah for the Next Man* (Swansea, Tasmania: Beachcomber Press, 2009), pp. 45, 54.
2 Gallagher, E.B., and Timmermans, T. *PS: Love me? The War Memoirs of Flight Sergeant Ed Gallagher* (Victoria, British Columbia: Tricia Timmermans, 2013), pp. 267-269.

3   *Ibid.*, pp. 248, 271-272, 287.

4   *Ibid.*, pp. 267, 269, 270, 287.

5   *Ibid.*, pp. 249, 331.

6   Ashworth, N., *The Anzac Squadron: A History of No 461 Squadron Royal Australian Air Force 1942–1945* (Perth: Hesperion Press, 1994), p. 21.

7   Davenport, *op. cit.*, p. 50.

8   Gallagher, *op. cit.*, pp. 286, 292-293.

9   Russell Baird Interview Transcript, dated 25.11.2003, Archive No. 1143, australiansatwarfilmarchive.unsw.edu.au, accessed 15.2.2019.

10 Southall, I., *They Shall Not Pass Unseen* (Sydney: Angus & Robertson, 1956), p. 10.

11 Gallagher, *op. cit.*, pp. 277-278, 284-285.

12 Southall, *op. cit.*, p. 14.

13 *Ibid.*, pp. 14-15.

14 Gallagher, *op. cit.*, p. 281.

15 Southall, *op. cit.*, pp. 14-15.

16 'Robert Veitch Stewart D.F.C.', www.rafcommands.com; & '77 Squadron Losses', www.bomber-command.info; both accessed 10.7.2017.

17 Gallagher, *op. cit.*, pp. 278, 284.

18 Southall, *op. cit.*, p. 16.

19 Gallagher, *op. cit.*, pp. 279-282.

20 *Ibid.*, pp. 278-289.

21 Dudley-Gordon, T., *Coastal Command at War* (London: Jarrolds, 1942), pp. 127-128.

22 Southall, *op. cit.*, p. 17.

23 Russell Baird Interview Transcript, dated 25.11.2003, Archive No. 1143, australiansatwarfilmarchive.unsw.edu.au, accessed 15.2.2019.

24 Baff, K.C., *Maritime is Number Ten: A History of 10 Squadron RAAF, The Sunderland Era* (Adelaide: K.C. Baff, 1983), pp. 217-219.

25 Holm, M., 'Kampfgeschwader 40', www.ww2.dk, accessed 14.7.2017.

26 Ashworth, *op. cit.*, p. 127.

27 Baff, *op. cit.*, p. 219.

28 NAA: A705, 163/132/172 & 163/144/180.

29 Baff, *op. cit.*, p. 220.

30 *Ibid.*, pp. 220-222.

31 Franks, N. L. R., *Search, Find and Kill: Coastal Command's U-boat Successes* (Bourne End, Bucks: Aston Publications, 1990), pp. 67-69.

32 Baff, *op. cit.*, pp. 220-221.

33 'R.Smg. Luigi Torelli', www.regiamarina.net, accessed 9.7.2017.

34 Baff, *op. cit.*, p. 223-224.

35 White, J., *The Milk Cows: U-boat Tankers at War 1941–1945* (Barnsley: Pen & Sword, 2009), p.238.

36 Wynn, K., *U-boat Operations of the Second World War, Vol.1: Career Histories, U1-U510* (London: Chatham Publishing, 1997), Vol.1, p. 86.

37 'U-105', uboat.net, accessed 9.7.2017.

38 Price, A., *Aircraft Versus Submarines in Two World Wars* (Barnsley: Pen & Sword, 2004, pp. 62-63, 85-86, 92.

39 Hendrie, A., *The Cinderella Service: RAF Coastal Command 1939–1945* (Barnsley: Pen & Sword, 2006), p. 94.

40 Price, *op. cit.*, pp. 85-86.

41 Mallmann Showell, J. P., *Dönitz, U-boats, Convoys: The British Version of His Memoirs from the Admiralty's Secret Anti-Submarine Reports* (London: Frontline Books, 2013), pp. 93-94.

42   Terraine, J., *Business in Great Waters: The U-boat Wars 1916–1945* (London: Mandarin, 1989), p. 12.

43   Padfield, P., *War Beneath the Sea: Submarine Conflict 1939–1945* (London: Pimlico, 1995), pp. 282-283.

44   Baff, *op. cit.*, pp. 238, 240.

45   Gallagher, *op. cit.*, p. 290.

46   Davenport, *op. cit.*, pp. 52-53.

47   '58 Sqn Coastal Command losses August 1942', www.rafcommands.com, accessed 18.7.2017.

48   Baff, *op. cit.*, p. 229.

49   Holm, M., 'Bordfliegergruppe 196', www.ww2.dk, accessed 13.7.2017.

50   Goss, C., *Bloody Biscay: The History of V Gruppe/Kampfgeschwader 40* (Manchester: Crécy Publishing, 2001, p. 23.

51   Davenport, *op. cit.*, p. 53.

52   Davenport, *op. cit.*, p. 53.

53   'UK SYKO Device', in 'Cryptographic Equipment', www.campx.ca/crypto, accessed 25.7.2018.

54   Davenport, *op. cit.*, p. 53.

55   Ashworth, *op. cit.*, p. 30.

56   Baff, *op. cit.*, pp. 233-234.

57   Gallagher, *op. cit.*, pp. 286-287.

58   NAA: A705, 163/111/57.

59   Baff, *op. cit.*, p. 235.

60   'Jagdgeschwader 2: Victories (1941/42)', www.cieldegloire.com, accessed 11.3.2018; Donald Caldwell, *The JG 26 War Diary 1939-1942* (London: Grub Street, 1996), pp. 263-264.

61   Ashworth, *op. cit.*, pp. 33, 65.

62   Greenhous, B., Harris, S. J., Johnston, W. C., and Rawling, W. G. P. *The Crucible of War 1939–1945: The Official History of the Royal Canadian Air Force, Vol. III* (Toronto: University of Toronto Press, 1994), pp. 389-391.

63   Timothy A. Walton, 'Eyes Of The Ospreys: An Analysis Of R.A.F. Coastal Command's Operational Research Section In Counter-U-boat Operations', dated 6.12.2015, www.ijnonline.org, accessed 24.7.2017.

64   Ashworth, *op. cit.*, pp. 64-66.

65   Gallagher, *op. cit.*, p. 302.

66   NAA: A705, 163/168/155 & 163/96/159.

67   Baff, *op. cit.*, p. 239.

68   V./KG40 is used for readers' convenience here, as this group-sized unit was not formed until January 1943, prior to that, it existed in squadron-form only, designated as 13./KG40—Holm, M., 'V./KG40', www.ww2.dk, accessed 14.7.2017.

69   Goss, C., *Bloody Biscay: The History of V Gruppe/Kampfgeschwader 40* (Manchester: Crécy Publishing, 2001), pp. 23, 225, 244.

70   All previous crew casualties involved flying accidents—Baff, *op. cit.*, pp. 130-131, 147-148, 151-153, 176-178.

71   Kingsland, R., *Into the Midst of Things: The Autobiography of Sir Richard Kingsland* (Canberra: Air Power Development Centre, 2010), p. 55.

72   Baff, *op. cit.*, p. 231.

73   Baff, *op. cit.*, p. 235.

74   Russell Baird Interview Transcript, dated 25.11.2003, Archive No. 1143, australiansatwarfilmarchive.unsw.edu.au, accessed 15.2.2019.

75   Ashworth, *op. cit.*, pp. 30-31.

76 Herington, J., *Air War Against Germany and Italy 1939–1945* (Canberra: Australian War Memorial, 1954), p. 286.

77 Gallagher, *op. cit.*, p. 304.

78 Docherty, T., *Dinghy Drop: 279 Squadron RAF 1941–46* (Barnsley: Pen & Sword, 2007), p. 20.

79 NAA: A705, 163/155/103, & 163/91/375.

80 Southall, *op. cit.*, pp. 29-30.

81 'Three airmen adrift for week in dinghies', *Weekly Times*, dated 26.8.1942, trove.nla.gov.au, accessed 11.3.2018.

82 Pitchfork, G., *Shot Down and in the Drink: RAF and Commonwealth Aircrews Saved from the Sea 1939–1945* (London: The National Archives, 2005), pp. 18-23.

83 Docherty, *op. cit.*, p. 20.

84 Pitchfork, G., *Shot Down and in the Drink: RAF and Commonwealth Aircrews Saved from the Sea 1939–1945* (London: The National Archives, 2005), p. 28.

85 Herington, *op. cit.*, pp. 290-292.

86 'Three airmen adrift for week in dinghies', *Weekly Times*, dated 26.8.1942, trove.nla.gov.au, accessed 11.3.2018.

87 NAA: A705, 163/155/103.

88 Herington, *op. cit.*, p. 292.

89 Ashworth, *op. cit.*, pp. 22-24, 241.

90 Kingsland, *op. cit.*, p. 55.

91 Ashworth, *op. cit.*, p. 241.

92 Gallagher, *op. cit.*, pp. 304-305.

Chapter 5

1 Teague, D. C., *Strike First They Shall Not Pass Unseen* (Plymouth: Dennis C. Teague, 1982), pp. 5-6.

2 Baveystock, L., *Wavetops at My Wingtips: Flying with RAF Bomber and Coastal Commands in World War II* (Shrewsbury: Airlife, 2001), chapters 4-10.

3 *Ibid.*, pp. 136, 138-141.

4 Russell Baird Interview Transcript, dated 25.11.2003, Archive No. 1143, australiansatwarfilmarchive.unsw.edu.au, accessed 15.2.2019.

5 Baveystock, *op. cit.*, pp. 149-150, 137-145.

6 Russell Baird Interview Transcript, dated 25.11.2003, Archive No. 1143, australiansatwarfilmarchive.unsw.edu.au, accessed 15.2.2019.

7 Baveystock, *op. cit.*, pp. 142, 152.

8 NAA: A705, 163/96/167.

9 Goss, C., *Bloody Biscay: The History of V Gruppe/Kampfgeschwader 40* (Manchester: Crécy Publishing, 2001), pp. 225, 244.

10 Holm, 'V./KG40', www.ww2.dk, accessed 14.7.2017.

11 Baveystock, *op. cit.*, p. 150.

12 Franks, N.L.R., *Search, Find and Kill: Coastal Command's U-boat Successes* (Bourne End, Bucks: Aston Publications, 1990), p. 73.

13 Baff, K.C., *Maritime is Number Ten: A History of 10 Squadron RAAF, The Sunderland Era* (Adelaide: K.C. Baff, 1983), p. 244.

14 Baveystock, *op. cit.*, p. 141.

15 Terraine, J., *Business in Great Waters: The U-boat Wars 1916–1945* (London: Mandarin, 1989), pp. 370-371.

16 Baff, *op. cit.*, pp. 250, 404, 417.

17 Davenport, P., *Hurrah for the Next Man* (Swansea, Tasmania: Beachcomber Press, 2009), pp. 54-55.

18 Baff, *op. cit.*, pp. 249, 254.

19 *Ibid.*, p. 248.

20 *Ibid.*, pp. 248-249.

21 *Ibid.*, p. 255.

22 Terraine, *op. cit.*, pp. 496-499.

23 Herington, J., *Air War Against Germany and Italy 1939–1945* (Canberra: Australian War Memorial, 1954), p. 422.

24 *Ibid.*, pp. 425, 417.

25 Greenhous, B., Harris, S. J., Johnston, W. C., and Rawling, W. G. P., *The Crucible of War 1939–1945: The Official History of the Royal Canadian Air Force, Vol. III* (Toronto: University of Toronto Press, 1994), pp. 394-395.

Chapter 6

1 Baff, K.C., *Maritime is Number Ten: A History of 10 Squadron RAAF, The Sunderland Era* (Adelaide: K.C. Baff, 1983), p. 262.

2 Herington, J., *Air War Against Germany and Italy 1939–1945* (Canberra: Australian War Memorial, 1954), pp. 421, 536-537.

3 Southall, I., *They Shall Not Pass Unseen* (Sydney: Angus & Robertson, 1956), p. 51.

4 Baveystock, L., *Wavetops at My Wingtips: Flying with RAF Bomber and Coastal Commands in World War II* (Shrewsbury: Airlife, 2001), pp. 153, 159-163.

5 Kingsland, R., *Into the Midst of Things: The Autobiography of Sir Richard Kingsland* (Canberra: Air Power Development Centre, 2010), p. 52.

6 Herington, *op. cit.*, p. 528.

7 *Bomber Command Continues: The Air Ministry Account Of The Rising Offensive Against Germany July 1941–June 1942* (London: His Majesty's Stationery Office, 1942); *The Mediterranean Fleet, Greece To Tripoli: The Admiralty Account Of Naval Operations April 1941 to January 1943* (London: His Majesty's Stationery Office, 1943); *Libyan Log: Empire Air Forces— Western Desert July '41–July '42* (Cairo: Thoth Bookshop, 1942); *Coastal Command: The Air Ministry Account of the Part Played by Coastal Command in the Battle of the Seas 1939–1942* (London: His Majesty's Stationery Office, 1942); Dudley-Gordon, T., *Coastal Command at War* (London: Jarrolds Publishers, 1942).

8 Dudley-Gordon, *op. cit.*, chapters 2, 7 and 9.

9 *Ibid.*, chapter XIV.

10 *These Eagles: Story of the RAAF at War* (Canberra, Australian War Memorial, 1942).

11 *Ibid.*, pp. 60-67.

12 Michael Paris, 'The R.A.F. on screen 1940-1942', www.historytoday.com, accessed 30.11.2017.

13 Baff, *op. cit.*, pp. 260-261.

14 *Ibid.*, pp. 216, 219, 250, 256.

15 *London Gazette* No. 35759, www.uss-bennington.org, accessed 17.7.2017.

16 Baff, *op. cit.*, pp. 203-204, 404.

17 *Ibid.*, pp. 215, 245, 259.

18 Kingsland, *op. cit.*, p. 53.

19 Churchill, W., *The Grand Alliance* (London: Reprint Society, 1950) p. 477.
20 Gallagher, *op. cit.*, p. 303.
21 Southall, *op. cit.*, p. 45.
22 Ashworth, *op. cit.*, p. 38.
23 Gallagher, *op. cit.*, p.277.
24 Southall, *op. cit.*, p. 45.
25 Teague, *op. cit.*, pp. 62-63.
26 Ashworth, *op. cit.*, p. 43.
27 *Ibid.*, pp. 42-43.
28 Gallagher, *op. cit.*, pp. 244, 267, 312, 389.
29 Ashworth, *op. cit.*, p. 43.
30 Teague, *op. cit.*, p. 144.
31 NAA: A11271, 139/2/P1 PART 1.
32 NAA: A705, 166/6/19 & 166/17/25.
33 Docherty, T., *Dinghy Drop: 279 Squadron RAF 1941–46* (Barnsley: Pen & Sword, 2007), pp. 35-36.
34 NAA: A705, 166/6/19, & 166/17/25.
35 Gallagher, *op. cit.*, p. 372.
36 NAA: A705, 166/6/19.
37 Terraine, *op. cit.*, p. 405-408.
38 Padfield, P., *War Beneath the Sea: Submarine Conflict 1939–1945* (London: Pimlico, 1995), p. 305.
39 Terraine, *op. cit.*, p. 501.
40 Dimbleby, J., *The Battle of the Atlantic: How the Allies Won the War* (London: Viking, 2015), pp. 353, 355-356.
41 Joubert de la Ferté, P., *The Fated Sky* (London: White Lion Publishers, 1977), p. 241.
42 Terraine, J., *The Right of the Line: The Royal Air Force in the European War 1939–1945* (London: Sceptre, 1988), p. 440.
43 Padfield, *op. cit.*, p. 313.
44 Holm, M., 'Flugzeugbestand und Bewegungsmeldungen III./KG40'; 'Flugzeugbestand und Bewegungsmeldungen 5./BFGr. 196'; & 'Flugzeugbestand und Bewegungsmeldungen V./KG40', in www.ww2.dk, accessed 19.7.2017.
45 Hendrie, A., *The Cinderella Service: RAF Coastal Command 1939–1945* (Barnsley: Pen & Sword, 2006), pp. 215, 218.
46 Terraine, *op. cit.*, pp. 418-419.
47 Hendrie, *op. cit.*, pp. 215, 210.
48 Orange, V., *Slessor Bomber Champion: The Life of Marshal of the RAF Sir John Slessor* (London: Grub Street, 2006), pp. 80-98.
49 Cooper, A., *RAAF Bombers Over Germany 1941–42* (Sydney: Rosenberg, 2016), pp. 29, 45-46, 57.
50 Greenhous, B., Harris, S. J., Johnston, W. C., and Rawling, W. G. P., *The Crucible of War 1939–1945: The Official History of the Royal Canadian Air Force, Vol. III* (Toronto: University of Toronto Press, 1994), p. 393.
51 Franks, N.L.R., *Search, Find and Kill: Coastal Command's U-boat Successes* (Bourne End, Bucks: Aston Publications, 1990), pp. 76-80.
52 Southall, *op. cit.*, pp. 57-59.
53 Walton, 'Eyes of the ospreys'.
54 Roskill, *War at Sea*, Vol. II, p. 85.
55 Teague, *op. cit.*, p. 145.
56 Davenport, *op. cit.*, pp. 56, 58-60.
57 Gallagher, *op. cit.*, pp. 316-317.

58 Ashworth, *op. cit.*, p. 55.

59 Davenport, *op. cit.*, pp. 58-60.

60 *Ibid.*, pp. 60-62.

61 Baff, *op. cit.*, pp. 451-453.

62 Gallagher, *op. cit.*, pp. 196, 268.

63 Ashworth, *op. cit.*, p. 144.

64 Southall, *op. cit.*, p. 56.

65 Ashworth, *op. cit.*, pp. 88-89.

66 Baff, *op. cit.*, pp. 332-333, 356-357.

67 Webster, C., and Frankland, N., *The Strategic Air Offensive Against Germany 1939–1945*, Vol. I (London: H.M.S.O., 1961), pp. 251, 312, 178-180.

68 Herington, *op. cit.*, pp. 422-428.

69 Franks, *Search, Find and Kill*, pp. 76-80.

70 White, J., *The Milk Cows: U-boat Tankers at War 1941–1945* (Barnsley: Pen & Sword, 2009), p. 130.

71 'Radar equipment for ASW use on aircraft', dated 23.6.1942, in NAUK: ADM 219/537; quoted by John D. Salt, 20.6.2011, in 'ASV Radar Detection Ranges vs. U-Boats?', theminiaturespage.com/boards, accessed 24.7.2017.

Chapter 7

1 Franks, N.L.R., *Search, Find and Kill: Coastal Command's U-boat Successes* (Bourne End, Bucks: Aston Publications, 1990), pp. 79-80.

2 Herington, J., *Air War Against Germany and Italy 1939–1945* (Canberra: Australian War Memorial, 1954), p. 533.

3 Up to the end of March 1943, No. 10 had accrued 16,529 hours, of which 3,153 were non-operational—10 Squadron ORB, NAA: A9186, 25.

4 Jessica Urwin, '"A fleeting Opportunity To Strike": The Combat Experiences Of Australians Serving In RAF Coastal Command During The Second World War', p. 22, www.awm.gov.au, accessed 16.1.2019.

5 NAA: A705, 166/6/112.

6 Baff, K.C., *Maritime Is Number Ten: A History Of 10 Squadron R.A.A.F., The Sunderland Era* (Adelaide: K.C. Baff, 1983), p. 302.

7 Davenport, P., *Hurrah for the Next Man* (Swansea, Tasmania: Beachcomber Press, 2009), p. 67.

8 In fact, having been SASO HQ Coastal Command until January 1943, Baker was at the time Air Officer Administration, HQ Technical Training Command—'Air Vice-Marshal G. B. A. Baker', www.rafweb.org/Biographies, accessed 3.10.2017.

9 Baff, *op. cit.*, p. 274.

10 Davenport, *op. cit.*, pp. 2, 68.

11 'U-119', uboat.net, accessed 3.10.2017.

12 Blair, C., *Hitler's U-boat War: The Hunted, 1942–1945* (London: Cassell & Co., 1998), pp. 273, 276-277, 357.

13 Davenport, *op. cit.*, pp. 67-68.

14 Baff, *op. cit.*, p. 275.

15 Jones, G. P., *The Month of the Lost U-Boats* (London: William Kimber, 1977), p. 63.

16 Wynn, K., *U-boat Operations of the Second World War, Vol. 1: Career Histories, U1-U510* (London: Chatham Publishing, 1997), Vol. 1, p. 277.

17 Baff, *op. cit.*, p. 276.

18 Franks, *op. cit.*, p. 82.
19 Ashworth, N., *The Anzac Squadron: A History of No 461 Squadron Royal Australian Air Force 1942–1945* (Perth: Hesperion Press, 1994), p. 96.
20 Wynn, *op. cit.*, Vol. 1, p. 309.
21 Mallmann Showell, J. P., *Dönitz, U-boats, Convoys: The British Version of His Memoirs from the Admiralty's Secret Anti-Submarine Reports* (London: Frontline Books, 2013), p. 135.
22 Nijboer, D., *Graphic War* (Erin, Ontario: Boston Mills Press, 2005), p. 120.
23 Urwin, "A Fleeting Opportunity To Strike", p. 14, www.awm.gov.au, accessed 16.1.2019.
24 Baff, *op. cit.*, p. 276.
25 Wynn, *op. cit.*, Vol. 2, p. 116.
26 Blair, *op. cit.*, p. 319.
27 Baff, *op. cit.*, p. 280.
28 *Ibid.*, p. 281.
29 Pitchfork, G., *Shot Down and in the Drink: RAF and Commonwealth Aircrews Saved from the Sea 1939–1945* (London: The National Archives, 2005), p. 28.
30 Baff, *op. cit.*, p. 281.
31 Goss, C., *Bloody Biscay: The History of V Gruppe/Kampfgeschwader 40* (Manchester: Crécy Publishing, 2001), p. 229.
32 Baff, *op. cit.*, p. 281.
33 Ashworth, *op. cit.*, p. 73.
34 Goss, *op. cit.*, p. 229.
35 Baff, *op. cit.*, p. 281.
36 'U-666', uboat.net, accessed 12.10.2017.
37 Goss, *op. cit.*, p. 229.
38 Franks, *Conflict Over The Bay*, p. 49.
39 Southall, I., *They Shall Not Pass Unseen* (Sydney: Angus & Robertson, 1956), p. 64.
40 Ashworth, *op. cit.*, p. 99.
41 Franks, *op. cit.*, p. 50.
42 Southall, *op. cit.*, p. 65.
43 Franks, *op. cit.*, p. 51.
44 Southall, *op. cit.*, p. 64.
45 *Ibid.*, pp. 65-66.
46 'Emergency landing by Sunderland "E" for Emu', Accession No. F04759, www.awm.gov.au, accessed 17.10.2017.
47 Southall, *op. cit.*, pp. 66-67.
48 Docherty, T., *Dinghy Drop: 279 Squadron RAF 1941–46* (Barnsley: Pen & Sword, 2007), pp. 51-52.
49 Ashworth, *op. cit.*, p. 100.
50 Southall, *op. cit.*, pp. 67-69.
51 'Sunderland "E" for Emu', www.pistonheads.com, accessed 16.10.2017.
52 Southall, *op. cit.*, pp. 70-72.
53 Ashworth, *op. cit.*, p. 102.
54 Southall, *op. cit.*, pp. 72, 74.
55 Ashworth, *op. cit.*, p. 102.
56 'Emergency landing by Sunderland "E" for Emu', Accession No. F04759, www.awm.gov.au, accessed 17.10.2017.
57 Ashworth, *op. cit.*, p. 263; Hendrie, *Short Sunderland*, p. 160.
58 Southall, *op. cit.*, p. 64.
59 Davenport, P., *Hurrah for the Next Man* (Swansea, Tasmania: Beachcomber Press, 2009), pp. 68, 73.

60 *Ibid.*, 73, pp. 68, 70-71, 73.
61 NAA: A705, 166/32/106.
62 Goss, *op. cit.*, pp. 230, 249.
63 NAA: A705, 166/32/106.
64 Goss, *op. cit.*, p. 249.
65 Gallagher, *op. cit.*, p. 217.
66 Baff, *op. cit.*, p. 285.
67 NAA: A705, 166/7/108.
68 Baff, *op. cit.*, p. 285.
69 'U-528', uboat.net, accessed 12.10.2017.
70 'U-463', uboat.net, accessed 12.10.2017.
71 Wynn, *op. cit.*, Vol. 2, p. 38.
72 Blair, *op. cit.*, p. 319.
73 *Ibid.*, p. 292.
74 *Ibid.*, p. 274.
75 *Ibid.*, p. 319.
76 Franks, *Search, Find And Kill*, pp. 85-86.
77 Bowman, M. W., *Deep Sea Hunters: RAF Coastal Command and the War Against the U-boats and the German Navy 1939–1945* (Barnsley: Pen & Sword, 2014), p. 171.
78 Franks, *op. cit.*, pp. 81-86.
79 Mallmann Showell, *op. cit.*, p. 136.
80 Padfield, P., *War Beneath the Sea: Submarine Conflict 1939–1945* (London: Pimlico, 1995), p. 329.
81 Rohwer, J., *War at Sea 1939–1945* (Chatham Publishing, 2001), p. 150.
82 Blair, *op. cit.*, pp. 758-761, 775, 782.
83 As reflected in the sub-titles of clay Blair's two-volume, *Hitler's U-boat War*, namely *The Hunters* and *The Hunted*—see bibliography.
84 Rohwer, *op. cit.*, p.158.

Chapter 8

1 Blair, C., *Hitler's U-boat War: The Hunted, 1942–1945* (London: Cassell & Co., 1998), pp. 361, 381, 274.
2 Franks, N. L. R., *Search, Find and Kill: Coastal Command's U-boat Successes* (Bourne End, Bucks: Aston Publications, 1990), pp. 87-96.
3 Southall, I., *They Shall Not Pass Unseen* (Sydney: Angus & Robertson, 1956), p. 87.
4 '02.06.1943 No 461 Squadron Short Sunderland GR3 EJ134 N F/Lt Colin Braidwood Walker', aircrewremembered.com, accessed 25.4.2018.
5 Goss, C., *Bloody Biscay: The History of V Gruppe/Kampfgeschwader 40* (Manchester: Crécy Publishing, 2001), p. 231.
6 Davenport, P., *Hurrah for the Next Man* (Swansea, Tasmania: Beachcomber Press, 2009), p. 2.
7 Southall, *op. cit.*, p. 96.
8 '02.06.1943 No 461 Squadron Short Sunderland GR3 EJ134 N F/Lt Colin Braidwood Walker', aircrewremembered.com, accessed 25.4.2018.
9 Southall, *op. cit.*, p. 97.
10 Goss, *op. cit.*, pp. 229-230, 249-250.
11 '02.06.1943 No 461 Squadron Short Sunderland GR3 EJ134 N F/Lt Colin Braidwood Walker', aircrewremembered.com, accessed 25.4.2018.
12 Goss, *op. cit.*, pp. 231-234.

13 *Ibid.*, pp. 230-238.

14 NAA: A705, 166/6/190.

15 Wynn, Kenneth, *U-boat Operations of the Second World War, Vol. 2: Career Histories, U511-UIT25* (London: Chatham Publishing, 1998), p. 10.

16 Blair, *op. cit.*, pp. 391-393.

17 Wynn, K., *U-boat Operations of the Second World War, Vol. 1: Career Histories, U1-U510* (London: Chatham Publishing, 1997), pp. 88, 302.

18 'U.454. Interrogation of Survivors', www.uboatarchive.net, accessed 21.10.2017.

19 Wynn, *op. cit.*, Vol. 1, p. 302.

20 NAA: A705, 166/25/59.

21 NAA: A705, 166/25/59.

22 Baff, *op. cit.*, pp. 298-300.

23 NAA: A705, 166/32/162.

24 Baff, *op. cit.*, pp. 298-300.

25 'U.454. Interrogation of Survivors', www.uboatarchive.net, accessed 21.10.2017.

26 Wynn, *op. cit.*, Vol. 1, p. 88.

27 Ashworth, N., *The Anzac Squadron: A History of No 461 Squadron Royal Australian Air Force 1942–1945* (Perth: Hesperion Press, 1994), p. 115.

28 *Ibid.*, pp. 115-116.

29 Franks, N. L. R., *Conflict Over the Bay: Momentous Battles Fought by RAF and American Aircraft Against the U-Boats, Bay of Biscay May–August 1943* (London: Grub Street, 1999), pp. 157-158.

30 Franks, *op. cit.*, p. 158.

31 Wynn, *op. cit.*, Vol. 1, p. 88.

32 Blair, *op. cit.*, pp. 393, 402-403.

Chapter 9

1 Baff, K. C., *Maritime is Number Ten: A History of 10 Squadron RAAF, The Sunderland Era* (Adelaide: K.C. Baff, 1983), p. 302.

2 Goss, C., *Bloody Biscay: The History of V Gruppe/Kampfgeschwader 40* (Manchester: Crécy Publishing, 2001), p. 234.

3 Baff, *op. cit.*, pp. 302-304.

4 NAA: A705, 166/27/197.

5 Goss, *op. cit.*, p. 234.

6 NAA: A705, 166/3/91.

7 NAA: A705, 166/6/112.

8 Goss, *op. cit.*, p. 236.

9 NAA: A705, 166/6/112 & 166/37/182.

10 Baff, *op. cit.*, p. 309.

11 Southall, I., *They Shall Not Pass Unseen* (Sydney: Angus & Robertson, 1956), p. 17.

12 Baff, *op. cit.*, p. 284.

13 Ashworth, N., *The Anzac Squadron: A History of No 461 Squadron Royal Australian Air Force 1942–1945* (Perth: Hesperion Press, 1994), p. 122.

14 Baff, *op. cit.*, pp. 282-284, 305-309.

15 Conferences at HQ Coastal Command on 20 August, at Pembroke Dock on 3 September, at Mount Batten on 5 and/or 8 October—10 & 461 Sqn ORBs, NAA: A9186, 25 & 148; Ashworth, *op. cit.*, p. 122.

16 'Porcupines', *These Eagles*, pp. 60-64.
17 Holm, M., 'Flugzeugbestand und Bewegungsmeldungen', V./KG40, www.ww2.dk, accessed 25.2.2018.
18 Goss, *op. cit.*, pp. 247-254.
19 Davenport, P., *Hurrah for the Next Man* (Swansea, Tasmania: Beachcomber Press, 2009), p. 77.
20 Goss, *op. cit.*, p. 252.
21 Ashworth, *op. cit.*, p. 119.
22 Jones, R. V., *Most Secret War: British Scientific Intelligence 1939–1945* (London: Coronet Books, 1978), pp. 491-494.
23 Holm, 'Kampfgeschwader 40', www.ww2.dk, accessed 11.5.2018.
24 Goss, *op. cit.*, pp. 225ff, 244ff.
25 *Ibid.*, p. 235.
26 Davenport, *op. cit.*, pp. 3, 70.
27 Russell Baird Interview Transcript, dated 25.11.2003, Archive No. 1143, australiansatwarfilmarchive.unsw.edu.au, accessed 15.2.2019.
28 Ashworth, *op. cit.*, p. 119.
29 Davenport, *op. cit.*, p. 73.
30 Ashworth, *op. cit.*, p. 119.
31 Davenport, *op. cit.*, p. 4.
32 Ashworth, *op. cit.*, p. 120.
33 Goss, *op. cit.*, p. 235.
34 Ashworth, *op. cit.*, p. 121.
35 Hendrie, A., *Short Sunderland in World War II* (Shrewsbury: Airlife Publishing, 1994), p. 160.
36 Davenport, *op. cit.*, p. 5.
37 *Ibid.*, p. 3.
38 Goss, *op. cit.*, p. 236.
39 Ashworth, *op. cit.*, p. 121.
40 Goss, *op. cit.*, pp. 236-237.
41 Storr, A., *RAAF Fatalities in Second World War in Number 10 Squadron RAAF Based in the United Kingdom* (Canberra: Alan Storr, 2006), p. 8.
42 Davenport, *op. cit.*, pp. 6-7.
43 Goss, *op. cit.*, pp. 225ff, 244ff.
44 *Ibid.*, p. 238.
45 'FO JA Cruickshank VC—210 Squadron', www.rafcommands.com, accessed 15.5.2018.
46 Ashworth, *op. cit.*, p. 127.
47 *Ibid.*, pp. 122-128.
48 Wilson, S., *Anson, Hudson & Sunderland in Australian service* (Canberra: Aerospace Publications, 1992), p. 167.
49 Goss, *op. cit.*, p. 238.
50 NAA: A705, 166/6/279 & 166/7/205.
51 Goss, *op. cit.*, pp. 228-239.
52 NAA: A705, 166/8/254.
53 Baff, *op. cit.*, pp. 313-314.
54 *Ibid.*, pp. 317, 407.
55 Franks, N. L. R., *Search, Find and Kill: Coastal Command's U-boat Successes* (Bourne End, Bucks: Aston Publications, 1990), pp.98-101.
56 Baff, *op. cit.*, pp. 317, 319.
57 Goss, *op. cit.*, p. 239.
58 NAA: A705, 166/8/309.

59 Goss, *op. cit.*, p. 239.
60 NAA: A705, 166/10/148.
61 Baff, *op. cit.*, p. 322.
62 *Ibid.*, pp. 320-321.
63 *Ibid.*, pp. 319-322.

Chapter 10

1 Egerton and Wood in January; Gillies in February, Beeton and Thorpe in March; Miedecke, Roberts and White in April; Griffiths in June, Mainprize and Rossiter in July, and Marks and Brown in September.
2 McKenzie, Saunders, Gerrard, Fry, Skinner, Jennison, Lees and Behrndt.
3 Jennison, Lees and Behrndt.
4 Croft, Dowling and Howe.
5 Walker, Wood, Manger, Smith, Marrows, Singleton, Baird, Clarke, and Weatherlake.
6 Niestlé, A., *German U-boat Losses During World War II: Details of Destruction* (London: Frontline Books, 2014), pp. 66, 69, 79, 117, 145.
7 Hendrie, A., *The Cinderella Service: RAF Coastal Command 1939–1945* (Barnsley: Pen & Sword, 2006), pp. 230, 232, 234.

Bibliography

Air Ministry, *Coastal Command: The Air Ministry Account of the Part Played by Coastal Command in the Battle of the Seas 1939–1942* (London: HM Stationery Office, 1942)

Ashworth, N., *The Anzac Squadron: A History of No 461 Squadron Royal Australian Air Force 1942–1945* (Perth: Hesperion Press, 1994); *How Not to Run an Air Force! The Higher Command of the Royal Australian Air Force During the Second World War,* Vol. 1 & 2 (Canberra: Air Power Studies Centre, 2000)

Baff, K. C., *Maritime is Number Ten: A History of 10 Squadron RAAF, The Sunderland Era* (Adelaide: K.C. Baff, 1983)

Baveystock, L., *Wavetops at My Wingtips: Flying with RAF Bomber and Coastal Commands in World War II* (Shrewsbury: Airlife, 2001)

Beesly, P., *Very Special Intelligence: The Story of the Admiralty's Operational Intelligence Centre 1939–1945* (Annapolis: Naval Institute Press, 2000)

Blair, C., *Hitler's U-boat War: The Hunters, 1939–1942* (New York: Random House, 1996); *Hitler's U-boat War: The Hunted, 1942–1945* (London: Cassell & Co., 1998)

Bowman, M. W., *Deep Sea Hunters: RAF Coastal Command and the War Against the U-boats and the German Navy 1939–1945* (Barnsley: Pen & Sword, 2014)

Bowyer, C., *Sunderland at War* (Shepperton, Surrey: Ian Allan, 1989)

Clark, C., 'R.A.A.F. Support For An Australian Maritime Strategy Before World War II', seminar paper presented to Air Power Development Centre, 26 April 2012.

Claymore, T., *Ships with Wings* (Cassell: London, 1943)

Cooper, A., *RAAF Bombers Over Germany 1941–42* (Sydney: Rosenberg, 2016)

Coulthard-Clark, C. D., *The Third Brother: The Royal Australian Air Force 1921–39* (Sydney: Allen & Unwin, 1991); *McNamara V.C.: A Hero's Dilemma* (Canberra: Air Power Studies Centre, 1997)

Davenport, P., *Hurrah for the Next Man* (Swansea, Tasmania: Beachcomber Press, 2009)

Dimbleby, J., *The Battle of the Atlantic: How the Allies Won the War* (London: Viking, 2015)

Docherty, T., *Dinghy Drop: 279 Squadron RAF 1941–46* (Barnsley: Pen & Sword, 2007)

Dudley-Gordon, T., *Coastal Command at War* (London: Jarrolds, 1942)

Ewer, P., *Wounded Eagle: The Bombing of Darwin and Australia's Air Defence Scandal* (Sydney: New Holland Publishers, 2009)

Franks, N. L. R., *Search, Find and Kill: Coastal Command's U-boat Successes* (Bourne End, Bucks: Aston Publications, 1990); *Conflict Over the Bay: Momentous Battles Fought by RAF and American Aircraft Against the U-Boats, Bay of Biscay May–August 1943* (London: Grub Street, 1999)

Gallagher, E. B., and Timmermans, T., *PS: Love me? The War Memoirs of Flight Sergeant Ed Gallagher* (Victoria, British Columbia: Tricia Timmermans, 2013)

Gallop, A., *U-Boat 1936–45 (Type VIIA, B, C and Type VIIC/41): Owners' Workshop Manual* (Yeovil, Somerset: Haynes Publishing, 2014)

Gillison, D., *Royal Australian Air Force 1939–1942* (Canberra: Australian War Memorial, 1962)

Goss, C., *Bloody Biscay: The History of V Gruppe/Kampfgeschwader 40* (Manchester: Crécy Publishing, 2001)

Greenhous, B., Harris, S. J., Johnston, W. C., and Rawling, W. G. P., *The Crucible of War 1939–1945: The Official History of the Royal Canadian Air Force*, Vol. III (Toronto: University of Toronto Press, 1994)

Hendrie, A., *Short Sunderland in World War II* (Shrewsbury: Airlife Publishing, 1994); *The Cinderella Service: RAF Coastal Command 1939–1945* (Barnsley: Pen & Sword, 2006)

Herington, J., *Air War Against Germany and Italy 1939–1945* (Canberra: Australian War Memorial, 1954)

Hewitt, J. E., *Adversity in Success* (Melbourne: Langate Publishing, 1980)

Jay, A., *Endurance: A History of RAAF Aircrew Participation in Liberator Operations of RAF Coastal Command 1941–1945* (Maryborough, Queensland: Banner Books, 1996)

Jefford, C. G., *Observers and Navigators and Other Non-Pilot Aircrew in the RFC, RNAS and RAF* (London: Grub Street, 2014)

Jones, G. P., *The Month of the Lost U-Boats* (London: William Kimber, 1977); *Autumn of the U-Boats* (London: William Kimber, 1984)

Jones, R. V., *Most Secret War: British Scientific Intelligence 1939–1945* (London: Coronet Books, 1978)

Joubert de la Ferté, P., *The Fated Sky* (London: White Lion Publishers, 1977)

Kingsland, R., *Into the Midst of Things: The Autobiography of Sir Richard Kingsland* (Canberra: Air Power Development Centre, 2010)

MacKenzie, S. P., *Flying against Fate: Superstition and Allied Aircrews in World War II* (Lawrence, Kansas: University Press of Kansas, 2017)

Mallmann Showell, J. P., *Dönitz, U-boats, Convoys: The British Version of his Memoirs from the Admiralty's Secret Anti-Submarine Reports* (London: Frontline Books, 2013)

McCarthy, J., *A Last Call of Empire: Australian Aircrew, Britain and the Empire Air Training Scheme* (Canberra: Australian War Memorial, 1988)

Niestlé, A., *German U-boat Losses during World War II: Details of Destruction* (London: Frontline Books, 2014)

O'Brien, P. P., *How the War Was Won: Air-Sea Power and Allied Victory in World War II* (Cambridge: Cambridge University Press, 2015)

Orange, V., *Slessor Bomber Champion: The Life of Marshal of the RAF Sir John Slessor* (London: Grub Street, 2006)

Padfield, P., *War Beneath the Sea: Submarine Conflict 1939–1945* (London: Pimlico, 1995)

Pitchfork, G., *Shot Down and in the Drink: RAF and Commonwealth Aircrews Saved from the Sea 1939–1945* (London: The National Archives, 2005)

Price, A., Aircraft Versus Submarines in Two World Wars (Barnsley: Pen & Sword, 2004)

Rawlings, J. D. R., *Coastal, Support and Special Squadrons of the RAF and Their Aircraft* (London: Jane's, 1982)

Rohwer, J., *War at Sea 1939–1945* (Chatham Publishing, 2001)

Roskill, S. W., *The War at Sea 1939–1945, Vol. II: The Period of Balance* (London: HMSO, 1956)

Slessor, J., *The Central Blue: Recollections and Reflections by Marshal of the Royal Air Force Sir John Slessor* (London: Cassell & Co., 1956)

Southall, I., *They Shall Not Pass Unseen* (Sydney: Angus & Robertson, 1956)

Stephens, A., *Power Plus Attitude: Ideas, Strategy and Doctrine in the Royal Australian Air Force 1921–1991* (Canberra: Australian Government Printing Service, 1992); *The Royal Australian Air Force* (Melbourne: Oxford University Press, 2001)

Storr, A., *RAAF Fatalities in Second World War in Number 10 Squadron RAAF Based in the United Kingdom* (Canberra: Alan Storr, 2006)

Teague, D. C., *Strike First They Shall Not Pass Unseen* (Plymouth: Dennis C. Teague, 1982)

Terraine, J., *The Right of the Line: The Royal Air Force in the European War 1939–1945* (London: Sceptre, 1988); *Business in Great Waters: The U-boat Wars 1916–1945* (London: Mandarin, 1989)

White, J., *The Milk Cows: U-boat Tankers at War 1941–1945* (Barnsley: Pen & Sword, 2009)

Williams, R., *These Are Facts: The Autobiography of Air Marshal Sir Richard Williams* (Canberra: Australian War Memorial, 1977)

Wilson, D. J., *The Eagle and the Albatross: Australian Aerial Maritime Operations 1921–1971*, PhD Thesis, University of New South Wales, 2003

Wilson, S., *Anson, Hudson & Sunderland in Australian Service* (Canberra: Aerospace Publications, 1992)

Wynn, K., *U-boat Operations of the Second World War, Vol. 1: Career Histories, U1-U510* (London: Chatham Publishing, 1997); *U-boat Operations of the Second World War, Vol. 2: Career Histories, U511-UIT25* (London: Chatham Publishing, 1998)

Index

Service ranks given are those at first mention in text